Fusion 3 Bible

Fusion 3 Bible

David Hague

IDG Books Worldwide, Inc.
An International Data Group Company

Foster City, CA ✦ Chicago, IL ✦ Indianapolis, IN ✦ New York, NY

Fusion 3 Bible

Published by
IDG Books Worldwide, Inc.
An International Data Group Company
919 E. Hillsdale Blvd., Suite 400
Foster City, CA 94404
www.idgbooks.com (IDG Books Worldwide Web site)

Library of Congress Catalog Card No.: 97-074806

ISBN: 0-7645-3132-8

Printed in the United States of America

10 9 8 7 6 5 4 3 2 1

1E/SU/QW/ZY/FC

Distributed in the United States by IDG Books Worldwide, Inc.

Distributed by Macmillan Canada for Canada; by Transworld Publishers Limited in the United Kingdom; by IDG Norge Books for Norway; by IDG Sweden Books for Sweden; by Woodslane Pty. Ltd. for Australia; by Woodslane (NZ) Ltd. for New Zealand; by Addison Wesley Longman Singapore Pte Ltd. for Singapore, Malaysia, Thailand, Indonesia, and Korea; by Norma Comunicaciones S.A. for Colombia; by Intersoft for South Africa; by International Thomson Publishing for Germany, Austria, and Switzerland; by Toppan Company Ltd. for Japan; by Distribuidora Cuspide for Argentina; by Livraria Cultura for Brazil; by Ediciencia S.A. for Ecuador; by Ediciones ZETA S.C.R. Ltda. for Peru; by WS Computer Publishing Corporation, Inc., for the Philippines; by Unalis Corporation for Taiwan; by Contemporanea de Ediciones for Venezuela; by Computer Book & Magazine Store for Puerto Rico; by Express Computer Distributors for the Caribbean and West Indies. Authorized Sales Agent: Anthony Rudkin Associates for the Middle East and North Africa.

For general information on IDG Books Worldwide's books in the U.S., please call our Consumer Customer Service department at 800-762-2974. For reseller information, including discounts and premium sales, please call our Reseller Customer Service department at 800-434-3422.

For information on where to purchase IDG Books Worldwide's books outside the U.S., please contact our International Sales department at 650-655-3200 or fax 650-655-3297.

For information on foreign language translations, please contact our Foreign & Subsidiary Rights department at 650-655-3021 or fax 650-655-3281.

For sales inquiries and special prices for bulk quantities, please contact our Sales department at 650-655-3200 or write to the address above.

For information on using IDG Books Worldwide's books in the classroom or for ordering examination copies, please contact our Educational Sales department at 800-434-2086 or fax 317-596-5499.

For press review copies, author interviews, or other publicity information, please contact our Public Relations department at 650-655-3000 or fax 650-655-3299.

For authorization to photocopy items for corporate, personal, or educational use, please contact Copyright Clearance Center, 222 Rosewood Drive, Danvers, MA 01923, or fax 978-750-4470.

is a trademark under exclusive license to IDG Books Worldwide, Inc., from International Data Group, Inc.

ABOUT IDG BOOKS WORLDWIDE

Welcome to the world of IDG Books Worldwide.

IDG Books Worldwide, Inc., is a subsidiary of International Data Group, the world's largest publisher of computer-related information and the leading global provider of information services on information technology. IDG was founded more than 25 years ago and now employs more than 8,500 people worldwide. IDG publishes more than 275 computer publications in over 75 countries (see listing below). More than 90 million people read one or more IDG publications each month.

Launched in 1990, IDG Books Worldwide is today the #1 publisher of best-selling computer books in the United States. We are proud to have received eight awards from the Computer Press Association in recognition of editorial excellence and three from *Computer Currents'* First Annual Readers' Choice Awards. Our best-selling *...For Dummies®* series has more than 50 million copies in print with translations in 38 languages. IDG Books Worldwide, through a joint venture with IDG's Hi-Tech Beijing, became the first U.S. publisher to publish a computer book in the People's Republic of China. In record time, IDG Books Worldwide has become the first choice for millions of readers around the world who want to learn how to better manage their businesses.

Our mission is simple: Every one of our books is designed to bring extra value and skill-building instructions to the reader. Our books are written by experts who understand and care about our readers. The knowledge base of our editorial staff comes from years of experience in publishing, education, and journalism — experience we use to produce books for the '90s. In short, we care about books, so we attract the best people. We devote special attention to details such as audience, interior design, use of icons, and illustrations. And because we use an efficient process of authoring, editing, and desktop publishing our books electronically, we can spend more time ensuring superior content and spend less time on the technicalities of making books.

You can count on our commitment to deliver high-quality books at competitive prices on topics you want to read about. At IDG Books Worldwide, we continue in the IDG tradition of delivering quality for more than 25 years. You'll find no better book on a subject than one from IDG Books Worldwide.

John Kilcullen
CEO
IDG Books Worldwide, Inc.

Steven Berkowitz
President and Publisher
IDG Books Worldwide, Inc.

Eighth Annual
Computer Press
Awards ≥1992

Ninth Annual
Computer Press
Awards ≥1993

Tenth Annual
Computer Press
Awards ≥1994

Eleventh Annual
Computer Press
Awards ≥1995

IDG Books Worldwide, Inc., is a subsidiary of International Data Group, the world's largest publisher of computer-related information and the leading global provider of information services on information technology. International Data Group publishes over 275 computer publications in over 75 countries. More than 90 million people read one or more International Data Group publications each month. International Data Group's publications include: **ARGENTINA:** Buyer's Guide, Computerworld Argentina, PC World Argentina; **AUSTRALIA:** Australian Macworld, Australian PC World, Australian Reseller News, Computerworld, IT Casebook, Network World, Publish, Webmaster; **AUSTRIA:** Computerwelt Osterreich, Networks Austria, PC Tip Austria; **BANGLADESH:** PC World Bangladesh; **BELARUS:** PC World Belarus; **BELGIUM:** Data News; **BRAZIL:** Annuário de Informática, Computerworld, Connections, Macworld, PC Player, PC World, Publish, Reseller News, Supergamepower; **BULGARIA:** Computerworld Bulgaria, Network World Bulgaria, PC & MacWorld Bulgaria; **CANADA:** CIO Canada, Client/Server World, ComputerWorld Canada, InfoWorld Canada, NetworkWorld Canada, WebWorld; **CHILE:** Computerworld Chile, PC World Chile; **COLOMBIA:** Computerworld Colombia, PC World Colombia; **COSTA RICA:** PC World Centro America; **THE CZECH AND SLOVAK REPUBLICS:** Computerworld Czechoslovakia, Macworld Czech Republic, PC World Czechoslovakia; **DENMARK:** Communications World Danmark, Computerworld Danmark, Macworld Danmark, PC World Danmark, Techworld Denmark; **DOMINICAN REPUBLIC:** PC World Republica Dominicana; **ECUADOR:** PC World Ecuador; **EGYPT:** Computerworld Middle East, PC World Middle East; **EL SALVADOR:** PC World Centro America; **FINLAND:** MikroPC, Tietoverkko, Tietoviikko; **FRANCE:** Distributique, Hebdo, Info PC, Le Monde Informatique, Macworld, Reseaux & Telecoms, WebMaster France; **GERMANY:** Computer Partner, Computerwoche, Computerwoche Extra, Computerwoche FOCUS, Global Online, Macwelt, PC Welt; **GREECE:** Amiga Computing, GamePro Greece, Multimedia World; **GUATEMALA:** PC World Centro America; **HONDURAS:** PC World Centro America; **HONG KONG:** Computerworld Hong Kong, PC World Hong Kong, Publish in Asia; **HUNGARY:** ABCD CD-ROM, Computerworld Szamitastechnika, Internetto online Magazine, PC World Hungary, PC-X Magazin Hungary; **ICELAND:** Tolvuheimur PC World Island; **INDIA:** Information Communications World, Information Systems Computerworld, PC World India, Publish in Asia; **INDONESIA:** InfoKomputer PC World, Komputek Computerworld, Publish in Asia; **IRELAND:** ComputerScope, PC Live!; **ISRAEL:** Macworld Israel, People & Computers/Computerworld; **ITALY:** Computerworld Italia, Macworld Italia, Networking Italia, PC World Italia; **JAPAN:** DTP World, Macworld Japan, Nikkei Personal Computing, OS/2 World Japan, SunWorld Japan, Windows NT World, Windows World Japan; **KENYA:** PC World East African; **KOREA:** Hi-Tech Information, Macworld Korea, PC World Korea; **MACEDONIA:** PC World Macedonia; **MALAYSIA:** Computerworld Malaysia, PC World Malaysia, Publish in Asia; **MALTA:** PC World Malta; **MEXICO:** Computerworld Mexico, PC World Mexico; **MYANMAR:** PC World Myanmar; **NETHERLANDS:** Computer! Totaal, LAN Internetworking Magazine, LAN World Buyers Guide, Macworld Netherlands, Net, WebWereld; **NEW ZEALAND:** Absolute Beginners Guide and Plain & Simple Series, Computer Buyer, Computer Industry Directory, Computerworld New Zealand, MTB, Network World, PC World New Zealand; **NICARAGUA:** PC World Centro America; **NORWAY:** Computerworld Norge, CW Rapport, Datamagasinet, Financial Rapport, Kursguide Norge, Macworld Norge, Multimediaworld Norge, PC World Ekspress Norge, PC World Nettverk, PC World Norge, PC World ProduktGuide Norge; **PAKISTAN:** Computerworld Pakistan; **PANAMA:** PC World Panama; **PEOPLE'S REPUBLIC OF CHINA:** China Computer Users, China Computerworld, China InfoWorld, China Telecom World Weekly, Computerworld Weekly, Game Software, PC World China, Popular Computer Week, Software Weekly, Software World, Telecom World; **PERU:** Computerworld Peru, PC World Profesional Peru, PC World SoHo Peru; **PHILIPPINES:** Click!, Computerworld Philippines, PC World Philippines, Publish in Asia; **POLAND:** Computerworld Poland, Computerworld Special Report Poland, Cyber, Macworld Poland, Networld Poland, PC World Komputer, PORTUGAL: Cerebro/PC World, Computerworld/Correio Informático, Dealer World Portugal, Mac*In/PC*In Portugal, Multimedia World; **PUERTO RICO:** PC World Puerto Rico; **ROMANIA:** Computerworld Romania, PC World Romania, Telecom Romania; **RUSSIA:** Computerworld Russia, Mir PK, Publish, Seti; **SINGAPORE:** Computerworld Singapore, PC World Singapore, Publish in Asia; **SLOVENIA:** Monitor; **SOUTH AFRICA:** Computing SA, Network World SA, Software World SA; **SPAIN:** Communicaciones World España, Computerworld España, Dealer World España, Macworld España, PC World España; **SRI LANKA:** Infolink PC World; **SWEDEN:** CAP&Design, Computer Sweden, Corporate Computing Sweden, Internetworld Sweden, it.branschen, Macworld Sweden, MaxiData Sweden, MikroDatorn, Nätverk & Kommunikation, PC World Sweden, PCaktiv, Windows World Sweden; **SWITZERLAND:** Computerworld Schweiz, Macworld Schweiz, PCtip; **TAIWAN:** Computerworld Taiwan, Macworld Taiwan, NEW ViSiON/Publish, PC World Taiwan, Windows World Taiwan; **THAILAND:** Publish in Asia, Thai Computerworld; **TURKEY:** Computerworld Turkiye, Macworld Turkiye, Network World Turkiye, PC World Turkiye; **UKRAINE:** Computerworld Kiev, Multimedia World Ukraine, PC World Ukraine; **UNITED KINGDOM:** Acorn User UK, Amiga Action UK, Amiga Computing UK, Apple Talk UK, Computing, Macworld, Parents and Computers UK, PC Advisor, PC Home, PSX Pro, The WEB; **UNITED STATES:** Cable in the Classroom, CIO Magazine, Computerworld, DOS World, Federal Computer Week, GamePro Magazine, InfoWorld, I-Way, Macworld, Network World, PC Games, PC World, Publish, Video Event, THE WEB Magazine, and WebMaster; online webzines: JavaWorld, NetscapeWorld, and SunWorld Online; **URUGUAY:** InfoWorld Uruguay; **VENEZUELA:** Computerworld Venezuela, PC World Venezuela; and **VIETNAM:** PC World Vietnam. 5/7/98

Credits

Acquisitions Editor
Michael Roney

Development Editors
Hugh Vandivier
Katharine Dvorak
Tracy Thomsic

Technical Editors
Jim Looker
Marie Rosé

Copy Editors
Hugh Vandivier
Nate Holdread
Ami Knox

Project Coordinator
Tom Debolski

**Graphics and
Production Specialists**
Linda Marousek
Hector Mendoza
Christopher Pimentel

Quality Control Specialists
Mick Arellano
Mark Schumann

Proofreader
Arielle Carole Mennelle

Indexer
Ann Norcross

Cover Design
Murder By Design

About the Author

David Hague is the Development Manager and a partner in Shazian Enterprises, an Australian-based Web-authoring company. He is also a contributor to *Australian NetGuide Magazine* and the *Sydney Morning Herald* newspaper, and he has been a freelance journalist since 1986 for such publications as *PC World*, *Macworld*, *Australian Reseller*, and *Computerworld*. In addition, he has written and directed over 40 hours of television for training on such popular applications as Microsoft Access, Word, PowerPoint, Excel, and Autocad Lite. Adding to his busy lifestyle, David hosts a weekly radio show concentrating on Internet issues.

David lives on the Northern Beaches of Sydney, Australia with his wife and business partner, Sharon, and their dog, VB. You can view Shazian's Web site at www.shazian.com.au, and you can e-mail David at david@shazian.com.au.

This book is dedicated to my wife, Sharon, without whose help, love, and patience it would have taken much longer than it did.

Foreword

Remember when the biggest challenge to building a Web site was to get text and graphics to appear on the same page? NetObjects Fusion solved that and more when it first appeared in 1996. Since then, the product has evolved to handle virtually every type of media, database, component, and commerce functionality you can imagine.

Why? Because Web sites are bulking up to meet business requirements. Sites are larger, more visually exciting. They're alive with animation and special effects. They provide information on demand, and enable site visitors to conduct business and complete transactions through a browser. Calling these software applications "sites" is like calling Australia a mere "island."

NetObjects Fusion 3 is now a heavyweight. Together with NetObjects Fusion ProPack, you have everything you need to build a business Web site with rich media, dynamic database connectivity, and advanced scripting and programming. You're able to publish your site to run correctly on all browsers, and can optimize the generated HTML for the latest 4.0 browsers.

Speaking of Australia, our friend and veteran site builder David Hague has devoted the last year to producing a comprehensive book on NetObjects Fusion 3, a Herculean effort in and of itself. In the Fusion 3 Bible, he's covered the product thoroughly, especially in the rich media areas — a particular expertise of David's. I think you'll find the Fusion 3 Bible a useful and enjoyable resource as you build and update your next Web site.

One final thought: Every day, we at NetObjects ask ourselves what we can do to better enable and support people who design and build Web sites. We hope NetObjects 3 and the *Fusion 3 Bible* provide you many of the things you need. And rest assured, we're just starting.

Dave Kleinberg
Executive Vice President, Products
NetObjects, Inc.

Foreword

As the Internet and World Wide Web flourish, users continue to try to find better and better tools with which to publish information they wish to share with others on the Web. Net-savvy people don't think of Web pages; they think of possibilities.

NetObjects Fusion has revolutionized the way Web pages are published. Fusion authors don't get bogged down in finicky HTML code one page at a time. Fusion puts people in command of the whole Web site, with facilities such as point-and-click, drag-and-drop formatting, and dozens of professional page themes.

Tapping into his personal storehouse of knowledge as a Web site developer, training video scriptwriter, and director, David Hague fully opens the possibilities of Fusion 3 in the *Fusion 3 Bible*. What begin as tutorials for the novice segues into hands-on workshops of techniques suited to the most advanced user, all written in a style that newcomers and experts alike will find refreshing and informative.

If you are using or contemplating using NetObjects Fusion, or simply intrigued by its decidedly different approach to Web development, this book is sure to hold your interest and become a valuable information resource.

David Flynn
Managing Director, The WordSmith Group

Preface

Welcome to *Fusion 3 Bible*. In this book you discover how to create that killer Web site using the latest — and best, in my opinion — Web-authoring development program available today: NetObjects Fusion 3 for both the PC and Macintosh.

Fusion uses a completely different metaphor and look and feel than any other similar Web-authoring program on the market. Because of this, I have to say at the outset:

+ If you are an experienced Web author, able to mark up HTML code in your sleep, for the time being put aside everything you have learned. Instead, enjoy the experience of not having to worry about whether that `<TD>` tag is closed or a `<COLSPAN>` value is correct. Enjoy approaching a site from a content perspective, not a coding one.

+ If you are using Fusion for your first attempt at Web pages, look forward to concentrating on what to put on the site and not how to program it. You will be dealing with text, images, animation, and sound — not computer code.

+ If you are a Web developer somewhere between the previous two types, you will see how to create Web sites that rival the very best the Internet has to offer. You will not need to understand the complexities of table commands, how to write HTML for Java applets and special effects, or how to code image maps.

I hope you enjoy *Fusion 3 Bible* as much as I have enjoyed researching (playing!) and writing it.

Have I Bought the Right Book?

If you have a passing interest in creating Web pages and are considering using NetObjects Fusion to do so, this is absolutely the right book for you.

Even if you don't use Fusion but rather another (gasp!) authoring tool, buy the book anyway. You'll see what Web authoring should be: fun and creative.

How This Book Is Organized

Fusion 3 Bible is organized into six parts. Part I covers the background to Web authoring: what it is, how it works, and the elements you can place on Web pages.

Part II provides a quick tour of NetObjects Fusion. It explains Fusion's separate modules and their functions, and it explores the Fusion interface.

The fun really starts in Part III, using a hands-on approach to create a basic Web site. In this section you're introduced to the commands and functions that make Fusion such a delight to use.

In Part IV, once again using a hands-on approach, you create a new Web site as the framework for the more advanced topics covered in Parts V and VI, which include forms, frames, multimedia, rich media objects, and data publishing.

The book also contains three appendixes. These provide information on installing Fusion and finding available resources to help dedicated "Fusioneers" (which by the end of the book I hope you will certainly be). There are also details on the contents of the CD-ROM that accompanies this book.

What's on the CD-ROM

Bundled into the back of the book is a CD-ROM that contains the trial version of NetObjects Fusion 3, as well as what I consider extremely useful complementary applications to Fusion: trial versions of NetObject's ScriptBuilder, Infini-D from MetaCreations, and Flash 2 from Macromedia, among others. Use these applications to create elements to jazz up your Fusion Web page. The CD-ROM also contains various NFX Components and Fusion templates to help you create your site. I've also included all of the "parts," or files, mentioned in the book that contain text, images, databases, and other elements used in the tutorial sections. Use these files to follow along, hands-on, with the exercises in the book.

Conventions Used in This Book

To aid in the readability of the book, I have tried to keep the tone conversational. In addition, I have used as many figures as possible to illustrate actions, commands, results, and anything else that would benefit from a screen shot. I believe the more visual I can make the book, the easier it is to absorb the information, and therefore the more valuable the book is to you.

Throughout the book you will also notice the following icons, which I include to further point out specific notes, tips, or other information:

The Note icon highlights a point of interest about the current topic. It's like saying, "Oh, and by the way . . . ."

The Tip icon adds further comment about the topic being discussed. This is a sort of "Have you heard you can also . . . ."

The Hot Stuff icon makes you aware of shortcuts and really snappy ways of doing things. It's like saying, "Pssst . . . wanna hear a secret?"

"Danger, Will Robinson!" This icon points out areas where certain things *may* go wrong if you try them. You won't find these icons often, but you will find a few.

This icon is especially designed for users of earlier Fusion versions. It points out new and improved features that make the Fusion 3 interface so easy to use.

This icon directs your attention to where you can find further information in the book or from a separate source, such as the Web.

How to Use This Book

If you have no knowledge of Web authoring, Part I provides a background to what this exciting new medium is all about and explains its concepts.

Because a Web page or site can be constructed in many different ways — from using a high-end program like Fusion to something as basic as a simple text editor — you must become familiar with the way Fusion works. Because of this, I suggest everyone read Part III. From there, experienced Web authors can leap straight into Part IV, which helps you add features such as links, tables, forms, and frames to your pages.

I guess this sounds like Part II is optional, but it's actually a good quick reference section for the Fusion interface and the various views that compose it.

Once you are familiar with the user interface and the commands and functions used to create a basic Web site in Fusion, Part V helps you add multimedia and NetObjects special components to Web pages. Part VI shows you how to work with your site's assets, preview your work in a browser, and publish your site.

Tip

Experienced users of earlier versions of Fusion will find they can dive right into Part IV. Although a lot of old ground is covered, Fusion's exciting new interface and command structures are covered in depth starting with Part IV.

Feedback

I am my own worst critic, but I do value any further input from you, dear reader — bouquets *and* brickbats! Please feel free to write to me c/o IDG Books Worldwide, or better yet, e-mail me at david@shazian.com.au.

Acknowledgments

A lot of water has passed under the bridge since I started this book. For starters, I got married and moved. These are traumatic events in most people's lives, but in the middle of writing a book when a major revision version was brought out . . . !

Various other things also turned what was originally a three-month concept into a much longer project, but I got there with the help of some very special people.

As is usual, I have many more people to thank for their assistance in creating this book than either a) I can remember or b) will fit in the space graciously allowed! Despite this, there are people who must be thanked come what may.

First, thanks must go to the terrific people at IDG Books Worldwide who took this project on board in a very short space of time.

Major thanks also go, of course, to NetObjects for creating what is without question the best Web-authoring program available today. Kudos particularly to its online technical support staff who helped during the course of this book, in particular Matt, Marie, Kristine, Ken, and Bernard. In the later stages, Buzz and Andrew also gave valuable assistance. Believe me, you have not seen product support until you have experienced the Fusion support newsgroups. You guys are the best. Thanks!

Not the least of people to thank is my wife, Sharon, who — especially in the later stages when deadlines became days and not months or weeks — put up with a very stressed author in some very odd moods. And thank you to my faithful hound, VB, who now has his own Web page and e-mail address.

To Mike Roney at IDG Books Worldwide: Mike, I am indebted to you for your support, guidance, assistance, encouragement, and patience. As Australians say, "Your blood's worth bottlin'."

A great deal of gratitude to my editor, Hugh Vandivier. Hugh had his own dramas to contend with as the deadline loomed, and these must also have placed a huge strain on his well-being. Hugh, thanks a million. Without your expert help and guidance — not to mention friendship, although we never met — I don't know where this would have ended.

In the later stages, Jim Looker and Marie Rosé leapt into the fray to help with technical editing, and my heartfelt thanks also to them.

My whole Internet experience culminating (so far) in this book would not have come about without the help of Sean Howerd, the founder of OzEmail. Sean, you are running Australia's and possibly the world's best ISP. Good luck for the future, and thanks for the past (and hopefully future!) assistance.

To anyone else I have forgotten, my apologies but also my heartfelt thanks.

Contents at a Glance

Contents

Part V: Using Rich Media   411

Introducing Web Publishing

Over the past few years, Web publishing has gone from being an art that a rare few had the opportunity to charge money for to a commonplace practice that students, business people, academics, government departments, and just about every other sphere of humanity has found either indispensable or irresistible. All of a sudden, anyone, anywhere can freely publish information about what that person likes, thinks, or feels at a fraction of the cost of traditional paper-based publishing. Because of this, I liken Web publishing to the printing press of the Middle Ages. In this part, I discuss the history of the Web and the basics of Web publishing, emphasizing why I believe that on the Web, "content is king."

What Is Web Publishing?

Web publishing involves creating HTML-based "pages" containing combinations of text, graphics, sounds, animation, or video, and making them available to others for viewing and interaction via the World Wide Web on the Internet. With the invention of the printing press in the Middle Ages, printed matter was brought to the masses. In this latter part of the 20th Century, Web pages have created a similar revolution.

Note

HTML is an acronym for *Hypertext Markup Language*. HTML is a series of *tags* describing how the elements will appear on a Web page. Examples of tags include ones to create bold or italic text, define the file names of images, and specify colors for backgrounds or text.

More often than not, a set of Web pages — called a *Web site* — is based around a single theme. The first page in the site is known as the *home page* and is joined to all the other pages (shown in Figure 1-1) using a special command called a *hyperlink*. Hyperlinks are special areas on a Web page that when clicked with a mouse, let you navigate from page to page.

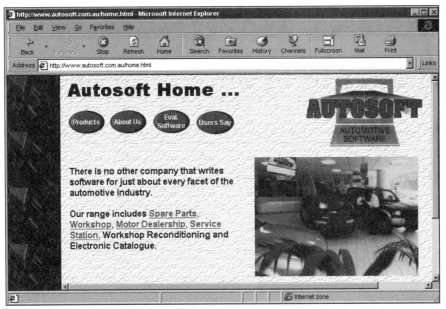

Figure 1-1: An example of a theme-based Web site produced with NetObjects Fusion.

Surfing the Net

Once created and tested, the pages are placed (or, more commonly, *published*) on a Web server making them available for viewing by anyone who is *surfing the Net*. Surfing the Net requires the use of a Web browser application such as Microsoft Internet Explorer (shown in Figure 1-2) or Netscape Navigator, and you can download these for minimal or no cost. Copies of these applications are also included in books (with software suites such as Microsoft Office), provided in magazines, or available via Internet service provider (ISP) startup kits. In fact, we're reaching the point where the local fast food restaurant might soon start giving this software away with every hamburger!

In fact, you may have received a "lite" version of Fusion if you have recently signed on with the Internet Service Provider CompuServe or bought a version of Netscape Navigator. NetObjects has made available a Personal Edition of Fusion as a free giveaway via these two companics.

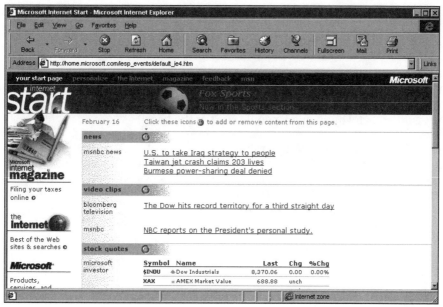

Figure 1-2: Internet Explorer 3 is one of the more popular Web browsers used to "surf the Net."

Dead Trees Versus Recycled Electrons

Web publishing has some similarities to paper publishing. You can display anything on a Web page that you can display on a traditional paper page, and you use the same basic design skills to create the layout in regard to colors, fonts, and so on. A Web page, however, is infinitely more flexible than its paper-based counterpart because in addition to text and images, Web pages can also contain sound, video, and most importantly, links to other pages.

While paper-based publishing *can* mimic some of the elements of a Web page — footnotes are an example comparable to links — the sheer volume of information available means this analogy would need you to access literally thousands if not millions of books to achieve the same net effect (if you'll pardon the pun).

When the Best Way to Get There Is Not a Straight Line

When browsing through a book or magazine, readers tend to progress in a linear fashion: they start at the front and advance page by page through the publication. (Newspapers are an exception, where despite the best of efforts, nobody has quite yet worked out why so many people start at the back!)

In contrast, Web pages are generally *not* linear in fashion. By clicking the hyperlinks on a page, a reader could be taken to another page in the Web site containing related information or to another site that may reside on a Web server on the other side of the world! Figure 1-3 is a schematic of a typical Web site showing the hierarchy of pages and its internal links.

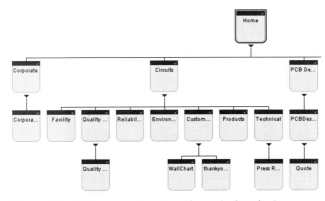

Figure 1-3: A diagrammatic view of a typical Web site showing its nonlinear structure.

Note

A *hyperlink* is a section of text, a graphic image, or some other object included in a Web page that when clicked with the mouse finds and loads another Web page. This page may be located on the current Web server or a site located on another Web server. This is what makes the World Wide Web so powerful.

Of Beatles and Web pages

I can best explain the advantages and flexibility of the "Web way" of presenting information by comparing it to the way information is presented in a book or a magazine.

If you want information on the history of the Beatles, your local library will probably have several books on the subject. These books, however, are totally dedicated to the one topic, and once you have finished reading, that is the end of the available information at that time.

In contrast, a Web site designed for the same purpose is potentially limitless, able not only to focus on the subject matter of the Beatles but also to connect to any other related subject, no matter how diverse. We can achieve this by using hyperlinks.

Using hyperlinks

Let's say you create a Beatles Web site similar to Figure 1-4, with pages containing biographical information and so on for each band member. You can then create hyperlinks on each of these pages that can be very diverse and have no immediately obvious connection to the subject at hand. From the (now Sir) Paul McCartney page for example, you might set links to the history of the bass guitar, a special site dedicated to the needs of left-handed people.

The John Lennon page might include a link to a site containing information about New York where he and Yoko Ono last lived, another link related to Eastern religions, and yet a third link to the 1960s peace movement.

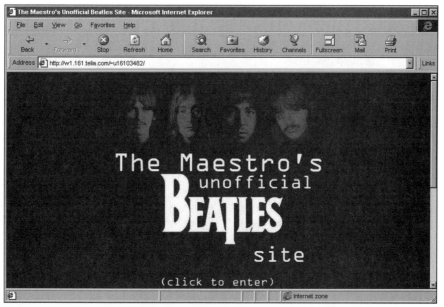

Figure 1-4: This Beatles page exists at http://w1.161.telia.com/~u16103482.

Yet other hyperlinks might allow the Web site visitor to download sound clips, view text files containing the lyrics of Beatles songs, display photos of album covers, or even see video animation from Yellow Submarine! The possibilities are endless on the Web.

As a result of this flexibility, the design and purpose of a Web site is limited only by the developer's imagination. The art of creating well-constructed, informative, and aesthetically pleasing Web sites is what Web publishing is all about.

The purists will hate this, but in my opinion, Web authoring and publishing is *not* about having "correct" HTML code. Content is king.

Uses of Web Sites

As what happens many times throughout history when a new technology is founded, when the World Wide Web first became available for popular use, it was the domain of hobbyists and enthusiasts. Announcing a new Web site caused great interest and generated lots of *hits*, regardless of the subject matter.

Note

A *hit* is recorded every time someone visits a Web site. *Web counters* let the owner of the site record just how many visits he or she receives. Some Internet Service Providers also allow the owner of the site to view its *logs*. These contain information such as where the visitor came from, the browser he or she is using, and other relevant facts. Programs such as The Surf Report are also available to chart this information and therefore expand on the usefulness of the standard logs. The Surf Report is available from `www.bienlogic.com/SurfReport/surfhome.html` and is shown in Figure 1-5.

Sites sprang up everywhere containing information on the author's hobbies or photos of his or her last holiday. Web pages were dedicated to pop groups, movies, games, sports, and just about every other leisure pursuit imaginable. More recently, the business, corporate, and government world has "found" the Internet — the Web in particular — and turned it into a vast billboard of information.

The possible reasons for having a Web site are infinite. When the printing press was invented, the ability to publish information was limited to the elite as the cost was so high. With the advent of the World Wide Web, the opportunity to publish information almost free of charge makes it available to anyone who wishes to inform, describe, comment, speculate, amuse, or even shock.

Individuals use the Web to tell about their holiday experiences, publish poetry, show off their newborn's photos, announce their wedding, or collate information on their favorite movie star. (See Figures 1-6 and 1-7 for some examples of Web sites.)

Figure 1-5: The Surf Report is an application used to gauge the number of hits on a Web site and provide full statistical logging.

Companies and corporations publish product data, price lists, newsletters, and branch locations or attempt to gain information via online surveys. Governments use the Web to inform populations about policies, direct people to appropriate departments, and even allow viewers of their sites to contact politicians directly via e-mail.

Religious organizations, welfare groups, and charities all use the Web to put their messages across. Sports franchises create Web sites to post results, newspapers have sites to update headline news, and television stations create Web sites to highlight their most popular programs, to sell station merchandise, and to promote their on-air personalities.

Figure 1-6: Publishing details of a wedding is popular, as is . . .

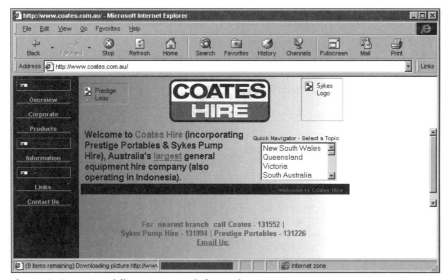

Figure 1-7: . . . providing corporate information.

Software companies have particularly taken to the Web, allowing visitors to download demonstration versions of their programs, providing support, or supplying updates. NetObjects first made Fusion available by this method. Figure 1-8 shows the Fusion download page at www.netobjects.com/download/index.html.

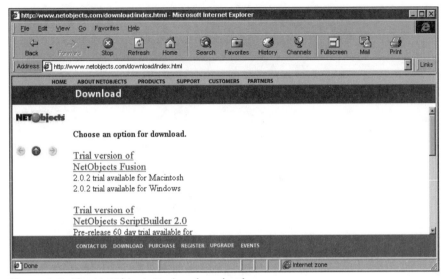

Figure 1-8: The NetObjects Fusion download page.

Benefits of Web Publishing

In the United States and elsewhere, entire television commercial campaigns are wholly dedicated to make viewers aware of a corporate Web site. Many newspaper advertisements contain the Web address of the advertiser in addition to standard copy. Business cards, letterheads, and even billboards all carry http:// or www Web addresses.

The reason is simple.

Information can be placed on a Web site far more cheaply than traditional advertising methods allow. In addition, the amount and *quality* of information that can be placed is far greater than otherwise possible. Finally, a Web site can be interactive, gaining valuable user feedback—not to mention names, addresses, and contact details!

Whereas a television or radio ad has a limited life before viewers and listeners "switch off," and print media ads only last the life of that publication, a Web site can be in place for perpetuity. Generally, an advertisement can only attempt to enthuse the viewer or listener to gain more information from another source (such as visiting the store, making a phone call, or writing a letter). A Web site, on the other hand, can contain every bit of information the owner of the site wishes to make available and can even let the visitor of the site buy the product or service on the spot. Online shopping, such as available from CD Universe shown in Figure 1-9, has transformed the way many of us buy goods today.

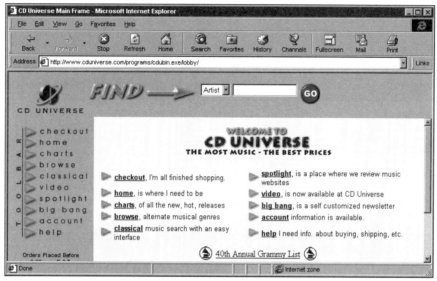

Figure 1-9: Buying music CDs online using a Web page.

A Web site is like a shop window

While the use of the Web for marketing, passing on information, or gathering feedback is gaining momentum and is undoubtedly a cost effective way of doing these things, normal marketing philosophy has to be applied to a Web site as it does to any other sort of advertising/marketing strategy. Just as repeatedly using a single television, radio, or print commercial (or never changing the display of the shopfront window) causes potential customers or visitors to become "sanitized," so does having the same Web pages face the public every time they visit your site. If you have nothing new to show, a visitor has no reason to return to your site.

For this reason, the design of a site should be flexible enough so that you can easily make changes to provide a fresh new look and feel. This should be achievable without seriously compromising the site structure and possibly losing the reason for the site's existence or its capability to convey the message you wish to put across.

At this, in addition to building Web sites, NetObjects Fusion excels.

Summary

✦ *Surfing the Net* is the term used to browse (or selectively view) World Wide Web pages on the Internet.

✦ Web browsers are computer programs used to surf the Net.

✦ Web publishing has similarities to paper-based publishing in concept but has the capacity to be far more flexible and interesting.

✦ *Hyperlinks* connect items on a Web page to another Web page.

✦ Web sites have a plethora of uses from entertainment to corporate information.

✦ Web publishing benefits include content diversity, minimal cost, and interactivity.

✦   ✦   ✦

Web Page Content

Creating Web pages carries the ultimate aim of producing a site that is functional, attractive, and above all informative. The content of the pages helps you to realize this goal. In Web parlance, content includes text, images, sound, animations, and specialized objects, such as Java applets and ActiveX controls.

Note

Java applets and *ActiveX controls* are components that can be inserted into a Web page. For example, both can load special programs that display certain file types such as 3-D objects, movie clips, and Acrobat documents. Java applets more particularly display special effects, such as rotating banners.

The available technology that allows authors to use more and varied types of objects on Web pages is improving all the time. Just a few years ago, for example, placing sound files on a Web page, while not unheard of, was at best a rare occurrence. The download time necessary before the viewer of the page could hear the sound was usually prohibitive.

Similarly, placing video on Web pages was only until recently in a similar state of complication. While still in its infancy, in probably six month's time video on pages will be the norm rather than the exception.

While trying to predict the future might be fun, it can either make you a hero but more likely a fool, and I'm no Arthur C. Clarke! Consequently, I will take the safe path and restrict myself to describing only those items that you can place on pages using Fusion's own tools elements. These items include text, graphics, sound, animations, and video.

This chapter is not a comprehensive tutorial, an in-depth study of the science of design, or even an explanation of the workings for some of the technologies available. Instead, this chapter provides a basic overview for those unfamiliar with what can constitute page content.

For more detailed information on a specific subject, any number of good books are available, and where appropriate, I have included references to those I have discovered.

Using Text

On most Web pages, the most common element is text, of course. We do live in a world of icons and images, but text is still the most common visual way of passing on information.

Note

I was talking with an old friend of mine who was once very resistant to *graphical user interfaces (GUIs)*. He observed that back in the Stone Age, mankind had no spoken language and communicated by way of pictures and images. Later, language evolved as did the written word. Now in the 20th century, we are back to pictures (icons) again. "Is this progress?" he asked.

When adding text to a Web page, there are several simple rules to follow. Some of these rules are constraints of the underlying HTML specifications that even Fusion is bound to follow. Others are visual or design rules, making it easier to view text; some are blatantly obvious, but others are a little more subtle.

When using text, use as minimal a number of words as possible to convey the message. Surveys have proven time and again that viewers of a Web site dislike having to scroll to continue reading. Also, *never* design a Web page that forces a reader to scroll to the right. This is a guaranteed source of contemptuous e-mail!

Fonts and typefaces

When placing text on a Web page, use a reasonable size font. Fusion's default is 12 point text, and this is satisfactory for most purposes. Also be aware that some readers may have less-than-perfect eyesight, including color blindness. Even for those of us whose vision is normal, non-contrasting colors, such as green and yellow, can be hard to read. Avoid them.

I am not going to attempt to teach the finer points of writing or typography here, as many excellent books cover this subject. I can recommend *Digital Type Design: The Page Designer's Guide to Working with Type* by Sean Cavanaugh (Hayden Books, 1996).

Today, the terms *font* and *typeface* are liberally exchanged with one another. For the sake of brevity and clarity, throughout this book I will refer to a *font family* as a singular typeface. For example, when I mention *Times New Roman*, I am speaking generically of all the different sorts of Times New Roman such as bold, italic, and so on unless otherwise stated.

Font restrictions

Many developers have spent enormous amounts of time and energy creating Web pages or sites, getting the layout just right, and finding or designing graphics that suit them perfectly. When viewed in a browser, the pages look fantastic!

They post the pages to the server, but shock! horror! the very next e-mail received tells in great and colorful detail how atrocious the site looks.

They check the site again. It looks great, but what could be wrong?

The answer is simple.

More often than not, they have used a font that is outside the display range of the standard Web browser. Sure, the developers have the font installed on their system, so when they view the site, it looks perfect. When another person views the site and does *not* have that particular font installed on his or her computer, however, the browser automatically replaces the correct font with its default font, normally Times New Roman. As a result, the layout, spacing, and other factors become totally unpredictable and usually produce terrible results. Figure 2-1 shows a Web site using a nonstandard font and how the browser reacts: not very favorably!

The latest HTML standard implementation using cascading style sheets circumvents a lot of font substitution problems. See the section entitled "Cascading style sheets."

To play it safe, use only Times New Roman or Helvetica (Arial) in either standard, bold, or italic. If you stick to this, you can pretty much guarantee that most browsers will display the text as you want it shown.

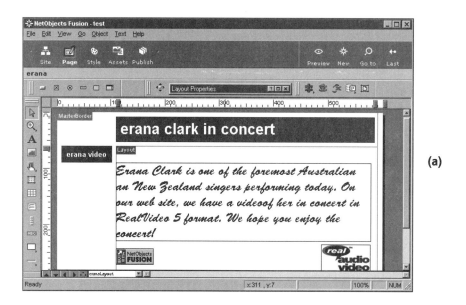

(a)

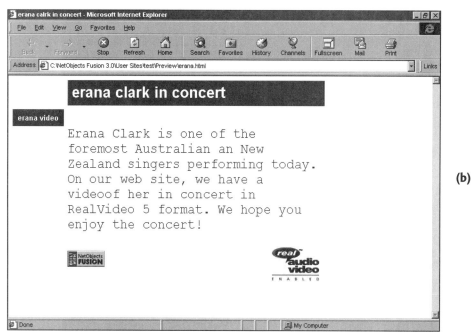

(b)

Figure 2-1: Using nonstandard fonts in Fusion (a) can produce unpredictable results in a browser (b).

Generally, a serif font such as Times New Roman is best used for body text, and a sans serif font (Arial or Helvetica) works best for headlines. Figure 2-2 shows an example of using these two fonts in this way. Serif fonts have "feet" at the corners of a letter, whereas sans serif fonts end smoothly. Note the differences in the letter *M*.

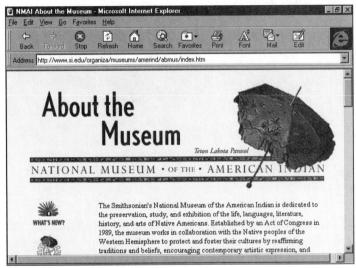

Figure 2-2: Example of a heading in Arial and body text in Times New Roman.

If you really must use a nonstandard font

If you feel that having a particular section in a specific font is important, (for example, where a company logo is being used), create it as a graphic in a program such as Adobe Photoshop or a shareware application like Paint Shop Pro and import it to the page.

Figure 2-3 shows a Web page that has standard text in the Arial typeface as well as a company logo and trademark created in Micrografx Picture Publisher using the Stop typeface.

Tip

If you have Word 6.0 or greater, a great facility exists called WordArt, which allows you to turn text into an amazing array of effects. Simply do a screen capture once you have created your text element and save the image as a GIF or JPEG file.

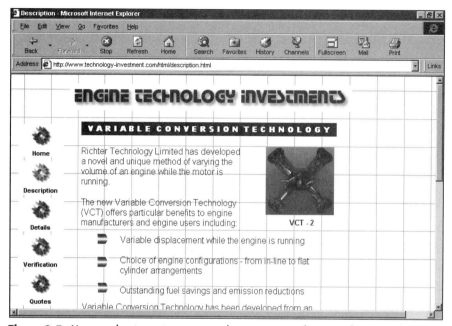

Figure 2-3: You can best create company logos or any other text that must have a nonstandard font in an image editing application and import them as a picture.

Cascading style sheets

A new HTML specification called *cascading style sheets* is partially designed to alleviate the problem of different fonts. Cascading style sheets allow the developer to specify several font styles in the HTML code for any particular piece of text. If the viewer does not have the first font locally installed, his or her browser will cascade down the list and attempt to find the second font nominated, and then the third, fourth, and so on until it finds one that it can display. If all of the nominated fonts defined in the style sheet fail, the browser will use the default font. I explain cascading style sheets in more depth in Chapter 8.

Using Graphics

When working with graphics images, browsers are far more unforgiving than they are with fonts. If the browser cannot display a particular graphics image, it simply ignores the image and displays a missing image icon instead (like the one in Figure 2-4).

Figure 2-4: The missing image icon.

So what sorts of images can a browser display?

Graphics aren't all created equal

Most browsers will cheerfully render and display two types of graphics files without a problem. These are known as *GIF* and *JPEG files*. GIF (*Graphics Interchange Format*) files are the most popular and owe their existence to the online service CompuServe. The second type, JPEG, was developed by the Joint Photographic Experts Group. See? *J-P-E-G*.

So what is the difference, if any, between these two types?

GIF files

A GIF is a highly compressed file best used for generic images on a Web page, such as buttons, diagrams, graphics (but not always photographs), and other visual elements. For most purposes, a GIF file is the best choice for graphics images on Web pages.

Over the years, GIF files have evolved into a couple of standards, GIF87a and GIF89a. Today, the most common in use is GIF89a, which not only allows a *static* image to be displayed but a series of images put together to simulate animation. These types of GIFs are called, appropriately enough, *animated GIFs*.

Tip

Due to a crossover point on file size efficiency, you're always wise to save photographs in both a GIF and JPEG format and check the file sizes.

Interlacing

Interlacing is a popular way of attempting to minimize the time lag that occurs when an image is being downloaded. Interlacing causes the image to appear line by line as it is rendered in the browser during download. Most popular graphics packages allow the interlacing of GIF files.

Although the time taken to download an image is the same as would be if it were not interlaced, the fact the viewer of the page can see something makes it *appear* to be faster. Due to this, you should, wherever possible, create GIFs that are interlaced.

Transparency

One great advantage of the GIF89a specification is a function called *transparency*, which is an image's capability to hide a particular color and therefore make it seem to be floating on the Web page. The transparency capability is available due to the way the GIF image is constructed. It is not the graphic that is transparent, but the capability to turn off a certain color.

Sound tricky? It's not really.

Images on a Web page can only be rectangular in shape. Surrounding an irregularly shaped image with a specific color and then making this color transparent makes it appear to the viewer as its natural shape. In Figure 2-5, the image on the left has no transparency attributes, whereas the one on the right has had the background color made transparent. This makes the object appear irregular in shape.

(a) **(b)**

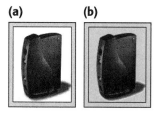

Figure 2-5: A GIF image showing both (a) nontransparent and (b) transparent attributes.

Many major image editing applications available like Micrografx Picture Publisher, Adobe Photoshop, or Paint Shop Pro let the Web developer make a GIF image transparent. For imported images, NetObjects Fusion also provides this functionality from its Standard toolbar.

Animated GIFs

Another major advantage of the GIF89a specification is its capability to create *animated GIFs*.

The easiest way to explain an animated GIF is to imagine the flip cards we used to play with as children. With these, a different image is placed on every card, and when they are flipped (holding them like a pack of playing cards and quickly running your thumb across the top), you see the illusion of movement as in a cartoon.

With an animated GIF, each of the "cards" is a separate file, holding one frame of the animation. An animated GIF creation program lets the developer place all of these frames (files) into a single file. When the file is placed on a Web page and viewed with a browser capable of displaying animated GIFs, the viewer of the page sees the complete animation. Figure 2-6 shows the first nine frames of an animated GIF containing a total of 14 frames.

Figure 2-6: The first nine frames from an animated GIF.

The program GIF Constructor Set (from www.mindworkshop.com) lets you create animated GIFs. Microsoft also has an animated GIF creation program available free of charge from its Web site at www.microsoft.com.

JPEG images

JPEG images are the second type of image that a Web browser can read and are acknowledged as being the best file type to use for photographic images.

Image compression

Unlike GIF files that are compressed automatically to the highest level possible under the specification, you can manually compress JPEGs. Of course, the higher the compression, the lower the quality of the image. In Figure 2-7, the image at left has been saved as a JPEG with minimal compression, while the one on the right has had 50 percent compression applied. You can easily see the loss of quality, even though the file size of the image with compression is much smaller.

(a)   **(b)**

Figure 2-7: Two JPEG images, one (a) with no compression and the other with 50 percent (b).

Note

At this time, you cannot make JPEGs transparent, but you can achieve interlacing via a relatively new specification called Progressive JPEG. Progressive JPEG is supported by Fusion 3.0.

Image editing tools

Many applications can help you create, modify, and edit both GIFs and JPEGs. By far, the most popular is a commercial application called Adobe Photoshop (see www.adobe.com), which has all of the functions and facilities you will ever need to create professional looking images.

Another professional program — and the one I use — is Micrografx Picture Publisher. (See Figure 2-8). Unlike Photoshop that is a stand-alone application, Picture Publisher is shipped as part of a package called the ABC Graphics Suite. Also included in the package is Designer, a high-end vector drawing program, ABC Flowcharter for creating every type of chart imaginable, Simply 3-D for creating 3-D text and images, and 2 CD-ROMs of clip art, giving over 30,000 images to use. See www.micrografx.com for more details.

Figure 2-8: Micrografx Picture Publisher is a high-end image-editing program.

Other companies such as Corel, Microsoft, and Macromedia also have applications available for this purpose. Corel has Corel Draw and Paint, Microsoft has some free-ware called Image Producer, and Macromedia has an excellent package for large images called Xres. Details — and in some cases trial versions — are available from their respective web sites at www.corel.com, www.microsoft.com, and www.macromedia.com respectively.

A trap for many new Web developers occurs when trying to get the best possible image: graphics are scanned at high resolutions giving correspondingly higher file sizes. Be aware that the computer monitor default display is 72 dots to the inch (dpi), so scanning at 600 or even 300 dpi and using the resultant image is not only a waste of time but a waste of bandwidth. Most Web professionals scan at 200 dpi, and then use their imaging software to reduce this to 72 dpi giving very acceptable results in the majority of cases.

If you have a large image, a neat trick is to display only a *thumbnail*—a physically smaller version of the image—and link this to a larger one. This lets Web site visitors choose whether they want to download the bigger image.

Inexpensive alternatives

For those who don't like spending money, though, a couple of very good shareware programs for image editing are available from the Net.

One of the best is Paint Shop Pro (as seen in Figure 2-9), which you can download at www.jasc.com/psp.html. Its many loyal users swear by it. Denying its shareware price is a feast of functionality that makes a lot of commercial image editing applications look pale in comparison.

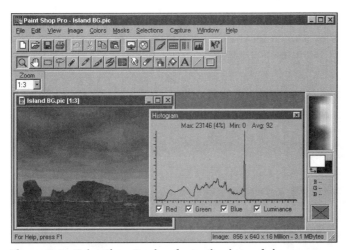

Figure 2-9: Paint Shop Pro is a fantastic piece of shareware with features rivaling packages costing hundreds of dollars.

Figure 2-10 shows another program, LView Pro, that is very popular and especially good for quickly creating transparent GIFs. LView Pro is a shareware application available directly from the Internet www.lview.com).

Figure 2-10: LView Pro is a Windows shareware application that is particularly good for quickly applying transparency to an image.

Using clip art

These days, if a graphics package does not include more clip art than you will ever need, it doesn't last long in the marketplace. The ABC Graphics Suite I use comes with more than 30,000 images! Most available commercial applications such as Corel Draw or Freehand have a similar quantity. In addition, you can buy any number of clip art packages from a variety of sources, and of course, the Internet itself is a great source of material. Before you can use clip art on a Web page, you usually need to convert it to either the GIF or JPEG formats as explained earlier in this chapter. Figure 2-11 shows some examples of clip art.

Figure 2-11: Clip art is a great source of images for use on Web pages. Beware of copyright infringements though!

Beware of copyright infringement

Be aware that copyright issues may apply if you use commercial clip art on your Web site. When using images from the Micrografx clip art library, for example, the licensing agreement stipulates that you meet certain conditions.

This may also apply if you "borrow" some images from another person's site.

Play it safe and read the copyright information supplied with your clip art. If you do borrow some images from another site, netiquette suggests you politely ask first!

Note

Netiquette is an abbreviation of "Net etiquette." It is a series of accepted but unwritten rules defining Net morals and ethics.

Using Multimedia

Multimedia is a generic term loosely describing any sort of content on a Web page consisting of sound, animation, or video. Although the word *multimedia* suggests combinations of these being "played" at the same time (*multi*), the term is also widely used to describe any singular use of these technologies.

Fusion supports many types of multimedia. Figure 2-12 shows the Fusion Advanced toolbar, where tools can place sound files, AVI or QuickTime video files, Shockwave or Macromedia Flash files, Java applets, ActiveX components, and on a Web page.

Figure 2-12: NetObjects Fusion's Advanced toolbar lets you place many types of multimedia elements on a Web page.

Using sound

Using sound on Web pages has become more popular as modem speeds have increased to allow the downloading of files in a reasonable amount of time. Most popular of all is the inclusion of a background sound on a Web page where a sound file (usually a music track) automatically plays when someone views that page. Other uses of sound files include welcome messages, clips of tracks from the latest pop music sensation, or even samples of sound effects that you can buy for inclusion on your own pages.

Sound file formats

Just as graphics images come in different formats, so do sound files.

Sound files on Web pages are normally one of three types: WAV files, AU files, or MIDI files. A fourth type you may also come across, AIFF files, are mainly Apple Macintosh-based files.

The WAV file

WAV files are most commonly produced by the use of the Windows Sound Recorder. You can also create any number of shareware sound editing programs such as Cool Edit and Goldwave, or high-end commercial applications including Sound Forge. Both music and speech can be recorded and played back as a WAV file.

The Windows Sound Recorder provides minimal options for editing any sounds that you capture. In contrast, Goldwave (shown in Figure 2-13) has enough editing and special effects tools to keep any budding sound engineer happy! You can obtain Botj Cool Edit and Goldwave off the Internet at www.sharewarejunkies.com.

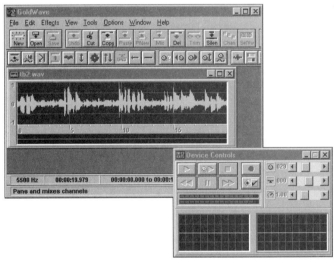

Figure 2-13: Goldwave contains a plethora of tools available to manipulate and edit sound files in both WAV and AU formats.

WAV files are not very efficient in their compression routines and are consequently very large in size. Differing qualities of sound can be stored in a WAV file, and the higher the quality, the larger the file size. As an approximation, a sound of 10 seconds in length in the highest possible CD level will generate a file size of around 200K.

AU files

AU files are slightly more efficient in their compression than WAV files, giving subsequently smaller file sizes. Not all browsers can automatically play back AU files, though. Both Cool Edit and Goldwave can create AU files, but the Windows Sound Recorder cannot.

MIDI files

MIDI files can be used only for music, and none of the sound editing packages I've just mentioned can produce MIDI files. They are highly efficient in their storage of music: a two minute track can be less than 30K in size. MIDI files have traditionally been created with a musical instrument that has a special interface and the output (the tune) saved onto a computer's hard disk.

Not everybody has a MIDI-compliant instrument, though, and even more of us are not musicians! Thankfully, some shareware packages have just recently become available that have a large sampling of MIDI tracks as part of a library (sort of a musical version of clip art). These programs let you modify the instruments that are used in a selected track, change the tempo (speed) and the pitch of playback, and include a number of special effects. By manipulating all of these factors in a MIDI file, anyone can easily generate unique, royalty-free soundtracks to use on their Web page.

The shipping version of NetObjects Fusion comes supplied with a small number of royalty free MIDI files that you can use on your Web pages.

RealAudio

A further sound file type that has come into prominence over the last few years is RealAudio. Without getting into technicality, RealAudio, by using a special server to process the sound file, lets sound *stream* from the RealAudio server to the user's browser.

Streaming is a process whereby the sound is played *as* it downloads instead of *after* it downloads. This negates the problem of having to wait for the full file before being able to hear anything. Another advantage is that RealAudio files can be very large indeed. Commercial servers contain files with entire 2 and 3 hour concerts, and many radio stations even broadcast live 24 hours a day in RealAudio. To obtain a list of these, have a look at `www.timecast.com/stations/index.html`. This Web site contains a fantastic repository of locations using audio (and video) on the Internet.

The commercial broadcast RealAudio Server software is beyond the reach of most people in terms of cost, but the RealAudio player is available for most common browsers free of charge from `www.real.com`. Thankfully, however, you do not necessarily need a RealAudio server to stream RealAudio files from your Web site. There is a relatively easy (albeit less efficient) method available using http:// protocols, which are covered in Chapter 21.

The RealAudio player (shown in Figure 2-14) lets the listener set the volume of the streaming file as well as fast-forward or rewind to specific sections of a RealAudio file.

Figure 2-14: RealAudio allows the streaming of sound files in a special format.

Using video

The use of video on a Web page is potentially one of the most exciting of the new technologies available. The two most common video formats currently in use are AVI from Microsoft and QuickTime from Apple Computer. There is a major drawback, however, in the massive file sizes required to make even 10 seconds of video. One megabyte of storage per 10 seconds of video is not uncommon. This makes for huge download times before the person viewing the Web page sees any action.

This is all changing as technology improves. The developers of RealAudio have released RealMedia 5.0, a combination RealAudio and RealVideo encoder and player. This allows you to take uncompressed video footage via a video capture card and effectively turn it into a streaming video file. As with RealAudio, the dedicated server software is quite expensive, but the player and encoder software is free of charge, and again, http:// streaming can be performed. Http:// streaming is covered in Chapter 21.

Hot
Stuff

For an example, take a look at www.mvclc.org.au/html/video.html, where a large number of church services have been encoded and placed for streaming download.

When video files are embedded into a Web page, they are not played back as part of the browser software. Video files need a special player to display the movie. Windows 95 comes with a Media Player capable of playing both AVI and QuickTime files (See Figure 2-15). Windows Media Player cannot display RealVideo files, though.

Figure 2-15: The Windows Media Player showing an AVI file.

Video editing tools

With video, you have hardware issues to consider as well as the software overheads. This is unlike most of the other software-driven technologies that are available to Web developers.

Video requires the use of a video capture card to grab the video signal and store it on the local hard disk as a movie file. This signal is captured from a source such as a camcorder or VCR player. Depending upon the quality of movie you require, these capture cards cost from a couple of hundred dollars to many thousands. A fast video card, lots — and I do mean *lots* (most professionals use hard drives with a capacity of 9 *gigabytes*!) — of hard disk space and knowledge of a video-editing package are also essential to make the effort worthwhile.

Adobe Premiere, shown in Figure 2-16 has become the standard for desktop-based video editing. It contains many editing and special effects filters but requires patience and perseverance to learn all its capabilities. U-Lead's MediaVision program is another excellent package, and a "light" version, that is bundled with many video capture cards.

Figure 2-16: Adobe Premiere is the de facto standard for creating and editing desktop video files.

Is there a better way?

For smaller video animations, one trick (assuming you have all the hardware and software requirements) is to use the GIF Construction Set software to convert a video (AVI or QuickTime) file into an animated GIF. While the final quality is not always fantastic, in many cases it is quite passable and has the added advantage of a much smaller file size than the equivalent AVI or QuickTime file.

Using animation

Another way of making animations and simulated video on Web pages is to use special software designed for this task. Two of the most popular are Flash and Director, both from the Macromedia company.

Macromedia Flash

Flash is designed for those who require animation on their Web pages. Figure 2-17 shows the Flash timeline where individual frames of an animation are built.

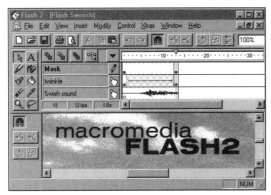

Figure 2-17: Macromedia Flash is an inexpensive and very effective way to add animation to Web pages.

Flash animations are created using either imported images or Flash's own suite of tools. With imagination, you can create very complex and exciting animations with Flash. A good example is the Microsoft Network Web site at `www.msn.com`.

To view Flash animation, the Web browser must have the Flash media player installed. You can obtain this free of charge from the Macromedia Web site at `www.macromedia.com`. Flash animation will stream to the Web browser when they are activated similar to the way RealAudio and RealVideo files do. They are also very small and therefore very efficient.

Just recently, Macromedia announced a joint venture with RealMedia to form a new specification called RealFlash. This effectively allows, for example, cartoons to be streamed from a Web site with true sound in real time. Warner Brothers is the first to do it, and seeing the Road Runner on a Web page just as you would see him on TV is quite an experience. You still don't feel sorry for the coyote though!

See `www.real.com/festival/index.html` for more details and a sample of the available cartoons.

Macromedia Shockwave and Director

Shockwave files created with Macromedia Director are specially converted files for use on the Web. Director is a very high-end authoring tool with a wide set of tools to create eye-popping animations, interactive applications, and multimedia projects. Once produced, Director files are converted to the Shockwave format, which allows them to be displayed in a Web page using a browser with a Shockwave plug-in.

Shockwave has become the standard for Web animations and multimedia. It's not for the casual user, as the learning curve is quite steep. This does not mean that Director is difficult, just that the breadth, scope, and potential of Director is so large. Master it though, and you are well on your way to being the next George Lucas!

Figure 2-18 shows a good example of the extent of the tools available in Director.

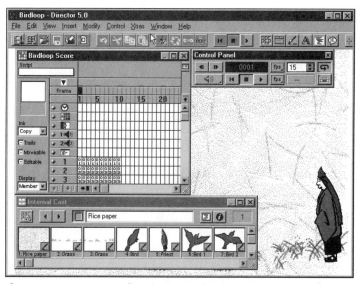

Figure 2-18: Macromedia Director is the de facto standard for creating Web-based multimedia applications and animations.

The Shockwave plug-in is free of charge and available from the Macromedia Web site at www.macromedia.com. A good introduction to Macromedia Director is *Macromedia Director 5 for Dummies* by Lauren Steinhauer (IDG Books, 1996). For Shockwave, have a look at *Shockwave for Director 5 for Dummies* by Greg Harvey (IDG Books Worldwide, Inc., 1996).

Using Dynamic Components

Fusion also allows the inclusion of Java applets, ActiveX controls, JavaScript code, and the proprietary objects, NFX components.

Java applets

Java applets are small programs that you can insert into Web pages to perform specific functions. These applets include banners (as seen in Figure 2-19), rotating images, and clocks. Java applets are written using the Java language developed by Sun Microsystems and have the benefit of being *platform-independent*. This means that a Java applet written on a Macintosh, for example, will run quite happily in a Web browser on a Windows 95, Windows NT, or UNIX-based computer.

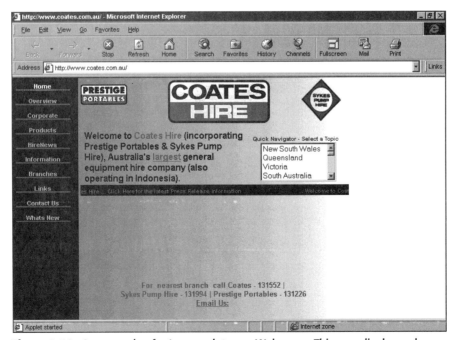

Figure 2-19: An example of a Java applet on a Web page. This one displays a banner that is changed by editing a simple text file.

ActiveX controls

Microsoft originally developed ActiveX controls from the older OCX controls used in the Visual Basic language. At this time, they can only be used successfully in Microsoft's Internet Explorer browser. From a trickle initially, a plethora of ActiveX controls is now available that you can embed into a Web page. One of the most common is the ActiveX control (as shown in Figure 2-20) developed by Adobe to display documents created in the Acrobat format.

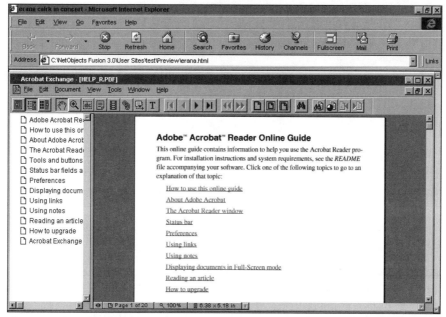

Figure 2-20: Adobe Acrobat uses an ActiveX control to display its documents inside a Web browser.

JavaScript code

Don't be confused! JavaScript has nothing to do with Java. Initially called LiveScript and developed by Netscape, JavaScript is a scripting program used extensively to add interactivity to Web pages. Working on the principle that everything on a Web page is an object (including status bars, windows, menus, and the contents of the page), JavaScript lets you control how these are manipulated. The earliest examples of JavaScript had a million and one Web sites displaying banner messages in the status bar at the bottom of the browser, but now experienced programmers use JavaScript for validating users or creating special effects.

JavaScript is not a hard language to learn particularly, and it is becoming increasingly popular as more demands are requested for interactivity on Web sites. Figure 2-21 shows the NetObjects ScriptBuilder application that is used to create JavaScript, a trial version of which is included on the CD-ROM that accompanies this book.

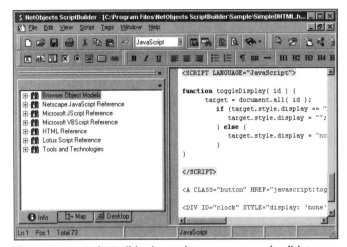

Figure 2-21: ScriptBuilder is used to generate and validate JavaScript code.

NFX Components

NFX Components are applets supplied by NetObjects. They are, in effect, a series of Java and Perl (another scripting language) applets. The NFX Components are available from the Component toolbar and include applets to create rotating and time-based images, message boards, interactive menu buttons, and so on. Figure 2-22 shows the Components palette. A sampling of NFX Components can be found on the CD-ROM that accompanies this book.

Figure 2-22: The NFX Component toolbar in NetObjects Fusion. Each icon represents a different NFX control.

Other Considerations

We need to consider two final things when defining Web page content: screen size and the number of colors to use.

Arguments rage regarding the use of screen resolution size when creating a Web site. Different surveys give different answers as to what is the most common screen resolution in use by those who access the World Wide Web: 640 × 480? 800 × 600? or 1,024× 768?

Second to this, what color depth should you use: 256 colors? 16.7 million? black and white?

Note

Screen resolution is measured in *pixels*. A single pixel is a dot of color on the computer monitor. A resolution of 640 × 480 therefore is a screen made up of 640 dots across and 480 dots deep.

Suggested resolution

Generally consideration dictates that Web pages should be designed with the lowest common denominator in mind, and in the case of screen resolution, this means 640 × 480. Using this resolution virtually guarantees that everyone will be able to see the full width of your pages.

While you *can* cram more onto a Web page at higher resolutions, the trade-off is that users running at a lower resolution must scroll to the right to see the rest of the page that is hidden from them. Figure 2-23 shows how a user running the standard 640 × 480 resolution will see a page designed at 800 × 600.

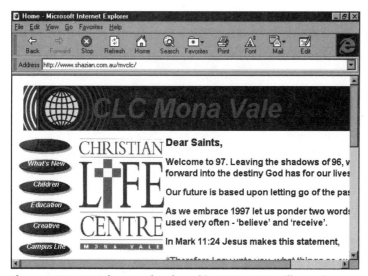

Figure 2-23: A Web page developed in 800 × 600 will not view correctly at lower resolutions without scrolling to the right.

How many colors should I use?

The same theory applies to colors. While an image on your screen may look fabulous in 16.7 million colors, the download time for your Web site visitors could be prohibitive.

Using 256 colors as against 16.7 million does not mean you have to sacrifice quality, though. It simply means a full palette of 65,536 colors is available to you, but only 256 can be displayed at any one point in time. This is more than adequate for most images you will display on a Web site. (Under Microsoft Windows, this is actually 216 as Windows reserves the rest for its own use, but this is academic in most cases).

The side benefit is that at this color depth, images are substantially smaller and will therefore download faster.

Summary

✦ Using NetObjects Fusion is an easy way to create pages containing text, graphics, sound, video, and animations.

✦ Wherever possible, restrict Web page sizes to 640 × 480 pixels.

✦ The number of colors used on a Web page should be restricted to 256.

Introducing NetObjects Fusion

P A R T

◆   ◆   ◆   ◆

In This Part

Chapter 3
The Fusion Difference

Chapter 4
The Fusion Interface

◆   ◆   ◆   ◆

In Chapter 2, I explored how NetObjects Fusion provides a never before seen approach to Web publishing by combining all the factors that enable Web site and page construction as well as ease of Web maintenance and management into a single package. In Chapters 3 and 4, I cover Fusion and its place above the other WYSIWYG (what you see is what you get) programs available for Web publishing.

In contrast to text editors (and their offspring), NetObjects Fusion is a program specifically designed to create Web pages and, more importantly, complete Web sites. Text editors are the traditional tools of choice for Web developers, but their very persona means that, as a developer, you need to concentrate on getting the underlying HTML code correct first. Unfortunately, as a result, more time is spent on this than the look and feel of the Web site. Consequently, you are forced to be a "code cutter" first and a Web designer second.

In addition, unlike packages that promise WYSIWYG Web publishing — but concentrate on individual pages that compose the site — NetObjects Fusion treats a Web site as a whole project. This lets you concentrate on the overall site and its interface, rather than mundane chores such as checking correct navigation from page to page or making sure that all the site's elements are referenced correctly. In Chapters 3 and 4 I delve into what makes Fusion stand out above the rest.

The Fusion Difference

If NetObjects Fusion has been installed correctly, you'll see an icon for the program on your desktop (shown in Figure 3-1). Simply double-click this icon to start Fusion.

After a moment, the Fusion splash screen will appear. Next, you'll see a dialog box (shown in Figure 3-2) asking for the type of site to open. You can either open a Blank Site, a site based on a template, or an existing Fusion Site.

More Info

For help installing Fusion, see Appendix A for all the details.

Figure 3-1: The Fusion icon on the desktop.

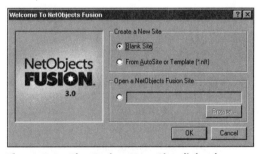

Figure 3-2: The Fusion New Site dialog box.

Note

The very first time you start NetObjects Fusion, the Welcome dialog box will open automatically. On subsequent launches, Fusion will load the last Web site you worked on and display the exact view you saw when you exited the program. If the last site loaded in Fusion has been moved or deleted, Fusion will revert to opening the New Site dialog box.

Note

If you are using the 30-day trial download of Fusion and not a fully registered and licensed version, you'll take another step between the splash screen and the dialog box (shown in Figure 3-2). You'll be presented with a dialog box containing the serial number of the 30-day trial version you have and a counter showing how many days are left before the trial version expires. The Cancel button in the dialog box will terminate this session of Fusion and the OK button will take you to the dialog box shown in Figure 3-2.

Danger Zone

Beware! If you try to cheat the 30-day trial version by resetting the time of your computer clock, Fusion will become totally inoperative. Not even resetting the clock to the correct date and time will help. There is no way to undo this. Also, once the 30-day period expires, you can never use that trial version on the same machine again.

Opening a Blank Site

A blank site initially contains a single blank page (the Home page) and is the most common starting point for a new site.

At this point, you are working from the NetObjects Fusion dialog box. The Blank Site radio button is selected by default, so just click OK. Fusion will next open the New Blank Site dialog box, allowing you to specify the name and location of the new site. I recommend you use the default for the location of new sites (the User Sites folder) as this makes it very easy to back up your files, as you only need to select this one folder.

Note

If you already have a site started and choose the New Site option from the File menu, choose the Blank Site option from the cascading menu to reach the New Blank Site dialog box.

Danger Zone

If you specify the name of a site that already exists, Fusion will prompt for confirmation to replace the existing site, as seen in Figure 3-3. *If you accept to overwrite, you cannot reverse this and the previous site of the same name will be irrevocably lost!*

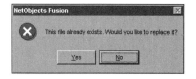

Figure 3-3: The Overwrite Site confirmation dialog box.

Fusion now displays the new site in Site view where the layout of the single home page is displayed as a single yellow icon surrounded by a blue border.

Opening a Site from a Template

An *Autosite* or *template* is a site file containing a preformatted set of Web pages in a particular site structure designed for a specific purpose such as a business presentation, company Internet, or department intranet. Figure 3-4 shows the folder containing the list of Autosite templates supplied with Fusion 3.0.

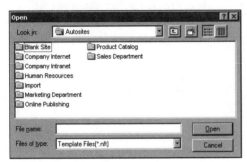

Figure 3-4: The AutoSites supplied with Fusion.

Using an AutoSite template aids dramatically in the construction of a Web site as all pages, styles, color schemes, and links between pages are already created for you.

If a template style does not exist for the site you wish to develop, you can save any site you create in NetObjects Fusion as an AutoSite template. This lets you build a library of often-used templates. Also, if you specialize in developing Web sites for a particular market niche, you can design a Web site with Fusion that satisfies the basic needs of that market and save this as an AutoSite template. This template is then available to use over and over for different clients, only requiring you to change styles, color schemes, or content as necessary. To save any site as a template, use the Export command from the File menu. Check out the "Exporting a site" section later on in this chapter.

Importing and Exporting an Existing Web Site

For those developers using Fusion to modify and update an existing Web site, NetObjects Fusion lets you import an existing site from either a local hard disk or from a remote location such as a Web server. In both of these cases, you need to know the exact disk location or URL of the site. You can convert imported sites into NetObjects Fusion format or leave them as native HTML code.

When you import a site, Fusion examines and copies the structure of the site and the content of each page, lays out the pages as close as possible to the original, and copies internal and external links.

Be aware that importing a complex site might take more processing time than you expect. If the source site was created in NetObjects Fusion, it is more efficient to import it as a template than to import the published HTML pages.

Importing from a local hard drive

If you want to import from a local site that was created with a different Web development program, select File ➪ New Site and choose From Local Import from the cascading menu (see Figure 3-5). You are presented with the dialog box shown in Figure 3-6.

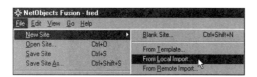

Figure 3-5: Selecting the From Local Import option.

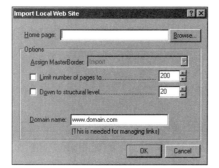

Figure 3-6: The Import Local Web Site dialog box.

To select the site, enter its Home page file name in the dialog box or use the Browse button to navigate to the file on the hard disk or network server.

The Assign MasterBorder field is only available when in Site view and importing a site into the current site. When importing a site in this way, instead of a new site being generated, the imported site is merged with the current site. For more details on MasterBorders, see Chapter 10.

The Limit number of pages to option is self-explanatory: it confines the imported Web site to a determined number of pages. Use the Down to structural level option to limit the "depth" of pages imported. As a Web site is a hierarchy of pages with the Home page at the top of the tree, each level of the hierarchy can be thought of as a number with the Home page being 0, the next being 1, and so on. To limit the levels imported to say 3, you'd enter this figure into this box.

The Domain name field requires some explanation. Fusion treats links as either *internal* or *external*. Links that reference a Web site out of the current domain are *external links*, and links inside the current domain are *internal links*. By filling in the Domain name field (assuming you have a domain name for the site to be imported, of course), Fusion will treat any links that exist in the site referencing this domain name as internal links.

Even if you have been building sites in other applications and they are stored locally, this can still be useful. For example, you may have built a site for a client who will ultimately have the domain name www.new_client.com. Even though this does not exist as yet, Fusion will treat all pages you have in the site that reference this domain as being internal to the site. In the imported site's Site view, this will give you much more flexibility to move or rename pages or create links to objects inside the site.

Using a domain name so that references will become internal also lets Fusion resolve the old problem of relative versus absolute path names.

Once you have entered all the information correctly, click the OK button. Fusion will request for an output file name it needs to create the site as a Fusion site. Once this is completed, Fusion will import the site and display it in Site view (as seen in Figure 3-7).

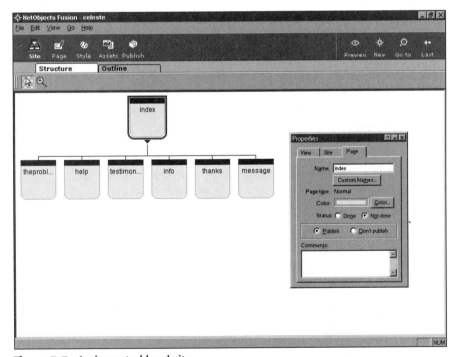

Figure 3-7: An imported local site.

Importing from a remote site

If you are importing a site from a remote location such as on an Internet service provider (ISP) server, the steps are very similar to importing from a local site. After selecting the From Remote Import option from the New Site command on the File menu, a dialog box opens (as shown in Figure 3-8).

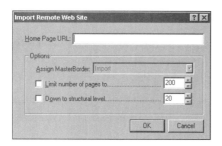

Figure 3-8: The Import Remote Web Site dialog box.

In the domain name field (named Home Page URL), you enter the domain name of the site including the page name (Index.html, from example).

Note You must be logged on to the Internet before you can import from a remote site. You must also not have securities against downloading, such as firewalls, proxies, or robot files.

As in importing a local site, once again you have options regarding the number of pages to import and to what level.

When you have completed all the details, click the OK button. Fusion will locate the domain and import the pages up to the level you have specified.

Once completed, Fusion will display the site in Site view.

Importing Web sites from previous versions of Fusion

If you have been using NetObjects Fusion version 2, version 3 can directly open the created NOD files. At this point you will be given two options (as seen from the dialog box in Figure 3-9): opening the older version directly and converting the original version 2 NOD file to version 3 or first making a copy and then opening the copy. I strongly recommend the second option for no other reason than having a backup of everything is a wise move!

Figure 3-9: Clicking No will completely update the Web site from a previous version of Fusion; clicking Yes will open up a copy in version 3.

Importing a template

As well as importing a complete site into an existing site, you can also import a template into an existing site. This is useful where you may have created a complete site on a modular basis and then want to merge all of the NOD files into a single Web site. Another use for importing a template is when you have created a series of pages that can be reused in different Web sites. A generic bulletin board system or guest book are examples of this where a set of pages can be saved as a template and then reused in different Web site you develop.

Limitations on importing

Once you have imported a site, depending upon its complexity — and especially if the imported site contained frames — you might have some strange looking results in certain areas such as in Figure 3-10.

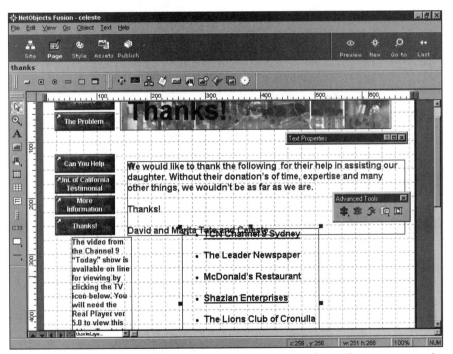

Figure 3-10: When importing sites, it is not uncommon to have elements appear in places that are not expected.

As a rule of thumb, the more complex the HTML used to create the original site, the more out of alignment elements on the imported pages may be. This especially applies to pages that make heavy use of percentage widths for positioning.

There is unfortunately no way to import a site perfectly. This particularly applies to designs that have been specifically defined for either Netscape Navigator or Microsoft Internet Explorer, as they both render slightly differently. Despite this potential drawback—which is no fault of NetObjects Fusion—importing an existing site into Fusion is still a much faster way to edit an existing site than starting from scratch.

Assets

All of the imported site's assets (its graphics, audio, video, and the like) will be displayed in the Assets view (as shown in Figure 3-11), and you can use these exactly as if you had placed them manually. If you are radically changing the imported site and discarding any of these assets, don't forget to check the Assets list before republishing and delete any now unused assets. Also, periodically delete the Preview Folder that Fusion creates every time a site is Previewed or published to remove any stray files or objects that may be left over from a previous publish/preview.

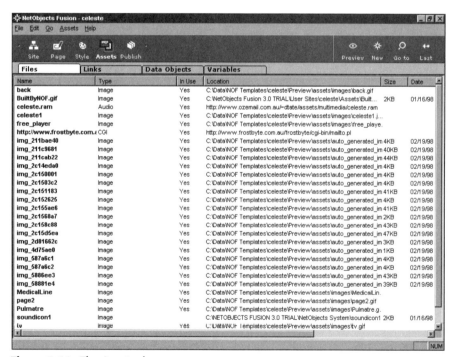

Figure 3-11: The Assets view.

Some thoughts on importing sites

Once a site has been imported from either a local or remote location, it is now a Fusion site for all intents and purposes. All the functions and facilities of Fusion are available to you to modify this site at will. Accepting the fact that not all sites, especially complex ones, will import absolutely perfectly, this is still the fastest way to modify existing sites.

It is worth noting at this point that I do *not* recommend trying to import a Fusion-generated site into another application. Why would you want to anyway? There is only one valid reason I can imagine.

The situation has happened in the past and no doubt will happen in the future in which clients of web developers suddenly will want to take over their own Web site maintenance and do not want to use Fusion for whatever reason. Because of the complexity of the code Fusion generates to give the pixel-level accuracy of placement of objects, many "lesser" Web authoring packages simply choke on the code giving completely unpredictable results.

Reference HTML

The Reference HTML option lets you refer to existing HTML pages you may have generated manually or perhaps with another Web authoring program. The HTML files you specify are copied and then used; the original files are not modified in any way. If you have specified that MasterBorders be applied to the Referenced HTML, Fusion will also add the necessary HTML to the copied file. The resulting HTML files are placed in the Publish or Preview folders.

For complete details on Publishing and the file folder options available please, see Part VI.

Exporting a site and creating templates

Fusion allows you to export a site to the local hard disk and save it as a template. Why would you do this?

A site that is exported is saved as a Net Objects Fusion template file with the *.nft* extension to the file, as distinct from the *nod* extension used for a standard NOD file. Saving as a template is very useful when a generic set of Web pages is created that would be applicable for inclusion in other sites or used as the basis for a new site.

Before exporting as a template, you should manually create the folder into which the exported template is to be saved. After a site is exported as a template, all assets and style details are exported to the new folder. This also gives a convenient way of backing up a site to a Zip disk or tape drive, as all elements of the site are now stored in a one-folder hierarchy.

With a normal NOD file, assets such as images, sound files, site style components, and so on are conceivably stored in a myriad of different locations on the hard disk. This makes it especially difficult to perform a backup of a site.

Creating a New Fusion NOD File

Whether a site is a single page or a hundred pages, Fusion must be instructed to create a new database or NOD file for the site before it is created. The NOD file contains all of the information relating to the site such as the number and names of pages, locations of attached external files, and any objects created using Fusion's own tools.

NOD is the extension used for the database file Fusion creates. For example, starting a new site called *starfleet* will create a NOD file called *starfleet.nod*. *N-O-D* stands for *NetObjects Database*. It is not too hard then to figure out that when a site is exported as a template (see earlier paragraphs) that the template file created has the *.nft* extension which stands for *NetObjects Template*.

You created the NOD file when you chose the New Site option. In the dialog box that opens, the file name you entered created the new site's NOD file.

For the purposes of this quick tour, we'll create a test site without using any preset templates. Instead, we'll use the new Blank site option by selecting its radio button and clicking OK. This opens the second dialog box mentioned earlier and shown in Figure 3-6. Type **test** in the File Name field of the dialog box. The dialog box should appear as it does in Figure 3-12. If all is correct, click the OK button.

Figure 3-12: The completed New Site dialog box.

Working with the NOD file

All the information needed to compose the final Web site is stored in a NetObjects Fusion database called a NOD file. It is called a *NOD file* simply because this is the extension NetObjects uses for the file name. For example, if your Web site is called *test*, the corresponding database NOD file is called *test.nod*.

Fusion will now create test.nod, the database file it uses to store its information on the site. This file will be placed in a folder called test, which in turn is located by default in the User Sites folder in the NetObjects 3.0 folder. Once the program has completed this task, it will open the Site view module of NetObjects Fusion and your screen should appear similar to Figure 3-13.

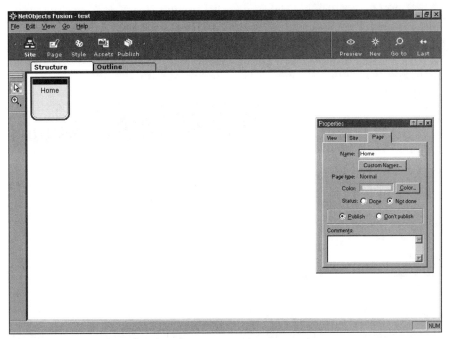

Figure 3-13: Site view showing the new test Home page icon.

The NOD file does not contain any of the HTML coding that Fusion generates when a site is published or previewed. What the NOD file *does* contain is information on the elements (assets) on pages in the site created using Fusion's tools. Additionally, pointers to external files that are included (such as graphics files, sound clips, video movies, Java applets, or ActiveX controls) are stored in the NOD file.

Because of this, you should regularly make copies of NOD files for sites that are currently under construction. Any damage to these files can take many hours of reconstruction, if such a reconstruction can be done at all.

Fusion includes an option in the Preferences palette for creating automatic backups of the NOD file every time it is saved. This option is set to be on by default. I recommend that you keep this option on. (Not that I think Fusion may crash and force you to use this file, but in my opinion you cannot ever have too many backups.) Note also that each of the backups created will take up corresponding disk space.

If you are loading a site that already exists, Fusion will start the new session in the view you were in when you last exited the program.

Managing external files

As Fusion keeps track of any external assets (files) in the NOD file, you should not move these to another location on your hard disk without updating the NOD file. If you inadvertently move a file in use to another location, Fusion will not be able to locate this file when you publish your site, and the result will be the dreaded broken GIF icon displayed in the browser. If Fusion cannot find an asset when in Page view, the asset will be replaced with a white box containing a cross and a red exclamation mark (as shown in Figure 3-14).

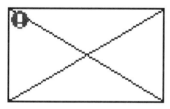

Figure 3-14: A Web page showing the missing figure symbol.

Use one folder per Web site

A recommended and proven procedure is to use one folder to store all external assets for any single Web site. An additional benefit to using this method is that backing up any individual site becomes a simple task of selecting only two folders to backup to tape, floppy, or Zip drive. The first folder is the User Site folder containing the NOD file, and the second contains all supporting files of external assets.

The NOD file and the completed Web site

When it comes time for Fusion to produce the code for the Web pages in a site (at either preview time or publishing time), each page is created sequentially from its description stored in the NOD file. You will remember that the NOD file is the database file maintained by the Fusion program containing all of the relevant information composing the current Web site, such as text, graphics, external files, headers, footers, color schemes, font styles, and so on.

Fusion creates a file containing a series of HTML tables for every page in the Web site. Individual cells in the table contain a single element from the page. To keep cells from collapsing when they do not contain any elements, Fusion inserts a special graphic into these cells called *dot_clear.gif*. This file is a transparent graphics image as wide as the table cell that it will fill and one pixel high.

Summary

✦ NetObjects Fusion is different from conventional HTML coding as it insulates the developer from the underlying code, instead allowing concentration on content and not programming.

✦ Sites can be created from scratch, from a template, or by importing an existing HTML site.

✦ The Fusion NOD file contains all the information contained in a Web site.

✦ A Fusion NFT file is a template of a Web site that can be used as the basis for a new site or inserted into an existing site.

✦ Correct management of external files used in a Web site is necessary to avoid errors in the NOD file.

✦   ✦   ✦

The Fusion Interface

♦ ♦ ♦ ♦

In This Chapter

The edit menu

The control bar

Site, Page, Style,
Assets, and
Publish views

♦ ♦ ♦ ♦

OK, all the preliminaries are over and done. Let's get down to business by taking a real look at NetObjects Fusion and explaining its basic layout.

No matter what version of Fusion you are using, your Fusion window will include two common features running through all the modules: the menu bar and the control bar (Figure 4-1). The actual commands or facilities available will vary from module to module, but the basic look of these sections stays the same.

Figure 4-1: The Fusion menu bar and control bar.

Tip

You may have a subwindow open at this time labeled Properties (as shown in Figure 4-2). If so, click its Close button to dismiss it for the time being. This will let you see more of the main Fusion window. You can restore it later (in Site view) by selecting View on the menu bar and choosing Properties Palette.

Figure 4-2: The Standard toolbar and Properties palette.

Tip

Instead of closing the Properties window completely, you can also double-click in its title bar — or click the middle button in the title bar that looks like an underline (see Figures 4-3a and b). This causes the main part of the window to roll up, leaving only the title bar in view (see Figure 4-4). You can then move this anywhere on the screen. To restore the Properties palette to its original state, simply double-click the title bar again (or click the middle button, which has changed to a box).

(a)   **(b)**

Figure 4-3: Roll up the Properties palette window either by double-clicking the title bar (a) or clicking the middle button on the title bar (b).

The rolled-up Properties palette

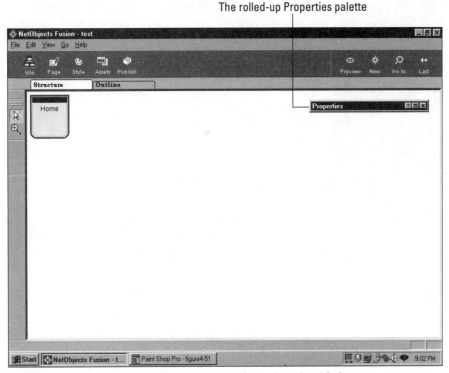

Figure 4-4: The rolled up Properties palette shows just the title bar.

The Menu Bar

Most of the commands for creating or importing sites in Chapter 3 are available from the main menu bar in Site view. It contains five menus: File, Edit, View, Go, and Help. We'll run through each one.

The File menu

When you click the File command on the menu bar, the drop-down menu displays options grouped in three sections, as seen in Figure 4-5 and as described in Table 4-1.

Figure 4-5: The File menu commands when in Site view.

Table 4-1
The Options on the File Menu

Option	Shortcut	What it does
New Site		This option contains four options for creating a blank site, a site from a template, from a local import, or from a remote import (see the next section)
Open Site	Ctrl+O	Opens an already created site
Save Site	Ctrl+S	Saves the currently open site
Save Site As	Ctrl+Shift+S	Saves a copy of the site or allows you to change the name of the site
Import Web Site		Lets you import a site not necessarily created in Fusion from a local site or a remote site
Import Template		Imports a template
Reference HTML		Lets you reference external HTML documents without converting them
Export Site		Lets you save the site as a template
Print Setup		Calls up a standard Windows Print Setup dialog box
Print Preview		Allows you to preview how the site schematic will print
Print		Prints the site in Site view
1 *file name* - 4 *file name*		Allows you to open the last four sites
Exit	Alt+F4	Allows you to exit the program

The New Site option

As you may remember, when starting NetObjects for the first time, a dialog box prompts you to enter a new site name. Figure 4-6 shows the New Site dialog box. The New Site option in the File menu is equivalent to this command, opening the dialog box so that you can enter the appropriate details. Once you have selected the New Site option, a cascading menu displays four options from which you can choose the source of the New Site (see Table 4-2).

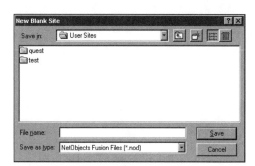

Figure 4-6: The New Site cascading menu.

Table 4-2
The New Site options

Option	What it does
Blank	Starts a site with a single empty Home page
From Template	Starts a new site based on either a Fusion supplied template (selected by choosing it from a dialog box) or from a site you have saved previously as a template
From Local Import	Imports an existing HTML site to edit or add to from a local (or network) hard disk
From Remote Import	Imports an existing HTML site to edit or add to from an Internet server by supplying its URL

The Open Site option

The Open Site dialog box lets you enter the full path name to open the NOD file for a site that already exists. As you can see from Figure 4-7, you can also use the standard navigation options to change to the folder containing the NOD file of the site. This option is most often used when you have been working on another site's NOD file and now want to modify or add to a different site.

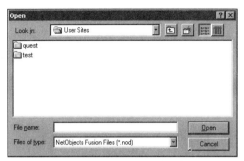

Figure 4-7: The Open Site dialog box.

The Save Site option

The Save Site command is self-explanatory. Use it often when working in a Fusion session to save an up-to-date copy to the hard disk of the site on which you are currently working.

When leaving a NetObjects Fusion session, the currently open file is automatically saved and backed up for you. You can disable these options on the Backup tab of the Preferences palette, which you can access from the Edit command on the menu bar. See the section in this chapter labeled "The Backup tab" for details.

The Save Site As option

The Save Site As option saves an exact copy of the currently loaded file to the hard disk but under a different name. This creates a duplicate of the current Web site on the hard disk or network drive. In the dialog box that opens when you select the Save As command, Fusion will prompt you for the new file name as shown in Figure 4-8

Once you have used the Save Site As command, you will then be working on a file that contains the name you applied as its "saved as" name. For example, if you were working on a file called test.nod. and used the Save Site As command to save the file as test1.nod, you would then be working on test1.nod and *not* the original file.

When using the Save Site As command, you cannot save the site to the same location with the same name (after all, that's what the Save Site command is for!). If you're using the same name for the site, you'd have to save the site to another location.

You won't be able to save the Web site under the same name to the same file with the Save As option like you can in other programs. Just use the Save option.

Many people use this option as a safety net as it ensures that if something does go wrong with the original site, you can at least load the copy and continue working with, hopefully, minimal loss of work or time.

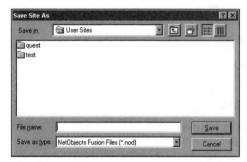

Figure 4-8: The Save As dialog box.

The Import Web Site and Import Template options

Using either the Import Web Site or Import Template command allows you to merge an existing Web site into the current one being built. When using the Import Web Site command, you have two choices from the cascading menu: import from a Local Site on a hard disk or import from a Remote Site on the Internet or intranet. By using Import Template, you can pull in a site previously built with Fusion and saved as a template. In contrast, importing a Web site causes Fusion to open a dialog box prompting for the domain of the Web site to be included into the current site.

Note

With either of these commands, the inserted site is placed in the site hierarchy with its Home page directly under the currently selected page.

The Reference HTML option

The Reference HTML command opens a dialog box (as seen in Figure 4-9) that lets you set the parameters for any HTML sites you import into Fusion. Such things as the URL of the Home page, the number of levels to import, how many pages, and so on are defined here prior to importing (as explained in Table 4-3). It is important to understand that the original HTML is *not* affected: it is actually copied into the Fusion site.

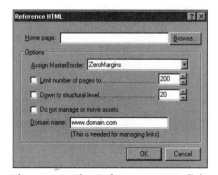

Figure 4-9: The Reference HTML dialog box.

Table 4-3
Options on the Reference HTML dialog box

Option	What it does
Home page	The Home page of the Site to be imported, usually the index.htm(l) page
Assign MasterBorder	You can choose a MasterBorder from the drop-down list. With the ZeroMargins set, no MasterBorders will be assigned to the imported HTML files. In other words, the files will come into the site totally unchanged.
Limit number of pages to	The maximum number of pages in the referenced site to import (200 is the default)
Down to structural level	The level in the hierarchy of the imported site to import (20 is the default)
Do not manage or move assets	Any referenced GIF files, JPG images, or other elements referenced in the HTML files are to remain as they are and not imported into the Fusion assets register
Domain name	Any domain name that may be available from the imported referenced HTML files, which are to be treated as internal (relative) links.

The Export Site command

The Export Site command (formerly called Export Site as Template in earlier versions of Fusion) creates a NetObjects Fusion template (NFT) file from the currently opened site. You can then use this template (which will contain all of the layouts, text, navigation controls, banners, and any external files used in the original site) as the basis for a new Fusion site. The Export Site command opens a dialog box (as shown in Figure 4-10) from which you can select the location of the Template file.

Figure 4-10: The Select Folder dialog box that opens after selecting the Export Site option.

If you click the Network button, all available network drives are also shown as locations where you can save the exported site.

To explain the differences between the Export Site command and the Save As command, you need to understand how Fusion controls and maintains its folder structure for a User Site. This is shown in Figure 4-11.

Figure 4-11: The User Sites folder structure.

All of the files Fusion uses internally for a site are kept in its User Sites folder and subfolders. What are *not* kept in this folder structure are any outside files you may have placed on a Web page. Examples include GIF or JPEG images, sound files, and so on. These are kept in their original locations on the hard disk. These files remain there until publishing time when they are copied into a totally Fusion organized and controlled folder structure on the Web server or local drive.

Note

If an image file placed on a Fusion page is ever modified — for example, adding text to it or any other sort of Fusion-enabled modification — a copy of the original file is created by Fusion and this becomes the asset file listed in the Assets view of Fusion.

When you use the Export Site command, Fusion creates a new folder with a name and location that the Web author nominates. It then gathers and *copies* all external files as well as all files it uses in the original User Site into this new structure. Figure 4-12 shows this new Folder structure. Notice the difference between it and Figure 4-11.

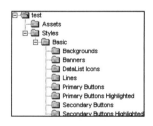

Figure 4-12: The Export Site folder structure.

The resulting database file (that was originally a NOD file) is also not a NOD file any longer. Instead, it now has the extension *NFT*, which stands for *NetObjects Fusion template*.

You can now use this as a safety backup of the original site. Because all the elements and objects composing the site are stored in a logical, single folder structure, you can transfer these folders and subfolders to a tape or zip drive, backup server, or even floppy disks at a pinch.

Although Fusion has an internal backup routine (activated whenever you close a NOF file), the Export Site command is a more useful tool for this purpose because it collates all of the files in the site into one folder and doesn't just make a copy of the NOD file.

The Print Setup option

The Print Setup command is the standard Windows or Macintosh command common to most applications. When selected, the dialog box (Figure 4-13) gives you the choice of deciding which printer and what parameters to use when printing the Web site schematic created in Site view.

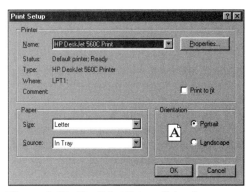

Figure 4-13: The Print Setup dialog box.

The Print Preview option

The Print Preview command lets you to see how your currently connected printer (selected using Print Setup) will print a copy of the Site view.

Figure 4-14 shows a typical corporate site in Print Preview mode.

The starting point of the printed output (the top of the tree in the printed schematic) is the currently selected page. For example, if your currently selected page is the Home page, Print Preview will show the site map of all pages in the site.

If Page 3 is the currently selected page, only Page 3 and its children will appear.

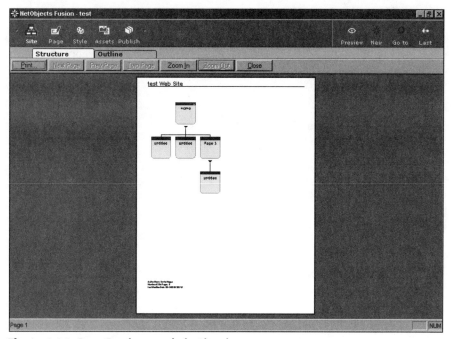

Figure 4-14: Page Preview mode in Site view.

The Print Preview option is helpful for making sure that you're printing the pages you want. Keep in mind that to print the entire site, you have to select the Home page. Otherwise, you'll only print out the page you've selected and its children, and not any of the pages beside or above it.

The Print command

The Print command is identical to the same option in all Windows or Macintosh applications and sends a copy of the Site view to the currently selected printer.

Completing the File menu

The final listings on the File menu refer to the last four sites that were opened in Fusion. To reopen one of these, simply select it on the File menu, and Fusion will replace the currently open site with the chosen one from the listing.

The Exit command

This command should be self-explanatory. With it, you can leave Fusion, and the open site will be saved automatically, unless you have AutoSave unchecked in the Preferences dialog. If this is the case, you will be prompted to save the site on exiting Fusion.

The Edit menu

The only commands available under the Edit menu (see Figure 4-15) while in Site view are New Page, Custom Names, and Preferences. Other options (which are currently grayed out) will become available as you progress through separate sections of NetObjects Fusion.

Figure 4-15: The Edit menu in Site view.

The New Page command

To add new pages to a site, use the New Page command. Every time you select this option (or its shortcut, Ctrl+N), Fusion will add a new page directly below the currently selected page. At the moment, the currently selected page is the Home page shown by its blue border.

You can find out more about adding pages in Site view in Chapter 5.

The Custom Names command

The Custom Names command opens a dialog box (as seen in Figure 4-16) that lets you add a title to the page and several of its elements.

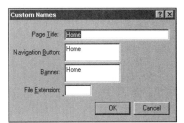

Figure 4-16: The Custom Names dialog box.

I'll have more about working with custom names in Chapter 5.

The Preferences command

The Preferences command opens the Preferences sheet containing three tabs: General, Page, and Backup.

The General tab

The General tab on the Preferences sheet (shown in Figure 4-17) contains commands that you can assign to the entire currently loaded Web site.

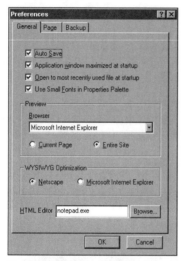

Figure 4-17: The General tab on the Preferences sheet.

When the Auto Save checkbox is checked, Fusion will automatically save any changes you make to the site when you exit the program, preview a page, change views, or publish a site.

If you make any major changes with this command turned on (to test a site's new look, for example), exiting the program will automatically replace the old site with the new. If you do not want these changes saved, make sure this option has been disabled before tinkering!

The "Application window maximized at startup" option will ensure that Fusion starts full screen whenever it loads. This is the same as clicking the full size window button at the top right corner of any Windows application.

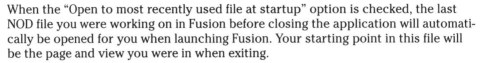

When the "Open to most recently used file at startup" option is checked, the last NOD file you were working on in Fusion before closing the application will automatically be opened for you when launching Fusion. Your starting point in this file will be the page and view you were in when exiting.

In Fusion versions 1 and 2, this was the default, and you could not disable this option.

To minimize the amount of space being used on screen by Properties palettes, checking the "Use Small Fonts in Properties Palette" option will cause all Properties palettes to use a smaller font, consequently reducing the physical on-screen size of the Properties palettes.

As I am sure you are aware, Web pages are viewed with a Web browser and the two most popular are Netscape Navigator and Microsoft Internet Explorer. There's no secret there. Because of this, Fusion has two preferences you can set relating to your browser of choice: Preview and Browser.

Previewing is where you can see what a page or site created in Fusion will look like in a Web browser before it has been moved to a Web server. Figure 4-18 shows a previewed Web page. Notice that the address of the page is not an Internet-based address but one that refers to a hard disk file.

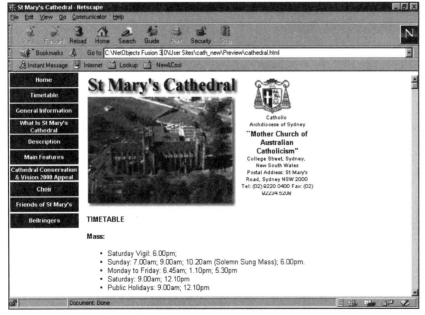

Figure 4-18: A previewed Web page.

Fusion needs to know which you prefer to use as a primary previewing browser. You make this choice by selecting it from the drop-down list on the General tab. When you choose the Preview option, you can also tell Fusion whether to generate the HTML code for just the current working page or the entire site.

With a large site, this may take many minutes to complete before you see the page you want, so I recommend selecting the Current Page option. (This is identical to holding down the Ctrl key when clicking the Preview button on the control bar.)

If you attempt to click a link in the browser once the page has been previewed and you have chosen to Preview only the current page, an error page (as seen in Figure 4-19) will be displayed detailing that the link has been disabled.

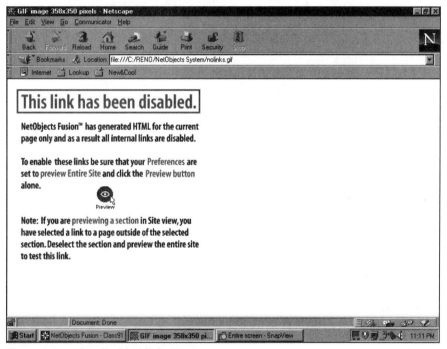

Figure 4-19: The disabled link page.

Tip

It is good practice to check the output of Fusion pages in both Netscape Navigator and Microsoft Internet Explorer before publishing. Why? Both browsers have some real differences between the way they each display various elements on Web pages. While a page may look perfectly good in one browser, it can look terrible in the other. If you have both browsers installed on your hard disk, it is a simple matter to change from one to the other via the Preferences command. Once you have changed the preference, preview again in the new preferred browser. I would recommend doing this particularly with pages containing tables and forms.

As I've just said, both Netscape Navigator and Microsoft Internet Explorer have subtle differences in the way they display Web pages. Because of this, you can specify for which of the two browsers you would like the Web pages to be optimized in the WYSIWYG Optimization box. Select your choice by clicking its radio button. Figures 4-20 and 4-21 illustrate some of these differences.

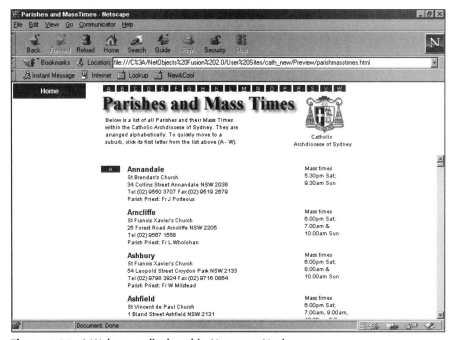

Figure 4-20: A Web page displayed in Netscape Navigator . . .

If you know your target audience is going to be using, for example, Microsoft Internet Explorer 4 on an intranet, for example, set the optimization for Internet Explorer 4. Fusion will create the pages taking into account certain rendering characteristics that are peculiar to IE4, especially as mentioned in regards to tables and forms.

The HTML Editor option lets you choose an HTML editor by browsing to its location on your hard disk. Under Windows 95, this is set to the Windows Notepad by default (in Macintosh, the default is SimpleText), but you can choose any editor you wish.

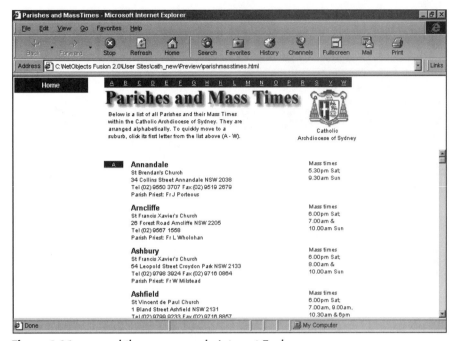

Figure 4-21: . . . and the same page in Internet Explorer.

Having stressed the point earlier in this book that Fusion does not require any HTML coding experience to create Web sites, this might seem like a strange option. But NetObjects Fusion version 2.0 and above let the Web author import external HTML code into a Web site (as shown in Figure 4-22). Another standard reason is for adding the Meta tags that the current crop of search engines require. Don't be too worried about this, though; I show all in due course.

For more information about Meta tags, refer to Chapter 17.

Instead of having to exit Fusion or manually load another application to modify any of this code, double-clicking the white square representing the HTML code loads the nominated HTML Editor.

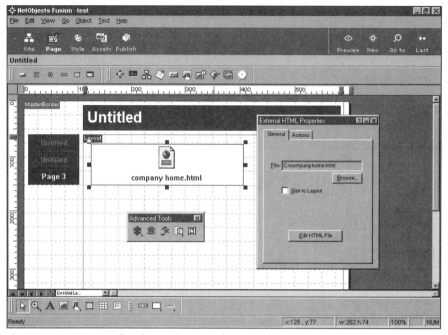

Figure 4-22: A page showing an imported HTML file.

The Page tab

The Page tab on the Preferences palette sets global settings that will apply to all sites opened in Fusion unless local settings override these. The options you can change on the Page tab relate to fonts, page sizing, and background images. Figure 4-23 shows the Page tab of the Preferences sheet.

Figure 4-23: The Page tab on the Preferences sheet.

The Browser Font Settings section of the Page tab allows you to set the default fonts in Fusion to match those defined in your browser. Matching fonts will ensure the pages you create in Fusion will look as they should in the browser. For example, if you normally use Times New Roman 10 as a proportional font and Courier New 12 as a monospaced font in your browser, change the settings in Fusion to match these.

Note

Of course, it is absolutely impossible to determine what fonts have been set as defaults in your site visitors' browsers.

When designing pages in Page view, a counter at the bottom left of the screen shows the exact x and y coordinates of the current cursor position (see Figure 4-24). You'll also see the dimensions of any object that you select. Changing measurement type allows you to use the one you prefer (pixels, inches, points, or centimeters). Personally, I recommend pixels.

x:436 , y:19

Figure 4-24: The counter in Page view showing the x and y coordinates of the cursor.

When Fusion starts a new site, as you know, it creates a blank Home page. The dimensions of this and any subsequently added pages in pixel units are determined by the values currently in the Default Page Size Width and Height fields.

Many arguments over a cup of coffee or something stronger have raged regarding just what these settings should be. At the risk of starting another, I personally use 640×480 pixels, as this is the lowest common denominator in use on the Web.

Note

I know, I know, many surveys have recently stated that 800×600 has overtaken this, but I am still betting that the number of users who use the Web at 640×480 is greater than those *new* users who have 800×600.

When in Page view, you can place and line up objects more accurately by turning on a *grid*. Overlying the physical Web page, the grid is a series of vertical and horizontal lines spaced exactly the same distance from each other. The grid is only used as a reference and does not appear as a part of the final Web page when published or previewed.

You can set the distance the lines from the grid are spaced with the Grid Size option on the Preferences sheet. You can set the Width and Height values of the grid to your preference using the spinner controls (or by typing them in directly).

If your browser adds a border to a page, you may need to tweak the Background Image setting. These values offset the width of this border. For example, if your browser sets a top border of 10 pixels, offsetting this with a value of 10 in the Top field will allow for this.

For those using either Netscape Navigator or Microsoft Explorer, the default settings of Fusion have been optimized for these two browsers and therefore should be left alone. Other browsers can offset any background images by between 6 and 16 pixels. If this is the case, you may need to experiment with these values to get the optimum for your browser.

If you have aligned elements on the page to areas in the background image, they can be shifted so that these alignments no longer are correct. If this happens, use the offset command to realign the page elements to the background. You will need to switch between Preview mode and Page view, adjusting the values until they are correct.

The Backup tab

New to 3.0

The Backup tab contains all of the options for setting the defaults for Fusion's automatic backup procedures. These include the location on your hard drive in which to place the backed up files, how they should be named, how many copies of a backup to keep at any time, and whether to compact the backups automatically.

Backup Location refers to a location on your hard drive where you prefer the backup files to be stored. To select a folder other than the default, click the Browse button to open a dialog box letting you navigate to another folder on the hard disk.

From the drop-down list in the File naming convention option, you can select one of two styles of names for the backup file name. The first is in the format *websitename-backup#.nod*, and the second adds a date and timestamp to the first. In this case, the # sign is the number of the backup file. If this is the third time a backup file has been created for a Fusion NOD file called starfleet, this file name would be starfleet-backup3.nod. If the full date and timestamp option is used, the file name would then be starfleet-backup03-16-0902AM.nod.

The Maximum number of backups kept option allows you to choose how many backup files are kept. For example, choosing three backup files as in the example above would cause the fourth backup to replace the first, and therefore the naming convention of this fourth backup would be starfleet-backup4.nod. The other two backups saved would be starfleet-backup2.nod and starfleet-backup3.nod.

If the Compact database upon exit option is checked, Fusion will use an internal algorithm to compact the NOD file thus minimizing file sizes. This option is the default and the recommended option.

The View menu

In the View menu (seen in Figure 4-25), you can display or hide the Standard Tools toolbar and the Properties Palette. By default, a checkmark shows that each is being displayed. Selecting again will remove the checkmark and hide the palette. This is the same as using the Window close boxes on the respective palettes.

Figure 4-25: The View menu.

We'll peruse the Standard toolbar and the Properties palette in Chapter 5.

The Go menu

The Go menu contains commands to take you all around Fusion. Figure 4-26 shows the Go menu, and Table 4-4 explains it.

Figure 4-26: The Go menu.

		Table 4-4
		The options on the Go menu
Option	*Shortcut*	*What it does*
Structure View		Lets you see a schematical page-by-page iconic layout of the site including the hierarchy of pages in the site tree
Outline View		Lets you see an outline and table of the site similar to that shown in the Windows 95 Explorer application
Site	Ctrl+1	Takes you to Site view, where you can create, delete, and arrange pages
Page	Ctrl+2	Takes you to Page view, where you can layout individual pages
Style	Ctrl+3	Takes you to Style view, where you can select or create a style for the site

(continued)

Table 4-4 (continued)		
Option	**Shortcut**	**What it does**
Assets	Ctrl+4	Takes you to Assets view, where you can look at the site's components, such as graphics, sound, and video files. Here you can also reassign files to an existing asset.
Publish	Ctrl+5	Takes you to Publish view, where you can prepare the site to post to an intranet or the Internet. The folder format to post to and other options specific to posting are set here.
Go To	Ctrl+G	Opens a dialog box that lets you search for pages in the site based on their page name or portions of that name
Last		Takes you to the last view used
Recent		Opens a dialog box with a list in order of the most recent Views you've visited and lets you select one to open
Preview	Alt+P	Converts the site into a series of HTML files and automatically displays them in the browser of your choice. This choice is made in the Preferences palette available off the Edit menu.

The first two sections of the Go menu are self-explanatory, so I'll explain the last two sections.

The Go To command

The Go To command is useful in that it opens a dialog box from which you choose a destination by typing parts of its name (as seen in Figure 4-27).

Figure 4-27: The Go To dialog box.

To use this command, enter either the first or last few letters of the destination page's name or a string of characters that are inside the name. For example, if you want to go to a page called Thermodynamics, checking the Begins With option checked and entering the characters **thermo** would find this page. If you have selected the Ends With option, typing **amics** would also find the page. Finally, if you choose Contains, typing **odyna** would find the page.

Note

If more than one page satisfies the search criteria used in the Go To command, Fusion opens a list box containing all of the page names that satisfy the search. You can then choose the one you want from the list. In addition, the Contains command would work with all three examples mentioned as they would all satisfy the criteria the Contains option expects.

The Last command

The Last command will revert to the last view open. For example, if you are in Site view but had changed to this from Page view, clicking the Last button would take you back to the previously opened Page view. The analogy is the Back button on your browser.

The Recent command

The Recent command displays a list of the most recently visited pages in the currently opened NOD file. To access any of these pages, simply select the one you want in the dialog box (shown in Figure 4-28) that opens and click the OK button. Fusion will open the selected page in Page view mode.

Figure 4-28: The Recent dialog box.

The Preview command

This command takes the NOD file, automatically generates HTML pages, and opens them in the browser that you chose in the Preferences dialog box. Depending upon what you selected in this dialog box, the Preview command will let you see the entire site in the browser (page by page) or only the selected page.

The Help menu

The Help menu has four options: Help Topics, NetObjects Fusion Web Site, Register NetObjects Fusion, and About NetObjects Fusion. Figure 4-29 shows the Help menu.

Figure 4-29: The Help menu.

Help Topics

When chosen, the Help Topics command opens a standard Windows or Macintosh Help topics dialog box letting you choose a particular Help Topic (shown in Figure 4-30).

Figure 4-30: The Help Topics dialog box.

NetObjects Fusion Web Site and Register NetObjects Fusion

Both of these options will load your currently selected Web browser (as nominated on the Preferences sheet) and attempt to connect you to the NetObjects Fusion Web site at www.netobjects.com. The first will take you to the home page of the site and the second to a special Web page where you can register your copy of Fusion.

About NetObjects Fusion

The About NetObjects Fusion option on the Help menu displays a dialog box (shown in Figure 4-31) detailing the NetObjects copyright message and the version number of the copy of Fusion you are running.

Figure 4-31: The About Fusion dialog box.

The Control Bar

Just underneath the standard menu bar is the control bar (shown in Figure 4-32), which is common to all of the views in NetObjects Fusion. The control bar contains a series of buttons on both the left and right of the screen. The buttons at left switch between the five views available in Fusion. As you click each in turn, Fusion switches between the Site, Page, Style, Assets, and Publish views.

Figure 4-32: The Fusion control bar.

On the left part of the control bar, you'll see a series of buttons labeled Site, Page, Style, Assets, and Publish, and on the right you'll see four buttons labeled Preview, New, Go to, and Last.

The first five buttons let you switch between modules by clicking the appropriate button. As each is clicked in order, the view of the current site will change between a map of the entire site (Site view); the currently selected page in the site (Page view); a list of available styles you can attach to a site (Style view); a list of objects, links, and other information in your site (Assets view); and a screen for publishing your site to a Web server (Publish view).

The last four buttons in the control bar (shown in close-up in Figure 4-33) Preview the current site or page in a Web browser, add a New page to the site, Go to a particular Web page, or return to the Last view displayed. We will be using these as we progress through the basics of creating a site.

Figure 4-33: Close-up of the right-side control bar buttons.

If you are not currently in Site view, click on the Site button to activate this module.

When using NetObjects Fusion, instead of working in a text-based programming environment, you are working in a graphical and visual one. Which particular mode you select in Fusion depends upon what functions of Web page or site creation you require at the time. These differing requirements are separated into logical views.

Site view

If you are mapping out the layout of a site and deciding what Web pages are necessary, you use the Fusion's Site view. Here, you can lay out the map of the Web site visually by adding or moving icons of pages to create a schematic of the site. Figure 4-34 shows the schematic of a possible corporate Web site in Fusion's Site view.

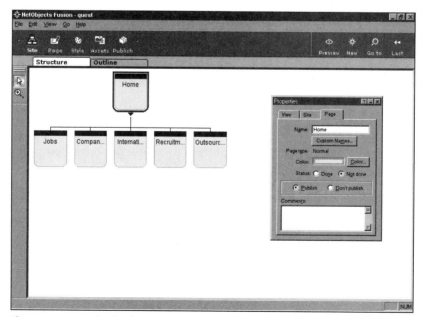

Figure 4-34: Fusion's Site view.

By default, Site view starts in a mode called Structure view shown by the highlighted tab at the top left of the Fusion screen and just under the control bar as highlighted in Figure 4-35. There are two modes in Site view: Structure view and Outline view. To make a particular view type current, click its tab.

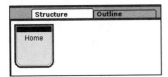

Figure 4-35: The Structure and Outline view tabs.

In Structure view, the hierarchy of pages composing the site is shown by yellow rectangular icons, each with a black bar at the top (as shown in Figure 4-36). Each icon represents a page in the site. The black bar inside the icon contains the name of that page. In Structure view, the currently selected page has a blue border surrounding it.

Figure 4-36: A Page icon as displayed in Site view.

At present — as we have just started a new site — only one page icon called Home is displayed. Fusion automatically creates the Home page whenever a new site is started, and it is the top page in the Web site's hierarchy. You cannot move or delete the Home page.

Each icon equals one page in the Web site. To show their relationships to each other in the hierarchy, page icons are connected together by lines. Familiar flowcharts to display the relationship between various departments or personnel in a company use the same metaphor.

A *Web page* is as any individual page in a complete Web site. Each icon in Site view is an individual Web page. The sum of all the icons (pages) in Site view is the Web site.

Chapter 5 provides contains more about working in Site view.

Page view

Page view is where everything happens! Well, the creative parts anyway: designing and placing the elements you want on a Web page in the site. With Fusion, using Page view allows the Web author to have full reign with his or her imagination and design capabilities without any need to worry about the normal constraints placed by the limitations of HTML coding. Using Page view is very similar to using such applications as PageMaker, Quark Xpress, or Microsoft Publisher. To assist, a truckload of tools is available, from which you can select several special palettes, such as Standard Tools, Advanced Tools, Form tools, and so on.

In Figure 4-37, you can see all of the tools and palettes available in Page view, as well as a sample of a Home page being laid out.

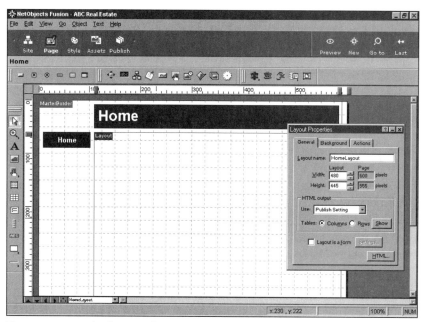

Figure 4-37: Fusion's Page view.

Switching to Page view from Site view

From Site view, you can enter Page view in many ways. The most obvious is to select the Page button on the control bar. In addition to this, though, you can also double-click any page icon in the Site view to go directly to that page in Page view. Finally, you can choose the Page option from the Go command on the menu bar or any of the other options here such as Go To or Last. If you select either the Page button on the control bar or the Page command on the Go menu, in both cases the currently selected page in Site view is the one that will be displayed in Page view.

Remember that the currently selected page in Site view has a blue border around its icon.

Chapter 6 provides more on working in Page view.

Style view

The contents of a Web page are a combination of background colors, textures, or images; banners; navigation controls; pictures; text; and increasingly video, animation, and sound.

When creating Web pages using a text editor, you need to code backgrounds, text, buttons, and images separately for each page in the site. This adds up to a lot of time in duplicate HTML coding or cutting and pasting HTML commands from one page to another. After creating a site, if even a simple change, such as a font color change, is needed you must manually alter every single page.

The use of styles in NetObjects Fusion eliminates this problem.

In Fusion, a *style* is a collection of images, colors, and text characteristics that can be applied to a Web page or site. Usual elements available in a style include a background color or image, banner, several types of navigation buttons and lines, and font definitions, such as color. Also included are details on link colors and data list bullets. Figure 4-38 shows the Fusion's Style view with a sample of the available styles listed.

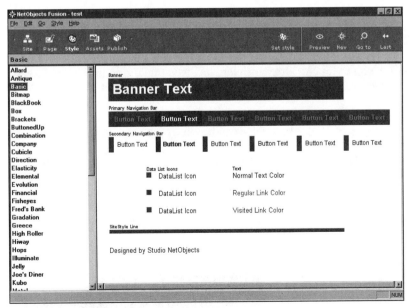

Figure 4-38: Fusion's Style view.

Fusion is supplied with many style themes that you can use in many different types of Web sites. To access the Style section in Fusion, you can either click on the Style button on the control bar or choose it from the Go menu.

The Style section is divided into two panes. The left pane contains a list of the available styles, and the right pane contains the various components that comprise the currently highlighted style. To see another style, select its name from the list in the left window and the right window will then display the information for that style.

Above the left pane is the name of the style currently assigned to the Web site. To the right and included in the standard control bar buttons is a Set style button. Clicking this will assign the currently selected style to the Web site.

If you change the style that is currently selected and then click the Page button, you will also be prompted via a dialog box if you wish to assign the newly selected style to the site.

When in Style view, you can modify any component of the style, including images and text color.

For a detailed description of creating, using and modifying styles, please refer to Chapter 7.

Assets view

Assets view (shown in Figure 4-39) lets you see what assets the current Web Site is using. In Fusion, an *asset* is anything that is a part of a Web site. This doesn't just include the obvious items such as graphics images or sound files, but also any imported HTML files, links to other pages or sites, applets, data list objects, and any Fusion-based variables you have assigned.

In the Assets view, you can alter or delete any asset included in the site. To access the Assets section, click its button on the control bar or select it from the Go option on the menu bar.

There are four types of assets in Fusion: files, links, data objects, and variables.

Selecting each of the buttons on the control bar gives a detailed list of the asset by type including its name, location on the hard disk (or network drive), size, date first created, and most importantly, whether it is still in use. To gain more detail on any asset, double-click it to display a dialog box showing on which pages of the site the asset appears as well as further information. This is shown in Figure 4-40.

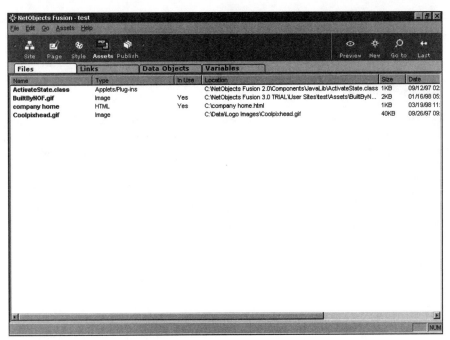

Figure 4-39: Fusion's Assets view.

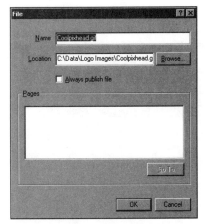

Figure 4-40: The Asset dialog box.

You should regularly check the asset listing for your sites and remove any unused assets. With a program such as Fusion where the capability to experiment with different styles and layouts is so easy and flexible, the list of unused assets can grow very quickly indeed. For example, if you assign a style to a site and subsequently change your mind regarding that style, any style components you have used may be included as an asset.

At publishing time, by default, all assets appearing in the list will automatically be sent to the Web server whether they are actually in use or not. This causes you to use disk space on the Web server unnecessarily, not to mention potentially increasing the site upload time. Removing unused assets will also assist in keeping the NOD file size as small as possible.

Chapter 26 fully covers the use of the Assets list and the management of the different types of assets.

Publish view

Publish view (shown in Figure 4-41) allows you to send your completed site to a Web or Intranet server or even your hard disk. You can achieve this by defining parameters for either Remote Locations — of which there can be any number — or your local computer. While you can create any number of remote locations, there is only one "My Computer" option, although you can redefine this at any time. To open the dialog box letting you create the parameters for either, click the Setup button on the control bar.

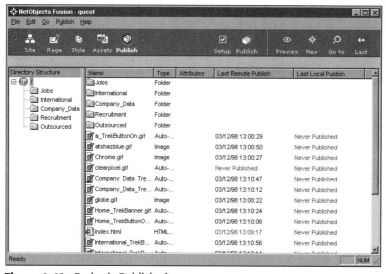

Figure 4-41: Fusion's Publish view.

In addition, you can also specify how the Web site is to be published. The various options such as Nested Tables, CSS and Layers, by Asset Type, and so on (accessed by clicking on the tabs in the Setup dialog box) are fully explained in Chapter 28.

The main window contains two panes: the left pane displays a list of folders containing files that the developer wishes to be published, and the right pane displays the list of files in the currently selected folder. Included in the right side buttons on the control bar is a Setup button and a Publish button (as shown in Figure 4-42).

Figure 4-42: Fusion's publishing buttons.

Clicking the Setup button opens a dialog box displaying three tabs: Directory Structure, HTML Output, and Server Locations. The Directory Structure tab (as seen in Figure 4-43) sets the directory structure types and the number of levels to publish.

Figure 4-43: The Directory Structure tab.

On the HTML Output tab, you can specify parameters such as how Fusion sends the final HTML files. It also contains options for comments, character conversion, and quote types (as seen in Figure 4-44).

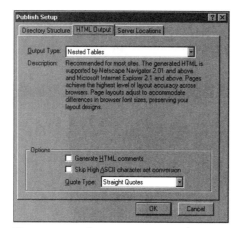

Figure 4-44: The HTML Output tab.

Using the Server Locations tab (see Figure 4-45), you can nominate the actual destination of the transmitted files (that is, the Web server to contain the Web site).

Figure 4-45: The Server Locations tab.

 For complete details on publishing, sites, please refer to Chapter 28.

Summary

✦ NetObjects Fusion consists of Site, Page, Style, Assets, and Publishing view modules.

✦ Site view maps out the layout of the Web site.

✦ Page view is where individual Web pages are composed.

✦ Styles are components that can be applied to a site as a whole, such as banners, backgrounds, navigation controls, font colors, and hyperlink colors.

✦ Asset view displays a list of all the entities contained in a Web site such as graphics files, links, Java applets, and so forth.

✦ Publish view is used to transfer the Web site from the local computer to a Web or Intranet server.

✦   ✦   ✦

Creating a Web Site

In Chapters 5 through 9, we get our hands dirty, metaphorically speaking, and start to create a site in NetObjects Fusion. First, a site is laid out in its entirety using the tools in Fusion's Site View. Then using styles, the overall look and feel of the site is created. Finally, text and graphics are added to the Home page.

If you are conversant with earlier versions of Fusion, I still recommend reading these chapters, as they cover important aspects of the dramatic changes in the visual interface of version 3 of NetObjects Fusion.

Creating a Web Site Structure in Site View

◆ ◆ ◆ ◆

In This Chapter

The Fusion Site
view module

Adding, moving,
deleting, and
renaming Web
pages

Page relationships

The Tools and
Properties palettes

◆ ◆ ◆ ◆

Now that we've explored the Fusion interface and learned a little about each view, we'll now examine each view and its related tools and facilities that create and manage Web sites.

Planning Your Site

The secret to good Web design is to create the site in distinct steps, planning each one very carefully. A logical flow would be the following:

1. Determine what sections will make up the site.

2. Plan what pages are needed for each section.

3. Decide on a look and feel for the site that will be consistent across all pages: for instance, the style of the site in terms of fonts, colors, headers, footers, and so on.

4. Gather all the necessary content to be placed on the pages.

5. Add the content to the pages.

6. Decide on both internal and external links.

7. Publish the site to a Web server for testing.

Working in Site View

Site view is where NetObjects Fusion displays the entire site as a schematic of the pages that compose the site and how each of these pages relate to each other navigationally. Each page in the site is shown in the diagram as a yellow page icon with its name below a black strip at the top. The currently selected page is also surrounded by a blue bounding highlight.

In Site view, you can add, delete, rename, or move new Web pages to different locations in the Web site's hierarchy. Figure 5-1 shows the new site just created.

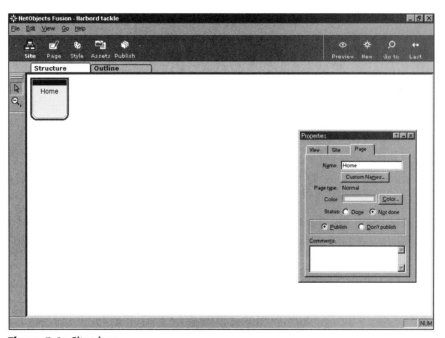

Figure 5-1: Site view.

Adding new pages

At present, the Web site only consists of one page: the Home page. To add new pages to a site, use the New button on the control bar (seen in Figure 5-2), which is identical to the New Page option in the Edit menu. Every time you click this button, Fusion will add a new page directly below the currently selected page with a line connecting them. At the moment, the currently selected page is the Home page shown by its blue border.

Figure 5-2: The New button will add a new page.

Tip

You can also add a new page by selecting a page and right-clicking the mouse (or by pressing ⌘+N on a Macintosh). When you do this, a popup menu appears (as shown in Figure 5-3) with the options for New Page, Delete Page, or Go To Page. The middle four options (Import Template, Import Local Web Site, Import Remote Web Site, and Reference HTML) let you insert an existing Web site into the currently open Fusion Web site. Finally, the What's This? option tells you a little bit about the Page icon (in this case). If you ever need some information about an object or command in Fusion, selecting the What's This? option displays a popup window of summary explanatory information.

Figure 5-3: A right-click will open a menu from which you can add a new page.

Clicking twice on the New button will add two new pages to this Web site, both connected to the home page. Figure 5-4 shows Fusion's Site view with these two pages added.

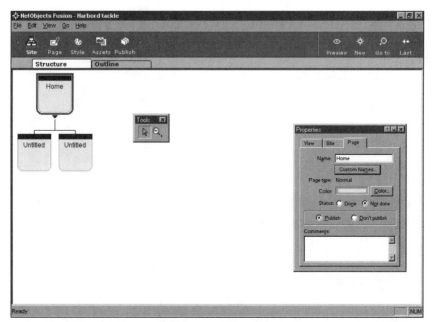

Figure 5-4: Site view after adding two new pages.

At this time, notice that both new pages are labeled Untitled. It is good practice to name pages immediately as you create them. You can rename pages at any time. You can change this to whatever name you like at any time. Be aware that the name you assign to a page in Site view will be the name of that page's HTML file created at either preview or publish time. If you have pages with the same name, when the pages are published — and you do not change any of the names at publish time — Fusion will publish these pages with sequential numbers appended to the name to distinguish them. For example, two pages called Untitled will be published as Untitled1.html and Untitled2.html.

Renaming pages

To change the name of a page (which will ultimately be the file name when Fusion generates the HTML code at publishing time), simply click on the word *Untitled* in the icon and type the new name. Figure 5-5 shows these two pages after renaming them Page 1 and Page 2.

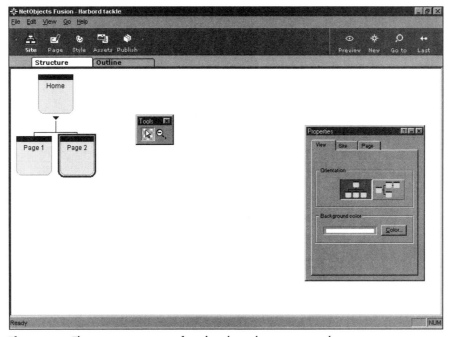

Figure 5-5: The two new pages after they have been renamed.

Deleting a page

Deleting a page is as simple as selecting it with the mouse (remember the currently selected page has a blue border) and pressing the Del key. In Windows, you can also use the popup menu by right-clicking when a page is selected. Try this: first select the Home page and add a new page by either clicking on the New Page button or from the popup menu using the right mouse key.

Once you have created the new page, select it and then delete it using the keyboard (or once again the popup menu via the right mouse button). Notice that a warning dialog box opens as shown in Figure 5-6. This is very important.

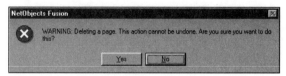

Figure 5-6: The Delete Page dialog box.

When you delete any page, you also automatically delete any pages connected below it and all their content. To delete the page, confirm this by clicking the Yes button in the dialog box.

You can never delete the Home page.

This operation cannot be reversed!

Until you are absolutely sure, it is best to set a page you feel you no longer need to Don't Publish and even make this page a different colored icon than the rest in the site. (See the sections on Icon color and the Publish/Don't Publish options to learn how to do this.)

Page relationships

Understanding the relationships between pages in a Web site is important as you use them in creating Navigation Bars (the navigational buttons Fusion places on the page). In the current Web site, the Home page is the *parent* to the other two pages. Inversely, the two new pages are *children* of the Home page. This relationship carries on logically as the nest of pages becomes deeper. For example, from Figure 5-7 if you select the leftmost of the new pages (Page 2) and add a new page called Page 3, Page 2 is now also a parent, and the new Page 3 is a child. If you do this, the Home page now also has a *grandchild* as well as children, and of course, the new page has a *grandparent* as well as a parent.

While this may not seem too important at this stage, when creating navigation controls for your Web site, the correct and logical positioning of individual pages in the hierarchy will make it much easier to create and maintain these controls.

If at any time you want to collapse the iconic representation of a Web site in Site view, pressing Ctrl and clicking on any of the small black triangles pointing to a connecting level below the current page will hide the lower levels. For example, by clicking on the small black triangle below the home page, all levels below this will be hidden and replaced by a plus sign. Clicking the plus sign will expand these levels back again. Figure 5-8 shows the current test Web site collapsed.

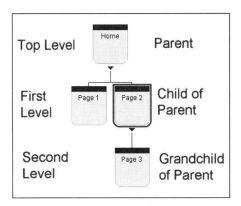

Figure 5-7: Page relationships in the Web site hierarchy.

Figure 5-8: A collapsed Web site.

Levels in a Web site

In conjunction with relationships is also the concept of *levels*. As you can see from Figure 5-7, the first two pages we created (Page 1 and Page 2) are on the first level of the Web site structure and *not* the second as you might imagine. Page 3 is on the second level. The first physical level in the Web site is the Home page. This level is unique as you cannot delete or move it and is referred to as the Top Level or as I call it, the Zero Level.

Note

When editing any Web page, all pages on the same level as the one being worked on are said to be on the *current level*. Any page one level above is on the *parent level*, and any page one level below is on the *child level*. Of course, as you change from level to level, the parent and child level reference changes relative to the current level.

Moving pages

Sometimes you'll find it necessary or desirable to move the location of a page in a Web site's hierarchy to a new position. When using a manual editor to modify the HTML code, if many pages in the site have links to a page that you need to move, it can be a logistical nightmare as the link code on each page must be modified. Luckily, NetObjects Fusion has a simple drag-and-drop method of moving pages while keeping the integrity of all links intact.

If you wanted Page 3 to become a child of Page 1, simply select the page and drag it over onto Page 1. When a red pointer appears beneath Page 1 as seen in Figure 5-9, release the mouse button and Page 3 moves to the new location with new connecting lines drawn from Page 1. At the same time, Fusion will automatically refresh the NOD database to update all references to links to this page on every other page. To see the red pointer, the mouse pointer must be inside the icon of the page you are moving to.

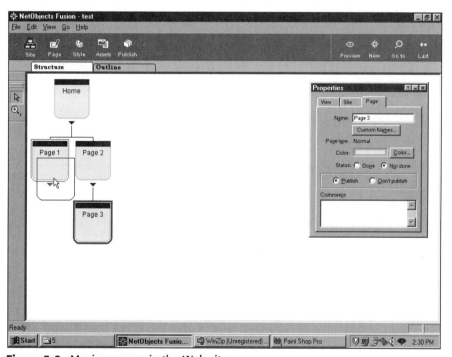

Figure 5-9: Moving a page in the Web site.

You can move pages in this fashion at any time you like. You have to agree that this beats manually changing references the old way, especially as this also moves any child pages and relocates them and all their links at the same time!

Note

You cannot copy and paste pages in Site view. You must create a new page, go to Page view, select and copy all the objects in the originating page and then paste them into the new one.

What You See in Site View

Site view is where the layout and design structure of a new or existing site all takes place. Using the tools here is what gives Fusion such a huge edge in Site creation and management in comparison to other products.

The Home page icon

When you first create a new site in Fusion, a single page called Home is displayed at the top of the Site view as an icon. The Home page is the starting point for the Web site and cannot be moved or deleted.

The Standard toolbar

A pair of palettes called the Properties and Tools palettes are available in Site view (shown in Figures 5-10 and 5-11). By default, these palettes are turned on, displaying as floating windows on top of the main window. To hide or close either palette manually, choose the View option on the menu bar and select or deselect the required palette.

Figure 5-10: The Tools palette.

Figure 5-11: The Properties palette.

The Standard toolbar (shown in Figure 5-10) runs down the right strip of the screen and contains three tools (two of which are visible), which are described in Table 5-1.

Table 5-1		
The Standard toolbar's tools		
Tool name	**Function**	
Select	Puts you in the mode so that you can point, select, drag, and drop page icons	
Zoom In	Zooms in on a site to see more detail	
Zoom Out	Zooms out of a site to see the bigger picture	

If you cannot currently see the Standard toolbar, open it by selecting Standard Tools from the View menu on the menu bar.

New to 3.0

As with all tool palettes in Fusion, the Standard toolbar has two modes available called *floating* and *docked*. When a palette is floating, you can move around the screen as a stand-alone window. When a palette is docked, it is attached to one of the edges of the screen. You can also position the tools anywhere in the sidebar you have established by dragging them to a new position.

By default, Fusion palettes start off docked. To make them floating, just click anywhere on a palette (but not on a tool in the palette), hold down the mouse button, and drag the palette away from its docked position.

Using the Select tool

The Select tool in Site view drags page icons around the site to relocate them. You also use the Select tool to select the page name field so that you can apply a new name to a page rather than the default "Untitled" name Fusion supplies.

Zooming in and out of a site

By now, you should be able to see that Site view is a great way to manage a Web site with its simple method of adding, moving, and naming pages. But what if the site grows so large that it can't fit in the visible page window?

This situation demands the Zoom tools on the Tools palette. Select the second magnifying glass by clicking on the magnification glass, holding down the mouse button, and dragging over the popout menu to the second icon with the minus sign. By clicking anywhere on the page while in Site view, the view will zoom out to show more of the site. Figure 5-12 shows the site after having zoomed out one level of zoom.

Keep clicking until it shrinks no further. The Web site should now look like Figure 5-13. Using these two tools, a zoom factor of six is available: you can see the smallest size to the largest possible size (or vice versa) by six mouse clicks in either direction.

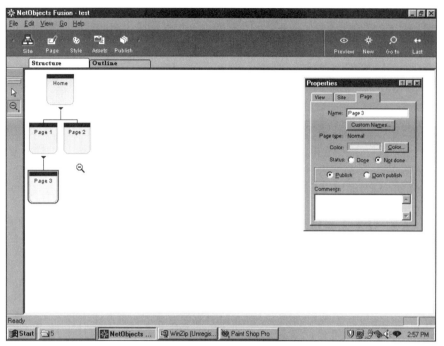

Figure 5-12: The Site after one level of zoom out.

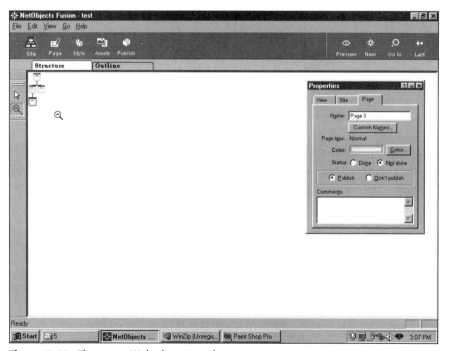

Figure 5-13: The same Web site at maximum zoom out.

If you wish to zoom into a site to see more detail—perhaps the site is so large you cannot read the page names—use the magnifying glass with the plus (+) to reverse the effect as seen in Figure 5-14.

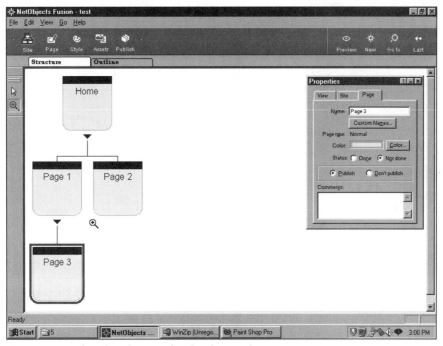

Figure 5-14: The Site after two levels of zoom in.

Tip

How do you remember which Zoom tool is which? Simple! Plus means bigger and minus means smaller.

Use the zoom tools to return the site map size to a size you are comfortable with by either zooming in or out. To toggle the Zoom tool, hold down the Alt key.

The Properties palette

The second palette available in the Site view module is the Properties Palette as seen in Figure 5-15. If this is not already open, choose the Window command on the menu bar, and select the Properties palette.

As the Properties palette in particular is quite large, the developers of Fusion have included a *roll-up function* for each palette. By double-clicking its title bar, the body of the palette "rolls up," leaving only the title bar displayed as seen in Figure 5-16. To roll down the body, double-click the title bar a second time. You can relocate the palettes anywhere on the screen by clicking and dragging their title bars, whether rolled up or not.

Figure 5-15: The Properties palette.

Note

Unlike the Standard toolbar, you cannot dock the Properties palette.

Figure 5-16: The Properties
palette rolled-up.

The Properties palette has three tabs on it: View, Site, and Page. Clicking on each
of these tabs will toggle between these sections letting you set the properties
available for each.

The Page tab

If it is not already in view, click on the Page tab. Each of the functions and attributes
of pages that can be modified are available on the Page tab. We'll now go through
these one by one.

The page Name attribute

At the top of the palette (Figure 5-15) is a field labeled Name, which contains the
name of the currently selected page or the default that Fusion sets (such as Home).
Changing the name in this field is equivalent to changing it by manually clicking the
page's title in its icon in the Site view just as you did when you changed Untitled to
Page 3.

The Custom Names button

Below this field is a button labeled Custom Names. Web Pages can have two types
of names: the field name (corresponding to the name in the field above the Custom
Names button) and a title. In Fusion, you can also create a custom name for a page.
This name will be used as an alias for that page in such elements as page banners
and navigation bar buttons.

A very simple example of where you might want different names is for brevity: you might want the Home page to be called "home," but you want "Critical Conditions: Psychopathology and Culture" to be shown in the title bar of the page when it is viewed in a Web browser. Using the custom names options allows this.

To change any of the Custom Names options, as well as the file extension to be used for a page, click the Custom Names button. A dialog box opens (as shown in Figure 5-17) that lets you add much more highly descriptive names than just the HTML page name allows. To wrap a name to the second line (when the name is too long to fit, for example) press Enter to add a line break.

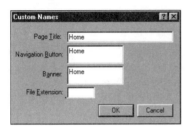

Figure 5-17: The Custom Names dialog box.

You'll see these names:

✦ Page Title (appearing in the title bar when the page is displayed in a Web browser)

✦ Navigation Button (appearing in any Navigation Bar buttons created automatically by Fusion)

✦ Banner (appearing in any banners included on a page)

For example, while you might leave the page name (file name) as Home, you might want to alter the Page Title to `ABC Real Estate - Home Page`, the Navigation Button field to `ABC Home`, and the Banner field to `ABC Real Estate - the No. 1 Choice!` Figure 5-18 shows these changes applied to the Custom Names dialog box.

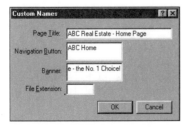

Figure 5-18: Changes made to the Custom Names dialog box.

Another option in this dialog box is to change the file extension used when the HTML page is created. By default, this is *html*, but some developers for example prefer to use *htm*.

Note   Changing the extension used in this dialog box only affects the change to the current page.

To assign any changes you have made, click the OK button.

Note   When in Site view, the application of these additional naming conventions is not apparent without reopening the Change Names dialog box from the Properties palette after selecting the Page required.

Icon Color

By default, any new page created in Site view has a yellow fill color to its icon. By selecting any page and using the Color option on the Properties palette, you can change this color. This option is especially useful for large Web sites where individual sections can display different colors for their icons to set them off from each other. To change the color of a page icon, select it and after clicking on the Color button, choose a new color as shown in Figure 5-19.

Note   This only changes the color of the icon in Site view and does *not* affect anything on the page, including its background color.

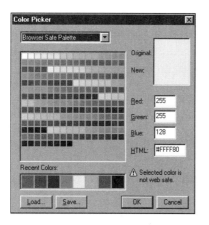

Figure 5-19: Choosing a new page icon color.

Using the color option, you can apply the same color to associated pages of the Web site that are displayed inside the page icon. While the use of this is arbitrary, you can use this feature any way you wish. This is just one suggestion that I personally find useful.

I use it to distinguish between different sections of a site. For example, in a corporate Web site, red might be used for the marketing division, blue for human resources, green for feedback, and yellow for product information (as seen in Figure 5-20).

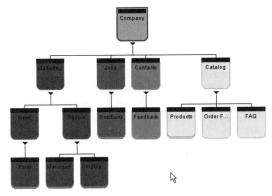

Figure 5-20: Using different colors to distinguish parts of a Web site.

Page Status

Another useful site management option on the Properties palette in Site view is the Status option. You can use the Done/Not Done radio buttons to distinguish sections of a site. When you have completely finished editing any single page, select the Done button and a small check mark will appear in the top left corner of the page's icon as shown in Figure 5-21. This gives the developer a quick visual indication of how the development of the site is progressing.

Note

One great thing about using Fusion is that because it releases the scope of your design imagination rather than having to worry about HTML coding, no Web site is ever finished. You will continually think of ways to improve it!

Figure 5-21: A Page icon with its Done attribute applied. Note the check mark.

The Publish/Don't Publish options

The Publish/Don't Publish radio buttons do not quite work the way you might expect and is a potential trap for the unwary! They are notorious for causing confusion, even among experienced Fusioneers.

If a page is set to Don't Publish, at Publishing time this page and its contents are not moved to the Web server or intranet server. On the surface, this may seem an easy way to publish a single page out of an entire site.

Fusioneer is a term coined by no-one-knows-who and used as an affectionate name for those of us who have flocked to NetObjects Fusion as our Web authoring tool of choice.

Because reposting an entire site can take some time, especially with a large site, many first time users wrongly assume that if he or she sets the Don't Publish attribute for all pages other than the ones they have made changes to, only the changed pages will be sent to the server. Nothing could be further from the truth!

However, when Fusion detects a Don't Publish selection on a page in the Web site, *all* references to that page in all other pages in the site are automatically removed. This includes all links and navigation controls. Because of this, use the Don't Publish option prudently. It is mainly used for publishing sites that are still under development to exclude pages in these sites that are not yet complete.

In this way, the Web author can disable any references to those pages in the published version of the site.

When a page has had the Don't Publish attribute applied, a red dot appears in its page icon as shown in Figure 5-22.

Figure 5-22: A Page icon showing the Don't Publish attribute applied.

The Comments field

Finally, the Page tab contains a field that lets you add some comments regarding the currently selected page. None of the information you might enter into this field is used anywhere else: it is not sent to the Web server or intranet server at publishing time and is purely for the Web author's reference purposes. Figure 5-23 shows the Home page with some comments applied by the Web author.

Figure 5-23: The Page tab comments field is used for reference purposes.

The Site tab

You can view the Site tab on the Properties palette by clicking on its name. The Site tab contains statistical information relating to the current site. Figure 5-24 shows a Site tab for a typical corporate Web site.

Figure 5-24: The Properties palette in Site view showing the Site tab.

The Author's Name field

The Site tab in the Properties palette contains only one field that the Web author can modify. This is the location allowing that person to place his or her name as the Web author. When individual Fusion generated sites are grouped together at a later stage making a single combined larger site, this option is useful as a reference as to who developed which sections.

This field, apart from being a reference point, has another use. NetObjects Fusion versions 2 and above have the facility to place "variables" on a page. I explain these variables in detail in Chapter 12, but basically they allow you to place values as those shown on the Site tab onto any page in the Web site. If any of these values change, Fusion will update the Web page automatically.

Other Site tab options

The remaining information in the Site tab is generated automatically by Fusion and details the site name, creation and last modified dates, and the current number of pages in the site. These values are also allocated to internal variables that can be used on Web pages.

The View tab

You can see the View tab in the Properties palette by clicking on its name. The View tab (as seen in Figure 5-25) contains only two options.

Figure 5-25: The View tab
on the Properties palette.

Site Map Orientation

The first of these options alters the orientation of the site map to either a horizontal or vertical viewpoint. (This option is not available when using the Outline view instead of the Structure view.) To change the current orientation, click on the button containing the icon of the orientation you prefer.

Site view has two options available to display the Web site schematic in different ways. The default is called *Structure view* and is seen in a *top down* or Portrait orientation: the Home page appears at the top of the schematic with subsequent pages and levels running down the page from top to bottom. Figure 5-26 shows the Web site in this view. We have been using this particular view up until now.

If you prefer to have a Landscape orientation view instead, you have this option from the Properties palette View tab. The Landscape view is shown in Figure 5-27.

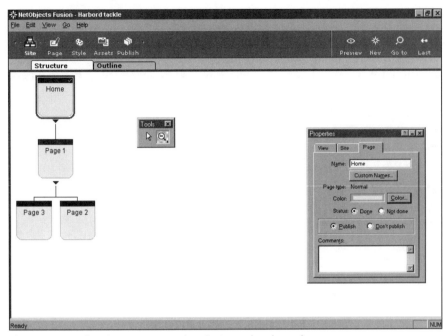

Figure 5-26: Site view Structure view in Portrait orientation.

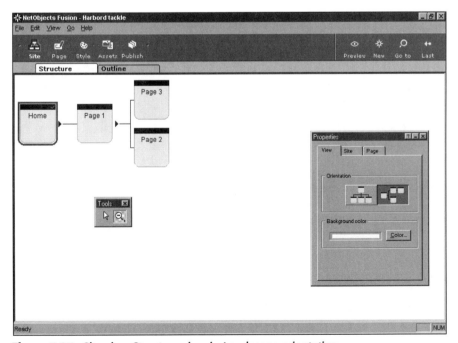

Figure 5-27: Site view Structure view in Landscape orientation.

Window Background Color

The second option changes the background color of the main window in Site view from its default white. Clicking on the Color button opens a separate window shown in Figure 5-28 containing boxes showing the colors available. To set a new color, select it in this window followed by clicking the OK button. This does not affect the background color of the individual pages in the site.

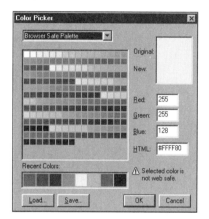

Figure 5-28: Changing Site view's background color.

Outline view

Two modes are available while in Site view: Structure view and Outline view. To my way of thinking, of the two, the Structure view is the most flexible and probably the one you will use most, but I could be wrong! It's your call. To change from Structure view to Outline view, just click on the Outline tab.

Outline view is useful if you are working with a large site. In some cases, the size of a site — particularly an imported one — might exceed the physical area the Structure view can display. Outline enables you to work more easily with large sites.

Outline view (shown in Figure 5-29) is similar to the structure of your hard disk when it is displayed in the Windows Explorer program. Some readers may also be familiar with the outlining mode available in Microsoft Word or another word processing program.

Note

Outlining is a useful way of showing a document's structure while it is being created and is apparently one of word processing's best kept secrets!

Outline view shows a horizontal stacked view of the pages in a Web site from left to right. If a page has children attached to it, these show further down the hierarchy but *across* the page. As a page containing children contains either a "+" or "-" sign in its iconic representation in the display, you can quickly see at a glance which pages do or do not have further branches.

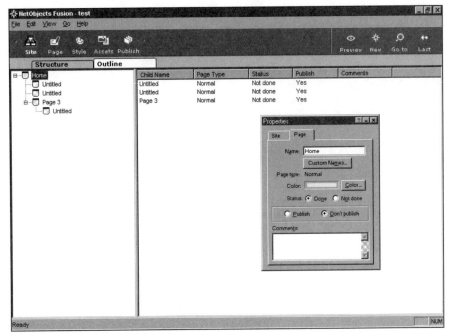

Figure 5-29: Site view's Outline mode.

If you want to collapse or expand sections of the site, just click on the small yellow box to the left of the page icon. When this box shows a minus sign, it is fully expanded. When showing a plus sign, it means there are further pages below this one, but this level is currently collapsed. Clicking this yellow box acts as a toggle, switching between collapsed and expanded mode with each click.

Note

In Outline view, you can still perform all of the tasks available in Structure view such as adding, moving, or deleting pages. Outline view does not feature any zoom options or a top down to landscape orientation facility.

More Info

Right-clicking on a page while in Outline view pops up the same menu as in Structure view.

Setting Site Preferences

Site Preferences are set on the Preferences palette, which you can access by choosing from the Edit menu on the menu bar. The Preferences palette is divided into three tabs: the General Tab, the Page Tab, and the Backup Tab.

The General tab

The General tab contains options that relate specifically to the site as a whole.

Auto Save

Checking the Auto Save box causes Fusion to continually save the site as you are working on it.

There are pros and cons to this feature. Say you make massive changes to a site and then decide that you don't want those changes to be kept. If Auto Save is turned on, you cannot go back to the last previously saved site and start over. On the positive side though, say the unforeseen happens such as a power failure. If Auto Save is checked, at least you know that the last three hours worth of work hasn't gone down the bit bucket somewhere.

Application window maximized at startup

When this option is checked, Fusion will start in a full screen window.

Open to most recently used file at startup

To have Fusion automatically load the last used site when it starts, check this box.

Use small fonts in Properties palette

You can shrink the size of the Properties palette if it is taking up too much space on the desktop. Just select the Preferences option from the Edit menu and choose the Use Small Fonts in Properties Palette option. This option shrinks the Properties palette approximately a third smaller on the desktop. This is especially useful when running in 640×480 pixel screen resolution.

Picking a Preview browser

From the list of available browsers in the Preview section, select the browser you wish to use as your preview browser.

Tip

When previewing sites, it is best to firstly preview with Netscape Navigator and then change this setting to Internet Explorer — or vice versa. This will ensure that you don't miss any browser-specific idiosyncrasies that may affect the site.

Setting WYSIWYG optimization

As Netscape and Microsoft browsers display Web pages slightly differently, use this option to optimize Fusion for your browser of choice. Fusion will then display all objects in Page view as they would appear in the browser.

Picking an HTML editor

Why would you have an option to use an HTML Editor when Fusion is supposed to negate that need? Sometimes you may import existing HTML into a page, and this code needs to be changed from some reason. Rather than having to leave Fusion, load an editor, change the code, save it, return to Fusion, and reload the code into the page, you can instead double-click the object on the page representing the code. Fusion will then load the editor that you have specified in this field so that you can edit directly.

The shipping version of Fusion comes with Allaire's HomeSite, which is the best to use by far, but you can set this field to whichever editor you prefer. To find the editor on your hard disk, click the Browse button and navigate to the application to set its name in this field.

The Page tab

The Page Tab contains settings that are related to objects that are used in Page view.

Browser font settings

The font settings you select here will force Fusion to use these as the default fonts. It is best to select the fonts settings that you have installed in your browser for these two options to retain conformity.

Proportional

This setting tells Fusion which font to use as the basic Proportional font and defaults to Times New Roman.

Fixed Width

This setting tells Fusion which font to use as the basic Fixed Width font and defaults to Courier New.

General

The General section of the Page tab contains information relating to default page size and grid settings.

Measurement units

From the list of available measurement units, choose the one you prefer by clicking on it. I tend to favor pixels as my favorite measurement unit as this is the one I mostly use when I create in graphics in Picture Publisher or Photoshop.

Default Page and Grid Sizes

These options are pretty much a personal preference. Simply set them as you prefer. I use the default settings here and adjust the page size setting for individual pages when in Page view. The default values are set for a standard Web page when used in a 640×480 resolution. The differences accommodate such things as scroll bars, status lines, and so on that all rob real estate from the 640×480 area, leaving an effective 600×555 pixel layout area.

I prefer to use guides rather than the grid, but if you choose to use the grid, change these settings to alter the space between the grid intersection points. I leave this as the default as I rarely, if ever, use the grid for positioning.

Background image

Both Netscape Navigator and Internet Explorer leave a small amount of white space to the left and top edges when displaying a Web page. If you have an image as a background, this tends to leave a white gutter on these sides of the image when it is shown. To offset this, change these values as necessary (although the defaults will work in most cases).

The Backup tab

The Backup tab contains settings to define how your automatic backups of the Fusion database are handled.

Automatic backup

The first option, the Automatic backup checkbox, is simply an on-off switch. Do you want Fusion to automatically backup or not?

This is not the same as Auto Save option mentioned earlier. Auto Save merely saves the current file. Automatic Backup will create a mirror of the file when you exit Fusion.

Backup location

In this field specify where Fusion will store the backup files it creates. I suggest that for most cases, leave this field as the default Fusion provides.

Note

I do *not* recommend setting this field as a network drive of Zip or Jaz drives as Fusion is not configured toward these sorts of external devices.

File naming convention

By default, Fusion will name backup files with the same name you have used for the site plus a hyphen and then the word *backup*. Finally this is appended with a sequential number that indicates how many times this site has been automatically backed up. For example, the second backup (see maximum number of backups below) of a site called "Zeppelin" would be saved as "Zeppelin-backup2.nod."

If you wish to change this convention (which I do not recommend), alter this field to the convention you prefer.

Maximum number of backups kept

As backup files can take up a lot of hard disk space, Fusion allows the option of setting a value for the maximum number of backups it is to keep. In my experience, the default value of two is fine, but more is better, if you have enough hard disk space.

The Compact option

This is another recommended default: that is, keep this option checked. When you exit Fusion, it will automatically compact the NOD database file thus keeping file sizes to a minimum.

Danger Zone

In large sites especially, compacting can take a few minutes. It is imperative to the integrity of the file that you do *not* interrupt the compacting process. If you do, you run the risk of damaging the NOD file and having to revert to the backup.

Summary

✦ A blank site contains a single Home page containing no objects.

✦ Fusion templates let *like* Web sites or individual pages be constructed from previous site definitions.

✦ Fusion Site view displays a map of a Web site and is the module used to add, move, delete, and name Web pages in a site.

✦ Using the Zoom tools, the magnification of the view can be increased or decreased as required.

✦ Page relationships are the basis of navigation between pages in a Web site.

✦ Site view can be displayed in either a Structure view or Outline view.

✦ Levels of a Web site in either Structure or Outline view can be expanded or collapsed.

✦ The Preferences Palette accessible from the Edit menu is where all parameter settings for Fusion are defined.

✦ *Never* interrupt Fusion when it is compacting a database. If this option is taking too long, turn off the Compact database upon exit option on the Preferences palette.

✦   ✦   ✦

Designing a Web Page in Page View

Page view is the engine room of NetObjects Fusion where the major action happens. It is also the fun part where your imagination can run riot with Fusion giving you all tools necessary to become the Leonardo da Vinci of Web publishing. Unlike creating HTML pages using a text editor and code, you are using a familiar graphical interface where your canvas is a page, and the objects to be painted are drawn from a variety of sources such as clip art, image files, Fusion's own drawing tools, or external applications. There's no code here folks!

Changing from Site View to Page View

By now, you should be familiar with the concept of switching to a new view in Fusion by simply clicking its button on the control bar or choosing it from the Go command on the menu bar. When in Site view, you have a third way to change to Page view for the particular page you want to edit: simply double-click the selected page in the site schematic.

In version 3.0 of Fusion, you can also navigate to another page by clicking the right mouse button and selecting the Go To option.

At the same time, the Page Properties palette and Standard toolbar open. If these are not visible, select them individually from the View menu. Figure 6-1 shows Fusion's Page view with a blank page.

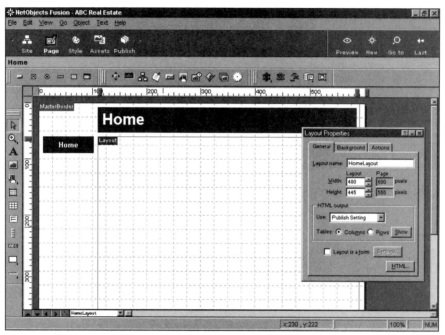

Figure 6-1: Fusion's Page view.

For those who have used applications such as Microsoft Publisher, QuarkXPress, or Adobe PageMaker, the Page view mode should look quite familiar as it has the same style of interface. The main part of the window contains a representation of the Web page, and on this representation element you place the content of the page. Page content can include text, images and graphics, or rich media objects such as Shockwave or Macromedia Flash animation, Java Applets, ActiveX controls, MIDI or other sound files, and even video files.

In Page view, placeholders for individual elements such as graphics images or text are drawn on the page at the required locations. The contents for the placeholder are then inserted, or, alternatively, if the element is an external object such as an image, its file name is specified via a dialog box.

With Page view, you can place elements with pixel-level accuracy. You are also working with text, graphics, animation, sound files, and so on and therefore don't have to worry about the code or the restraints and limitations of HTML. This results in much richer content and layout for a Web site in a much shorter time frame than traditional page coding methods allow.

What You See in Page View

When you create a site based on the Blank Site template, Fusion automatically applies the Basic style. A *style* is a preset definition of colors, fonts, navigation controls, and other elements. With the Basic style applied, the page will already have a banner at the top of the page, a vertical Navigation Bar, a "Built With NetObjects Fusion" icon, and a text-based navigation bar at the base of the page when you initially access Page view.

Tip

If you cannot see the entire page, you may need to use the Zoom tools on the Standard toolbar. If this is not open, select it from the Standard toolbar. If it is open but all you can see is the title bar of its window, double-click the title bar to "roll down" the palette.

The representation of the Web page consists of a large, white page separated into two sections. The inner section is called the Layout, which is where all objects such as text, graphics, links, and so on are placed for *this* page only. Anything located in the Layout area will *only* appear on the current page (unless manually duplicated to other pages) when the HTML code is generated at publishing time. This area is for placing content that is unique to an individual page.

The MasterBorder area

The margin surrounding the Layout section is called the *MasterBorder*. The MasterBorder is designed to contain objects such as text, graphics, and so on that will be common to *all* pages that share the same MasterBorder style. This is useful for elements you want repeated across multiple pages such as dates, links or copyright information. It functions just like headers and footers in a word-processing document.

MasterBorders are designed to facilitate creation of sets of Web pages that share common elements. These include — but are certainly not restricted to — banners, navigation buttons, contact information, dates of creation and modification, separator lines, and so on. Instead of laboriously placing these objects on every page and making sure the alignment, font styles, colors, hyperlinks, and so on are correct for each page, you just need to place each of these elements on the MasterBorder once.

Once you place an element in a MasterBorder, all pages that share that MasterBorder will show this element on the page. If you modify any element in a MasterBorder, this modification will also apply to all pages sharing the MasterBorder.

This means of course, if you need to make a modification to any element, you only need to change it once, which is a huge time saver.

As mentioned, you can define as many MasterBorders in Fusion as you need in your Web site. For example, in a Corporate Web site, you might have a set of pages for a Human Resources Department and another for Engineering. In the Web site, both of these sections would have their own MasterBorder elements and styles, perhaps containing separate telephone extension information, buttons, text styles, and even colors relevant to the departmental pages to which they are applied.

MasterBorders are very flexible. They can be any width or height you like, and with a single mouse click, they can even be converted into frames containing their own background images, colors, or textures. Figure 6-2 shows the MasterBorder Properties dialog box.

Figure 6-2: MasterBorders become frames with a single mouse click.

Fusion can define as many MasterBorders as required and apply them to any number of pages. In addition, you can create new MasterBorders using an existing MasterBorder as the basis.

In Fusion version 3, you can delete MasterBorders that you no longer require. I recommend this as it will reduce the size of the NOD file.

MasterBorders are one of the most powerful and timesaving features of Fusion. By intelligent use of MasterBorders, you not only save time creating Web sites than with traditional hand-coding methods (or by using any of the newer breed of Web authoring applications), but you can create much more accurate pages.

Frames

MasterBorders have another function as well. They are basic building blocks for adding frames to Web pages. *Frames* segment sections of a Web page off, with each *pane* or *window* of the frame being given individual control. The most popular use of frames is to supply a static pane inside a single frame containing navigation controls for the Web site. While the content of other panes on the page may change, the navigation frame constantly displays the same information. Figure 6-3 shows a frame-based page.

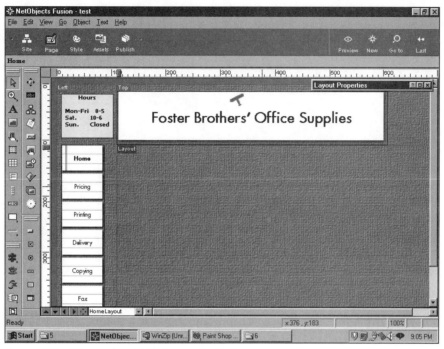

Figure 6-3: A frame-based Web page in Fusion.

The Layout area

In the Layout section of the page (the area inside the inner rectangle seen in Figure 6-3), you place elements such as text, graphics, buttons, links that are specific to this page: that is, they will appear on this page and this page only, unless manually placed on other pages.

The page — the white area — consists of two rectangles, one inside the other. (Depending upon your screen resolution, you may not see all of the two rectangles making up the entire page. If so, you will need to move to the right and down using the scroll bars to see the rest of the page.) Notice the banner at the top of the page, a vertical row of buttons down the left side, and a "Built with Fusion" icon and the single word *Home* at the base. I'll talk more about these in a moment.

Layout templates

A Layout section can be as wide or as deep as necessary, and any individual page can have as many layouts defined as required. Multiple layouts can test different constructions — or even language versions — of a Web page. By using multiple layouts, you can save a constructed page's current Layout while you build another. At any time, you can recall previously saved layouts for that page.

The list of currently available layouts is at the bottom left of the page representation (as shown in Figure 6-4). Just to the right of the page navigation controls is a small dropdown list, and I do mean small! Because of this, Figure 6-4 has been magnified a little. This is the layout template list. When you first create a Fusion page, it has only one layout template based on the currently selected style, but you can assign as many layout templates as you like to any single page.

Figure 6-4: The Layout template list.

To add a new Layout to this list, click on the arrow to the right of the dropdown list of layouts, and choose the Add option from the list. To rename the new layout from the default name of "Untitled Layout" to a more meaningful name, change it in the Layout name field on the layout Properties palette. To switch between different layouts, simply select the required Layout from the list. When you publish your site, the currently active layout for the page is the Layout that is published.

Note   Only objects in the layout section of the page can be saved as a Layout. Any objects placed in MasterBorders will remain for all pages no matter which layout is currently selected.

Note   Don't be confused between *layout templates* and *styles*. Styles apply to all the pages in a site, whereas a layout template applies only to an individual page. In fact, a template applies *only* to the page you are currently viewing in Page view.

Layout templates let you experiment with a page's look without losing the original design. For example, you might create a page containing the usual Navigation Bars, images, and text, but when finished you're not too sure if you quite like the design. No problem. With Fusion, changing a design is easy, but what if the new one is no better (or is worse!) than the last?

Using layout templates, you can save the original and apply a new design to the page. If after finishing the second design, you decide the first was preferable after all, instead of having to start anew, simply load the layout template you previously saved from the Layout template list box.

Navigation controls

While you can certainly switch from page to page by toggling between Page view and Site view, Fusion supplies a set of page navigation controls directly available from the Page view window.

By using these page navigation controls, you can also see how the MasterBorder area on this page is common to all of the other pages in the current site.

The direction arrows

At the bottom left of the main window (right by the layout template list), you'll see a series of four arrows: up, down, left, and right (as shown in Figure 6-5).

Figure 6-5: Fusion's page navigation buttons.

When using these controls, clicking the up arrow will take you to the page in the site hierarchy that is directly above the current page. Clicking the down arrow will take you directly down one level, and clicking the left and right arrows will move to the next page in these directions on the same level. Look at the Site view of a sample Web site on Figure 6-6.

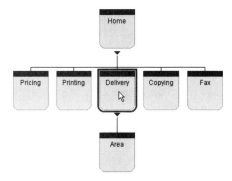

Figure 6-6: Site view of a sample Web site.

If you are currently on the Delivery page in Page view, clicking the up arrow will take you to the Home page, the down arrow will take you to the Area page, the left arrow will take you to the Printing page, and the right arrow will take you to the Copying page.

If you click on a page navigation control and nothing seems to happen, this means that Fusion cannot navigate to any further pages either on the same level (left or right) or below or above (up and down).

The page navigation controls provide a quick and convenient way of changing from page to page. In a large site, however, you can sometimes find it a little disorienting as to exactly where in the hierarchy you are located. If this occurs, you could simply switch to Site view to get your bearings.

The navigation window

But you have a newer, faster way of seeing just where you are. To the right of the page navigation buttons is another button with four arrows on it. By clicking this, a navigation window opens that shows a scaled version of Site view. Using this window, you can select pages and navigate the site exactly as you can in the full Site view by double-clicking its icon (shown in Figure 6-7).

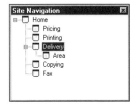

Figure 6-7: The Site Navigation window opened on the page.

For some strange reason, using the navigation bar to move to a graphics-heavy page is a slow process. If you know the page has a lot of graphics, it's faster to get there by switching to Site view (or using the navigation window) and selecting the page in question by double-clicking its icon.

Toolbars

NetObjects Fusion version 3.0 has four separate Tools palettes, called Standard, Advanced, Component, and Form. You can make them visible by selecting them from the View option on the menu bar. To dock a Tools palette, simply drag it to the position you want it on the top, bottom, left, or right of the screen. To undock the palette and make it floating, click anywhere on it (but not on a button) and drag it to a new location in the Fusion application window. Figure 6-8 shows all four toolbars as floating palettes, and Figure 6-9 shows them docked to all four sides. I personally prefer to have all the toolbars docked to the left as this seems the most natural.

The various toolbars are the command center of Page view because collectively they contain all of the tools that you need to place elements onto a Web page. Many of the toolbar buttons also have a series of options available once they are selected and once you have placed an object. These options are available on the Properties palette. For example, in Figure 6-10, a picture has been selected and the Effects tab on the Properties palette contains options for transparency and for adding text inside the image.

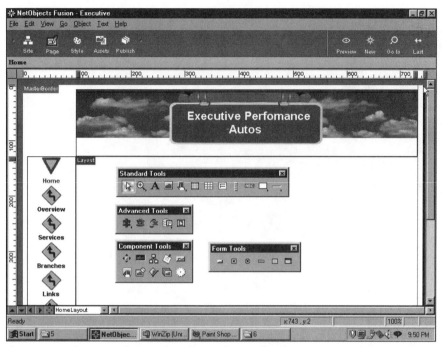

Figure 6-8: The Page view Tools palettes shown floating.

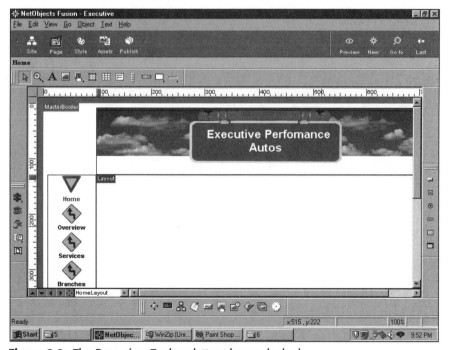

Figure 6-9: The Page view Tools palettes shown docked.

Figure 6-10: The Properties palette changes after placing an image with the Picture tool.

Tip

If any toolbar is not displayed, just select it from the View ➪ Toolbars cascading menu on the menu bar.

By selecting the appropriate button on any of the individual toolbars, you can easily create the location of text, images, form fields, Navigation Bars, banners, graphics, or rich media content on the page. Unlike standard HTML coding (without very fancy table and cell coding) that restricts you to left, right, and center alignment options, Fusion lets you define *exactly* where you want to place any object.

Tip

Clicking and holding down some buttons on the toolbars (the ones with the right-pointing triangles) displays a pop-out list showing more options for that tool (as shown in Figure 6-11). Simply select the tool you want. As you move the mouse pointer over the available buttons (and while still holding down the mouse button), a tool tips description will appear describing that particular tool.

Figure 6-11: Selecting from a tool's sub-tools menu by holding down the left mouse button.

The Standard toolbar

The Standard toolbar (seen in Figure 6-12) contains the basic tools you will be using in Fusion, as described in Table 6-1.

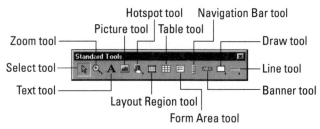

Figure 6-12: The Standard toolbar.

<table>
<tr><th colspan="2">Table 6-1
The Standard toolbar's tools</th></tr>
<tr><th>Button</th><th>What it does</th></tr>
<tr><td>Select tool</td><td>Selects an object on the page</td></tr>
<tr><td>Zoom tool</td><td>Magnifies (or shrinks) the viewing size of the page</td></tr>
<tr><td>Text tool</td><td>Adds a text box to a page</td></tr>
<tr><td>Picture tool</td><td>Adds a graphics image to a page</td></tr>
<tr><td>Hotspot tool</td><td>Adds an area to a graphic that becomes a hyperlink</td></tr>
<tr><td>Layout Region tool</td><td>Adds a special region on a page (used to group objects or become a form)</td></tr>
<tr><td>Table tool</td><td>Creates a grid of cells to contain text or graphics or both</td></tr>
<tr><td>Form Area tool</td><td>Draws an area on a page to contain form controls</td></tr>
<tr><td>Navigation Bar tool</td><td>Adds a Navigation Bar to a page</td></tr>
<tr><td>Banner tool</td><td>Adds a Banner heading to a page</td></tr>
<tr><td>Draw tool</td><td>Draws rectangles, circles, and irregular polygons on a page</td></tr>
<tr><td>Line tool</td><td>Adds lines, arrows, or horizontal rules to a page</td></tr>
</table>

The Select tool

The Select tool is the default tool in Page view and selects, moves, or resizes any objects that have been placed on a page. In conjunction with the select tool, you can also use the four arrows on the keyboard to nudge an object pixel by pixel up, down, left, or right.

Tip

To nudge a selected item by a distance of 10 pixels rather than a single pixel (which is what the arrow keys do), hold down the Shift key when pressing the arrow key in any direction.

The Zoom tool

Similar to the equivalent tools in Site view, clicking the Magnifying Glass with the + symbol in its center zooms the page to a larger magnification. The Magnifying Glass with the – sign has the opposite effect, zooming out so that you can see more of the page on the screen. To the bottom right of the main Fusion window, a status box shows the current percentage of magnification in use.

The Text tool

When the Text tool is selected, the mouse pointer changes to a cross mark when placed over the document. To place text, place the pointer at the top left of the area to contain the text and drag a rectangle to the bottom right corner. Once you have defined the text area, a cursor appears inside the rectangle letting you type your text as shown in Figure 6-13. When in text insertion mode, the Properties palette contains options for changing font size, style, typeface, color, justification, and so on.

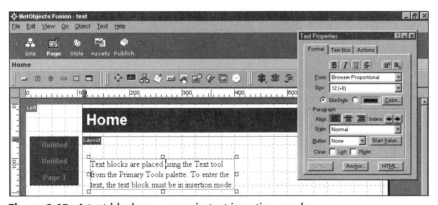

Figure 6-13: A text block on a page in text insertion mode.

You can later move text blocks anywhere on the page by choosing the Arrow tool, selecting the text block, and dragging it to a new location. You can also use the arrow keys on the keyboard for incremental pixel-by-pixel movements of a text block (or hold the Shift key at the same time to move the text block in increments of 10 pixels).

When selecting text blocks with the mouse, click the mouse button once to select the block. Once a text block is selected, black *handles* will appear at each corner and at the center top and bottom sides of the object. You can now move the text block using either the Arrow tool or the arrow keys on the keyboard.

If you see clear or white handles around the text block, you are in text insertion mode for the object (double-click the text box to get into edit mode). To exit this and enter text block select mode, single click anywhere on the bounding box of the text block.

Once you've selected a text block, you can modify the physical shape of the text block at any time by dragging any of its handles.

You can turn any section of text into a hyperlink or target of a hyperlink using the Link and Anchor buttons on the Properties palette. For more details on creating hyperlinks and anchors, please read Chapter 11.

The Picture tool

The Picture tool places an image on a Web page. To use this tool, select it from the Tools palette and draw a rectangle on the page. This will be the image's placeholder.

Unlike the Text tool, you do not have to draw the placeholder to the size of the image. No matter how large or small you create the Picture placeholder, the image will always be inserted at 100 percent of its size.

Once you've defined the picture's location on the page, a dialog box opens requesting the file name of the image. Type the file name or use the dialog box to navigate to its location on the hard disk and click OK. Figure 6-14 shows the placing of an image.

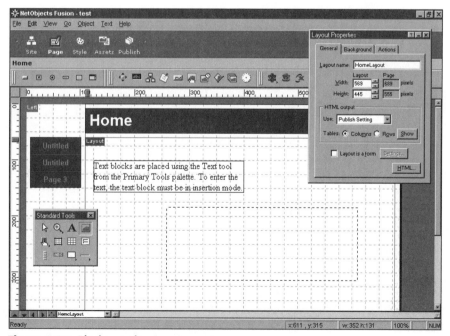

Figure 6-14: Placing an image on a page.

Once you've placed an image with the Picture tool and the image is selected, a new tab called the Effects tab appears in the Properties palette. On the Effects tab, you can apply Alt tags to an image to modify the transparency of an image if it is a GIF image, add text to the inside of the image, rotate it in 90° increments, and add a border.

Whereas Web pages require images to be either GIF or JPEG files, most image file types such as BMP or TIFF files are supported by NetObjects Fusion. After being placed, images other than GIF or JPEG will automatically be copied to a new GIF or JPEG file (depending on which format you chose) and named automatically by Fusion. This copy of the original file is placed in the Assets folder of the current user site. This copying process does not affect the original image.

Remember that images placed on a page are *not* stored in the NOD file; only the pointer to the file's location is stored. Because of this, if the original file is modified, this will reflect in its display on the page; if the original file is deleted or moved, the page will show a blank placeholder with a cross through it as shown in Figure 6-15.

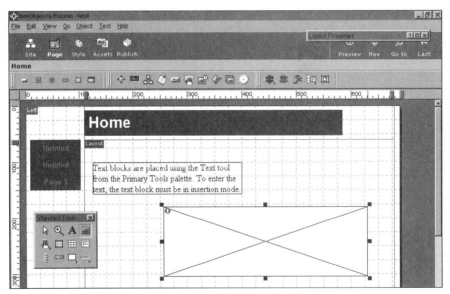

Figure 6-15: A page displaying an error when it cannot find a placed image.

If you inadvertently delete or move an image on your hard disk, by selecting any blank placeholder you can discover the original file name that was at the location by looking in the Properties palette.

Alt tags display a description of an image when it is downloading and when the visitor to the Web site has turned off his or her images option. In later browsers (versions 4 and greater or Navigator and Explorer), the Alt tag is also displayed when the user moves a mouse pointer over an image on a Web page.

More important, many sight impaired people use synthesizers to "read and speak" the text of a Web page. If no Alt tag is available, they have no way of knowing what an image is, or if it even exists. Good Web design protocol always dictates that you provide an Alt tag on any image.

Alt tags are discussed more fully in Chapter 9.

The Hotspot tool

The Hotspot tool creates regions on a graphic that, when clicked, link to another Web page in the current site, an anchor in the current site, or a separate URL altogether. This is called client-side imagemapping and is discussed in much greater detail in Chapter 14.

For example, you might have an image of the United States with hotspots set up over each state. Clicking on a state in the image will take you to a specific web page for that state.

The Layout Region Tool

The Region tool is one of those funny tools that initially makes you scratch your head and wonder what on earth it does.

With the Region tool, you can create a subsection on a page and place elements inside that subsection. The beauty of the Region tool is that once you have done this, all of the elements inside that region are effectively grouped, thus allowing you to move the region anywhere on the page as one entity.

Another benefit is that you can apply left and right word wrap to text around objects and they are more than a little useful for creating multiple forms on a page. There is more to the Region tool than meets the eye! Stay tuned or leap straight to Chapter 16.

The Table tool

Tables are grids of cells in rows and columns and mainly display tabular information such as price lists, calendar events, and other repetitive information. Tables are especially useful for data that need to be aligned horizontally or vertically in a regular fashion. Table cells can contain either text or images, and the contents of a cell can be aligned to the left, right or center. You can separately define individual backgrounds, cell widths, and cell heights for different cells.

To create a table, select the Table tool from the Tools palette. After drawing the location of the table's boundary on the page, a dialog box opens (as shown in Figure 6-16) requesting the number of rows and columns required for the table.

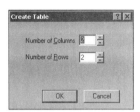

Figure 6-16: The Create Table dialog box.

You can modify or format the number of rows and columns in a table, the size of individual cells, and a cell's contents and background color at any stage after you've created a table by right-clicking and choosing the option from the popup menu.

Figure 6-17 shows a formatted table in Page view.

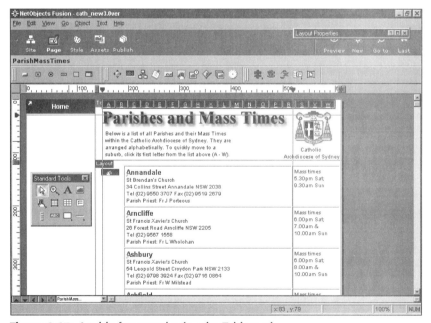

Figure 6-17: A table formatted using the Table tool.

The Navigation Bar tool

Navigation Bars are a series of images (or a text block) that a user clicks to navigate to other pages in a Web site. Fusion creates Navigation Bars automatically, based on the current Style sheet setting (although this can be altered), and they can be either vertical or horizontal in orientation. You can fully define the hierarchical page levels displayed in a Navigation Bar, including First Level, Parent Level, Child Level, the home page, and so on.

To place a Navigation Bar, select the Navigation Bar tool from the Standard toolbar and draw a rectangle on the page (usually inside a MasterBorder). A rectangle drawn with its horizontal axis longer than the vertical axis will create a horizontally oriented Navigation Bar. If the vertical axis is longer than the horizontal one (the rectangle is deeper than it is wide), a vertically oriented Navigation Bar will be created (as in Figure 6-18).

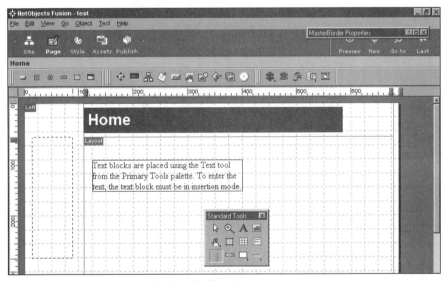

Figure 6-18: Creating a vertical Navigation Bar.

A Navigation Bar can be located anywhere on a Web page, but it will most usually appear in a MasterBorder area. Just as you do with text or images, draw a rectangle at the location you want the Navigation Bar to display. The size of the rectangle drawn does not affect the final size of the Navigation Bar.

Once you've created a NavBar, the General tab of the Properties palette contains several options for that NavBar. For example, if the Navigation Bar contains a button (or text link) to the current page, you can apply borders and alter the spacing value of images or text. In any single style, you have two choices of buttons you can apply to a Navigation Bar, labeled Primary and Secondary.

Figure 6-19 shows the Navigation Bar tab on the Properties palette.

Figure 6-19: The Navigation Bar tab on the Properties palette.

Tip

You are not limited to a single Navigation Bar on a page. By setting the properties of the buttons in the Navigation Bar, separate Navigation Bars can have links to different sections of a Web site.

The Banner tool

Banners are graphics images usually placed at the top of a Web page that describe the name or purpose of a page. In Fusion, the banner image is defined according to the current style sheet setting (although this can be altered) and normally contains the name of the page. By default, this is the name you supplied in Site view when the page was created, but you can modify this using the Custom Names button on the Properties palette while in Site view or Page view. For example, you may prefer having the banner contain your company name or a Web site description rather than "Home."

Banners are placed identically to a Navigation Bar, with specific tabs applicable for banners appearing in the Properties palette as seen in Figure 6-20.

Figure 6-20: The General tab for Banners on the Properties palette.

The Draw tool

The Draw tool places basic images on a page such as rectangles, circles, and polygons. Clicking on the Draw tool button on the Standard toolbar pops out a bar of available tools for placing graphics.

After placing a Draw object, you can use the General tab on the Properties palette to modify its interior and border colors, change line thickness, or place text inside the body of the object.

You can also use draw objects as hyperlinks or the destination of a hyperlink using the Link and Anchor buttons on the Properties palette.

The Line tool

The Line tool selects either standard drawn lines, SiteStyle lines, or rule lines to place on Web pages. Drawn lines can be of different thickness and color and can also contain arrow heads and tails. SiteStyle lines are graphics images stored as part of a SiteStyle (see Part III for more details on Site Styles). An HR rule is the equivalent to the HTML <HR> command. An HR rule can also have varying thickness in addition to having a shading option.

The Advanced toolbar

The Advanced toolbar (seen in Figure 6-21) contains many tools that let you place graphics, sound, animation, and data lists on your pages. Table 6-2 shows the tools of the Advanced toolbar.

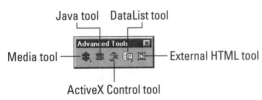

Figure 6-21: The Advanced toolbar.

Table 6-2
The Advanced toolbar's tools

Button	What it does
Media tool	Adds sound, video, or Shockwave elements to a page
Java tool	Adds Java applets to a page
ActiveX Control tool	Adds ActiveX controls to a page
DataList tool	Connects an external database to a page
External HTML tool	Connects external HTML files to a page

Note

Shockwave files are special files created in Macromedia Director, Macromedia Flash 2, or Macromedia Authorware and converted to Web use via "shocking" them: a process that makes them Web savvy. Generally, they are multimedia files containing combinations of sound, video, animation, or user interactivity.

The Media tool

Media can include Shockwave, QuickTime, video, or sound that is placed on a Web page. When you select the Media tool on the Advanced Tools palette, a pop-out menu appears containing a button for each of these types as shown in Figure 6-22.

Figure 6-22: The Tools palette with the Media tool selected.

To define the location on a page of a media object, draw a rectangle on the page at the location where you want an icon for the file to appear and enter the file name into a dialog box. The size of the rectangle is not relative to the object itself.

When viewed in a browser, in most cases the user clicks on the icon to activate the media object.

The Java Applet tool

You can place Java applets onto a Web page with the Java Applet tool. Many thousands of other Java applets are available from the Internet — most of them free — that you can use to add special effects and interactivity to your Web pages, and of course, you can write your own. To search the Internet, as there are literally hundreds of locations dedicated to Java applets, use a search engine such as AltaVista or HotBot and use the keywords "Java applet."

To add a Java applet, select the Java tool and draw a rectangle where the applet will be placed on the page. A dialog box will open prompting for the location of the applet on the hard disk. When you have chosen this, use the Properties palette General tab to place the parameters the applet requires as seen in Figure 6-23.

What is Java?

Java is a computer language primarily used to create small programs to embed into Web pages. Its major advantage is that it is platform independent: a Java applet written on a Macintosh, for example, will run without any modification on a PC and vice versa. The disadvantage, in my opinion, is that it is not an easy language to learn. There are many good books describing the Java language, and I can highly recommend *Java Programming for Dummies* by Donald J. and David Koosis (IDG Books Worldwide, 1997).

Figure 6-23: The Java applet parameter dialog box.

A Java applet is usually defined in its programming to be a specific display dimension. This especially applies to applets that provide visual effects. In this case, the size and location of the rectangle drawn to place the applet is important. To find out this size, check the documentation or read.me file supplied with the applet.

For a more detailed description of using the Java applet tool, refer to Chapter 24.

An excellent source of information on Java and Java applets is JavaWorld at www.javaworld.com.

The ActiveX tool

ActiveX is a Microsoft technology that is an extension of the *object linking and embedding* (OLE) functionality originally built into Windows applications such as Excel or Word. From a relatively slow start, ActiveX controls are now available for many functions including visual effects, user control and navigation, element display on a Web page, and control of external files from inside the Web browser.

ActiveX components are installed on a Web page similarly to Java applets. Simply select the ActiveX tool, draw a rectangle where you want the control placed on the page, and complete the parameters in the General tab on the Properties palette (see Figure 6-24) for the control.

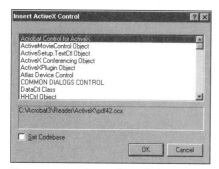

Figure 6-24: The ActiveX dialog box.

Remember that not all browsers support ActiveX controls at this time. At the time of writing, Internet Explorer 3 and 4 do "as-is." Netscape Navigator does not without a plug-in, and even then, not all are guaranteed to work. For the most up-to-date information (and it is changing all the time) if you use Netscape Navigator, visit its Web site at www.netscape.com and do a search for "ActiveX."

For a complete description of using ActiveX controls in Fusion, refer to Chapter 24.

The Data List tool

A *data list* is an object placed on a Web page that refers to the data object, which contains the definition of a database connected to a Fusion Web site. A data list holds such information as the file name and location of the database, data filtering and sorting parameters, and field display and navigation configuration. To be connected, a database must be ODBC-compliant, such as Microsoft Access or Lotus Approach.

To create a data list, select the Data List tool and draw a rectangle at the location on the page where you wish the index of the data to appear. A series of dialog boxes open allowing you to set all of the appropriate parameters for the filtering and sorting of the data from the database. Figure 6-25 shows the Data List dialog box.

When complete, Fusion creates an index on the page. The contents of the index depend upon the options selected in the dialog boxes.

From the information referenced in the Data List, Fusion also automatically creates a special set of Web pages called *stacked pages*. For each record in the database matching the search and sort parameters previously set, one stacked page is created.

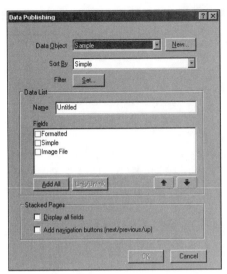

Figure 6-25: Adding a data list object.

Once the stacked pages have been created, you use the Data Fields tool to place fields from the database onto the pages. Figure 6-26 shows a stacked Web page containing data fields.

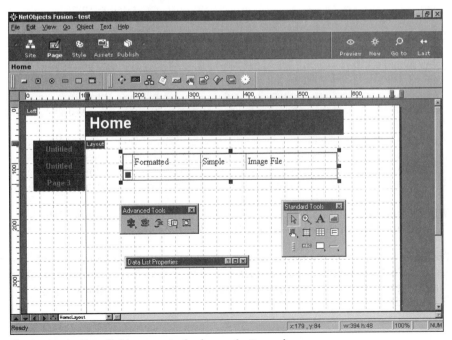

Figure 6-26: Data fields on a stacked page in Page view.

All stacked pages are identical in their format and therefore only one of the stacked pages needs to be formatted with data fields. This also applies to any other elements you want on the stacked pages, such as background colors, graphics images, and so on.

Any changes made to a stacked page's layout will affect all the stacked pages created using the one Data List.

Unlike using other tools such as Cold Fusion, the database remains on the local hard disk or network drive and is not published to the Web server. Because of this, the data is not live, only receiving any updates when the Web site is republished to the Web server.

Chapter 20 contains full details on adding and configuring data lists, data fields, and stacked pages using databases.

The External HTML Tool

The external HTML tool lets you incorporate existing HTML pages into a Fusion page. Why would you do this? Perhaps an example will best illustrate.

The local horse trotting and pacing track in Sydney can automatically generate an HTML document of the race results from its electronic timing equipment at the end of a race. This is then e-mailed to me (I maintain the Web site for the organization). Instead of laboriously having to retype everything already done, using the Insert HTML tool, I simply import the results page into the existing Fusion page.

To see this in action, take a look at `www.haroldpark.com.au/html/results.html`.

The Component toolbar

The Component toolbar (seen in Figure 6-27) contains all of the tools necessary to add specialized interactive elements supplied with Fusion. Table 6-3 details the tools you can find on the Component toolbar.

Figure 6-27: The Component toolbar.

Table 6-3
The Component toolbar's tools

Button	What it does
DynaButtons tool	Adds dynamic navigation controls
TickerTape tool	Adds a scrolling ticker tape message
SiteMapper tool	Adds a Java applet displaying a graphical map of the site
Message Board tool	Adds a bulletin board to the page
Form Handler tool	Adds a custom form to a page
Picture Rollover tool	Adds images that change when the mouse pointer moves over them
Time Based Picture tool	Adds images that change dependent upon the time
Picture Loader tool	Places a picture from a remote location
Rotating Picture tool	Adds images that change at specified time intervals
NetObjects Components tool	Adds custom third-party controls

The DynaButtons tool

DynaButtons are interactive menu buttons that "change state." When a DynaButton becomes active by moving the mouse pointer over it, it will change from the Primary button image used in the attached SiteStyle to the Secondary button image. In addition, a DynaButton displays the name of the page in the site to which it is linked.

Up to 20 DynaButtons can be assigned on a page in a single group, and each of these 20 can have a further 20 sub-buttons attached.

The TickerTape tool

The TickerTape tool allows you to assign a series of scrolling messages to a region on a Web page. The height and width of the TickerTape is totally configurable, as is the color of any message, border or background to the control. The only thing that is fixed is the font style with TickerTape using a built-in LED-style font.

The SiteMapper tool

The SiteMapper tool places a button upon a Web page that when clicked displays a graphical map of the site in a separate window. Pages in the site can be navigated to by double-clicking it on the map. Pages can also be displayed in a familiar Windows Explorer-style hierarchy. There is a search facility to find page names in the site.

The Message Board tool

The Message Board tool lets you build an interactive bulletin board system on your Web site. Messages and threads can be built up, with messages displayable in various ways such as by topic. To use the Message Board system, your web site must have access to a cgi-bin directory.

The Form Handler tool

The Form Handler tool is primarily a series of scripts attached to the Submit button on a form. It lets you assign the contents of a form to either a text file on the Web server or to dispatch the contents of a form to an email address. Again, you must have access to a cgi-bin directory to use the Form Handler tool.

The Picture Rollover tool

The Picture Rollover tool assigns more than one image to a region on a Web page. The image that is actually displayed depends upon certain conditions such as the mouse pointer entering the region or leaving the region.

The Time Based Picture tool

Similar to the Picture Rollover tool, the Time Based Picture tool will display different images in a region depending upon the time of day. For example, a series of 24 images can be defined, with the image changing to the next on the hour.

The Picture Loader tool

The Picture Loader tool defines a region on a Web page to contain an image that is in another location: for example, an image at a URL on another Web server.

The Rotating Picture tool

The Rotating Picture tool is yet another useful variation on the previous Picture tool. It allows a sequence of images to be set up as you would find in a slide show. Each image is displayed for a period of time before changing to the next.

The NetObjects Components tool

The NetObjects Components tool is used to add third party developed NFX components to a web page. There are a number of third party NFX components supplied on the CD that is enclosed with this book.

The Forms toolbar

Forms are special areas on a Web page containing fields, lists, buttons, checkboxes, and radio buttons. Forms are primarily used as a means to gain feedback from visitors to your site, provide an area where subscribers can submit information, or to send messages to a bulletin board system. You can place certain form elements, such as dropdown list boxes, on a page, and you can use JavaScript to perform special actions such as navigating to another page after selecting it from a list.

The Form toolbar (as seen in Figure 6-28) shows the tools you'll need to create a basic form and Table 6-4 shows what each tool does.

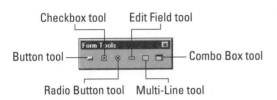

Checkbox tool   Edit Field tool

Button tool

Combo Box tool

Radio Button tool   Multi-Line tool

Figure 6-28: The Form toolbar.

Table 6-4	
The Form toolbar's tools	
Button	**_What it does_**
Button tool	Adds a Submit or Reset forms button to a form on a page
Checkbox tool	Adds a checkbox to a form on a page
Radio Button tool	Adds a series of radio buttons to a form on a page
Edit Field tool	Adds a single-line data entry field to a form on a page
Multi-Line tool	Adds a multiple-line data entry field to a form on a page
Combo Box tool	Adds a field allowing a choice of selections to a form on a page

The Button tool

There are two types of forms buttons: submit and reset. The submit button calls a script that processes the form and the reset button is used to cancel all forms input allowing the visitor to start over. Figure 6-29 shows a typical form.

More Info

In Chapter 16, there is a complete description and walk-through of creating forms.

Figure 6-29: A form on a Web page used to gain visitor feedback.

For forms to work, in most cases you need to have access to a special Web server facility called a *cgi-bin*. A cgi-bin contains *scripts* that process the information entered into a form and transmit it to its destination. A script is a computer program (commonly written using a language called Perl) that the form calls when the user presses a Send button.

The elements of the form (fields, checkboxes, radio buttons, and so on) are purely the visual part of the form. The Perl script does all the work, taking the content of each field and processing it according to what the Web developer wants. For example, the form on the Coates Hire "Contact Us" page (`http://www.coates. com.au`) gets the required information from the user via the form elements. The Perl script that is activated when the user clicks the Send button checks the state in which the user has stated he or she lives or works, and then sends the content of the form to the e-mail address of the Manager for that state.

You do not necessarily have to understand the Perl language to use forms. It is quite possible to call a Perl script from a location that is separate from where your Web site is hosted. A generic "Mail To" Perl script is available at `http://www. frostbyte.com.au/frostbyte/cgi-bin/mailto.pl` for example. This script looks for a form containing the fields "from" (for the user's e-mail address) and requires the developer to add the hidden fields "to", "sub" (for subject), and "nexturl"(for the page to navigate to automatically after clicking the Send button).

Note

While this script is freely made available by the author, Steve Frost, it is requested that rather than use it directly from his site (`www.frostbyte.com`) that you download it and place it in your own cgi-bin directory. All Steve asks is that you let him know you are using his script. Steve's e-mail is `steve.frost@frostbyte.com.au`.

To place the objects of a form onto a Web page, click the appropriate button on the Forms Tools palette. After choosing a form element and placing it on a page the parameters for the form object such as field size, labels, and actions are completed in the Properties palette.

The Checkbox tool

A checkbox is used on a form as a yes/no switch. For example, a checkbox might be used to ask whether visitors to the site want to receive regular mailings. If they check it by clicking it, they do. If they leave it blank, they don't.

The Radio Button tool

Radio buttons are used on forms to allow a single choice from a multiple-choice question. An example is where two radio buttons might be labeled Male and Female respectively. Only one radio button in a single group can be activated at any one time: in this example, if you clicked the Male radio button, the Female radio button would be de-selected and vice versa.

The Forms Edit Field tool

A forms edit field is a single line field where the visitor to the site can enter text.

The Multi-Line Edit Field tool

A Multi-Line Edit Field is used when a single line of information is not sufficient. An example of this might be where you wish to solicit comments from the person visiting the site and allow them several lines in which to enter these comments.

The Forms Combo Box tool

A Forms Combo Box is either a dropdown list or "spinner" control list where selections can be made from existing data. For example, a forms combo list might contain a list of states where the visitor lives, and he or she can select this from the list rather than typing the entry into a single line forms edit field.

The Properties palette

New to 3.0

In Fusion 3, the Properties for an object are made visible by first selecting the object and then selecting the appropriate tab on the Properties palette. The title of the Properties palette will change to reflect the type of object selected.

Palettes are also used extensively in Page view and similar to Site view, a Properties palette is available. Just click F12 to see it (as shown in Figure 6-30). The Properties palette is a floating palette and can never be docked.

Figure 6-30: The Page view Properties palette.

In Page view, the Properties palette behaves exactly as it does in Site view: you can move it around the screen, double-click in its title bar to make it roll up, and so on. In Page view, however, the available tabs on the palette change depending upon which objects are selected and whether the MasterBorder or Layout section is the current location.

When no objects are selected on a page, the Properties palette displays three of four possible tabs: General, Background, and Actions. Figure 6-31 shows this display of the palette. Figure 6-32 shows the Properties palette if you click on the MasterBorder area of the page. Notice that the Background tab is replaced with the AutoFrames tab. Click back in the Layout section of the page to redisplay the Background tab.

Figure 6-31: The Properties palette when the Layout area is current.

Figure 6-32: The Properties palette when the MasterBorder area is current.

In effect, the General tab displays the general properties that you can alter for the currently selected area or object. If you have selected the Layout section, the General tab displays the available options for the Layout; if you have selected the MasterBorders section, the General tab displays the properties for the MasterBorder. Likewise, you'll see the properties when you select a graphics object, text, and so on.

New to 3.0

This is totally different from earlier versions where different areas and objects all had sections in what was called the Layout tab.

At this point, you might want to select different objects or areas on the page and see what options become available to you on the Properties palette. I'll discuss the individual details of these different options in depth as we progress. For now, simply be aware that the Properties palette is the engine room of Fusion for elements that constitute a Web page, and it is here that all characteristics and behaviors of graphics, text, backgrounds, and so on are defined.

The Object Tree

The Object Tree window (shown in Figure 6-33) is accessible from the View ⇨ Palettes command on the menu bar and shows all elements on a Web page in a hierarchical format. The top of the "tree" is the whole page. As you look down the tree, you can see the MasterBorder (with its elements cascaded below) and then the Layout (again with its elements cascaded below).

Figure 6-33: The Object Tree window.

Elements in the Object Tree can be moved up and down levels and while there are no immediate visual indicators on the page this has happened, it *is* important when using either the CSS and Layers functionality and actions. See Chapter 20 for more information on Layers and Actions.

Page Labels

The Page Labels option turns on or off the Layout and MasterBorder labels (shown in Figure 6-34). Page Labels also appear on any frames you add to a page.

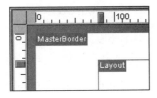

Figure 6-34: The MasterBorder and Layout labels.

Object outlines

The View menu contains other options that are also very useful when creating or editing Web pages. An *object outline* is a rectangle surrounding each element on a page and, when turned on, quickly allows you to see the exact perimeters of each element on the page (the dimensions of a selected object are shown in the bottom right status bar). This is especially useful when placing transparent GIF images, as the background may not be visually evident and therefore may potentially give a false impression of the image's true physical size.

Tip

As the Object Outline takes up one pixel when butting objects flush together, I recommend turning Object Outlines off.

Figure 6-35 shows the Home page with the Show Element Borders option turned on.

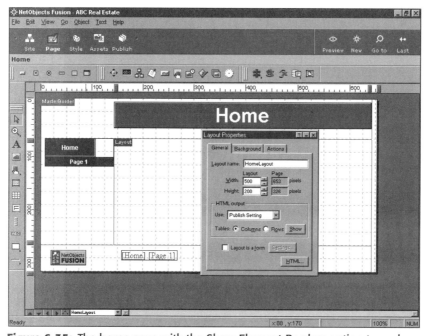

Figure 6-35: The home page with the Show Element Borders option turned on.

Object icons

Object icons are special symbols that Fusion places next to an element depending upon its properties. For example, if an element has a hyperlink attached to it, you have no way of visually knowing this without viewing its properties in the Properties palette. With the Object Icons option turned on, a small blue circle containing a white arrow is placed next to the object. Table 6-5 shows the object icons and what they signify. Figure 6-36 shows a page in Page view with the Object Icons option turned on.

Table 6-5		
The object icons		
What you see	**What it is**	**What it does**
	The link icon	Shows an object that has a hyperlink applied to it
	The anchor icon	Shows an object can be the destination of a hyperlink
	The HTML icon	Shows there is associated HTML in the object
	The HTML tag icon	Shows that an embedded HTML tag resides at this point
	The error icon	Shows there is another object overlapping the object on the page
	The embedded object icon	Shows another object is embedded in this object at this point
	The action icon	Shows an action has been applied to the object

Figure 6-36: A page with the Show Element Icons option turned on.

Rulers

Also available from the View menu and further aiding in accuracy, are a vertical and horizontal ruler. The dimensions shown on the ruler are determined by the settings on the Preferences palette (accessed by choosing it from the Edit menu). As the mouse moves around the page, an indicator shows on both rulers indication the respective horizontal and vertical position of the mouse. These x, y coordinates are also shown in the status bar at the bottom of the window.

Fusion 3 adds the capability to set page size and MasterBorder size on the ruler line. As Figure 6-37 shows, the rulers now contain margin tabs that you can drag to new locations effectively changing both the Page and MasterBorder sizing depending upon which are dragged.

Figure 6-37: The top horizontal ruler showing the Page and MasterBorder margin tabs.

Guides

Guides are used in conjunction with the rulers for precise alignment. Guides are horizontal and vertical lines that you can place anywhere on the page. To set guides, make sure the Rulers & Guides option is on via the View menu on the menu bar (see Figure 6-38).. Next, click anywhere on a ruler. Either a red (if you clicked in a MasterBorder area) or blue (when clicked in a Layout area) marker will be placed on the ruler line in association with a guide drawn down or across the page, depending upon whether you placed the guide on a vertical or horizontal ruler.

Figure 6-38: Setting the guides option from the View menu.

When the mouse is clicked on a guide's marker on the ruler line, a small yellow pop-up box will display the coordinate of the guide on that ruler. To move a guide, drag its marker to a new location on the ruler. To remove a guide, drag it off the layout area.

Figure 6-39 shows a Home page with the guides option turned on. Note the guides and their associated markers on the ruler.

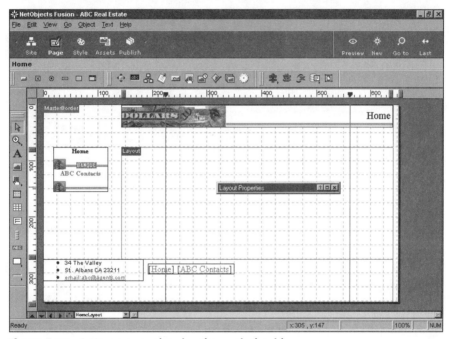

Figure 6-39: A Home page showing the vertical guides.

Tip

When aligning an element, position it by selecting it with the mouse and dragging the element to a new location. If pixel by pixel movement is necessary, you can nudge a selected element a pixel at a time using any of the four arrow keys on the keyboard.

When the Rulers & Guides option is set, Fusion lets you place vertical and horizontal guides on the page at any location you like. To place a guide, simply click on either a vertical or horizontal ruler at the position you want the guide to be placed. You can add as many guides as you like in this way.

The grid

You use a *grid* to align elements precisely to each other on the page, and it is represented on the page as a series of crisscrossed lines at exactly the same distance from each other (see Figure 6-40). You turn on the grid from the View menu.

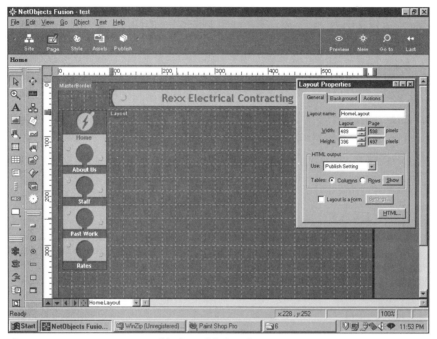

Figure 6-40: A Home page with the grid showing.

To change the default spacing values of the grid, open the Preferences sheet (Edit ➪ Preferences), click the Page tab, and use the spinner controls to increase or decrease the Grid Spacing values (which by default are set to 25).

Dimensions

At the bottom right of the main window in the status bar is a pair of values that help in exact physical placement by showing the current position of the mouse pointer in x and y coordinates. As the mouse pointer moves over the page, these values will change.

The unit of measurement of the numbers shown depends upon the settings on the Preferences sheet (as shown in Figure 6-41). The unit you will use is very much up to personal preference. I find that I tend to size images in image editing applications using pixels as reference values; using pixel measurements in Fusion retains conformity.

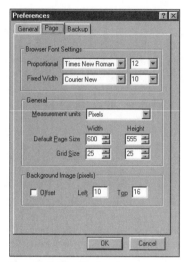

Figure 6-41: Setting measurement units.

The Snap options

In addition to turning on grids, guides, and rulers, Fusion lets you define snap options. The View menu contains the available snap options (see Figure 6-42). Turning on Snap to Grid or Guides causes any element when moved on a page to snap or jump to the nearest grid line or guide. The Snap to Objects option causes an object to snap to another object when placed close to it on a page.

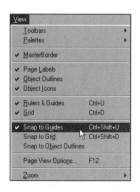

Figure 6-42: Setting the Snap options.

Setting Layout Properties

Before creating a Web site or page, you might first want to set several configuration options.

Layout name

By default, a page's layout is labeled by its page name. For example, the layout area for a page you have called Courier rates is called "Courier Rates Layout" unless otherwise changed. To change the name of an existing layout, enter a new name in the Layout Name field on the Properties palette (click anywhere in the Layout area but *not* on an element to display this palette).

Margins

How large should design your pages? Internet newsgroups are continually debating this topic, with no — ahem — resolution in sight as to what is or is not correct.

Personally, I prefer to use the lowest common denominator, which just about guarantees that no one will have to scroll any of my pages in his or her browser in any direction other than up or down. This means that I set all my Web pages at 640×480 resolution in 256 colors.

You may or may not agree. If you don't, you need to reset the default page size of Fusion (which is 640×480). This option is in the Preferences sheet located from the Edit menu on the menu bar and seen in Figure 6-43. The Preferences sheet has three tabs: General, Page, and Backup. The page size settings are on the Page tab. Either select the setting you wish to change and retype a new value or alternatively use the spinner controls to change to a new value. Each click of a spinner arrow will increment (or decrement) the existing value by one.

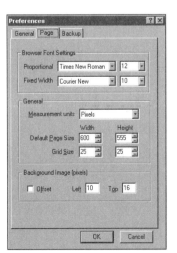

Figure 6-43: The Preferences sheet.

HTML output

The setting in the HTML Layout field on the Layout Properties palette determines a format the page is to be published in. The four options are:

✦ Publish Setting

✦ Nested tables

✦ Regular tables

✦ CSS and Layers

You choose the setting at this point (which will always be overridden at publishing time) so that you can change different publish formats to see how a page will look when previewed in that particular format. For more detail on the differences between these separate options, refer to Chapter 28.

Layout as a Form

When the Layout as a Form box is checked, the page can contain one and only form. For details on form creation, please refer to Chapter 16.

Background

The Background of a Layout is determined initially by the style that has been applied to the site. You can change this at any time from the applied style to either a solid color or a graphics image by selecting the appropriate option on the Background tab of the Layout Properties palette.

Background Sound

By checking the Background Sound box and specifying a file name in the dialog box that opens a sound file or MIDI file can be attached to the page. This will play once the page has loaded in a web browser. By also checking the Continuous Loop box in the file name dialog box, the sound will continue to play until the page is exited.

While this initially seems like a cool idea, after you have been to a Web page with background sound a few times — especially a looping sound — it can become a trifle annoying. Use with discretion!

For more information about adding sound to a page, have a look at Chapter 21.

MasterBorder and Layout relationships

MasterBorders and Layouts are two totally separate entities: changing any attribute on one will not affect the other and vice versa (with the exception of size and even then only the sum of the sizes making up the whole page will change).

Switching between saved layouts will also not affect a MasterBorder or its elements.

To find out more about MasterBorders and their relationship with the Layout area, flip over to Chapter 10.

Summary

✦ MasterBorders contain elements that are common to all pages containing the same MasterBorder.

✦ Layout Areas contain elements that will appear on the current page only.

✦ The grid, guides, and rulers assist in exact placement and alignment of elements.

✦ The snap options assist in locating objects in positions relative to each other.

✦ Element borders and icons are visual aids showing element perimeters and specialist properties such as hyperlinks.

✦ Different types of publishing formats can be specified for previewing purposes.

✦ Background sounds can be added to a page.

✦ A Layout can be a container for a form.

✦   ✦   ✦

Working with Styles

A style in Fusion is a set of elements or descriptions that follow a particular theme. Fusion comes supplied with a large number of different styles covering a variety of different themes. A typical *style* contains a series of buttons used for Navigation Bars, graphics images for Banners, lines and DataList icons, and text attributes such as typeface and color for normal text as well as links. Figure 7-1 shows the Fusion Basic style.

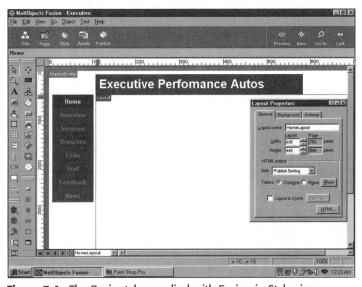

Figure 7-1: The Basic style supplied with Fusion in Style view.

At the very start, it is important to understand that when Fusion applies a style, it applies to the entire site and not just to a page. As you can imagine, this is an enormous time-saver: with a couple of mouse clicks, you can apply a completely new look no matter whether the site has two pages or 200.

Choosing a Style

To switch to Style view, select it from the Go menu on the menu bar or by clicking its button on the control bar. Figure 7-2 shows the Fusion Style view.

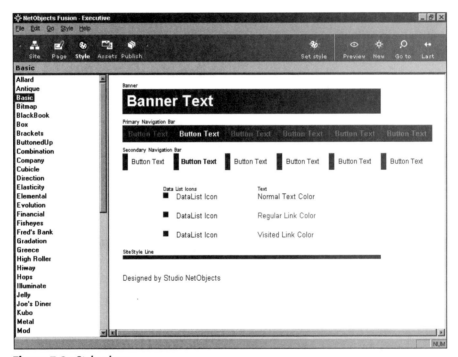

Figure 7-2: Style view.

Style view consists of two windows: the left window shows a list of all the different styles available, and the right window shows each of the elements in the selected Style. Fusion always applies the Basic style to any new site, and in most cases, we want to change this to reflect more accurately the look and feel we want for the pages. Table 7-1 shows all the SiteStyles you'll find in the left window.

Table 7-1			
The styles available in Fusion			
Allard	Antique	Basic	Bitmap
BlackBook	Box	Brackets	ButtonedUp
Combination	Company	Cubicle	Direction
Elasticity	Elemental	Evolution	Financial
Fisheyes	Fred's Bank	Gradation	Greece
High Roller	Hiway	Hopps	Illuminate
Jelly	Joe's Diner	Kubo	Metal
Mod	Nautica	Paper	Plain
Presentation	Reger	Remote	Ripple
Scotch	Simple	SlowMetal	Smile
SoHo	Stadium	Subway	Surf's Up
SweetStone	Switchplate	Tech	Texture
Totu	Traditional	Train	Trans World
Trek	Venezia	Wintergreen	

To find the style you want, scroll down the list until you can see its name and then select it with the mouse.

The right window shows the following elements:

✦ a Banner

✦ two types of buttons (known as *primary buttons* and *secondary buttons)*

✦ DataList icons

✦ colors for text, hypertext links, and visited hypertext links

✦ a separator bar

You can modify every aspect of each of these elements as required, including the typeface, font color, size, and even the images used. I'll cover that in a few sections.

Setting a Style

To apply a different style to the current site, scroll down the list of styles until you find one that suits, make sure it is selected with the mouse, and click on the Set Style button on the icon bar. You can also select the Page icon in the control bar. You'll see a dialog box like the one in Figure 7-3. If you don't want Fusion to prompt for this confirmation in the future, click in the checkbox at the lower left of the dialog box.

Figure 7-3: A dialog box asking to set the selected style as the SiteStyle.

Let's use an example of a bank called ABC Financial site, one of the supplied Fusion styles is far more suited than the Basic style currently assigned. This style is called, Financial. Figure 7-4 shows the Financial Style. To apply this Style, select it from the list and click the Set Style button.

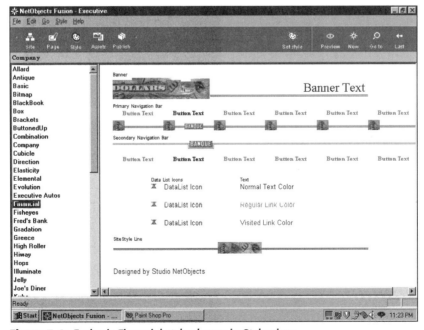

Figure 7-4: Fusion's Financial style shown in Style view.

Switching back to Page view now shows the style incorporated into the site (see Figure 7-5). Try doing *that* with any other Web authoring tool! One click, and the entire site has been revamped. Cool huh?

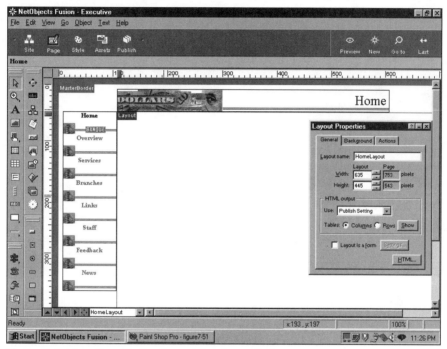

Figure 7-5: The site with the Financial style applied.

Creating a New Style

You can also create your own styles using the New Style option from the Style menu. Simply give the style a new name (as shown in Figure 7-6). The new style will be added to the list in the left window, and the right window displays blank placeholders for all the style elements (shown in Figure 7-7). To fill in the placeholders, double-click each style element and supply the requested parameters.

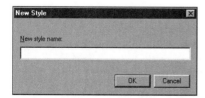

Figure 7-6: The New Style dialog box.

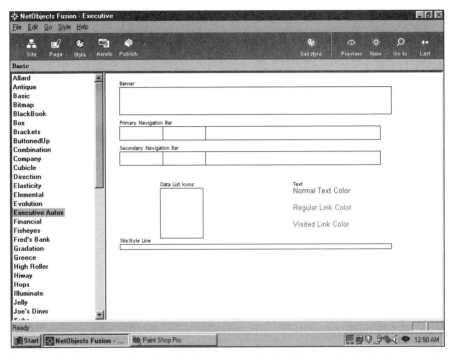

Figure 7-7: The new style showing the empty placeholders ready for their parameters to be added.

Any graphical objects that are part of a style (such as banners and buttons) are stored in separate files in the NetObjects Fusion 3/Styles/*Stylename*/*Element* folder. For example, the Primary Button for the Basic style is stored in the file NetObjects Fusion 3/Styles/Plain/Primary Buttons/PlainButton.GIF (as shown in Figure 7-8).

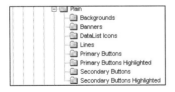

Figure 7-8: Style elements are stored in their own files and folders.

Copying a Style to Modify

If you are going to make permanent changes to any part of a style, you should copy that style to preserve the original version. To do this, follow these steps:

1. Open Windows Explorer and go to the NetObjects Fusion 3/Styles folder.

2. Create a new folder in the Styles folder by selecting File ➪ New ➪ Folder. Give it the name of the new style.

3. Open the style folder that you want to modify and select all its contents (press Ctrl+A).

4. To copy the contents, hold down the left mouse button and the Ctrl key and drag all of the contents of the existing style's folder into this new folder (as seen in Figure 7-9). (You can also press Ctrl+C, open the new folder, and press Ctrl+V.)

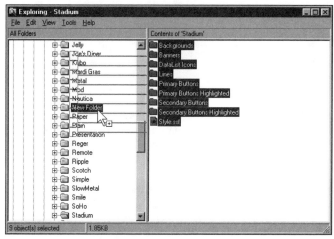

Figure 7-9: Dragging the contents of the current style's folder into the new folder. (Notice the plus sign signifying a copy.)

5. To complete the creation of a new style, select the Add Style to List command from the Style menu in Fusion, navigate to the folder you just created, and import the *.ssf file for the style.

Doing this leaves the original style intact just in case you want to use its defaults again. If you *do* make any changes to these defaults, any other sites that use the style will inherent these changes whenever such a site is republished.

Note

Macintosh users can select the folder of the style to copy, select the File ➪ Duplicate command, and change the name to the new style.

Editing a Style

As I've mentioned before, when in Style view, you can modify any element of the style, including images and text characteristics. To modify an element, simply double-click it. If the element you are changing is a banner, button, line, icon, or background, when editing you have the opportunity of nominating a different image file to replace the one supplied by Fusion (as shown in Figure 7-10).

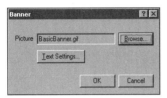

Figure 7-10: Editing the Banner element in a Fusion style.

For text that is used inside the banner and buttons, you can assign different colors and typefaces as well as characteristics such as bold, underline, italic, and strikethrough. Finally, you can change the colors Fusion will assign to hyperlinks in the Web site: both the color of unvisited links as well as visited ones.

Be sparing with your changes to a style supplied with Fusion, especially if you plan to use the same style in a different site. Changes made to a style will reflect in any other site having that style assigned to it. You're better off copying the original style as we did in the last section.

When modifying font attributes, Fusion will load all the fonts stored on your hard disk into memory. Because of this, if you have a large number of fonts installed, you may experience a small delay while this occurs.

This is best illustrated by way of an example.

You're designing a Web site for Executive Performance Autos, so you logically pick the Hiway style. On the Home page, though, the company name is too big for the banner (see Figure 7-11). What do you do? Follow these steps:

Figure 7-11: The company name is too big for the banner.

1. First, you can wrap the text. Just select the Custom Names option from the Edit menu and insert a return after the "Performance." The Banner field should now look like Figure 7-12.

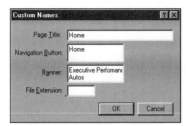

Figure 7-12: Making a wrap in the Custom Names dialog box.

2. The name is *still* too big (see Figure 7-13). Now, you go to Style view, double-click on "Banner Text," and click Text Settings. You'll see the dialog box in Figure 7-14.

Figure 7-13: The text is still too big.

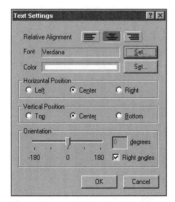

Figure 7-14: The Text Settings dialog box.

3. Press the Set button on the same row as the Font field. In the dialog box that opens, you'll see that the Font Size is 24. Press the up arrow a few times and select 16. Press OK, OK, and OK.

4. Press the Page icon on the control bar to view the results (as seen in Figure 7-15).

Figure 7-15: The company name now fits in the banner!

Remember that if you changed the font on the Hiway style, all sites using it will display banners in 16-point type.

By creating a dummy style where the banner is a plain white graphic, you can use any fancy font you like for a headline (assuming you use a white background. If you use a different colored background change the banner color accordingly). Instead of having to use Photoshop or some other image editing program to create banner graphics for every page in the site, simply apply the font you want to the style (say Olde Englishe) and then this font will be used as the banner heading for each page automatically. It's a simple but effective trick!

Removing a Style

If for some reason you need to remove a style from the list of available styles, select it with the mouse and choose the Remove Style From List option from the Style menu on the menu bar. From experience, I don't recommend removing styles because you just never know when it will come in handy! I would be lost without the Tech style, for example, as I think it has the best Navigation Bar buttons for generic use.

Updating the Styles List

If you *do* remove styles and want them back, there is a quick way to do this without manually importing each style one by one.

Again from the Style menu on the menu bar, choose the Update Styles List, and Fusion will automatically update the list with all styles that reside in the Styles folder on the hard disk.

Summary

✦ Assigning a style applies a consistent look and feel to a site.

✦ When a style is applied, all elements are applied to all pages in the site.

✦ Styles can be copied to form new styles.

✦ Individual elements of a style can be modified, such as color and text attributes.

✦ New styles can be created from scratch with custom graphics and text attributes.

✦ Styles can be removed from the styles list when not needed.

✦ The Styles list can be updated with all styles residing in the Styles folder after they may have been removed from the Styles list.

✦   ✦   ✦

Adding Text

Without text, a Web site would have an interesting effect I agree, but the fact remains that text is the one common denominator for getting information to a Web site's visitors.

Using Fusion, the addition and manipulation of text across the entirety of a site is a dream. For example, let's say you have built a client site that consists of a couple of hundred Web pages. All of a sudden the client decides that he wants all the body text (that is text that is not a heading) changed from light blue to dark blue. If you understand how Fusion deals with text, you can achieve this with a couple of mouse clicks.

Likewise, as text in placed on a page in blocks, it is also quite easy to simulate many of the effects used in magazine and newspaper production such as pseudo-wrapping of text around images.

Sound good? Read on!

Adding a Text Block

To add text, you need to draw a text box on the page first. Select the Text tool from the Standard toolbar (see Figure 8-1) and draw the text box where you want it on the page. You don't need to make it perfect — you can resize it later. The depth of the text block is immaterial as it will always default to the amount of text entered, with a minimum of one line.

Tip

If you do want a text block to have a specific size — say deeper than the actual number of lines of text in the block — create the text block the size you want and click the Lock height option on the Text Properties palette.

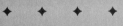

Figure 8-1: Selecting the Text tool
from the Standard toolbar.

When the Mouse button is released after defining the text block, Fusion automatically enters text edit mode: a rectangle appears containing a flashing cursor on the page (as shown in Figure 8-2), ready to accept the text.

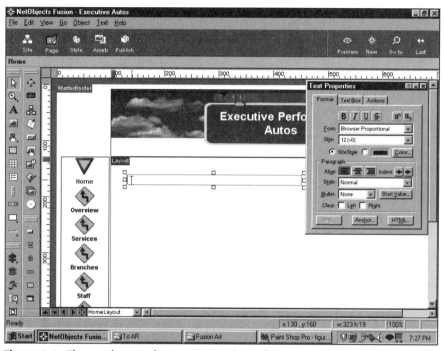

Figure 8-2: The text box on the Home page is ready to accept keyboard input.

Adding paragraph text

With the text box open and the cursor flashing, you can now enter text from the keyboard. It's just that simple!

For an example, just type the word **Welcome** in the text box.

Note

Whenever you press the Enter key, Fusion inserts a new line and carriage return, effectively creating a double blank line. This is equivalent to the HTML <P> tag. If you require only a carriage return (equivalent to the HTML <BR> tag), hold down the Shift key when pressing Enter.

At any time, you can use any of these standard word processing features:

   ✦ Find
   ✦ Replace

✦ Spell Check

✦ Word Count

You can access any of these from the Edit menu, and they apply only to the page you are currently on.

Importing text

You can also import text from an external file. To do this, we'll use a text file called welcome.txt on the CD-ROM included with this book. Select the text file in Windows Explorer or the Mac Finder and drag it onto the page under the Welcome! text block. (This maneuver may be a bit tricky: you'll have to open the Windows Explorer folder on top of the Fusion screen. In Macintosh, you may need to reduce the Fusion window to see the finder.) The text block containing the text will be created automatically (as in Figure 8-3).

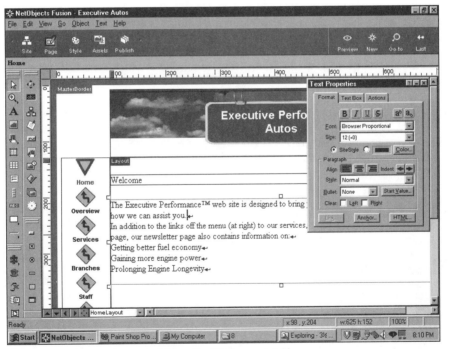

Figure 8-3: The text imported from the Welcome.txt file.

Formatting Text

At present, none of the text is formatted beyond the default font (which is listed as "Browser Proportional," or Times New Roman), 12 point in size and black. This is bland to say the least! The page will have much more visual impact if each line of the text is centered on the page, the first line is in a bigger font size, the three "choice" lines are lined up with bullets applied, and the entire text is in bold.

Note

Make sure you don't select just the text block. If you do, it will be shown with black, square handles at each corner. To select the text itself, double-click the text block and then drag the mouse pointer over the text to be changed.

Tip

To select sections of text quickly, try the following: for a single word, double-click the word; for a paragraph, triple-click any word in the paragraph; and for all the text in a text box, press Ctrl+A. For Ctrl+A to work, the text box must be in insert mode shown by the flashing cursor.

Danger Zone

The fonts available in the font list are the fonts installed on your computer. Be aware that if you choose a font outside the default browser fonts of Times, Arial (Helvetica), or Courier, visitors to your pages may see only the font that is defined if they also have it installed on their computer. If not, the text will revert to their default browser font, usually Times New Roman on a Windows machine or Times on a Macintosh.

Applying formatting

The first row of buttons in the Text Properties palette applies various formatting to text. Figure 8-4 shows the buttons.

Figure 8-4: The text formatting buttons on the Text Properties palette.

For example, to make the "Welcome" text bold, select it with the mouse and click the Bold button on the Text Properties palette. (The Bold button is the button labeled with a *B* at the top left. If you wanted to make the text italic, you would repeat this procedure, but instead click the Italic button (the one with a large *I*)).

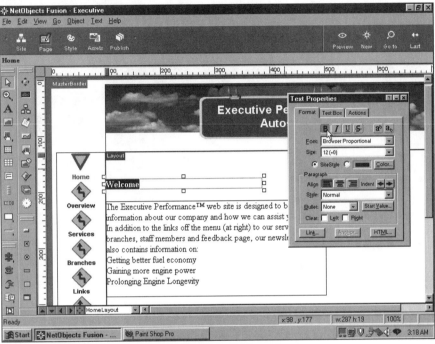

Figure 8-5: Making the "Welcome" bold.

Applying a font

The bold attribute is fine, but Times Roman (the font type) is not particularly suited to a headline; a sans serif font, such as Arial or Helvetica, is better for this purpose. To alter the font type, select the text to change and choose the new font from the font list on the Format tab of the Properties palette. Figure 8-6 shows the Welcome text changed to the Arial font instead of the standard Times Roman font.

Arguments rage over which are the best fonts to use under different circumstances. At the school I went to, sans serif fonts were taught as best used for headlines and banners, and a serif font for body text. But trends and styles change: for example, I prefer using a sans serif font such as Arial or Helvetica for body text. You also may have noticed lately a penchant among the advertising types for using a fixed length font such as Courier.

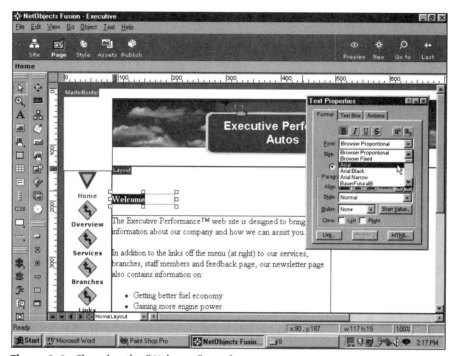

Figure 8-6: Changing the "Welcome" text font.

Note

While I believe there is a place for fixed length fonts such as Courier, I try to steer clear of them as they can give unpredictable results in browsers.

The fonts that are available to you in the Font list depend upon the fonts you have installed in your computer.

Danger Zone

Be careful when choosing a font type for a style. If visitors to your site do not have this font type installed on their computers, they may see unpredictable results viewing a page due to their browser substituting font types.

Adjusting the font size

The text size is set to the default 12 point in Fusion. To alter this, select the "Welcome" text and choose a new font size. To change the font size, select a new value from the Size dropdown list on the Text Properties palette.

To increase the impact of the "Welcome" (once it has been selected), change the point size to 18 in the Font Size dropdown list as shown in Figure 8-7.

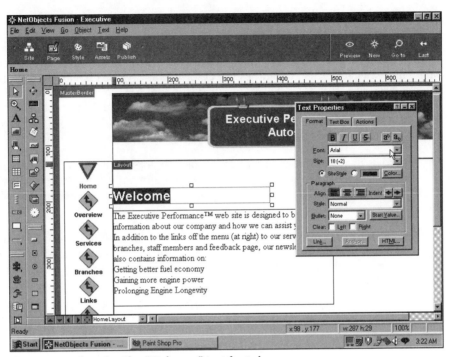

Figure 8-7: Changing the "Welcome" text font size.

Note

In Fusion, the font size is shown in a different manner than is normally displayed in such applications as word processing programs. With these, a font size is generally depicted as a value such as 10, 12, or 36. The higher the number, the bigger the font. In Fusion, font sizes are shown as a value that is either zero or a positive or negative number. Examples include –1 or +2. These values represent an increment size increase (or decrease) over the base font size that is generally 12 point. Under these circumstances then, a font size of 0 is equivalent to 12 point, +1 equals 14 point, +2 equals 18 point, and –1 equals 10 point.

New to 3.0

To make it easier to identify which sizes you can choose, Fusion version 3 shows both values in the font size list.

Adding a color

Color is an important aspect of presentation, and of course you can change the color of any font you use on a Web page so that the mix of colors of your text and any images is pleasing to the eye — or as grating as you want depending upon the effect you are trying to create!

Before I continue, though, you should be aware of a very important aspect to color in Web pages. When choosing a color for any element on a page, you have three possible color palettes you can choose from: Browser Safe, Windows System, and Custom Palettes. I strongly recommend that where possible you use the Browser Safe palette because this guarantees the color will always be displayed correctly when viewed in a browser. The reason for this is that Netscape Navigator has been designed to only display a fixed set of 216 colors. Using a color out of this range from either the Windows System or Custom Palettes may not display in the exact color you originally applied.

The Windows System Palette displays a list of all colors available to your specific computer. The colors available depend upon your currently set Display settings. The Custom Palette is a special palette of colors you create yourself using your favorite colors.

Applying a color to text is simple. For example, if you wanted the Welcome text to be in another color than the one specified in the applied SiteStyle, select the text and click on the color button on the Text Properties palette. (For more information on styles refer to Chapter 7).

Once you have clicked the Color button, the Color Picker will open (as shown in Figure 8-8).

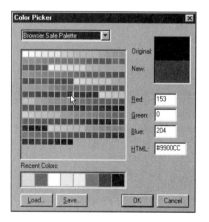

Figure 8-8: The Color Picker dialog box.

At the top of the color picker window is a drop down list to select the color palette to use. The center shows the available colors in that palette, and the bottom row shows the current colors in use in the Web site.

To assign a new color to the selected text, simply choose it by clicking its swatch in the Color Picker.

If you do choose a color that Fusion considers is not a "browser safe" color, a warning message will appear in the bottom right of the Color Picker.

Aligning and indenting text

Once you have created text, applied a font, and chosen a color, you can then use the alignment and indenting tools to set the position of the text. You can align text to the left, right, or center of the text box by selecting the text and choosing the option you require from the Text Properties palette.

To center the Welcome text, select it with the mouse and choose the Center alignment button on the text Properties palette. The text will be centered, just like in Figure 8-9.

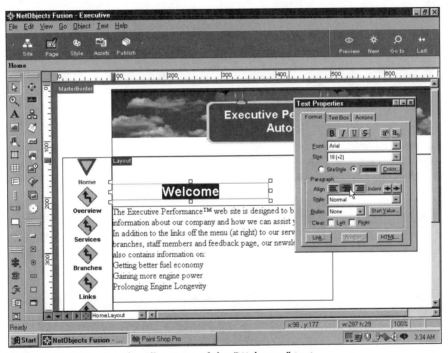

Figure 8-9: Changing the alignment of the "Welcome" text.

Note

Unlike word processing or page layout programs, in HTML you cannot justify text so that the edges of the text are flush left and right.

You can also indent text using either the left or right indent buttons next to the alignment buttons. For each click on an indent button, the select paragraph of text will be indented 40 pixels in the direction shown by the arrow. (Note, however, that the entire paragraph will be indented; HTML cannot "tab" paragraphs.)

Applying a paragraph style

Fusion comes supplied with several paragraph styles that you can edit to create new styles or define completely new styles from scratch. Paragraph styles are similar in concept to the style sheets used in most common word processing applications. Simply, Paragraph styles are preconfigured attributes that you can apply to sections of text such as font size and type, color, alignment, and so on (not to be confused with Fusion styles that are applied to pages). Table 8-1 shows the paragraph styles included in Fusion.

Table 8-1 Paragraph styles				
Address	Code	Footnotes	Headings 1-6	Quotes
Caption	Credits	Formatted	Normal	Subheads

A paragraph style will override any other formatting previously applied to the text.

For the Welcome heading, we'll eliminate what we've done before (hey, it's an example) and use a style of Heading 2. We apply it by selecting it from the Style dropdown list on the Format tab of the Properties palette (as shown in Figure 8-10).

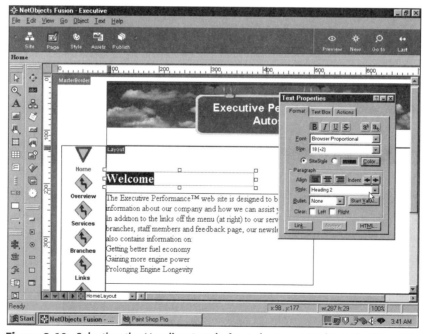

Figure 8-10: Selecting the Heading 2 style from the Format tab on the Properties palette.

The newer HTML specifications allow for a functionality called Cascading Style Sheets (CSS). Due to the way Fusion uses styles and the option to publish pages using the CSS and Layers function, Cascading Style Sheets are fully supported by Fusion. This functionality, though, requires Web pages be viewed with a version 4 or greater browser (Internet Explorer or Netscape Navigator). I discuss Cascading Style Sheets in more detail in Chapter 19.

Editing a current style

To retain conformity throughout the site, the text characteristics applied to this text block should be used on all pages: that is, the text formatted to Arial (or Helvetica on a Macintosh), 10 point, and black. At present, the default paragraph style is set to Browser Proportional default that is usually Times Roman, 12-point black. To change these values, you need to edit the style itself by choosing the Edit Text Styles command from the Text command on the menu bar. From the dialog box that opens, clicking the Change button will open a second dialog box (seen in Figure 8-11) showing a full description of the style, plus buttons to let you change the Paragraph and Font settings for the style. Here, you can also change the style's name, modify it based on a format from another style (with the Based on dropdown list), and tell Fusion what style to use for the paragraph immediately following any formatted with this style.

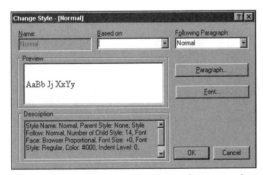

Figure 8-11: Changing the Normal Paragraph style.

One way to make sure the desired characteristics are applied to each text block created is to change the text attributes manually every time you add some text. This is very time-consuming and prone to error. It is not hard to miss a block every now and then. If this happens, the offending page looks very unprofessional when finally published and leaves the author open to criticism for not attending to detail! For this reason, the styles editing functionality of Fusion is brilliant!

A much faster and safer way is to edit the attributes for the Normal paragraph style. Alternatively, if you want to keep this one intact (a very good idea considering it may affect other sites using this style), create a new style.

Creating a new style

You add a new style to the list by once again choosing the Edit Text Styles command from the Text menu and choosing the New button from the dialog box that appears. The second dialog box (as seen in Figure 8-12) is very similar to the one shown when editing a style and has the same buttons. You can make changes using standard Windows or Macintosh dialog boxes to set font attributes, colors, and paragraph formats.

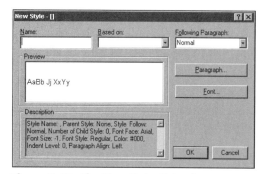

Figure 8-12: The New Style dialog box.

If you already have a style, the Edit Text Styles command lets you use this style as the basis for a new style, and this is often the fastest way to create a new style.

Once you have assigned a name to the new style and clicked the OK button to close the dialog box, it appears in the Paragraph Style list on the Format tab of the Properties palette. You must select a section of text and not a text block. Figure 8-13 shows a new style added to the list.

Figure 8-13: The new Style added to the Paragraph Style list.

Every time you add a new text block to a page, you can apply this style to the text by clicking anywhere in the text block (putting the text in insert mode) and selecting the style from the list on the Text tab of the Properties palette.

Tip

When creating a new style or modifying an existing style, a very useful option in many cases is the Following Paragraph box. This lets you specify which style to apply automatically to the paragraph immediately following any paragraph assigned the style you have currently added or modified.

Formatting bullets

The bulleted list will start with some lead-in text. This is followed by another press of the Enter key to start a new line. Each item in the list is then typed with a further Enter after each item.

The text for the list is given below. Although the spacing between items may seem a little large, once the bulleted style is applied to these items, the style will correct this spacing factor.

> Getting better fuel economy
>
> Gaining more engine power
>
> Prolonging Engine Longevity

These are the last three lines of the Welcome.txt file you imported.

The next step is to apply the bulleted style to the list items. First, you might have to replace the "soft" returns with hard returns: these show up as left arrows in Edit mode. Using the mouse, drag over the three list items to select them. To apply the bullet to each item in the list that is now selected, choose a bullet character from the Bullet list on the Text tab of the Properties palette (as seen in Figure 8-14).

Figure 8-14: The Bullet list on the Format tab of the Properties palette.

Once you've applied the bullet, the text closes up to a single line format, and Fusion places the selected bullet character at the start of each line in the list. Figure 8-15 shows the completed text block.

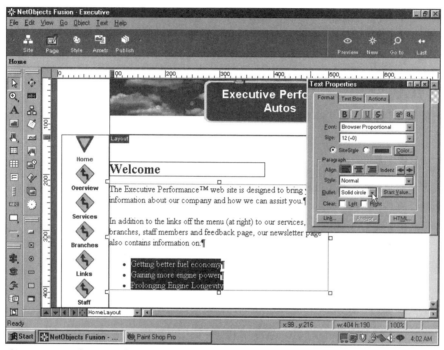

Figure 8-15: The completed text block with its bulleted list.

If you are using sequence bullets, Fusion 3 provides the Start Value button on the Format tab of the Text Properties palette. With it, you can tell Fusion at what number to start the bullet numbering. This is especially useful when each element in a bulleted list contains more than one paragraph. Under ordinary circumstances, Fusion adds a new bullet when a new paragraph is added. To circumvent this, simply turn the bullet option off for subsequent paragraphs, and turn it back on again with a new Start Value for the next actual bulleted paragraph. You might also want to indent all paragraphs in a bulleted list that are not bulleted so they line up with the bulleted items. Read on to see how this is done.

Wrapping

I mentioned at the beginning of this chapter that using Fusion's tools, in many cases it is possible to mimic conventional magazine layouts with wrapping text around graphic elements. You can achieve this by first placing a graphics element inside a text box—didn't know you could do that, did you?—and then entering the text as shown in Figure 8-16.

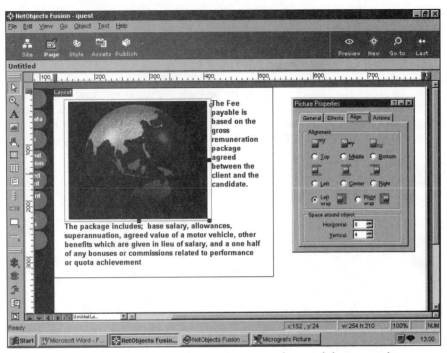

Figure 8-16: Inserting a graphics element into a text box and then wrapping text around it.

To wrap the text around the element, choose an element wrap option from the Align tab on the Picture Properties palette. To see this tab (as shown in Figure 8-17), you must first select the graphics element.

Figure 8-17: The Align Tab where text wrap options for a graphic element are selected.

Clear Left, Right

When you use this option, in some cases you may want a paragraph following a wrapped paragraph to start clear of a wrapped graphic element. This is what the Clear Left and Right buttons on the Text Properties palette do.

When you click the Left check box, the text will restart at the first left margin position that is clear of a wrapped graphics element. When you click the Right check box, the text will restart at the first right margin position that is clear of a wrapped graphics element (see Figure 8-18a).

If both the Left and Right checkboxes are checked, the text will restart at a margin position when both the left and right margins are clear of a wrapped graphics element (see Figure 8-18b).

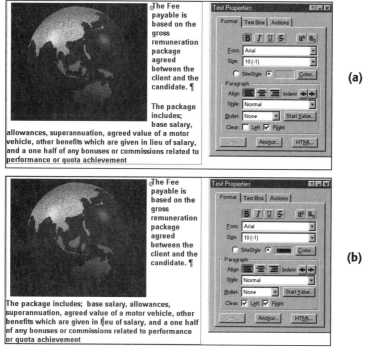

Figure 8-18: The Right Clear option (a) and Both Clear options (b) set.

Adjusting text box options

If you thought these options gave great control over your text, there are even more fine-tuning options available on the Text Box tab of the Text Properties palette to complete the picture.

Background color

By default, the background to the text box is transparent when you enter text into a text box on a page: whatever image or color you have set for the background of the page will show through. If you want a solid background color to be the background of a text box instead, the Background color button on the Text Box tab of the Text Properties palette lets you choose a background color. When clicked, the Color Picker opens and is used in exactly the same way as we did earlier when changing the color of the text.

Text inset

After you enter text into a text box, the text will flow from the extreme edges of the text box, depending upon the left, right, or center alignment options you have set. For example, if you set the alignment to left, the start of each line will be at the exact edge of the perimeter of the text box. If you need to indent this so that there is white space between the text and the edge of the text box, use the Text Inset spinner control. Each click of the spinner will inset one pixel between the text and the text box.

Lock height

If you want a text block to have a specific size — say deeper than the actual number of lines of text in the block — create the text block to the size you want and click the Lock Height option on the text Properties palette. Clicking this option will also stop the text block from resizing in a browser when, for example, the browser is displaying a text font smaller than expected.

This option is also useful when designing pages before any content is applied. You can place and move around empty text boxes and text boxes the size of intended graphics images so that you can experiment with different roughs of layouts.

Size to Layout

When a Text Box is selected, clicking the Size to Layout checkbox will expand the text box to fill the entire width of the Layout area.

Use this with caution as any other elements on the page will immediately be placed behind the text box that has been expanded to the size of the layout. If this occurs, when the page is viewed in a pre-4.0 version browser, totally unpredictable results will occur with all elements that are being overlapped by the text box being repelled to new locations.

Positioning Text

Once the text box is correctly formatted, you just need to position it on the page accurately. For this, we will use the Rulers & Guides option of Fusion. If this option is not currently set, select it from the View menu option. To place a guide, click anywhere on one of the rulers and the guide will appear complete with a marker on the ruler line allowing you to drag the guide to any position on the page (as shown in Figure 8-19).

Guide

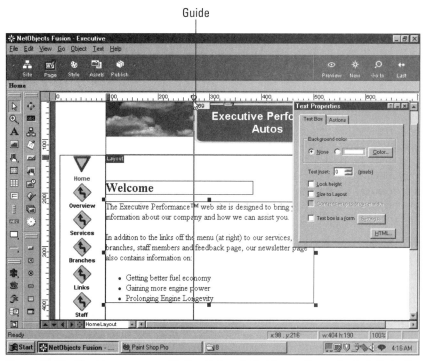

Figure 8-19: The Home page with the Rulers & Guides option selected. Note the guides placed on the page and the guide marker tab on the rulers.

The correct location for the Welcome text box is to align it to the left and flush it with the capital E of the word Executive appearing in the banner. To position a guide as a reference point, move the mouse pointer over the vertical guide marker on the ruler line. Press the left mouse button and drag the guide to the new location flush with the left of the E in the banner (as seen in Figure 8-20).

To make sure the text box will snap to the guide, turn on the Snap to Guides option on the View menu. To move the Welcome text box, click and hold the left mouse button down until the black handles appear around the box and then move it to the guide using either the mouse or the arrow keys on the keyboard. Figure 8-21 shows the page with the text box in the correct location.

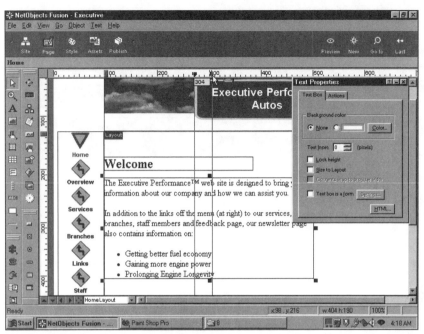

Figure 8-20: The guide moved to the position where the text box will be aligned.

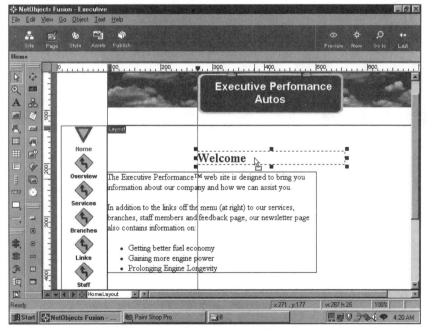

Figure 8-21: The Welcome text box in the correct location.

Now, do the same for the other text box (as shown in Figure 8-22).

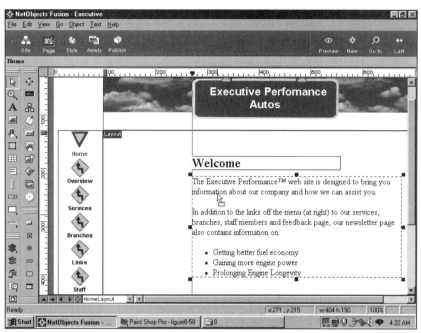

Figure 8-22: The Welcome text box in the correct location.

Sizing a Text Box

The final step is to size the text box containing the Welcome message. Correct sizing makes sure that the box is not using more white space on the page than is necessary. If you do not keep the size of elements in check, elements may end up overlapping, thus producing unpredictable results when previewed or published.

To size the text box, single click it and hold the mouse button down until the black handles appear around the box. Clicking and dragging any of these handles can size the text box sized so that word *Welcome* fits comfortably inside with no extra wasted space (as seen in Figure 8-23).

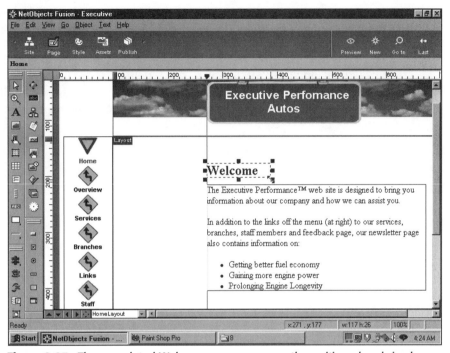

Figure 8-23: The completed Welcome message correctly positioned and sized.

Summary

✦ Text is added using the text tool from the Standard toolbar.

✦ Guides aid in exactly placing the dimensions of a text block or other element on a page.

✦ The text attribute controls such as alignment, bold, and font styles are available off the Format tab of the text palette.

✦ Using nonstandard fonts may produce unpredictable results.

✦ To size a text block, select it and drag the handles to a new position.

✦ Enter inserts a line feed and a carriage return (an HTML <P> tag).

✦ Shift+Enter inserts a carriage return only (an HTML <BR> tag).

✦ Use bullets to offset and highlight important points.

✦ Styles define text and paragraph attributes.

✦ Font sizes are shown as plus or minus figures to signify sizes greater or less than the base font size of 12 point.

✦ Text boxes can have a different background color applied.

✦ Use the Lock Height control to fix the size of the text box.

✦ Graphics can be embedded in a text box and text then wrapped around the graphic element. Text paragraph positioning is determined by the Clear Left, Right, and Both checkboxes.

✦   ✦   ✦

Adding Graphics

Without a doubt, the capability to add graphics to a Web page has caused the World Wide Web to become the success that it has. Without graphics, the Web would be a dull place indeed!

The use of graphics and the facilities available to Web authors has improved greatly since those first primitive images climbed out of the primordial digital soup. In the early days of the Web, only simple images could be placed on a Web page, and aligning these in any shape or form was a nightmare of HTML coding. Today, several different formats are supported, which include animated images, image maps letting an author turn an image into a clickable control center, and even images that change according to certain criteria or conditions. Even video is just a series of images.

Using Fusion's new Actions Feature (described in Chapter 19), you can apply attributes to static images causing them to dissolve into view, fly in from a specific direction, and much more.

We'll explore the more exotic of these graphics types in Chapter 14. For now, we'll concentrate on the basic image, what options you are given, and how best to make use of these to get the best looking graphics for the minimum download time.

JPEG Versus GIF Files

For static images, the HTML specification supports two types of files: JPEG and GIF.

Strictly speaking, JPEG is not a file type but a compression format. As the extension JPG is normally used for files saved using the compression format, for the sake of brevity, I will refer to them as a file type. No e-mails from the purists please!

JPEG files (the letters are the initials of the *Joint Photographic Experts Group*, the inventors of the file type) are best used for photographs and are of an image type called *lossy*. As the description suggests, with JPEG files, there is some loss in quality of the image from the original. This quality loss occurs when a JPEG file has compression applied to it to make the file smaller and thus decreasing Web download times. The higher the compression, the lesser the quality of the image.

GIF files (standing for *graphics interchange format*) on the other hand are automatically compressed to the highest possible order before quality loss occurs. GIF files are best used for standard graphics images created in such applications as Micrografx Picture Publisher, Photoshop, and so on.

With all graphics, there is always a trade-off between quality and size. This can also happen between graphics types. Many arguments ensue regarding which format is best for what, and the Internet newsgroups are full of discussion on this point. With any graphic, I personally find it best to save it in both a GIF and JPEG format, compare the files sizes against the quality and use the best at that time to meet the need.

Bitmaps and other graphics types

While it is true that HTML only supports JPEG and GIF files — strictly speaking, the browsers support these file types — Fusion does, however, allow you to place other image file types onto pages. When you place an image of a different type, say a Windows BMP file or a Macintosh PICT, Fusion automatically creates a GIF or a JPEG file copy of the original (depending on which option you chose) and stores this in the User Sites folder. The original is not modified or altered in any way. A dialog box opens letting you decide into which format — JPG or GIF — you would like to convert the file.

The naming convention Fusion uses for internally generated files is built in. The resulting file will use the original name but change the suffix. For example, if you place a file called BlueThunder.BMP and you decide to change this to a JPG file in the dialog box that opens, the new copy of the file will be called BlueThunder.JPG. Remember that both files will be held in Fusion's Assets register.

The images Fusion uses for Nav Bars and banner also uses this naming convention when they are created. In addition, if a standard GIF or JPEG image has text placed inside it using the Text in Element option (explained later), the resulting image is also automatically generated and named.

Importing a Standard Graphic

For purposes of illustration, we'll place a graphics image of a high performance vehicle on a page. (This image is called car.gif and is located on the CD-ROM supplied with this book.) To import either a JPEG or GIF image to a page, use the Picture tool on the Standard toolbar. Similar to placing text, draw a rectangle on the page at the location the picture is required.

Note

The size of the rectangle drawn to contain the image does not indicate the size of the image. Fusion will place the image at its full size and not to the size of the rectangle you've drawn. The rectangle top left corner defines where the top left of the image will appear.

Selecting the Picture tool is shown in Figure 9-1.

Figure 9-1: The Standard toolbar showing the Picture tool.

After defining the rectangle for the picture's location, Fusion opens a dialog box requesting the location of the file containing the image as seen in Figure 9-2. The dialog box defaults to JPG, JPEG, GIF, and PNG file extensions, but you can override these in the drop-down File Type list box.

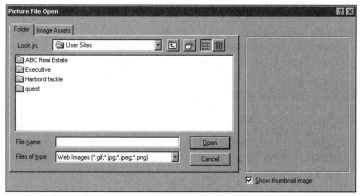

Figure 9-2: The Open Picture File dialog box.

Either type the file name into the field or navigate to the folder containing the file. After choosing the file, clicking the Open button will place the image at the location on the page. Figure 9-3 shows the image placed on the page.

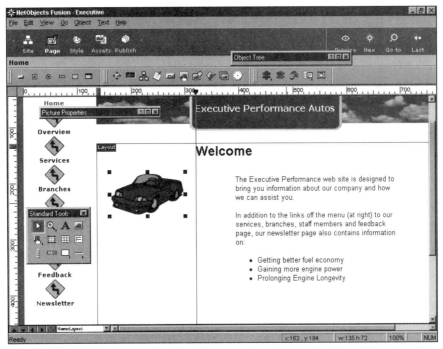

Figure 9-3: The car image placed on the page.

When you have placed and selected an image, you'll see a new set of options for the picture on the Properties palette (as seen in Figure 9-4). The three tabs (General, Effects, and Actions) contain all of the settings that you can alter to affect the way a picture or graphic appears on the page. These options include aligning, tiling, stretching, and rotating an image as well as providing locations to enter Alt tags or text inside the image. Actions are special commands used to provide animations and interactivity of images. Full details on actions is available in Chapter 19.

Figure 9-4: The Picture Properties palette.

Aligning an Image

I mentioned earlier that the size of the rectangle drawn using the Picture tool off the Standard toolbar has no bearing on the resultant image size. This is true if you do not apply any other attributes, but it is possible to extend the rectangle (called the bounding box) after you have placed an image and use this size for special effects or alignment.

For example, let's say you need an image below a text block and precisely centered in alignment with the block. Using the guides to assist in exact placement, you can place one guide at each side of the text block and then drag the image bounding box to a new size snapping to each of these guides. Once you have defined the new size of the bounding box, making sure the image is still selected, click the Align button on the Picture tab of the Properties palette and choose the Center option from the dialog box. Figure 9-5 shows the Display area.

Tip

If you need to resize the bounding box of an image, you need to click the Stretch button on the Properties palette.

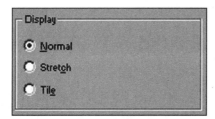

Figure 9-5: The Display area of the Picture Properties dialog box.

Manipulating a Graphic

Once you have placed an image on a page, three commands are available to modify this image. These commands are Normal (crop), Stretch, and Tile.

Stretching

When you have dragged an image's bounding box to a new size, clicking the Stretch radio button on the Picture Properties palette causes the image to stretch both horizontally and vertically to fill the new space. Figure 9-6 shows an image after stretching.

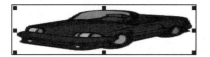

Figure 9-6: An image after applying stretching.

Tiling

Tiling an image, on the other hand, fills the new space made available by increasing the size of a bounding box with multiple copies of the image (as seen in Figure 9-7).

Figure 9-7: An image after applying tiling.

Rotating a graphic

Once you've placed and selected an image, you can use the Rotate option on the Effects tab of the Picture Properties palette to rotate an image around its center point in increments of 90 degrees. Each click of the spinner control will increase (or decrease the angle) of rotation. Figure 9-8 shows an image after being placed and 90 degrees rotation applied.

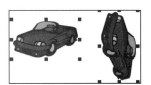

Figure 9-8: An image at 0 degrees and 90-degree rotation.

Adding Text to a Graphic

You can place text inside any image to act as a caption to that image. When you use this option, you can separately define the location of this text, its font type, size, and color. When placed in this way, however, the text becomes part of the image and is not a separate item as such, although it always remains editable.

To place text in an image, select it and click the Enable check box in the Text in element section on the Effects tab of the Picture Properties palette. "Your text here" appears in the image, and the Settings button is live (it is no longer grayed out). When clicked, the Settings button opens a dialog box (as shown in Figure 9-9) where you can enter the text and define its attributes.

At the top of the dialog box lies a space in which you enter the text to appear (entered using the keyboard). Below this is a series of buttons to set the alignment of the text to the left, center, or right of the picture. In addition to the alignment, a set of radio buttons lets you fine-tune the alignment in respect to vertical or horizontal orientation. You can also rotate text in increments of 1 degree around its central axis. If you check the Right angles checkbox, the rotational values are locked to 90 degree increments.

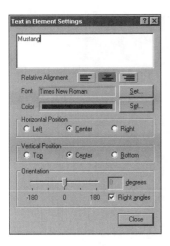

Figure 9-9: The Text in Element Settings dialog box.

Finally, using the Font and Color Set buttons, you can modify the style and appearance of the text using a series of dialog boxes. Figure 9-10 shows the Font settings dialog box for the Text in element command. Figure 9-11 shows the Executive Performance home page with the car graphic containing Text in element. To apply the settings for the Text in element command, click the Close button.

Tip

Because text applied to an image in this way becomes part of the image, this is a great way to use nonstandard fonts. For example, if you wanted a banner at the top of the page to use a calligraphic font, placing an image the same color as the background of the page and using the Text in element option lets you use any font you like. Being a graphic, even if the site viewer does not have this font installed on his or her system, that person will still see the text in its original font.

This method also ensures the browser will not change the size of the font you have used.

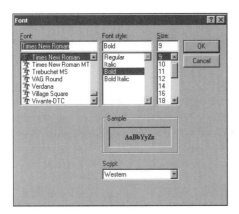

Figure 9-10: The Font settings dialog box for the Text in element command.

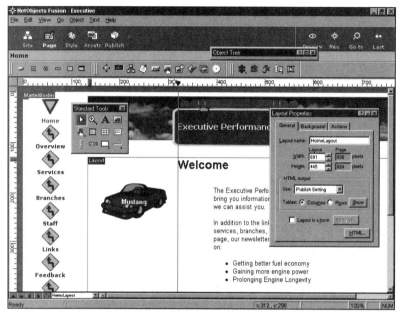

Figure 9-11: The Executive Autos Home page with Text in element.

Setting Alt Tags

Alt tags describe an image when, for any of a number of reasons, a browser cannot successfully display it. Instead of the image appearing, the text used as an Alt tag is displayed instead. The Alt tag will also appear in the placeholder for the graphic while the image is downloading. This gives the site viewer a clue as to what the image might be. Some users, for example, continue to use an older version of the Lynx browser that is totally text-based. Others, while using graphics-based browsers, sometimes turn off the image display capabilities to speed up the download of Web pages. Yet other people are vision impaired and use the information in the Alt tag to play through special software and voice synthesizers that tell them what an image contains. Because of these factors, it is very important to use the information in the Alt tag for an image. It is also accepted that not having Alt tags is a sign of Web development sloppiness!

Note   There is conjecture in some circles that not using the Alt tag may in fact violate Equal Opportunity and Access laws in some countries. As far as I am aware, it has never been tested in court, but just lately there have been numerous Internet newsgroup and mailing list messages on this subject.

To place an Alt tag in an image, type the text describing the image into the Alt tag field on the General tab of the Picture Properties palette once you have selected an image. Figure 9-12 shows an image in a Browser displaying the Alt tag and not the picture itself.

Alt tag

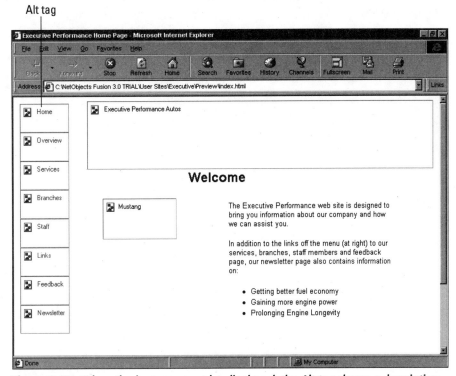

Figure 9-12: When the image cannot be displayed, the Alt tag shows a description of an image.

Setting Transparency

Transparency is used to turn off a color in an image making an irregular image appear to float on a Web page. Figure 9-13 shows an image displayed twice on a Web page. The image on the left has a black background, while the one on the right has no background, appearing to be a part of the background color of the page. In this particular case, the black of the image has been made the transparent color.

Figure 9-13: In the image on the right, the black background is transparent.

Currently, you can apply transparency only to GIF images, which is an attribute unique to GIF images. Selecting a color to be the transparent color in Fusion is a two step process.

First, select the image by clicking it and then choose the Effects tab on the Properties palette as seen in Figure 9-14.

Figure 9-14: The Effects tab on the Properties palette.

The Picture Properties palette contains an icon of an eye-dropper, which is the Transparency tool. Once selected, using its pointer, click on the color on the image that is to be transparent. This color will then appear in the Transparency color field on the Effects tab of the Properties palette.

To complete the operation, select the check box next to the selected transparency color.

If after these steps the image does not appear to have the transparency applied, the most common cause is that the source image used is not a GIF file, but a JPEG image instead. In this case, you need to use an application such as Photoshop, Lview, or Paint Shop Pro to convert the image. These applications also have the facility to create transparent GIF images.

Summary

✦ Web pages can only contain JPEG or GIF images.

✦ Fusion converts other image file types to GIF or JPEG files by choosing a type in a dialog box.

✦ Place graphics using the Picture tool on the Standard toolbar.

✦ Images can be aligned inside their bounding box.

✦ Stretching an image fills the bounding box with a single image.

✦ Tiling an image fills the bounding box with multiple copies of the image.

✦ Cropping an image shows only sections of the image.

✦ Images can be rotated in increments of 90 degrees.

✦ Text captions can be included inside an image.

✦ Use Alt tags to describe an image when it cannot be displayed in a browser or when it is downloading.

✦ Transparency allows a color in an image to be made transparent and lets the page background color show through.

✦   ✦   ✦

Enhancing a Web Site

Now that we have had a quick tour of Fusion, it is time to get really into the meat of things. Everything done previously was rehearsal; now it's showtime! In Chapters 10 through 19 I discuss how to work with Fusion's MasterBorders, create links, use Fusion's Draw and Line tools, as well as add functionality to a site. And in Chapter 20 I cover how to publish your finished site on the Internet.

Note that all the elements you'll place on the pages of the Web site created in Chapters 10 through 20 are stored in the Examples folder on the CD-ROM that accompanies this book. Also note that as Fusion uses absolute addressing of pointers to external files placed into the NOD file, you should copy the Examples folder and all its contents to your hard disk. If you choose not to do this, any time you load the Web site into Fusion, the CD-ROM *must* be located in your CD-ROM drive. If not, the NOD file will not work correctly and will show empty white boxes with an X through them where images and so on should appear. In addition, if you choose to publish the site, none of these elements will be in the final site on the Web server.

Working with MasterBorders

A complete understanding of MasterBorders is one of the major keys to getting the most out of Fusion's flexibility. A simple change to a MasterBorder can transform an entire site and in the process save many hours of mundane layout work. In addition, intelligent use of MasterBorder areas can change a site from being boring and very ordinary to one that really sizzles!

Starting Out with the Default MasterBorder

When you first define a Web site, as well as automatically creating a home page, Fusion also applies a default MasterBorder to the page. In this MasterBorder, the program places a page banner at the top MasterBorder, a default graphic Navigation Bar on the left MasterBorder, a "Built With NetObjects Fusion" icon, and a text Navigation Bar at the bottom MasterBorder.

The default MasterBorder comprises margins that completely surround the Layout area. These margins are set to the following:

✦ Left: 110 pixels

✦ Right: 10 pixels

✦ Top: 60 pixels

✦ Bottom: 50 pixels

The current MasterBorder margin sizes are displayed on the MasterBorder tab of the Properties palette as shown in Figure 10-1. If you cannot see the MasterBorder Properties palette, click anywhere inside a MasterBorder area.

Figure 10-1: The MasterBorder Properties palette.

A MasterBorder area can contain any element that you might also position in a Layout section. As mentioned earlier though, the difference is that any elements placed in the MasterBorder area will appear on *all* pages that share the current MasterBorder. In contrast, elements placed in a Layout area only appear on that page (unless of course you manually replicate elements on different pages).

You can define as many MasterBorders as you like. This is useful when creating a Web site with different sections that have common areas. For example, in a Web site devoted to sports, one MasterBorder might be defined for football, another for motor racing, and a third for ice hockey. Each can contain separate color schemes, Navigation Bars, or manually placed navigation buttons and other icons reflecting the different sports — and therefore sections — of the Web site.

Figure 10-2 shows two Web pages from the same site but with different MasterBorders applied to each.

Note

Although you may have a series of MasterBorders as I've described, in a single site they will still share the same SiteStyle. It is the *content* of the MasterBorder that changes.

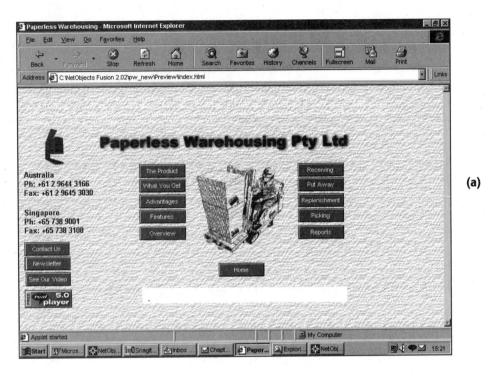

(a)

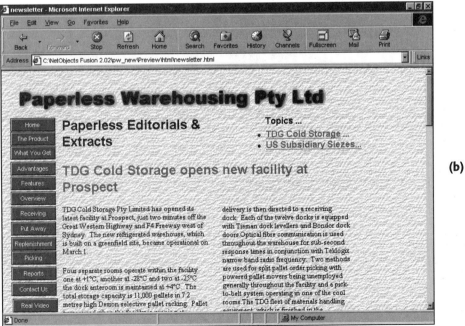

(b)

Figure 10-2: Two Web pages (a and b) from the same site but with different MasterBorders.

Frames separate a Web page into any number of individual *panes*, each containing its own information. For example, in a two-frame page, the left frame may contain a navigation menu, and the right frame may display text and graphics. As different menu items are chosen from the left frame, it remains static while the right frame changes to reflect the menu item chosen. You'll find an example of this type of frame usage at `http://www. bblawyers.com.au`

Using MasterBorders as headers and footers

As the concept of the MasterBorder also embraces page headers and footers, contact information (normally placed at the bottom of Web pages) and page banner graphics (at the top) can be varied from section to section. Using a MasterBorder means that you only need to define these sorts of elements once instead of having to manually add these elements to every page.

Using MasterBorders to create framed pages

In addition to supplying a common area for like pages, MasterBorders are also the starting point for adding frames to pages built with NetObjects Fusion. You can turn any MasterBorder area into a frame with a single mouse click from the AutoFrames tab on the MasterBorder Properties palette. For more detail on using MasterBorders as frames, see Chapter 18.

Sizing a MasterBorder

The first step in working with a MasterBorder is understanding how to change it to a new size. You can resize a MasterBorder in two ways:

✦ Manually enter the new dimensions required into the relevant field on the MasterBorder Properties palette (as shown in Figure 10-3).

✦ Drag the margin sizer on either the vertical or horizontal ruler to its new position (as shown in Figure 10-4).

I consider the second method much faster and more flexible, as you'll see.

Figure 10-3: Changing size from the MasterBorder Properties palette.

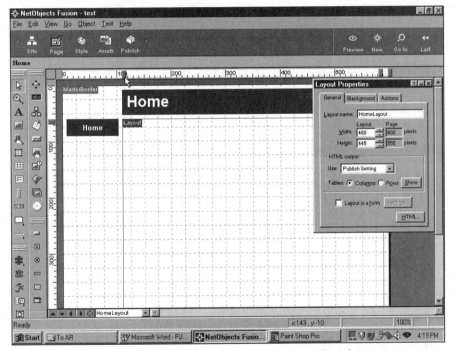

Figure 10-4: Changing size by moving the margin sizer on the ruler.

Note

Although the rulers are on by default, if for some reason they are not showing, select Rulers & Guides from the View menu (or Ctrl+U).

Manually changing a MasterBorder value

To change a value, either increment (or decrement) the current MasterBorder sizes by clicking on the up or down arrows for each area. Alternatively, you can drag over the current value with the mouse pointer and type a new value. If the new value is illegal (for example, an object may already be in a MasterBorder that is larger than the value you are attempting to set), the new value will be ignored and the original restored.

Dragging a MasterBorder

Many times, a Web page will have more white space than needed between the bottom of the text in the Layout section and the rule line in the bottom MasterBorder (as shown in Figure 10-5). If you knew the exact distance between the two, you could change the layout height value very quickly on the MasterBorder Properties palette. If you do not know this value, you could take an educated guess, enter this value into the field, and then use the spinner controls to decrement the value a pixel at a time until you reach the required location.

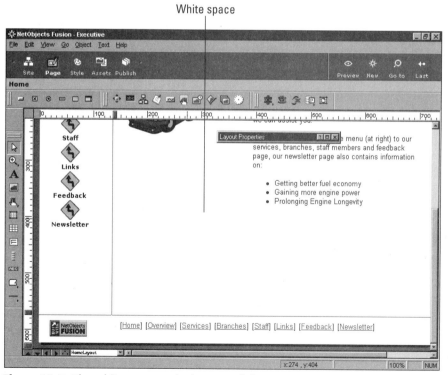

Figure 10-5: The white space at the bottom of the Home page.

Dragging the MasterBorder to a new location is a much faster option, however. To remove the white space, follow these steps:

1. Move the mouse pointer over the MasterBorder margin slider control for the bottom MasterBorder. This is on the left ruler.

2. Press and hold down the left mouse button.

3. Drag the margin slider control upward on the ruler until it is situated just below the last of the Layout text. A blue line displays the new location of the MasterBorder margin as it is being dragged. Figure 10-6 shows the Home page after moving the bottom MasterBorder.

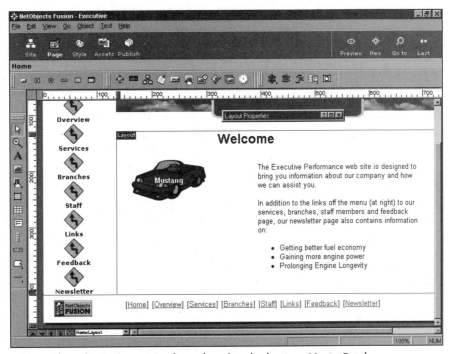

Figure 10-6: The Home page after relocating the bottom MasterBorder.

Note

Fusion prevents you from moving a MasterBorder farther than allowed. In this case, the maximum you can move it is to the base of the vertical Navigation Bar. If you change MasterBorder values manually rather than using the drag option, a warning dialog box opens describing the minimum value that you can apply and asks whether you would like this adopted automatically (as seen in Figure 10-7).

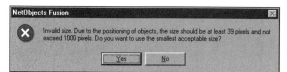

Figure 10-7: A dialog box appears if you've crossed the line.

Sometimes, for some mysterious reason, Fusion will not let you move a MasterBorder. One of two things may cause this. Firstly and most commonly, a page element is probably in the way. With the Executive Performance Home page, for example, any element between the bottom of the text and the original location of the MasterBorder would stop any new size going above the bounds of this element.

While this may seem obvious, such an element may be invisible. This would occur if, for some reason, text on the page was the same color as the background. This can happen when invisible objects are used as anchors. See Chapter 11 for more details on anchors.

To see whether any objects are in the path where you would like to move a MasterBorder, make the Layout section active by clicking in it (but not on an element in the layout) and press Ctrl+A. This will select all the elements in the Layout section (shown by their handles), letting you see if any are indeed invisible so that you take the appropriate action.

An even easier way is to make sure Object Outlines option (on the View menu) is checked. This places a border around all objects on the page.

The second reason a MasterBorder may not move is similar but not quite as obvious. As well as being restricted by elements in the Layout section, the top and bottom MasterBorders in particular are also restricted by the location of objects in the left and right MasterBorders.

For example, although 200 pixels of white space may lie between the bottom MasterBorder and the lowest element in the Layout section, if any elements are in either the left or right MasterBorder inside the space of this 200 pixel area, Fusion will not allow you to move the MasterBorder beyond its lowest point.

This was precisely the reason the MasterBorder on the Executive Performance home page could not move any further than it was: it was constrained by the position of the Navigation Bar in the left MasterBorder.

MasterBorder and Layout size relationships

The width and height of the Layout section are tied to the values applied to the four MasterBorder areas in terms of the total page width. To see this relationship, click anywhere in the Layout section and then select the General tab on the Properties palette. On the Properties palette are four sets of values as seen in Figure 10-8. You can manually alter the Width and Height of the Layout section by changing the values in their respective fields. You cannot change the values for the Page Width and Height.

Figure 10-8: The Width and Height settings for the layout section.

Fusion calculates the values for the Page Width and Height as the sum of the values of the appropriate MasterBorders plus the value of the height or width of the Layout area. By displaying this value, it is easy to see if the physical size of the Web page is starting to exceed the value you set in Page Size. If this did occur, the viewer of the page may need to scroll to the right (if, for example, the page width exceeded 640 pixels, and the viewer had his or her screen resolution set at 640×480).

To bring the total width back to a maximum of 640 pixels, you will need to adjust a combination of the layout width and the left and right MasterBorder's width.

Some Additional Information About Page Size

If you are targeting a 640 × 480 monitor, you need to make your page width somewhat smaller than 640 because other things are eating up the real estate devoted to the page's display. This includes the window edges, vertical scroll bar, and browser indent. Because these can vary from platform to platform and from browser to browser, a good rule of thumb is to make your width no greater than 620 pixels. Length is less of an issue because Web pages are designed for vertical flow. If you are interested in ensuring that the viewer on a 640 × 480 monitor sees all the primary or introductory content, however, that content should be contained in an area no larger than 380 pixels. This accommodates window edges and tool/control bars that use up screen space. Also, if you are using frames, you must account for the additional screen real estate lost when you add additional divider bars and/or scroll bars.

Using Object menu commands for quick sizing

The Object menu contains other options that quickly let you resize pages: the Size Layout to Objects, the Size MasterBorder to Objects, and the Restore Original Size commands.

The Size Layout to Objects command automatically reduces the size of the layout area to the minimum area occupied by the objects in the Layout area. The Size MasterBorder to Objects command performs the same function for the MasterBorder area.

Automatically increasing Layout or MasterBorder space

When the opposite needs to happen (increase the white space in the Layout or MasterBorder section), Fusion will automatically add the new amount of space needed when you place or drag the object to a new position. The most common reason for increasing the white space is when new elements are added that are larger than the current dimensions allow or existing elements are dragged or moved to new positions beyond the current dimensions.

MasterBorder sizing using auto-resize

If an element larger than the current width or height of a MasterBorder is placed in the MasterBorder, the MasterBorder will automatically expand to accommodate the size of the placed element. At other times, however, you may want to change the size of any of the MasterBorder margins manually.

Changing these values via the Properties palette can be tedious, especially when a large element has been placed on a page and later deleted. When this happens, you may need to resize the MasterBorder back to its original values by many hundreds of pixels. Using the MasterBorder tabs on the ruler, you can drag MasterBorder boundaries with the mouse pointer to new locations, thus setting a new margin size. Figure 10-9 shows the horizontal ruler and the right and left MasterBorder margin tabs.

Figure 10-9: The horizontal ruler showing the right and left MasterBorder tabs.

Using the MasterBorder margin sizer on the ruler line, it is much easier to drag a margin where you want. Move the mouse pointer over the MasterBorder margin sizer, press the left mouse button, and drag the margin until the margin value display box shows the value you want. Figure 10-10 shows this.

Note

Of course, if you increase the size of a MasterBorder, you are correspondingly decreasing the area of the Layout, but the opposite is not true.

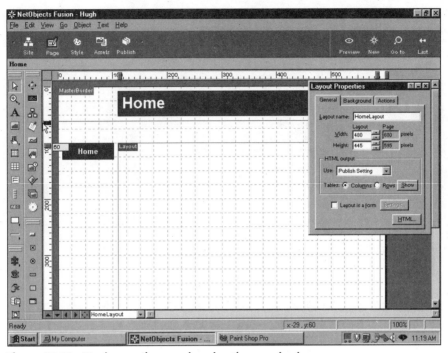

Figure 10-10: Moving up the margin using the margin sizer.

Note

Your mouse pointer may look different from those shown as there are many types of custom pointer icons available. Throughout this book, we are using the Microsoft 3D mouse pointer set. In addition, all measurement units are displayed in pixel values.

When a MasterBorder margin won't move

If at any stage you find you cannot move a MasterBorder by dragging it, this is probably due to an element inside the MasterBorder being larger than the size you are trying to drag to. The most common culprit is the text Navigation Bar created by Fusion as seen in Figure 10-11. Using the Hide Object from the View menu, you may also have a hidden object in the way. Use the Show All Objects command (also on the View) menu if this occurs.

Whenever a new page is added to a site, depending upon the display values for a default text Navigation Bar, this may increase in width by the addition of the new page and cause MasterBorders to alter their size beyond the boundaries you require. If this does occur, you should delete the default text Navigation Bar and define your own with the text tool and the Links tool on the Properties palette. Figure 10-12 shows a text Navigation Bar created in this way.

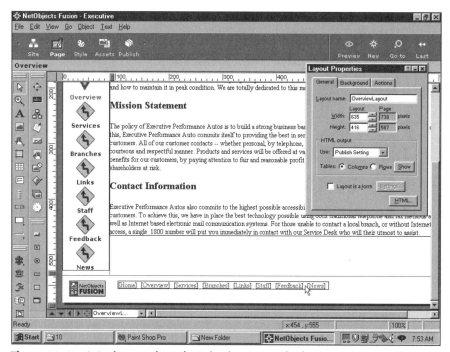

Figure 10-11: A Fusion text-based Navigation Bar at the bottom of a page.

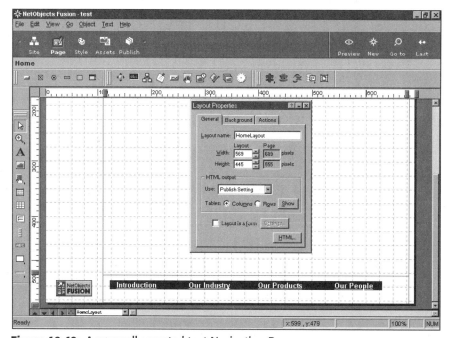

Figure 10-12: A manually created text Navigation Bar.

If you still cannot see why a MasterBorder boundary cannot be moved, click once in any MasterBorder area and press Ctrl+A. This will select all objects that are in the four MasterBorder margins. Black selection handles around it (as seen in Figure 10-13) define each object. You may have inadvertently created an object that is "invisible" (such as white text on a white background), an empty text box, or an image file with a transparent background larger than expected. Any of these may stop you from resetting MasterBorder values. Such an object is different, of course, from one you have hidden using the Hide Objects command.

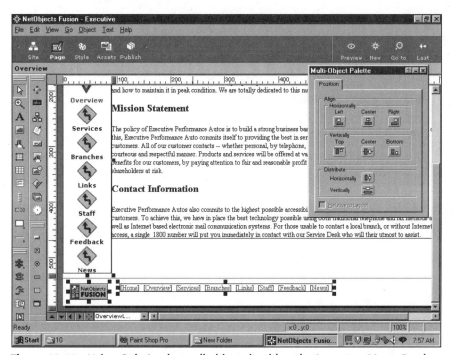

Figure 10-13: Using Ctrl+A selects all objects in either the Layout or MasterBorder areas.

Turning on the Object Outlines option on the View menu is another quick way to see if any objects are stopping you from resizing MasterBorder boundaries (unless of course you have a black object on a black background!).

Creating a New MasterBorder

The power of MasterBorders would certainly be diluted if only one were allowed per site! Thankfully, this is not the case: Fusion allows as many MasterBorders as you need. Once you define a set of MasterBorders for a site, you can call up the required MasterBorder and apply it to any individual page as needed.

Tip

When creating a new site, my preference is to define all of the MasterBorders I require for that site before adding any content to pages. Sure, you can never know exactly how many different types you will need or their total characteristics, but from experience I know that I need separate MasterBorders for at least the Home page, a forms page, and the first-level pages.

To create a new MasterBorder, follow these steps:

1. Open the MasterBorder Properties palette by clicking anywhere in any MasterBorder section of the page.

2. On the General tab, the Name field contains the name DefaultMasterBorder. Beside it, you'll see a button labeled Add/Edit (as seen in Figure 10-14). Click it.

Hot Stuff

Another way to access the MasterBorder Properties palette is to click anywhere on the gray area outside of the page.

Figure 10-14: The General tab on the MasterBorder Properties palette showing the Name field and the Add/Edit button.

3. Fusion opens a dialog box (shown in Figure 10-15) that lets you choose whether to Add a new MasterBorder, Rename an existing MasterBorder, or Delete a previously defined MasterBorder. At this time, we want to create a new MasterBorder based on the existing MasterBorder. To do this, click the Add button.

4. A second dialog box opens with a field for entering the name of the new MasterBorder and a dropdown list for selecting the MasterBorder upon which we'll base the new one (seen in Figure 10-16).

Figure 10-15: The Edit MasterBorder List dialog box.

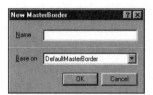

Figure 10-16: The New MasterBorder dialog box.

5. Once you have entered a name in the Name field, click the OK button.

Fusion creates a new MasterBorder for the page based on the MasterBorder chosen as the basis. The new MasterBorder will look exactly like the one on which you based it. Only the Name field will be different, showing the new name of the MasterBorder. You can now modify the new MasterBorder as you wish.

New to 3.0

Quickly creating similar MasterBorders for a site is a very powerful feature of Fusion. In older versions of Fusion, you had to copy all the elements in an old MasterBorder, paste them into a new MasterBorder, and manually set all the margin sizes to the correct values. This feature alone places Fusion head and shoulders above any other Web authoring program.

Note

You can manage your MasterBorders with the Rename and Delete buttons on the Edit MasterBorder List dialog box. Just make sure the correct name is selected from the list before selecting either of these buttons. The Rename button will open a dialog box where you can type a diffent name for the MasterBorder. The Delete button will display a dialog box confirming your desire to delete the MasterBorder name from the list.

Modifying a MasterBorder

If you want to make the new MasterBorder quite different from the original, you're best off starting with a clean slate by selecting all the elements that are currently in the MasterBorder and deleting them. The quickest way to do this is to click

Note

anywhere in the MasterBorder area (but not on an element) and press Ctrl+A. Once all the elements are selected, press the Del key to remove them.

You are no doubt asking why then did we base this new MasterBorder on the default MasterBorder used on the Home page? In this case, although the elements in the new MasterBorder will be different from the previous one, basing this new one on the default MasterBorder caused it to inherit the MasterBorder margin sizes, which is a huge timesaver!

Now you can add new banners, navigation bars, text, and graphics that you want duplicated on other pages.

Working with banners

Banners are like titles to the Web Page. They are pictures that contain the name of the page.

Because we just deleted all the MasterBorder elements, the page currently does not contain a banner. To add one, choose the Banner tool on the Standard toolbar (shown in Figure 10-17) and draw the location of the banner in the top MasterBorder. Make sure you have drawn a horizontal placeholder for the banner otherwise you may end up with a vertical banner creating an enormous top MasterBorder area!

Figure 10-17: Selecting the Banner tool from the Standard toolbar.

Tip

If you do this, instead of manually deleting the banner and manually resizing the MasterBorder, select the Undo command from the Edit menu (Ctrl+Z) and sequentially step back through all the commands you have performed.

The banner will appear in the style you have chosen for the site and the banner name you have chosen in Custom Names. If you want to change either of these, we'll get to that in a minute.

The Figure 10-18 shows the banner in place. It's set in Basic, the default style, and bears the name "Home," the default name.

Note

To change the font size and color of text embedded into a banner or navigation bar, you must edit the graphics elements defined in the style for these objects and use the available tools to alter these settings.

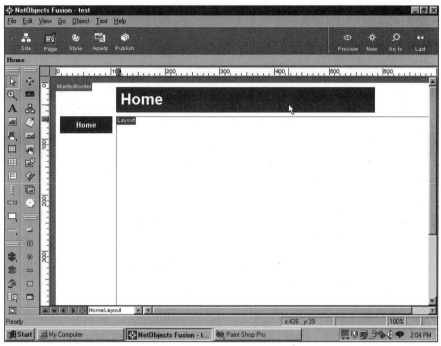

Figure 10-18: The Banner set in place.

Modifying the banner

In many cases, the automatic banner placed by Fusion will be quite satisfactory, but you have many options available to fine-tune a banner and its properties, including placement, orientation, content, style, spacing, and appearance.

All of these properties are modified or configured on the General tab of the Banner Properties palette (seen in Figure 10-19). Before the General tab for the Banner on the Properties palette becomes accessible, you need to select the banner on the current page by clicking it with the mouse.

Figure 10-19: The Banner Properties palette.

Adding a custom image as a banner

You can replace the current SiteStyle banner with a custom graphic at any time. You can do this one of two ways:

✦ Double-click the banner and select a new graphics image file to use as the banner.

✦ Use the Custom Image button from the Banner Properties palette to choose a new file.

The second option also supplies an Undo Customization button, so it is the preferred method.

If you change a banner in a MasterBorder to a custom image, all pages that share this MasterBorder will also have the new banner applied.

Using SiteStyles

If we wanted to change the actual image comprising the banner, we would simply click the Browse button and select a new image. In this way, you can create complete new styles out of any existing images you may have.

Changing banner text

First off, you may not like the title that appears on the banner. You can modify this by selecting the Custom Names option from the Edit menu. From the dialog box that appears, change the name in the Banner field.

If the text inside the banner is just a fraction too long, but there is room to have the remainder of the name on a second line in the banner, you can now wrap lines inside a banner. To do this, either go to Site view for the page and choose the Custom Names button, or if in Page view, press F12 to open the Page Properties palette and choose the Custom Names button.

In the text field for the Banner Heading, where you want the text to wrap, insert the cursor and press Shift+Enter.

Working with navigation bars

Like the MasterBorder, the *Navigation Bar* is a fundamental component of NetObjects Fusion. A Navigation Bar is a grouping of graphic or textual elements placed on a Web page that act as navigation elements for a Web site. Each element in a Navigation Bar (a single graphic or text entry) has a hyperlink dynamically assigned to it. When an individual element in a Navigation Bar is clicked while viewing the page in a browser, it automatically loads the Web page associated with that link. Figure 10-20 shows a typical graphics-based Navigation Bar in a Fusion-generated Web site.

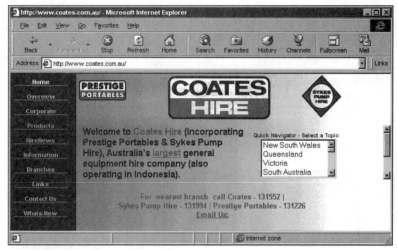

Figure 10-20: A typical Web page generated in Fusion with a left Navigation Bar.

The most important aspect of this is that the Navigation Bar specifically reflects the structure of the site and automatically updates with structure changes. You could group a bunch of images together and call them a navigation bar, but it certainly isn't the same thing as a NetObjects Fusion Navigation Bar.

As you have seen, every time a new Web site is created in Fusion, a Navigation Bar using buttons from the Basic style is automatically generated and placed in the left MasterBorder of the home page. Fusion also places a text-based Navigation Bar in the bottom MasterBorder.

Adding new Navigation Bar buttons

When you create a new site and Fusion adds a default Navigation Bar, it contains only one entry, a link to the Home page. As you add new pages, Fusion places additional buttons in the Navigation Bar on each page using the currently assigned style. By default, individual elements of both Navigation Bars point to the pages on the first level of the site. The default MasterBorder has the Navigation Bar in a vertical orientation down the left side of the page, but you can place a Navigation Bar horizontally, say, across the top of the page under the banner.

Adding Navigation Bars

Since the MasterBorder contains just a banner, we'll create the new Navigation Bar by selecting the Navigation Bar tool from the Standard toolbar (shown in Figure 10-21) and drawing the location of the Navigation Bar onto the page just to the left side of the Layout section. Fusion will place the Navigation Bar as shown in Figure 10-22.

Make sure you draw a vertically oriented rectangle as the Navigation Bar placeholder. As with the banner, the Navigation Bar will contain the site's selected style and custom page names selected for it.

Figure 10-21: Selecting the Navigation Bar tool from the Standard toolbar.

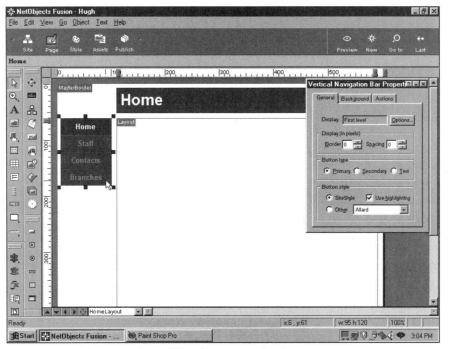

Figure 10-22: The page after adding the new Navigation Bar.

Setting the Navigation Bar options

In many cases, the automatic Navigation Bar placed by Fusion will be quite satisfactory, but you have many options available to fine-tune a Navigation Bar and its properties, including placement, orientation, content, style, spacing, and appearance.

All of these properties are modified or configured on the General tab of the Navigation Bar Properties palette (as seen in Figure 10-23). Before the General tab for the Navigation Bar on the Properties palette becomes accessible, you need to select the Navigation Bar on the current page by clicking it with the mouse.

Figure 10-23: The Navigation Bar Properties palette.

Setting the display level

The first option on the General tab of the Navigation Bar Properties palette is the Display option, which lets you define which pages in the site will have buttons on the currently selected Navigation Bar. The Options button opens a dialog box shown in Figure 10-24. At this point, the knowledge of the relationships between pages and levels becomes important.

Figure 10-24: The Nav Bar Display dialog box.

The Bar Display dialog box contains a radio button for each level that can be applied to the Navigation Bar: First, Parent, Current, and Child. The display also has a checkbox to include the Home page in the Navigation Bar and an orientation button to set the Navigation Bar as either vertical or horizontal.

For the purposes of demonstration, we'll use a sample Web site, called ABC Financial. Figure 10-25 shows how the site looks in Site view. We'll be changing the display levels of the Personnel page so you can see what happens to its Navigation Bar.

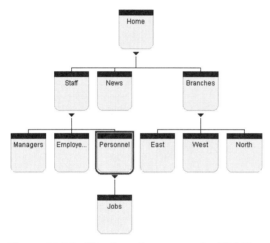

Figure 10-25: Site view of our example, ABC Financial.

First Level

The first level of a Web site contains all the pages that are directly connected to the Home page. This is the default setting for a Navigation Bar. In the ABC Financial site, the first level includes the Staff, News, and Branches pages (shown in Figure 10-26). (The Home page is included because the Include Home Page option is selected.

Parent Level

The parent level includes all pages one level above the current page. In many cases, this is the same as the first level (as it is in the ABC Financial Web site), but as pages are created further and further down the site hierarchy, the parent level differs for each level of pages.

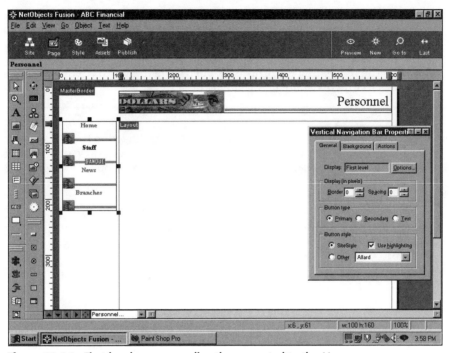

Figure 10-26: First-level pages are directly connected to the Home page.

Current Level

The current level contains the pages that are on the same level as the current page but connected to the same parent. For example, Figure 10-27 shows the Personnel page's Navigation Bar for the current level. This includes the Managers and Employees pages but not the East, West, and North pages.

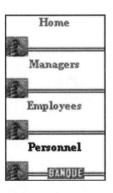

Figure 10-27: Current-level pages are on the same level as the selected page and have the same parent.

Tip

By default, a Navigation Bar will also show a button for the currently displayed page. If you select the Use highlighting option on the Navigation Bar Properties palette, this button will be displayed as a different graphic image to the rest of the buttons on the Navigation Bar. This is useful to give the visitor to the site visual feedback as to exactly where in the site he or she is.

Child Level

Finally, the child level contains pages that are directly linked to the current page but are one level below. Figure 10-28 shows the Personnel page's Navigation Bar for the child level. If the Jobs page had a child, it would not appear on the Navigation Bar.

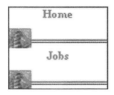

Figure 10-28: Child-level pages are one level below the current page.

If a Child Level setting is applied to the current Navigation Bar (which will apply to all pages as they share the same MasterBorder), the Navigation Bar will be correct for the Home page (the visitor can navigate to the Staff page) and the Staff or Branches pages. In other words, you can step down the hierarchy one level at a time. If the Home page checkmark is turned on, you can also return to the Home page at any time as this button appears on every page.

What happens when, for example, a visitor navigates to the ABC Managers page? This page has no children; therefore, the only option is to navigate back to the Home page. If a visitor to the site navigates to the Managers page but wants to view the News page, he or she would need to go back to the Home page and retrace steps. This is clumsy and doesn't actually invite people to navigate your site.

Change one, change all!

Remember though: changing a Navigation Bar on any level will affect other Navigation Bars on other pages using the same MasterBorder. Because of this, you should spend a little time thinking about which pages you want to appear on the Navigation Bar for each page. If you require different settings for Navigation Bars on different pages, you need to create a new MasterBorder for each Navigation Bar style.

Include Home Page

As mentioned, the dialog box for setting the levels of pages also contains a checkbox. When you tick this, this Navigation Bar will appear in all pages sharing this particular MasterBorder. As the Home page has been designed to show in this Navigation Bar on every page that uses the MasterBorder.

Horizontal and Vertical

You can use this option to change a vertical Navigation Bar to a horizontal one or vice versa. Be aware, though, that changing from vertical to horizontal Navigation Bar often kicks the Layout area over.

Setting a border for the Navigation Bar

If required, you can also place a border around the Navigation Bar. The Border control works very simply: the higher the number you set by using the spinner control arrows, the thicker the border around the Navigation Bar will be. Due to an HTML limitation, you cannot change the color of a Navigation Bar border, however.

Changing Navigation Bar spacing

Due to the text description underneath each button (particularly when vertical Navigation Bars are used), sometimes the spacing between the buttons can look a little cramped. You can see this when looking at the Navigation Bar in Figure 10-29. Not only are the buttons very close together, but the text describing each button's destination page doesn't fit inside the space.

Figure 10-29: The buttons are very close together and the text is cut off in this Navigation Bar.

A two-step procedure will correct this. First, remove the word *Properties* from the Custom Name of each of the two pages in question (Page 2 and Page 3), thus allowing the description to fit.

This is a simple matter of returning to Site view, selecting the first page to have its name modified, and clicking on the Custom Names button on the Properties palette Page tab. To delete the word *Properties*, double-click it in the button field and press the Del key. Click the OK button to close the dialog box.

The default spacing for buttons in a Navigation Bar is 3 pixels. Clicking on the up arrow in the spinner control until the spacing reaches 10 pixels gives a more balanced look to this particular Navigation Bar (as you can see in Figure 10-30).

Figure 10-30: The buttons look much better after trimming the names and increasing the Spacing.

Setting button type and style

Fusion places buttons on the Navigation Bar from the current style and uses the Primary buttons. You can change the buttons from Primary to Secondary or Text buttons from the Navigation Bar Properties palette. You can also change the style of the buttons and add highlighting as well.

Highlighted buttons

In addition to the Primary buttons available in a style, there are also Highlighted buttons. The option whether to use these is on the General tab of the Navigation Bar Properties palette: check the box to turn it on, and uncheck to turn it off. Figure 10-31 shows the Use Highlighting checkbox turned on.

Figure 10-31: The General tab of the Navigation Bar Properties palette with the Use Highlighting option checked.

So, when and how are highlighted buttons used?

Normally, if a Navigation Bar contains a button for the page that is currently loaded in a Web browser, that button is the same as every other button in the Navigation Bar. With the Use Highlighting option checked, the graphic image representing the button for the current page will be a different button type as seen dramatically in Figure 10-32.

Figure 10-32: A Navigation Bar using highlighted buttons.

The image used for the highlighted button varies from style to style. By switching to Style view, you can see that in the two rows of buttons, one in each row is substantially different from the others. On each row, appropriately named "Primary Navigation Bar" and "Secondary Navigation Bar," the second button is different from the others on that same row. This is the highlighted button image that will appear when the Use Highlighting option is checked. Figure 10-33 for example shows the Primary, Secondary, and Highlighted buttons for the Joe's Diner style.

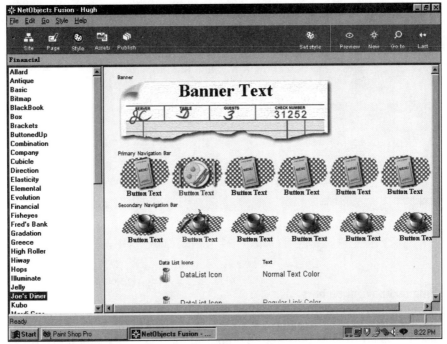

Figure 10-33: The different button types for the Joe's Diner style. Note the Highlighted buttons (the plate of bacon and eggs and the full cup of coffee).

Secondary buttons

Each Style has two button types available for Navigation Bars. Unless otherwise told, Fusion uses the top row of these buttons in the style (called the Primary buttons) when it creates a Navigation Bar. The second row is appropriately enough called the Secondary button, and you can choose these instead of the Primary button if you prefer. Both Primary and Secondary buttons have Highlighted versions.

The option to use either the Primary or Secondary buttons is available on the Navigation Bar tab of the Properties palette.

Using buttons from other styles

As well as being able to select either the Primary or Secondary buttons for a Navigation Bar from a style in addition to choosing whether to have highlighting of buttons, you can also apply buttons from any other style.

The dropdown list on the Navigation Bar tab of the Properties palette gives a complete listing of all styles available to the site. To choose either the Primary or Secondary button (including the Highlighted option) from another style, select it from the list and make sure the Other Style radio button is checked (see Figure 10-34). The new buttons will immediately be applied to the page.

Figure 10-34: The Style options on the General tab of the Navigation Bar Properties palette.

Using text navigation bars

As well as having a graphical Nav Bar, it is also good practice to place a text-based Nav Bar on each page, usually at the base of the page in the bottom MasterBorder. One reason for using text as well as graphical Nav Bars is to cater for those who either do not use a graphics capable browser or choose to turn off the graphics capabilities of their browser. With no graphics, visitors to the site in either of these categories will have no means to navigate around the site.

In some cases, a graphics-based Navigation Bar is not appropriate such as when building a intranet-based Web site where all the users of the site have only a text-based browser. (This is rare, I know, but it could happen!)

Under this circumstance, a text Navigation Bar would be preferable and the option to substitute text for graphics is available on the Navigation Bar tab of the Properties palette. Figure 10-35 shows an example of a text-based Navigation Bar.

Text Navigation Bars for the Visually Impaired

A further consideration to use a text-based Navigation Bar is to assist those who are visually impaired. Many of these people use voice synthesizers to "read" the page out loud to them through a speaker attached to their PC.

Special software scans the text of the page in a Web browser and digitizes it for the synthesizer. Of course, graphic buttons are not text and therefore cannot be scanned. It makes good sense therefore to assist the visually impaired by having a text-based Navigation Bar on your pages.

The same theory applies to the importance of using Alt tags on graphics images on a Web page.

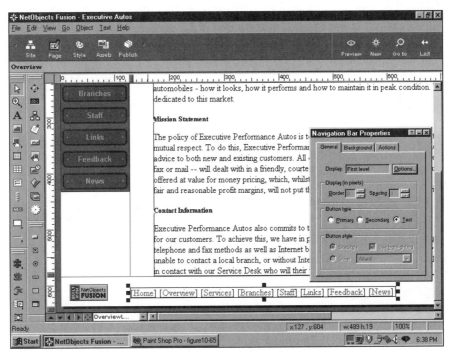

Figure 10-35: A page using a text-based Navigation Bar.

Placing a text Nav Bar in Fusion is easy. Simply place the Navigation Bar where you want it in exactly the same way you placed the previous graphical Navigation Bar. Once the Navigation Bar is displayed on the page, make sure it is selected and then choose the Text radio button in the Button type section of the Properties palette. The graphical Navigation Bar will be converted to a text-based one.

The font style (typeface), color, and text attributes used in a text-based Navigation Bar depend upon the Normal paragraph style for the style in use. (For details on changing the style, see Chapter 7).

You cannot select and edit a text Navigation Bar as you can normal text, nor can you embed carriage returns to make the text wrap to a new line if the number of entries in the Navigation Bar exceeds the preferred page width. If a text Navigation Bar grows too large, it is better to use standard text blocks, linking the appropriate sections of the text using the Links button on the Text tab of the Properties palette. See Chapter 11 for more information on linking text blocks.

Changing background

The Background tab on the Navigation Bar Properties palette also lets you add a fill color to a Navigation Bar. You have two options: a color you choose or no fill color (the default).

If you want to specify a particular color as the background of the Navigation Bar, choose this by clicking the first radio button and selecting a new color from a pop-up Color Picker chart (shown in Figure 10-36).

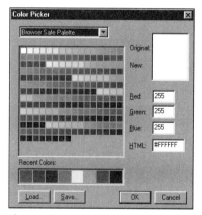

Figure 10-36: Setting a fill color for a Navigation Bar.

In many cases, though, the background color will not show due to the nature of the graphics images used in the style for navigation bars. This option is better used in text-based navigation bars.

Creating a Navigation Bar from scratch

When you need to use special descriptions in Navigation Bar buttons and the Custom Names functionality is not sufficient, creating your own navigation bar is usually more convenient. Just follow these steps:

1. Select the Picture tool from the Standard toolbar.

2. Draw the image in the MasterBorder and select the image to place from the Picture File Open dialog box.

3. If you've had problems placing a long page name on a button, click the Stretch radio button in the Picture Properties palette and drag the handles to elongate it.

4. For the other buttons, just duplicate the image by pressing copy and paste for each other image you need.

5. To place text in the image, click the Effects tab of the Picture Properties palette and use the Text in Settings option.

6. Use the Link button on the General tab of the Properties palette to supply the link to the destination page.

I provide more detail about links in Chapter 11.

You don't need to sacrifice the look and feel of the site as you can still use the style buttons that the automatic Navigation Bar uses. To do this, first find the folder on your hard disk containing the image you are after (you can check this by switching to Style view, double-clicking on the style you want, and double-clicking the button type. The dialog box will show you the path to the GIF file of the button). Second, switch back to Page view, use the Picture tool to draw a placeholder at the location where you want the button to be located, and then use the Link tool on the Properties palette to add the link manually.

Applying the New MasterBorder to Other Pages

Applying an already configured MasterBorder to a page is as simple as a single mouse click. Simply navigate to a page that requires the new MasterBorder using the page navigation buttons at the bottom left of the Fusion window. Next, click anywhere in a MasterBorder area so that the MasterBorder Properties palette appears and select the new MasterBorder from the dropdown list (as seen in Figure 10-37).

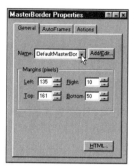

Figure 10-37: Applying a MasterBorder to a page.

Summary

✦ You can define as many MasterBorders as required, and you can base them on existing MasterBorders.

✦ Name MasterBorders with meaningful titles.

✦ Apply a new MasterBorder from the MasterBorder Properties palette.

✦ MasterBorder margins can be dragged to a new position on the Rulers.

✦ MasterBorder size values can be entered manually onto the MasterBorder tab of the Properties palette.

✦ Banners are used to signify a web page's purpose.

✦ Navigation bars automatically reflect the site's structure allowing easy access to pages in the site.

✦ Different levels of navigation can be defined for automatic Navigation bars.

✦ Custom page name text can be added to both Navigation Bars and Banners (including text wrapping with Shift+Enter).

✦   ✦   ✦

Creating Hypertext Links and Anchors

Hypertext links (see Figure 11-1) are areas of text on a Web page that, when clicked, take the person browsing the page to another part of the current Web site or to a page on a totally different Web site. A link created to a location in the current site could take the site visitor to the top of another page in the site or to a specific location (or anchor) on the current or another page. To create a link to specific locations in the current site (as distinct from a link to a page) also involves specifying destination anchors in addition to a hyperlink.

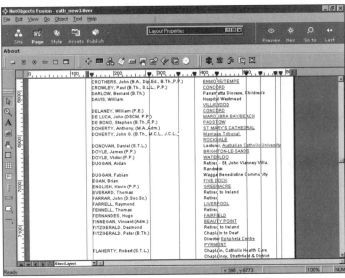

Figure 11-1: Hypertext links are often the areas of the text that are underlined.

Links are what the World Wide Web is all about. They make navigation through a single or number of sites (popularly called *browsing* or *surfing*) possible.

Adding Simple Hypertext Links

Creating text-based links in Fusion is easy. To add simple hypertext links, follow these steps:

1. In Page view, select the text to be the link.

2. Click the Link button on the Text Properties palette.

3. In the Link dialog box that opens (as shown in Figure 11-2), enter the correct destination of the link. Fusion gives you four types of links:

   - internal links
   - smart links
   - external links
   - file links

4. Click the Link button, and the text will appear with an underline.

That's it! There's no messy coding or having to refer to file path names.

Figure 11-2: The Link dialog box.

Note

Depending on your local settings and whether you have made any changes to the style applied to the site, the underlined text may also change color after you have defined a link.

Tip

The link color is determined by the style currently in use or by the browser's settings (in our example, the Hiway style makes the link red). To change the color to another, go to Style view, double-click the Regular Link Color of the style, and choose another color from the Color Picker dialog box. If you want to preserve the style's look and feel, though, simply select the text after the link has been applied and choose another color from the Text Properties palette.

Internal links

An *internal link* is one that, when clicked, takes the viewer to another part of the same site. This is the most common type of link and the first tab you see when the dialog box opens. To create an internal link, select the page to link to from the available list.

For example, in Figure 11-3 the word *services* in the second paragraph (highlighted) can become a hypertext link. When clicked, the site visitor is taken to the company services in exactly the same way as if the visitor had clicked a menu option.

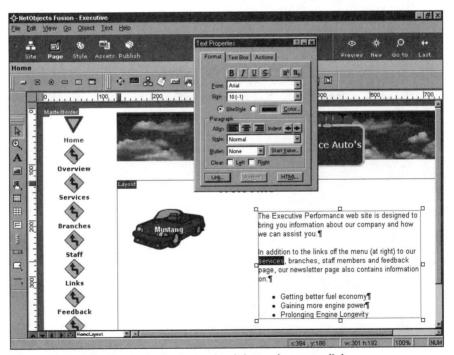

Figure 11-3: Selecting text prior to turning it into a hypertext link.

To turn the word *services* into a link, follow these steps:

1. Drag the mouse over the text box and double-click it to enter Edit mode.

2. Select the text you want to become the hyperlink (as shown in Figure 11-3).

3. Click the Link button on the Text Properties palette. The dialog box shown in Figure 11-4 opens.

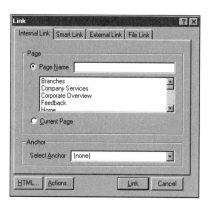

Figure 11-4: The Internal Link tab of the Link dialog box.

4. On the Internal Link tab of the Link dialog box, Fusion displays all of the pages available in the current site. To create the link, select the page from the scroll list that this link will refer to (as shown in Figure 11-5) and click the Link button.

Figure 11-5: Selecting the page to link to.

When Fusion has closed the Links dialog box, the word *services* in the text is now underlined. This signifies that it is a link. To create hypertext links for other words in the second paragraph to pages in the Web site, repeat the previous steps, and in the Links dialog box select the corresponding page.

Smart links

Smart links are unique to Fusion. They are not links in the sense of an HTML specification but rather a way of telling Fusion which page in the hierarchy of the pages in the Site map will be linked.

Examples of smart links include Next Page (the next page to the right in the current level of the site map), Up (up one level in the hierarchy), and Home (to the home page). A good use of smart links is on pages that simulate a magazine or newsletter style of approach such as at `www.sydneymarkets.com.au/freshtimes10/home.html`. To apply a smart link, follow the same procedure as you would with an internal link, except click the Smart Link tab (shown in Figure 11-6).

The Blank option is a special smart link that lets you assign a null link to an element. After doing this, you can apply special HTML scripts or actions to a link using the Actions tab on the Properties palette. See Chapter 20 for more information on actions.

Figure 11-6: The Smart Link tab of the Link dialog box.

External links

An *external link* is a link to a page (usually a home page) in another Web site altogether. Fusion also classifies special links that send e-mails, download files, and perform other special functions as external links. Figure 11-7 shows the External Link tab of the Links dialog box.

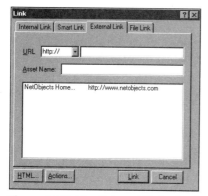

Figure 11-7: The External Link tab of the Link dialog box.

Fusion allows many types of external links. Of these, the two most common are links to other Web sites and mailto: links. You can also apply these types of links:

http://	javascript:
ftp://	gopher://
mailto:	snews://
news://	telnet://
shttp://	rlogin://
https://	tn3270://
file:///	wais://

Either way, the method of creating such links are all exactly the same.

Creating mailto: links

When a visitor to a site clicks on a mailto: link, the coding in the link opens that person's e-mail program and automatically fills in the destination e-mail address that is coded into the link. The visitor then enters his or her message and clicks on the send button, which sends the e-mail and closes the e-mail program.

Creating a mailto: link is the same as creating any other external link. The difference is the type of link selected. In the Built With Fusion link, the link type selected from the dropdown list was an http:// link. A mailto: link, therefore, would create a mailto: link. This makes sense really!

A common use of a mailto: link is to supply a contact reference point in the bottom MasterBorder of pages. Many sites use the bottom left portion of the MasterBorder to place their full address details including a mailto: link.

For the Executive Performance Autos home page, Figure 11-8 shows a typical address. This has been placed in the Default MasterBorder, and therefore will not appear on the first-level pages as they have their own MasterBorder definition.

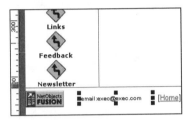

Figure 11-8: The address information on the home page.

To turn the e-mail address into a mailto: link, select it with the mouse and click the Link button on the Properties palette. As the mailto: link is an external type, you need to select the External Link tab (shown in Figure 11-9) to complete the operation. From the dropdown list of link types, choose the mailto: link, and finally, enter the destination e-mail address into the field to the right of the list. To apply the link, click the Link button.

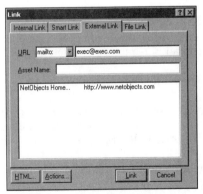

Figure 11-9: The External Link dialog box showing the completed mailto: link.

File links

In some cases, you may need to have a link to files stored on the Web server and provide the facility for visitors to the site to download these files to their computers. In this case, you create the link the same way as you would a hypertext link to a Web site, except that in the link field, you specify the full path name of the file to be downloaded. Figure 11-10 shows an example of a link to a file called instructions.doc that is being stored on a Web server. This option is often used to link to demonstration versions of software that the site visitor can then download.

Figure 11-10: The File Link tab of the Link dialog box.

Attaching Links to Graphics

You can attach links to graphics as easily as you can for text. The method of creating links from graphics objects is the same. You can tell whether a graphic has a link attached to it because it will contain a small blue circle and white arrow.

Tip

If this indicator does not appear, turn on the Object Icons option from the View menu.

When you display the page in a browser, though, you have no visual indicator that a graphic may be a link until you move the mouse pointer over such a link. It changes to a pointing finger, and the link's destination shows in the browser's status bar.

Whenever Fusion creates a new site, it automatically creates an external link on the Home page to the NetObjects Fusion home page at www.netobjects.com. This is the Built with NetObjects Fusion icon placed at the bottom left of the home page as seen in Figure 11-11.

To see the link attached to the Built with NetObjects Fusion icon, select the graphic with the mouse (it will show black handles when selected) and click the Link button on the Properties palette. The Link dialog box will open for the link as shown in Figure 11-12.

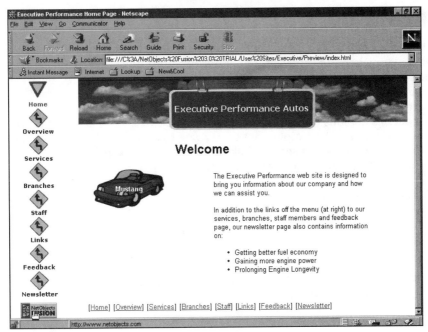

Figure 11-11: The Built with NetObjects Fusion link.

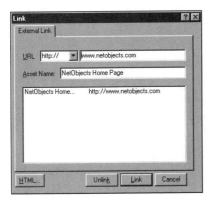

Figure 11-12: The Built with NetObjects Fusion link in the Link dialog box.

As this link has already been defined, only the External Link tab appears on the Links dialog box. At the left of the dialog box is a dropdown list where you can select the type of link. Most links to other Web pages will be http:// links.

More Info

One major time-saver with links is that Fusion classifies them as an asset. I explain more fully in Chapter 26, but in the case of links, this simply means that Fusion stores a link's definition internally. This allows it to be selected from the assets list as many times as needed without having to retype the URL of the link every time it is used.

Adding Anchors

While I personally do not believe it is good practice to have very long Web pages (that is, ones where the site visitor continually scrolls down to view the content), sometimes it is unavoidable. The most common reason for long Web pages is when you cannot logically break up large amounts of text into smaller pages such as in `www.dtec.nsw.gov.au/HSCRecommend/chap1.htm` (as seen in Figure 11-13). This page contains copious quantities of text that can be viewed by scrolling down the page. For those who simply want to navigate to a section of text inside the document, however, you'll see text links at the top of the page labeled Comments, Criticism, Considering, Statements, and Proposed Equity.

Each of these, when clicked, will take you to the appropriate section of the text. The destination that is defined for the link is called the *anchor*.

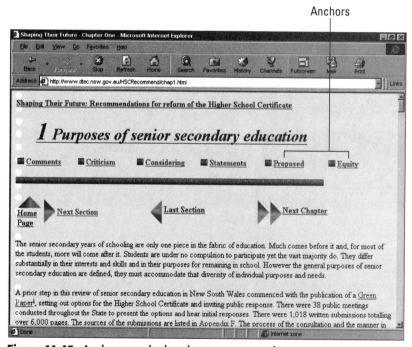

Figure 11-13: Anchors used when large amounts of text are on a page.

Another example is `www.coates.com.au/html/wa.html` (see Figure 11-14), where the client specification necessitated that the long pages have all their branch details on the one page but that visitors be able to navigate quickly to the one they want to see. In this example, the regions are listed across the top of the page, and the anchor is defined in the textual heading for that region (for example, *Goldfields*).

Anchors

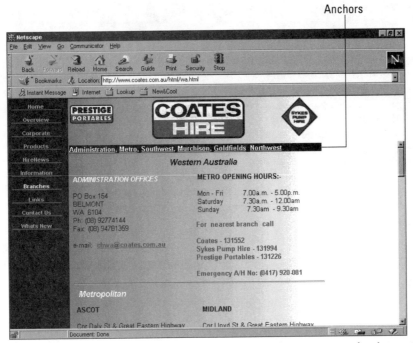

Figure 11-14: Anchors let users navigate to the section on a page that interests them.

To aid the visitor in navigation on these types of pages, the Web author uses NetObjects Fusion's anchors facility feature.

Anchors *are* hypertext links, but they point to an element on a page. The element pointed to can be on the same or a different page in the current Web site or on a page in another Web site entirely. Because of this, anchors also operate as navigation tools that point visitors to specific sections (as distinct from a page) in a site. Examples include footnotes, diagrams, and so on.

Anchors to the same page

For purposes of example, we'll add text to a page with navigation controls that will point to its separate sections. Each of these sections will contain an anchor.

The text is located in a file called co.txt in the Text folder on the CD-ROM included with this book (or your hard disk if you copied it over from the CD-ROM).

The Corporate Overview contains text consisting of an Introduction, Mission Statement, and Contact Information. To let a visitor to the site navigate directly to any of these sections without having to scroll down the page, we place links across the top of the page that point to the individual sections. These sections have an anchor applied to them, and the links across the top of the page point to the respective anchors.

Prepping the Imported Text

First, set up a blank Web page with the Hiway style. If you recall from Chapter 8, you import text by dragging it from the Windows Explorer (or Mac Finder) onto the Web page. Position the text block, leaving room under the banner. Select each of the three headings (Introduction, Mission Statement, and Contact Information) and make them bold (Ctrl+B). Insert a line of text in that area between the banner and the imported text. Type **Introduction (5 spaces) Mission Statement (5 spaces) Contact Information** into the text box and make everything bold. Your page should look like Figure 11-15. Now you're ready to continue.

Before we turn the top line of text into links, we need to define the anchors. The imported text contains three headings corresponding to the labels. We will use these as the anchors.

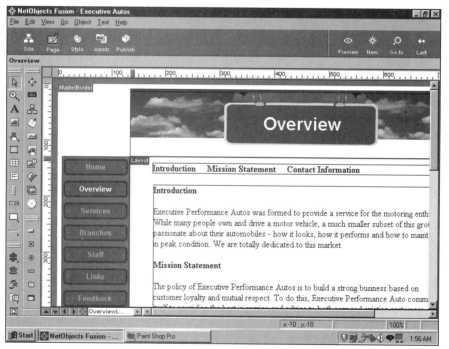

Figure 11-15: The Web page ready to add anchors.

To create the anchor for the Introduction section, double-click the imported text block to get into Edit mode and click on the word Introduction and position the cursor at the beginning of the word. On the Properties palette, click the Anchor button to open the Add Anchor dialog box (as shown in Figure 11-16). Finally, supply a name in the field that will identify this particular anchor. The space underneath the field name displays a list of all the anchors that have been defined for the current page. Once you have defined the anchor name, you can close the dialog box.

Tip

It is helpful to use anchor names that easily identify the position of the anchor. I find it best to use the name of the link that will refer to the anchor. For example, in the case of the Introduction label, I would also call the anchor "Introduction." To see which elements on pages have anchors applied to them, turn on the Object Icons option on the View menu. Repeat the process for the other two anchors. Keep in mind that anchors cannot have any spaces in them. Also, if you are navigating to an anchor on another page, you must also select the page containing the anchor. Elements containing anchors will show a small icon of a red circle with an upside down *T* inside it when Objects Icons are turned on from the View menu.

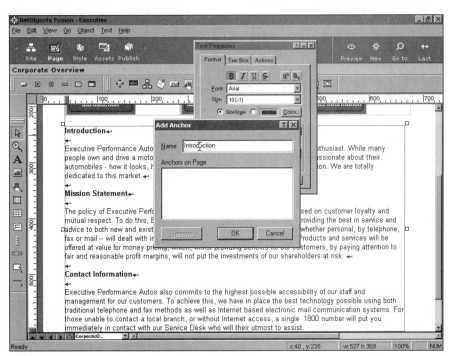

Figure 11-16: The Add Anchor dialog box.

With the anchors set, we can now link the first label at the top to this section. This operation is very similar to creating a standard link with one extra step:

1. Select the Introduction text on the top line of text.

2. Click the Link button on the Text Properties palette.

3. On the Internal Link tab, choose Introduction from the Select Anchor dropdown list.

4. Click the Link button.

Figure 11-17 shows the settings for the button to link to the Introduction anchor.

If you have turned on the Object Icons option on the View menu (which is on by default), the Introduction heading will have a small red circle with an upside-down white *T* signifying an anchor.

Repeat this process with the other two labels. The final product should look like Figure 11-18.

Figure 11-17: The Link dialog box for the Introduction button and anchor.

Anchors to a different page

Linking to anchors on another page in the Web site follows the same basic set of steps used to link to anchors on the current page. The one difference is when selecting the anchor in the Link dialog box.

At this step, select the page in the list that contains the anchor. The dropdown list will then display a list of available anchors for that particular page. Now you can select the anchor required. If no anchors have been defined for the selected page, the list of anchors is grayed out.

Figure 11-19 shows the Links dialog box when selecting an anchor on a different page.

Anchors

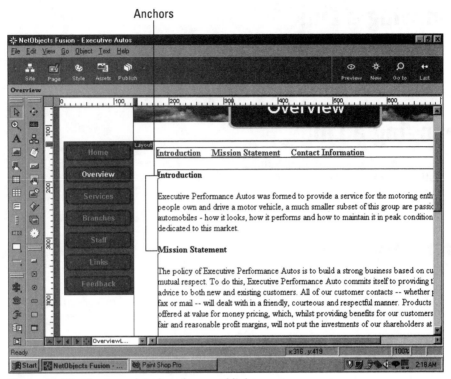

Figure 11-18: The completed anchors and links.

Figure 11-19: Selecting an anchor on a different page.

Removing a Link

If you've already set a hyperlink, the Link dialog box will show an Unlink button. Clicking this button will sever this link and let you define another for the graphic object. The original will still stay in the assets list for future use.

Changing a Link

If you have already specified a link and wish to change it, simply click the Link button again and choose the Unlink button on the Link dialog box. You can then add the new, updated link.

Summary

✦ Internal links are links to pages in the current Web site.

✦ External links link to other sites, create mailto: links, or other more specialized links such as to newservers, gopher sites, and so on.

✦ Smart links are used primarily for stacked pages.

✦ File links are used to link to a file stored on the Web server or elsewhere.

✦ Links can be created from either text or graphics.

✦ Adding anchors.

✦ Use anchors to link to text or elements on a page.

✦ Links can be to anchors on the same or different pages.

✦ Use View ➪ Object Icons to show the location of anchors.

✦   ✦   ✦

Working with Special Characters, Variables, and HTML Tags

Many times when you're using text blocks, you'll need to add a special character to a page. Examples of such characters include the registered trademark (™) and copyright (©) symbols. In addition, special text variables, such as Date Last Modified and Date Created, can add extra viability and functionality to a Web site. Finally, because the HTML specification is an ever-evolving animal, new HTML tags may appear from time to time that you may find useful but are not able to use in the visual environment of NetObjects Fusion. Certainly scripts could incorporate them, but in reality they may be more trouble than they are worth.

Fusion caters to all these situations in another, much easier way. The functionality of Fusion makes using these options easy to implement using special commands available from the Text menu, which is available when you're in Text insert mode or when a text block is selected while in Page view.

Adding Symbols

Special symbols are used frequently in typography, from the common copyright symbol (©) to more complex characters such as fraction signs. Their absence, particularly from special text such as a company name or logo, can make a Web site look a little amateurish and unprofessional. NetObjects Fusion makes adding these sorts of symbols easy.

To see how easy it is to add symbols, place the trademark symbol (™) next to the company name, Executive Performance, on the home page shown in Figure 12-1. Although a large number of symbols is not generally available, such as those provided in word-processing programs, for example, Fusion has a built-in list that should cover most needs.

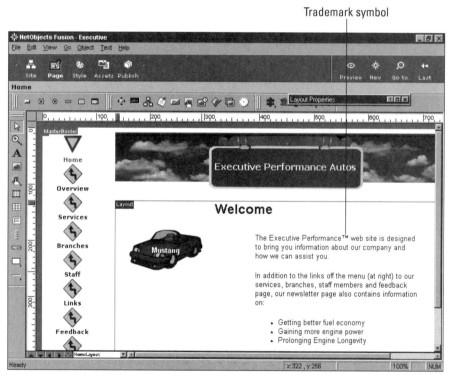

Figure 12-1: The trademark symbol is added to the name of the company in the text of the Home page.

To insert the trademark symbol, place the cursor at the location in the text block where you want the symbol to appear. Then choose Text ➪ Insert Symbol from the menu bar (see Figure 12-2).

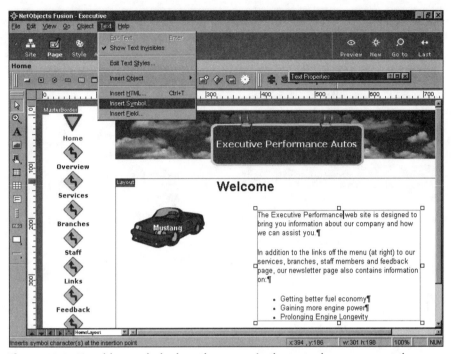

Figure 12-2: To add a symbol, place the cursor in the text where you want the symbol to appear and then choose Text ⇨ Insert Symbol from the menu bar.

Fusion opens a scrolling list box of all the symbols available, as shown in Figure 12-3 and listed in Table 12-1. Simply select the symbol required and click the Insert button. The symbol is added to the text at the position of the cursor.

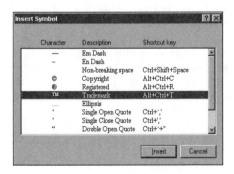

Figure 12-3: The trademark symbol is selected from the displayed scrolling list of available symbols.

	Table 12-1	
	Special Characters You Can Insert into Text	
Character	*Description*	*Shortcut key*
—	Em dash	
–	En dash	
	Non-breaking space	Ctrl+Shift+Space
©	Copyright	Alt+Ctrl+C
®	Registered trademark	Alt+Ctrl+R
™	Trademark	Alt+Ctrl+T
...	Ellipsis	
'	Single Open Quote'	Ctrl+ `,'
'	Single Close Quote	Ctrl+','
"	Double Open Quote	Ctrl+`+"
"	Double Close Quote	Ctrl+'+"
'	Single Straight Quote	
"	Double Straight Quote	

Adding Fields

A field (also called a *variable*) is slightly different than a symbol in that its value can change as time goes by. For example, after inserting the Number of Pages field, its value displayed on the Web page containing the variable will increase or decrease whenever new pages are added or deleted from the site. Similarly, the Now field will constantly change as the computer's clock is updated.

You can also define your own fields. This is extremely useful in such areas as telephone numbers, addresses, or even personal names. If the definition of the field changes, such as a change in address or telephone number, all references to the field in the site will also be updated whenever you publish the site to the Web server.

System variables

Probably the most common system variable added to a site is the Site Modified variable. This field keeps track of the last date any changes were made to the site. When the site is published to the Web server, the field updates a text block containing this date. Figure 12-4 shows a site with the Site Modified variable installed.

The Site Modified field

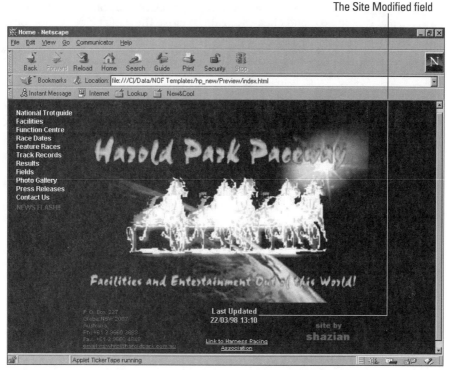

Figure 12-4: The Site Modified field is displayed on a Web page.

To insert the Site Modified field, follow the same basic steps to install a symbol:

1. Place the cursor in the text box at the position where you want to insert the field.

2. Select the Insert Field command from the Text menu on the menu bar.

3. Select the field Type from the drop-down list.

4. Select the Field you want from the available list.

When you choose the Insert Field command in Step 2, a dialog box opens, as shown in Figure 12-5. The available fields are listed in three separate groups: Date & Time, Site & General, and User defined Variable. Each of these fields is chosen from a drop-down list box at the top of the dialog box. To insert the Site Modified field, select Date & Time from the Type list box and choose the Site Modified field, as shown in Figure 12-6.

With the Date & Time fields, you can also apply formatting options to alter or configure the way the field will display in the Web browser. To access the available formats, click the Date Format button in the Insert Field dialog box to open a second dialog box containing these formats. Figure 12-7 displays the Date & Time format dialog box. Choose the style you prefer, click the OK button to close the Date Format dialog box, and click OK again to close the Insert Field dialog box.

Figure 12-5: The Insert Field dialog box.

Figure 12-6: Selecting the Date Last Modified field.

Figure 12-7: The Date Format dialog box.

The formatted field appears at the position in the text specified by the current cursor position.

After you have inserted a field, you can treat it and format it as you would any other text. Fields can have different fonts, colors, alignments, and other attributes applied as needed. Simply select the Field with the mouse and use the options available from the Format tab of the Text Properties palette.

Now that you've included the Site Modified field on the page, every time you modify the Web site on the Web server by posting a new version using Fusion's FTP client, the field automatically updates to reflect this change.

User-defined variables

User-defined variables can be very useful indeed. Not only can they be great time-savers when building a site, but they can also contain special characters that save having to insert a symbol over and over again.

One area where I use user-defined variables a lot is the address and phone/fax number that is usually placed in the footer of pages on a Web site, as shown in Figure 12-8. All this information is created once as a field and then placed in the appropriate MasterBorder as necessary.

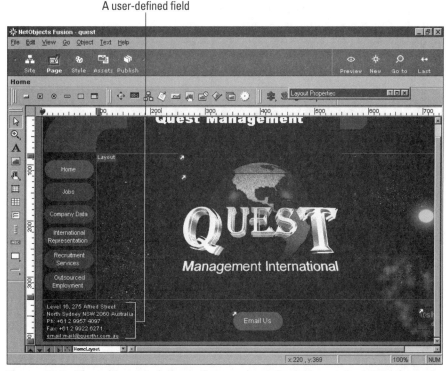

Figure 12-8: The address and phone/fax number information at the left of the main Web page is a user-defined field.

If any of the information in the field changes — for example, all telephone numbers in the Sydney region recently added a 9 to the front of them — all you need to do is change the field. Wherever this field appears in the site, it will update automatically.

To create a user-defined field, follow the same basic steps for inserting a system field:

1. Place the cursor in the text box at the position where you want to insert the field.

2. Select Insert Field from the Text menu on the menu bar.

3. Select the user-defined field from the lists of available fields, and then click the New button.

4. Define the field (or paste it from the Clipboard).

5. Click the OK button to close the dialog boxes. The field is inserted into the text at the position selected.

As I mentioned, you can also have symbols appear as a part of a field. As an example, you can turn the "Executive Performance™" text you created earlier into a user-defined variable. You can then add this in the text wherever the new name with the trademark symbol is required.

To turn this existing text into a field, simply select it with the mouse and copy it to the Clipboard, as shown in Figure 12-9.

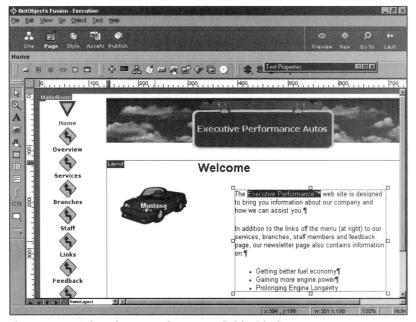

Figure 12-9: Select the text to become a field with the mouse.

Second, choose the Insert Field option from the Text menu on the menu bar to open the Insert Field dialog box, as shown in Figure 12-10. Select the User defined Variable option from the list.

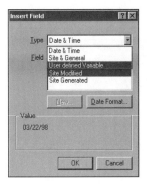

Figure 12-10: The User defined Variable option chosen in the Insert Field dialog box.

Next, click the New button to define a new user-defined field, and name the field by typing in the space available. Follow this by placing the cursor in the Value field. You can now paste the contents of the Clipboard, the text selected earlier, into the Value field, as shown in Figure 12-11.

Figure 12-11: The contents of the Clipboard are pasted into the value field to define the field. Note that the ™ character appears as a |.

Close the Insert Field dialog box by clicking the OK button. The text assigned to the field is displayed on the page. You can detect which sections of text are fields from the text's gray background making up the field's value, as shown in Figure 12-12.

Tip

When pasting the text into the Value field, you will not be able to use the Edit ➪ Paste command with this dialog box. Instead, you have to use the Ctrl+V key combination (⌘+V on a Macintosh) on the keyboard.

As before, once you have placed a field, you can treat it and format it as you would any other text. You can apply different fonts, colors, alignments, and other attributes to fields as needed. Simply select the field with the mouse and use the options available from the Format tab of the Text Properties palette.

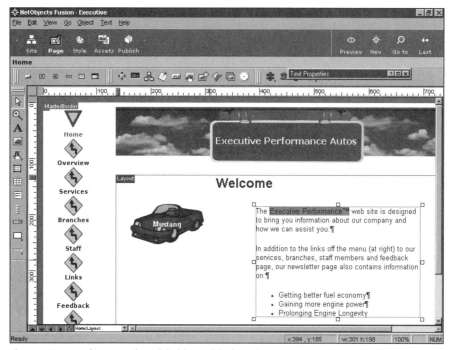

Figure 12-12: The completed field is added to the page and shown by its gray background.

Adding HTML Tags to Text

Most times there is little need to use Fusion's Insert HTML option, but, as I mentioned at the beginning of this chapter, the HTML specifications are changing all the time. Under these circumstances, an HTML tag may become available that you want to use but cannot implement using the standard Fusion commands or features.

This is where the Insert HTML command comes in handy. To demonstrate this command, add a simple Italic tag (<I>) to the Executive Performance™ variable you just created.

To insert the tag for the Italic HTML command, place the cursor just before the variable's contents (as shown in Figure 12-13) and choose the Insert HTML button from the Text Properties palette.

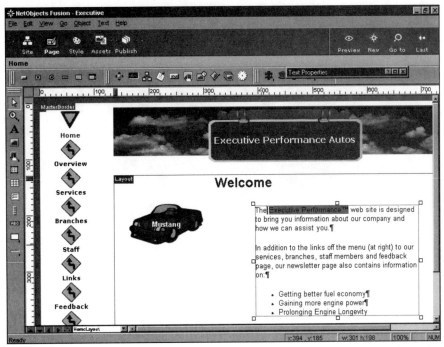

Figure 12-13: To insert the HTML tag, place the cursor in front of the text where that action of the tag will take place.

When you choose this command, the dialog box shown in Figure 12-14 opens, enabling you to enter the <I> tag into the field. You can then close the dialog box and repeat the operation *after* the variable to insert the closing Italics tag (</I>). See Figure 12-15.

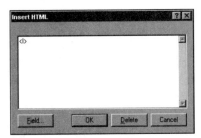

Figure 12-14: The Insert HTML dialog box.

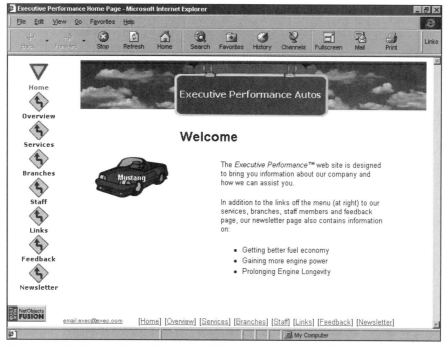

Figure 12-15: The text/variable after adding the opening and closing HTML tags.

Note   The preceding example is a simple usage of adding HTML tags to text. It was not really needed in this case because you could have easily selected the trademark symbol and clicked the italics button on the Format tab of the Text properties palette.

Summary

✦ Symbols are inserted using the Insert Symbol command available from the Text menu on the menu bar. A text box must be in insertion mode or selected.

✦ Fields are inserted/defined from the Insert Field command available from the Text menu on the menu bar.

✦ HTML commands and tags are inserted using the HTML button available from the Format tab on the Text Properties palette.

✦   ✦   ✦

Using Fusion's Draw and Line Tools

When the need arises to place primitive shapes on a page, use the Draw and Line tools from the Standard toolbar, which let you create such shapes as:

- ✦ Rectangles
- ✦ Rounded rectangles
- ✦ Ellipses
- ✦ Polygons
- ✦ Lines
- ✦ Arrows
- ✦ HTML rule lines (or separators, the ⟨HR⟩ tag in HTML)

Shapes can have different colors, fills, and line thickness defined, as well as many styles of arrowheads for lines. Shapes can also be defined as links to other Web pages or to sections on a page.

Creating Shapes

Selecting the Draw tool and holding down the left mouse button on the Standard toolbar (shown in Figure 13-1) pops out a palette to the right of the main Draw tool. Each button on the pop-out palette represents a type of shape.

Figure 13-1: The Draw and Line tools on the Standard toolbar.

Creating a shape using any of these tools is simple. Select the type of shape required, move the mouse pointer to the required location of the shape on the page, and draw by holding down the left mouse button and dragging the shape to the size required. As the mouse pointer moves, a dotted image of the selected shape appears on the page. After releasing the mouse button, the completed shape appears. Figure 13-2 shows examples of each of the available shapes drawn on a page.

Figure 13-2: Samples of the available shapes from the Draw tool.

The one exception to this method is the irregular polygon tool. Polygons are drawn in a series of steps where each drag and click of the mouse creates one side of the polygon. To finish a polygon, double-click the mouse. See Figure 13-3.

Figure 13-3: Creating an irregular polygon.

Editing drawn objects

Once a shape is on a page, you can easily edit it to change its size or, in the case of irregular polygons and ellipses, even its shape. When you select a drawn object with the mouse, a series of handles appear at each vertex or corner of the shape (with circles, a handle appears at each corner and sides of an imaginary rectangle around the circle). Figure 13-4 shows each of the shapes with their handles visible.

Figure 13-4: Selecting shapes displays their handles, which enable you to edit the size or appearance of the shapes.

To resize a shape, drag any of the handles to a new position.

Tip   When editing drawn shapes, make sure you only move the handle required to a new position. If you don't select the handle exactly, Fusion assumes you want to move the entire shape to a new location on the page.

Applying fill colors, border colors, and border sizes

After you have scaled a shape to the size required and moved it to the correct position on a page, you can apply further attributes, including its line width and fill colors. Different types of shapes have different attributes available, which are applied to a selected shape from a tab on the Properties palette corresponding to the type of shape being edited.

Figure 13-5 shows the Properties palette with a tab for an irregular polygon.

Figure 13-5: The Polygon tab on the Properties palette.

With the exception of rules and lines, the Properties tab for each of the shapes is identical. Each tab contains separate controls for setting the fill color of the shape, changing its border (line) thickness and color, and setting the Text in Element option (see Chapter 9).

Creating Lines

You can create lines approximately the same way you create shapes with the Draw tool. By selecting the Line tool on the Standard toolbar and choosing the line type you want, Fusion lets you create three different types of lines: an HR rule, a line, and a SiteStyle line.

When coding by hand, many Web authors use a rule line to separate sections of Web pages. The rule is created using the <HR> tag. To simulate the <HR> tag on a page, a graphics box was usually placed at the position required (using the Rectangle tool). The HR rule gives a representation of a three-dimensional line from user-defined start and finish points. The Line Shape tool lets you draw a normal line, define the thickness and color, and also set arrow head and tail styles.

Finally, the Line: SiteStyle tool is designed to let you place a line defined in the currently set Style (to see this style, click the Styles button on the icon bar) at a particular location on the page.

Adding an HR line

To add an HR line, choose the Line HR tool from the Standard toolbar. The mouse pointer changes to a cross. Holding down the left mouse button, click and drag the pointer from the start to the finish points you require on the page. For example, place a separator between the text in the layout of the Home page and the information in the bottom MasterBorder.

Note

If you haven't already guessed, *HR* stands for *horizontal rule*. As the name implies, you can only draw HR lines horizontally.

Tip

Of course, you could place the rule in the Layout section, but you would have to repeat this process on every page. Figure 13-6 shows the rule placed in the MasterBorder.

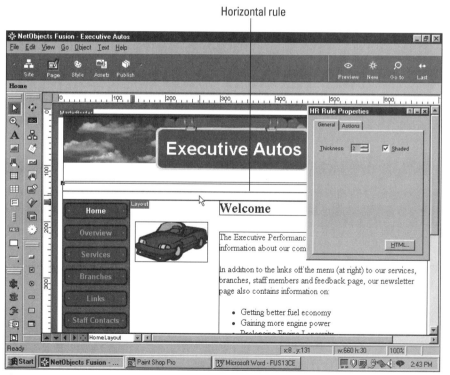

Figure 13-6: A horizontal rule placed as a separator in the MasterBorder.

As you place the rule line, notice that the Properties box changes. From the Properties box you can change the line's thickness and shading.

The shading of an HR rule takes on the color, or the variations on the color, of the background in Netscape Navigator. In Internet Explorer an HR line is always gray or whatever color has been set as the default background color for the browser. This color can be changed by adding a COLOR attribute using the HTML button on the Properties palette and adding the attribute to the Inside Element Tag. For more information on adding HTML to objects, see Chapter 11.

Adding a line

To draw a simple line on a page, select the Line: Draw tool from the Standard Tools menu. The cursor changes to a cross. Holding down the left mouse button and dragging draws a line from one point to the location where you release the mouse button. After you place the line, the Properties palette switches to Line Properties, which has a number of options available, enabling you to customize the line as shown in Figure 13-7.

Figure 13-7: The Line Properties palette.

The first option is the line width. Changing the value (the default is two pixels) increases or decreases the width of the line accordingly. Below the width box are three options for color: line, head, and tail. I'll get to head and tail in a moment, but for now, clicking the Line Color button lets you choose a color for the line from the standard color picker palette.

Clicking the All parts use one color checkbox automatically makes the line and any heads or tails added to the line the same color as the line color selected for the line.

Adding an arrow

In addition to thickness and colors, lines drawn using the Line: Draw tool can also have an arrow head and tail, which you can specify on the Properties palette after the line is drawn and selected. Head and tail arrowheads can be the same or another color as the line itself. The head and tail arrowheads can also be of different styles. A style for either a head or a tail is selected from the two drop-down lists on the Line properties palette. Figure 13-8 shows a blank page with a number of different line and arrow styles added.

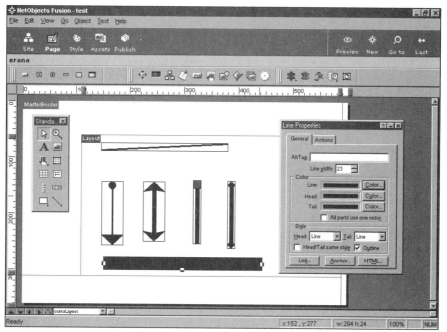

Figure 13-8: Some different line and arrow combinations created using the Line tool with head and tail options.

Because a line is considered a graphic object (as are all the shapes available with the Line tool), you can also define an Alt tag for a line on the Properties palette. A line can also act as a link—just click the Link button.

Note

By holding down the Shift key when drawing the line, it will be constrained to either 90 degrees (horizontal drawing) or 180 degrees (vertical drawing).

Adding a SiteStyle line

When selected, the Line: SiteStyle tool draws the LineStyle on the page from the currently active style (to see the active style, click the Style button on the icon bar). Apart from actions, which I explain in Chapter 19, you cannot apply any other attributes to a placed Line: SiteStyle.

Figure 13-9 shows the three different types of lines on a blank Web page. For the Line: SiteStyle I've used the ButtonedUp style (it looks like a zipper).

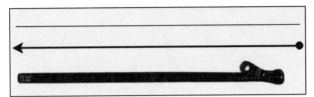

Figure 13-9: Three different Line Styles on a blank Web page.

Summary

✦ Fusion's Draw and Line tools are used to create rectangles, ellipses, polygons, lines, arrows, and rule lines.

✦ Draw objects can have their line and fill colors modified.

✦ Lines can use differing styles of arrowheads and tails, either of the HR type or the line type defined in the SiteStyle.

✦   ✦   ✦

Creating an Image Map

By now you should be familiar with using an image as
a link. Simply place the graphic at the location on
the Web page you want it, and use the Link button on the
Properties palette to define the link. But this method is only
good for defining one link per graphic. What if you want more
than one link within your graphic?

"When would I need that?" you ask.

Probably the most common use for multiple links is when you
place an image on a page, and where you click the image
dictates what link to what location is activated. Figure 14-1
shows an example of using an image in this way. Many Web
developers also use this method to define links on menu bars
where the graphic image is relevant to the style of the site.
An image used to hold several different links is called an
image map.

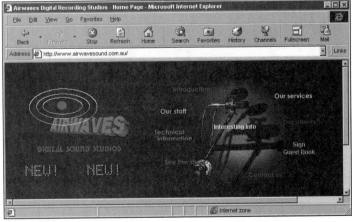

Figure 14-1: Clicking different sections of the microphone stand
image takes you to different Web pages in the site.

Using Image Maps as Navigation Controls

Like anything else, however, the best way to explain a concept is to demonstrate it. Consequently, to explain and show how to use an image map, place a map of the United States on the Branch Locations page of the Executive Performance Web site. After you've completed the image map, a visitor to the site can click the map in an area containing a link and be taken to a page describing the details of each individual location.

Adding the graphic

You can find the graphic you want to use on the CD-ROM enclosed with this book. Insert the CD-ROM into your CD-ROM drive and copy the USA.gif file, found in the Examples folder, to your hard drive. Then simply place this file on the page the same way you would place any other graphic image, using the Picture tool as shown in Figure 14-2.

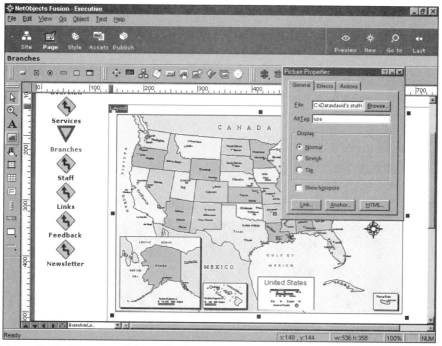

Figure 14-2: The map of the United States placed on the page.

It is now time to add the hotspots to the graphic. *Hotspots* are the regions placed on the graphic that will contain the links. The hotspots in conjunction with the graphic make up the image map.

Executive Performance has branches in Washington (West), North Dakota (North), and Ohio (East). In this example, separate Web pages for these regions were created when the site was originally mapped out (see Figure 14-3). (If you look at the site in Site view or open the Site Navigation window, you see three child pages off the Branches page.) After the image map is created for each region, clicking a region takes the visitor to the respective Web page.

The three branch Web pages

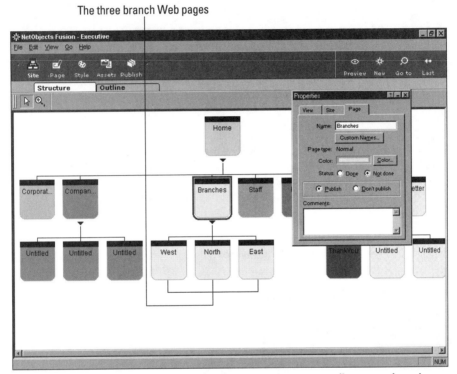

Figure 14-3: The site map showing the three pages corresponding to each region.

Adding rectangle hotspots

As mentioned earlier, a *hotspot* is defined as an area on the graphic that, when clicked, acts as an independent link to another Web page. This page may be either local or remote. (You can also activate cgi scripts from a hotspot, but that's another story. See Chapter 17 for more details on cgi scripts). The tools to define the image — known as hotspot tools — are located on the Standard toolbar, as shown in Figure 14-4. Three types of shapes can be defined as hotspot areas: rectangular, circular, and polygonal. For the first state in which Executive Performance has a branch operation, Washington, you need to draw a rectangular hotspot on the graphic and create the link to the West Web page.

Figure 14-4: The image map tools on the Standard toolbar.

To create the hotspot, select the rectangular hotspot tool (the far left tool on the Tools palette). To draw the perimeter of the link location, hold down the mouse button while drawing the size of the rectangle you require on the graphic. Figure 14-5 shows the rectangular area being drawn around Washington.

 — Rectangular hotspot   **Figure 14-5:** Drawing the rectangular hotspot around Washington.

When the area has been defined, the links dialog box automatically opens, enabling you to define the link. Links created using image maps can be of any type you have used previously: internal, smart, or external. For this hotspot the link will be internal, as the link will be to an existing page in the Web site.

The Washington link will join to the Web page called West. Select this page in the list and click the Link button to complete the operation. Figure 14-6 shows the page selected as the link in the Link dialog box.

Figure 14-6: Selecting the link destination for the Washington hotspot.

Once you have created the link, the area is shown by a border on the graphic image, as shown in Figure 14-7.

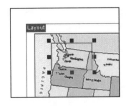

Figure 14-7: The completed hotspot area for Washington State.

Adding circular hotspots

If a circular hotspot area is required, the steps to create it are exactly the same as for a rectangular hotspot, except that you use the circular hotspot tool. Unlike many drawing tools in such programs as Micrografx Designer, Macromedia Freehand, or CorelDraw, you can't use any extra keys to constrain the dimensions of the circle. It cannot be changed into an ellipse, for example.

Adding polygonal hotspots

Creating irregular or polygonal hotspots, while technically the same as creating rectangular or elliptical ones, needs a little explaining due to the nature of the way in which Fusion draws the shape. You'll use the polygonal hotspot tool to draw the hotspot area for both North Dakota and Ohio.

When using the polygonal hotspot tool, instead of drawing the perimeter of the shape you are creating, the tool draws a succession of lines to create multisided objects. For example, the first line drawn creates a simple line. Clicking and drawing the second line forms a triangle, the third line a rectangle, the fourth a pentagon, and so on. When the entire shape has been defined, double-clicking the mouse button ends the drawing procedure. The Links dialog box opens, letting you define what link will be activated when a visitor to the site clicks the location of the hotspot on the graphic.

After you place a polygonal hotspot, you can reshape it to whatever physical dimensions you require, but you can't add any further points to the polygon. For example, once you have created a six-sided polygon, you cannot later edit it into a polygon of more or fewer sides. To do this, you must delete the existing polygon (by selecting it and pressing the Del key) and create a new hotspot. Deleting a hotspot also deletes its link information.

Figure 14-8 shows the irregular hotspot polygons in place for both North Dakota and Ohio.

 —Polygonal hotspot

Figure 14-8: The polygonal hotspots for North Dakota and Ohio in place on the graphic.

It is not necessary for the graphic you are using as the basis for the image map to be a standard .GIF or .JPG file. Animated .GIFs work just as well as image maps. If you have an artistic bent, you can use some wonderfully creative ways to create animated .GIF's that not only act as image maps but also, by their very animation, give visual feedback as to the sort of destination to which the visitor may be about to link.

Note Once a hotspot has been defined on a graphic, at any later time you can move it to a new location without losing the linking attributes of the hotspot. Select the polygonal area and drag it to the new location on the graphic. If needed, you can even copy and paste it onto another graphic using the Edit ➪ Copy and Edit ➪ Paste commands on the Edit menu.

Tip You can also define a hotspot as an anchor. After creating the hotspot, choose the Anchor button (after making sure the hotspot is selected) and enter a name for the hotspot's anchor.

Danger Zone Hotspots are a valuable tool in that they allow much greater use of graphics content on pages as links to other sections of a Web site. Be aware, however, that if a visitor is browsing with the image display facilities turned off, and there are no substitute navigation tools, such as a text Nav Bar, he or she will have no way of knowing how to see the rest of your site. This also applies to those site visitors, such as the visually impaired, using synthesizers to read the text of a Web page.

Summary

✦ Image maps are used to add multiple links to a graphic.

✦ Image map hotspots can be rectangular, circular, or polygonal in shape.

✦ Hotspots can be named anchors as well as links.

✦ Hotspots can be moved, copied, and pasted without losing their link definitions.

✦ Remember to allow text-navigation controls as well as image-map controls to a page.

✦   ✦   ✦

Working with Tables

When the HTML specification was revised to allow for the use of tables, all of us who were Web authors cheered mightily! At last we had some control over the location of elements on pages and spacing between those elements. Sure, the use of the dreaded ROWSPAN, COLSPAN, and other table commands made marking up elements in tables a laborious operation and very much a hit-and-miss affair, but at least they took away the bland-looking Web pages that pre-tables commands allowed us.

When Fusion appeared on the scene, however, all those long nights of hand coding went out the window because to create the same effects — or better — for elements on pages, nary a table command was in sight. Now, with Fusion, you just place the element where you want it. Easy!

Note

The current version of Fusion does not support splitting cells as per the ROWSPAN and COLSPAN commands in HTML. Having said that, the use of standard text boxes should solve this problem in most cases.

You may be wondering, "Do tables still have a place in Fusion? If so, where?" The answer is yes, but not in the same place they have been used in the past — to align objects or provide spacing. The standard tools supplied with Fusion do those things just fine.

When to Use Tables

If you need to use an object that is tabular in nature, such as that shown in Figure 15-1, tables are much easier to use than the standard text tools. You can also imaginatively use tables to create many other effects on pages that with other Fusion tools, while possible, would be time prohibitive.

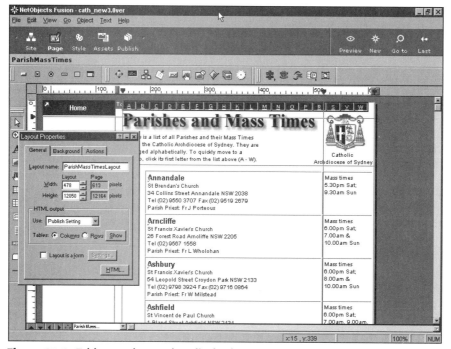

Figure 15-1: Tables can be used to display large amounts of text on a page.

Don't fall into the trap of using tables for everything, though, especially if you are comfortable with hand coding or have used other Web-authoring products that force you to use tables in areas where spacing and alignment are needed. As I mentioned at the start of this book, the single hardest thing about getting used to Fusion is getting out of the HTML mindset and into a publishing one. If you feel that a table is the only way to place a particular set of objects on a page (usually because this was the only way to do it in other products), think again about it. In many cases, using a table is the wrong approach, and Fusion provides better tools for the purpose you have in mind. In other words, tables in Fusion are used for tabular data and are *not* needed to gain spacing or alignment considerations.

Note

When I received my first copy of Fusion way back in version 1 days, I spent hours creating pages using tables for alignment, as I hadn't bothered to completely understand the Fusion paradigm. NetObjects support, which had been very patient with my tech support questions, finally and gently pointed out the error of my ways. It is without question the best support team in the world and never made me feel like a consummate goose—unlike other experiences I reckon we all have had.

Adding a New Table

To demonstrate how to add a table, we'll place one step by step. This table will show the opening times of the different branch locations of Executive Performance.

To add a table, select the Table tool from the Standard toolbar. Then draw the rough dimension of the table at the location on the page required, as shown in Figure 15-2.

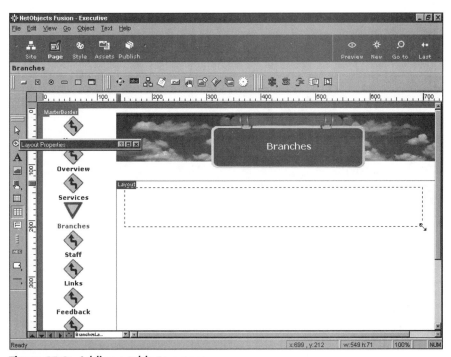

Figure 15-2: Adding a table to a page.

After you have drawn the dimensions of the table, the Create Table dialog box opens, requesting the number of rows and columns required for the table. For this table a column for each day of the week and one for the detail of the time blocks is required. Each day will be broken down into eight hourly segments. This means the table requires eight columns and eight rows, which you enter into the dialog box shown in Figure 15-3.

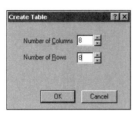

Figure 15-3: Set the size of the table in the Create Table dialog box.

After you click the OK button to close the dialog box, Fusion draws the table on the page and makes the Table Properties palette available, as shown in Figure 15-4.

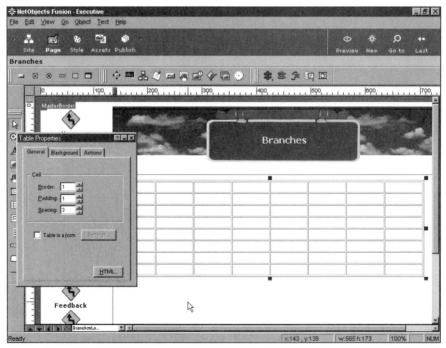

Figure 15-4: The table drawn on the page with its details showing in the Table Properties palette.

Entering Text in a Table

Except for the top row and left column, each of the cells in the table acts as a time block. When a block is colored, each of the branches is open at that time. When a block is clear, the branches are closed at that time. In this way a visitor to the Web site receives a quick visual indicator that is much easier to read than a figure- or time-based table. The first thing to do, therefore, is to add the header and side column text describing what each row or column describes.

Adding text to tables is as simple as double-clicking in a cell and typing. Fusion treats each cell in a table as an individual text block. Because of this, you can format text, assign text and background colors, and set alignments. There are also no restrictions to adding links and anchors to any text you add to a table cell.

Figure 15-5 shows the table with the text in the top row tiling each day of the week. To move from cell to cell when entering text, press the Tab key.

Unfortunately, you cannot choose multiple cells and apply formatting to these cells en masse. You must format each cell separately. While this may seem like a drawback, a little bit of the old lateral thinking soon makes you realize that this is a perfect place to use a style. After you enter the text, simply select the Edit Text Styles command from the Text menu, define the required style, and then attach it to each cell in the table.

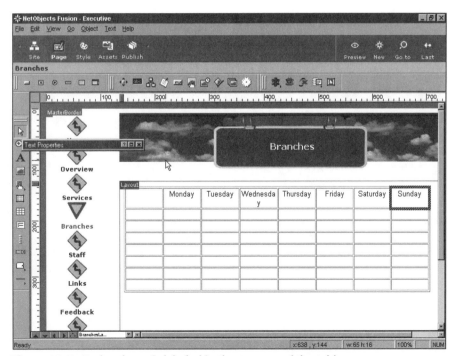

Figure 15-5: Each column is labeled in the top row of the table.

As you can see, the text is too wide for some of the cells and has wrapped to the next line in some cases. To circumvent this, you must select each cell (by double-clicking in it) and apply formatting to the text. Figure 15-6 shows the text formatted in Arial font in 8-point bold and centered in the cell.

Note

If you have defined a style for the correct sizing and alignment, this text wrap does not happen. Alternatively, you may want to format the first cell to see what properties are correct for the style and then create the style using these properties. You can then attach the style to the rest of the cells using the Style drop-down list on the Text Format palette of the Text Properties palette.

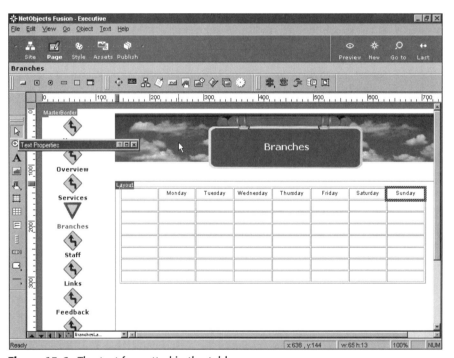

Figure 15-6: The text formatted in the table.

While applying formatting has worked for the majority of the cells, the cell for Wednesday is still too narrow. In this case you need to widen the column for Wednesday a fraction because the text is as small as you can make it.

Changing row and column sizes

To change a column width or row height, select the table (shown by black handles at each corner). There are two ways to select a table:

✦ Using the pointer tool, draw a rectangle (also known as a marquee) so that any part of it touches the table (but no other objects on the page).

✦ Using the pointer tool, click anywhere on the table and hold down the left mouse button for about a second (letting go of the mouse button immediately places you in insert mode for the cell you click).

Once the table is selected (shown in Figure 15-7), moving the mouse pointer over any cell border causes it to change into a double-headed arrow. When this occurs, you can click the border, hold down the mouse button, and drag the border to a new width or height. Figure 15-8 shows the widened border with *Wednesday* on one line.

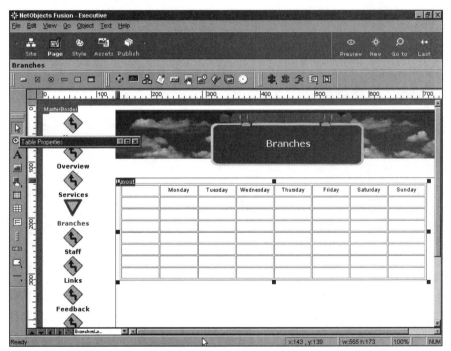

Figure 15-7: The table is selected, ready for the column containing Wednesday to be widened.

After you complete the days headings, you can add the times headings to the table's left-most column exactly the same way, as shown in Figure 15-9.

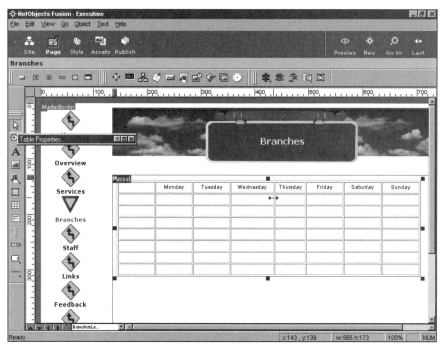

Figure 15-8: The table after the column is widened.

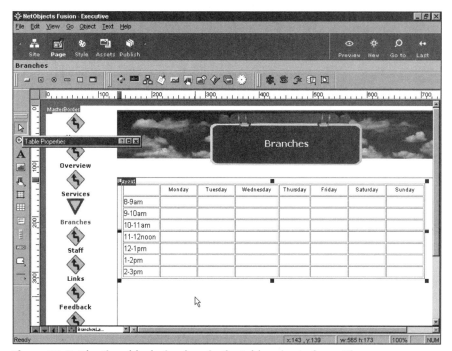

Figure 15-9: The time blocks in place in the table prior to formatting.

Adding rows and columns

As Figure 15-9 shows, the number of rows required has been miscalculated, and the table is two rows short. Thankfully, this is an easy problem to fix.

Right-clicking anywhere on a table pops up a menu with several commands specifically related to tables, as shown in Figure 15-10. When you choose the Add Row (or Add Column) commands from the pop-up menu, Fusion adds a new row directly below the currently selected row. With columns, the new column is added directly to the right of the currently selected column.

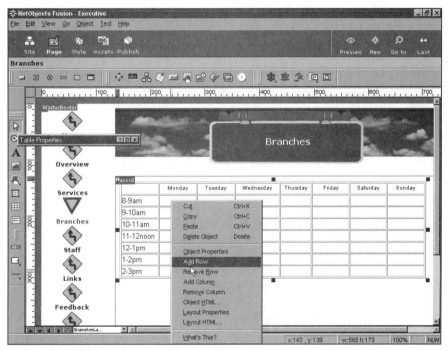

Figure 15-10: The Tables pop-up menu.

Adding two rows below the last row in the current table gives enough rows to complete adding the time blocks, which you can then format accordingly. Figure 15-11 shows how the table looks so far.

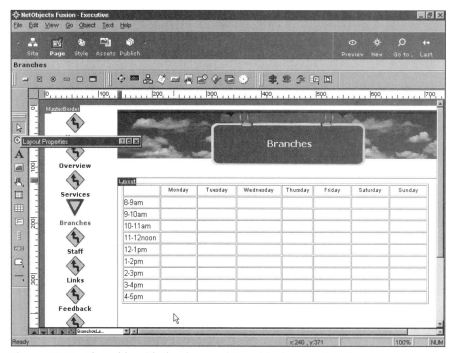

Figure 15-11: The table with the days and time blocks completed.

To delete rows or columns, place the cursor in the row or column to be deleted, right-click the mouse, and select the Remove Row or Remove Column option. The currently selected row (or column) will be deleted. Any elements you have in the cells of the row or column are also deleted, and Fusion gives no warning about this, so be careful when using these commands.

Changing background colors in cells

To distinguish between times the branches are open and closed, make these cells a different color. To do this, change the background cell color of those blocks signifying open times from the current default of white to dark blue.

To change the background of each cell that signifies the branch is open, double-click the cell. From the Text Box tab on the Properties palette, change the Background Color to a dark blue as shown in Figure 15-12.

As you may have noticed, there is also a Background color option on the Background tab of the Table Properties palette (see Figure 15-13). If you were to use this command instead, all the cells in the table would be filled with the color selected.

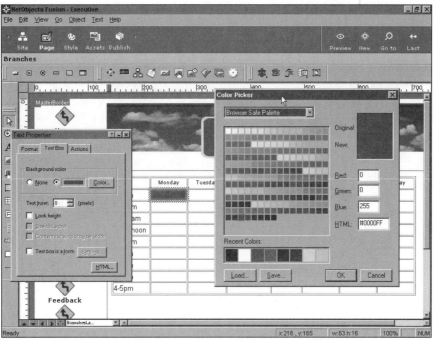

Figure 15-12: Changing the background fill color of an individual cell in a table.

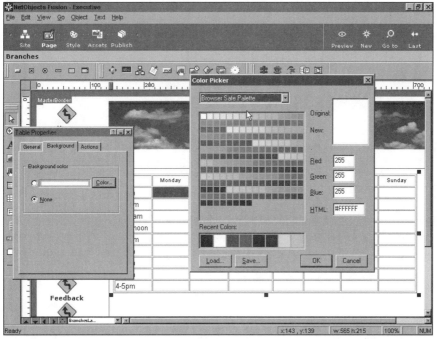

Figure 15-13: The Fill Background color command on the Table Properties palette.

Repeating these steps, you can now complete the rest of the cells in the table that require a color change. Figure 15-14 shows the completed table.

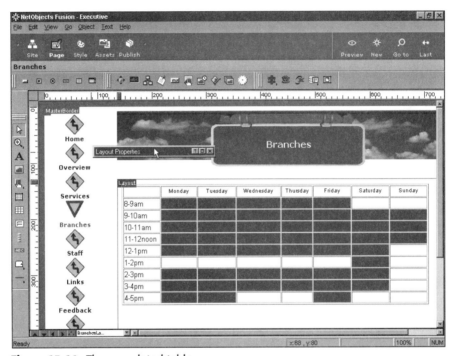

Figure 15-14: The completed table.

Before you leave tables, however, there is an important side aspect worth knowing. As I mentioned at the beginning of this book, the generated code Fusion creates for all pages in its default mode is heavily based on tables. This method achieves the pixel-level accuracy-of-element placement that Fusion is so good at mastering.

Some elements, when previewed or published, do not appear on the page exactly where they should. This problem appears to be a browser-dependent one — a page may appear perfect in Netscape Navigator but out of whack in Internet Explorer and vice versa.

You may have noticed that when the page layout is selected, on the Properties palette is an option for HTML output. This option determines how Fusion will publish the pages to the server. See Chapter 28 for more details. The available options are

✦ Publish Setting

✦ Nested Tables

✦ Regular Tables

✦ CSS and Layers

When either of the Nested Tables or Regular Tables options are selected (either here or in the Publish Setting mode of Fusion), the pages are created using tables for positioning. Listing 15-1 shows an example of the code Fusion creates for a nested tables page.

Listing 15-1: Fusion-created code for nested tables.

```
</TR>
  <TR VALIGN="top" ALIGN="left">
    <TD COLSPAN=9 HEIGHT =1></TD>
    <TD WIDTH=15 ROWSPAN=5><IMG id="Line5" HEIGHT=114 WIDTH=15
SRC="file:///C:/NetObjects Fusion 3.0/User
Sites/test/Preview/auto_generated_images/a_ArrowLine_1.gif"
BORDER=0 ></TD>
    <TD COLSPAN=4></TD>
  </TR>
  <TR VALIGN="top" ALIGN="left">
    <TD COLSPAN=9 HEIGHT =2></TD>
    <TD></TD>
    <TD WIDTH=15 COLSPAN=2 ROWSPAN=6><IMG id="Line7" HEIGHT=121
WIDTH=15 SRC="file:///C:/NetObjects Fusion 3.0/User
Sites/test/Preview/auto_generated_images/a_ArrowLine_2.gif"
BORDER=0 ></TD>
    <TD></TD>
  </TR>
```

Below the HTML Output list on the Properties palette you will also notice you can change the table orientation Fusion uses when creating the code from Rows to Columns. There is also a Show button that when clicked displays gray borders of the different table layouts on the page.

If you find you are having problems with object placement being shifted for no apparent reason when publishing or previewing, try changing the table orientation — assuming you are using this and not the CSS and Layers Publish option — from Row to Column or vice versa. In the majority of cases this will override the browser's insistence on placing the object where it wants it and places the object back where it belongs.

Defining Forms

A great use for tables (in my opinion) is for defining forms. A pet peeve of mine is seeing a Web page where the form elements (fields and such) don't line up properly. By defining a table as a form (click the option on the Properties palette after selecting the table), any form controls can be placed inside individual cells of the table, thus guaranteeing perfect lineup.

A simple table/form structure might be a two column table, with the cells in the left column containing the form field descriptions, and the cells in the right column containing the form field elements themselves.

Using a table is also a really neat way to color code forms on a Web page. For example, you may want to separate forms users fill out before downloading some software; the Windows forms could be color coded blue and the Macintosh forms red.

Tip

When using tables as the basis for a form, I recommend turning off the borders option and setting the spacing control to 0; otherwise, the form could look a little on the clunky side. You can use the padding option to space the elements of the form but continue to keep the continuity of the background color you have chosen.

Summary

✦ Tables are best used in Fusion for tabular text.

✦ Text in a cell can have any attribute normally applied, such as font styles, colors, and even links and anchors.

✦ Cells in tables can contain text or graphics.

✦ You can individually set background colors for cells in tables.

✦ You can change cell widths for a single row or column in a table but not individual cells.

✦ Fusion does not support the HTML COLSPAN and ROWSPAN commands.

✦ You can add rows and columns to a table.

✦   ✦   ✦

Working with Forms

Until now, all the elements you have added to a Web site have been *static*. In other words, with only one exception, these elements provide no interactivity — visitors to the site can do nothing but look at them. There is no feedback or any other visual indicator of anything happening when someone browses the site.

Note The exception is the mailto: link placed in the bottom MasterBorder, as mentioned in Chapter 11. You will remember that when this link is clicked, the Mail Client installed on the user's computer is started with the e-mail address of the recipient filled in automatically.

If you require feedback from visitors on the Web site — or perhaps, in the case of more sophisticated sites, you want the visitor to be able to fill out order forms, submit subscription information, and so on — a form is the way to go. Certainly you can use e-mail, but you have no guarantee you will receive all the information required, and it will definitely not be in an ordered format. Figure 16-1 shows a typical form on a Web page.

When Web pages were hand-coded in an editor, forms were the hardest parts to get just right. The HTML code necessary to define a form is confusing and convoluted, has to be exactly right, and is anything but fun to play with.

Fusion, on the other hand, makes adding a form to a Web site a simple point-and-click affair, allowing you to create even complex forms in minutes with only the minimum amount of coding.

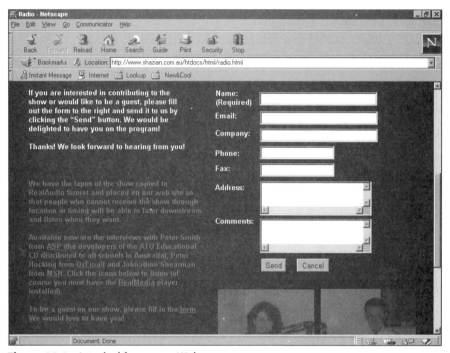

Figure 16-1: A typical form on a Web page.

Form Elements and Controls

A form *area* can contain the same element types as a Web page: text, graphics, multimedia, and so on. However, the elements of a form and the data they will contain when transmitted to the required destination — usually an e-mail address — are limited to special field types and controls available from the Form toolbar, as shown in Figure 16-2. These field types and controls include the following:

✦ Buttons

✦ Checkboxes

✦ Radio buttons

✦ Single-line text fields

✦ Multi-line text fields

✦ Combo boxes (drop-down lists)

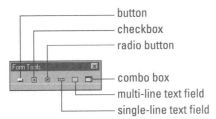

Figure 16-2: The Form toolbar.

You can place each of these elements on a Web page so that they are visible to the person filling out the form. You can also define components of the form that will transmit data but are invisible to the visitor to the page. This is useful when you want the form to place a specific subject name in the header of the resultant e-mail or to have the form copied (Cc) to a second recipient, for example. You can also use these *hidden fields* to specify the destination e-mail address of the form.

Finally, to control what the form does when the user clicks the control to send the information, Fusion has a special Settings section on the Properties palette. This section specifies the Perl or another cgi-based script that controls the form, the type of form, and other information.

CGI description

cgi stands for *Common Gateway Interface* and is the standard used for controlling forms. The way cgi is set up varies from Internet service provider to Internet service provider. Some have heavy restrictions on the use of cgi due to security worries, and others do not allow cgi scripting at all. For any form to work, cgi access must be available. If you have access to cgi, you will also have access to a folder on the WEB server called a cgi-bin, where all cgi scripts are held.

Perl is the most common language used for scripting. A discussion on Perl is beyond the scope of this book, but Appendix B contains details on reference material that will prove useful if you wish to learn the language.

Form area

Before you can define a form, you have to designate an area on a Web page as a *form area*. You can create such an area in many ways, most commonly by using the Layout Region tool on the Standard toolbar, which is shown in Figure 16-3. You can also designate an area with the Form Region tool by designating a table (as suggested in Chapter 15) or even a text block. You use the Form Region tool in this example.

Figure 16-3: The Form area tool on the Standard toolbar.

To create a form area, choose the Form Area tool from the Standard toolbar and define a rectangle on the Web page. A dialog box opens, as shown in Figure 16-4, requesting the type of form you require.

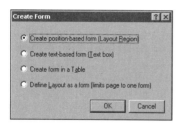

Figure 16-4: The Create Form dialog box.

For this exercise you will use a position-based (Layout Region) form. This form enables you to position the form's elements precisely on the page. Fusion also treats the Layout Region as a single entity, which lets you move the form as a single object on the page. A major benefit of this is that you can align all the form elements once and then move the entire form to a new location, if required, without laboriously realigning the elements.

If you had used the Layout Region tool instead of the Form Region tool, you would have bypassed the dialog box asking which type of Form you wanted.

If you select the fourth option in the Create Form dialog box (Define Layout as a form), you can define only one form per Web page.

When you have selected the option for the form area in the dialog box, click the OK button and the form area appears on the page. You can resize the form area at any time by dragging its handles to new locations.

Forms Edit Fields

The most common form control/field is the text field, which is similar in concept to those fields used to receive and store information in database products such as Access or Approach. Fusion calls a single-line text field on a form a *Forms Edit Field*. Forms Edit Fields are only a single line, so if you require more than one line of information for data entry, you need to use a multi-line field. Figure 16-5 shows a standard text field.

Figure 16-5: A single-line Forms Edit Field (text field).

Text fields must follow a naming convention expected by the cgi script controlling the form. For example, in the form to be added to the Executive Performance Web site, certain text fields are required on the form for it to work. These fields must exist on the form or as hidden fields (see later in this chapter for details on hidden fields) and include from, to, and subject fields.

You can define a default value for a text field. This is sometimes useful when a description of the information expected may help the person filling out the form see exactly what the field should contain. For example, for a text field in which the required content is a person's first name, the default value could be Enter Your First Name Here. The text you want to appear as the default text is entered into the Text box on the Edit Field Properties palette.

Text fields also contain two values to define their physical structure. The first value is the length of the field: the maximum number of characters a person entering data can type into the field. The second value is the maximum visible length of the field: the physical length of the field shown on the form when it is displayed in a Web browser.

Tip

Call me parochial, but when creating forms, think beyond the obvious when it comes to Edit Field lengths. I have lost track of the number of times State/Province fields only have two characters available, or a telephone number field has the U.S.-oriented 555-555-5555 format. Neither of these two types of fields is applicable in Australia, for example, which has three-character state abbreviations and, allowing for the country code, up to 11 digits for a phone number.

Multi-Line fields

The second type of field or control that can be placed on a form is the multi-line field that Fusion calls a *Forms Multi-Line Field*. All the considerations that apply to a text field also apply to a multi-line field, with the exception of the addition of a line height value. Figure 16-6 shows a typical multi-line field.

Figure 16-6: A Forms Multi-Line Field.

Note

When a multi-line field is defined, scroll bars are also created when the field is displayed in a Web browser. Because of this, if the aesthetics of the form are critical, some experimentation with the width and height values may be needed to make a multi-line field line up with other form elements.

Danger Zone

Be aware that Netscape Navigator and Microsoft Internet Explorer display form fields differently, especially multi-line fields. Figure 16-7 shows the same form displayed in Internet Explorer and Netscape Navigator.

Multi-line fields

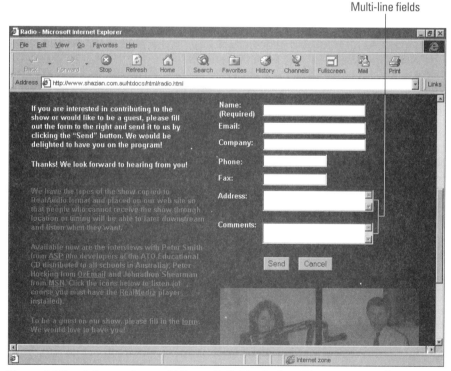

Figure 16-7a: A form using multi-line edit fields displayed in Internet Explorer.

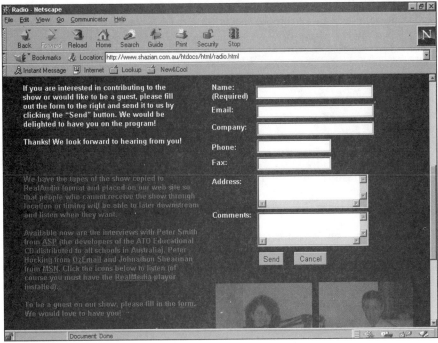

Figure 16-7b: The same form displayed in Netscape Navigator.

Checkboxes

Checkboxes, which are toggle fields, are used to display a yes/no value for a single field. Figure 16-8 shows an example of a checkbox. A checkbox appears on the form in a Web browser as a small square. When clicked once, the square contains a check; a second click will remove the check.

Please click any equipment you are interested in:	☐ Air Compressors	☐ Compaction
	☐ Concrete / Masonry	☐ Loaders/Forklifts/Bobcats
	☐ Electrical Tools	☐ Generators / Lighting
	☐ Access Equipment	☐ Booms / Lifts
	☐ Pumps	☐ Welding Equipment
	☐ Portable Toilets	☐ Portable Buildings
	☐ Containers	☐ General Equipment

Figure 16-8: A form using the checkbox control.

Checkboxes can have attributes applied to send whatever value the developer requires for either state of the checkbox (ON or OFF). An example might be Send Monthly Newsletter when the state of the checkbox is ON (checked).

Tip

Unlike earlier versions of Fusion, the checkbox name does not become an automatic label that appears on the page. A label for the checkbox field must be created manually.

Radio buttons

Radio buttons are similar in operation to checkboxes in that they also show a toggle (ON/OFF) effect. The difference is that a checkbox is a stand-alone field, whereas radio buttons are defined in groups. In any one group, only one of the radio buttons can be in the ON state.

If a radio button is clicked, it is turned on. If another radio button in the group is subsequently clicked, the first is automatically turned off, and the latest radio button clicked is turned on. This makes radio buttons useful for multiple choice questions on forms, such as defining an age group or location, as shown in Figure 16-9.

	○ NSW	○ VIC	○ ACT	○ QLD
Select your location:	○ WA	○ SA	○ TAS	○ NT
	○ Indonesia		○ Other	

Figure 16-9: Radio buttons in use on a form.

Once again, the developer can define what values are sent when the form is transmitted from individual radio buttons, depending upon their state. For example, a radio button group called Age Group might have three buttons in the group. The value sent if the first radio button is clicked might be 18-24; the second, 25-40; and the third, 40+.

Danger
Zone

When creating a series of radio buttons, it is imperative that you make sure all the radio buttons have the same Group name. If not, you may have *orphan* radio buttons that will be independent of the main group.

Combo boxes

Combo boxes enable the user to select a single value from a predefined set of values. Combo boxes can be displayed either as drop-down lists with scroll bars, or from a rotating list using spinner controls. Figure 16-10 shows both types of combo boxes.

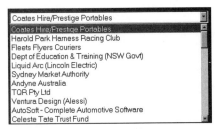

Figure 16-10a: A combo box using a drop-down list.

Figure 16-10b: A combo box using spinner controls.

The developer can easily define the default value for a combo box and has the option of restricting the person filling out the form to a constrained list. You can also let the visitor enter his or her own value. One example of letting the visitor enter his or her own value is when a list of common countries is displayed in a combo box, but the visitor to the Web site is from a country not available in the list. He or she can then manually enter that country, provided the developer included this option.

Buttons

Buttons primarily enable the person filling out the form to send the form or cancel it. When a button is placed on the form, it is displayed as a standard Windows or Macintosh button, with its name applied as its title (shown in Figure 16-11.)

Figure 16-11: Send and Cancel buttons on a form.

Buttons are defined as one of two types: Submit or Reset. When a user clicks a Submit button, it transmits the contents of the fields in the form to the e-mail destination nominated in the Hidden Fields section or defined in the underlying Perl script defined in the Settings section. A Reset button does as its name implies — it resets all data input information in the fields on the current form to null, thus allowing the user to start over.

Note

In addition to using standard buttons, it is also possible to nominate any graphics image on a form as a Submit button in Fusion.

Hidden fields

Hidden fields are placed as a part of the structure of the form using the Forms Settings dialog box (shown in Figure 16-12). Common uses for hidden fields include the destination e-mail address, the subject of the message, and sometimes a nomination of which Web page the form came from, which is useful for a quick statistics check if a Web site has many forms on it.

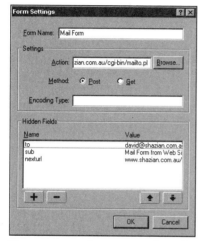

Figure 16-12: The Form Settings dialog box showing some typical hidden fields and settings.

Form settings

The Settings section of the Form Settings dialog box, shown in Figure 16-12, specifies the specific cgi script to be used for the form. You can also name a form, which is optional. Naming a form is useful if you are also using other scripting languages such as JavaScript or VBScript and want to physically reference the form in a script. To access the Settings section of a form, the Form area must be selected. The Settings button will then appear on the Properties palette.

In this context, *script* is defined as code written using Perl, JavaScript, or VBScript. It should not be confused with Fusion scripts, which are sections of HTML code that the Web developer applies to objects on a Web page using the HTML button on the Properties palette.

Now that all the components of a form have been identified, here's a brief overview of how everything comes together to get a form and its contents from the Web browser to the destination to which it is intended. In the settings section, a script — most commonly one written in the Perl language — is nominated as the controller of the form. This script contains all the coding that dictates how a form and its contents are processed.

When the site visitor clicks the Submit button on a form, control is passed to this script. (The location of the script is usually the contents of the Action field on the Settings properties palette). If the script to control the form is on your local hard disk, the File section specifies this script file location. This way, Fusion can successfully access the script and move it to the remote Web server at publishing time. If, however, the script controlling your form is located on a Web server (for example, you may be using a script your Internet service provider makes available to all users), the Action field will contain the location of the cgi script on the Web server.

To explain further, here's a simple example. Say you have a form on a Web page with two Forms Edit fields. One field expects data to be a person's name, and the second, the person's e-mail address. You have obtained a generic Perl script called `mailto.pl` that will process this form and send it as an e-mail message to a nominated destination.

In this example, in addition to the two Forms Edit fields on the Web page, you would also have at least one hidden field in the Settings section. The hidden field would be called "To," in which the destination e-mail address would be defined. In the Actions field on the Settings properties palette would be entered the full path name to the Perl script — for example, **www.shazian.com.au/htdcos/cgi-bin/ mailto.pl**.

When the visitor to the site clicks the Submit button (after filling out the two fields making up the form), the `mailto.pl` Perl script "grabs" the data in the two fields and sends it as e-mail to the target specified in the Hidden field containing the destination e-mail address.

The key to all of this is the Perl script. This example is very simple, of course, and in actual practice the Perl script would probably check such things as whether the two Forms Edit fields contained data and whether the e-mail Forms Edit field contained a valid e-mail address format.

Forms can be one of two types: Post or Get. Loosely, a *Post* form is primarily used for feedback styles of forms such as will be designed for the Executive Autos Web site. A *Get* type, on the other hand, is mainly used for higher-level scripting applications in such areas as search engines, online shopping systems, and so on.

The final field in the Setting dialog box is for an encoding type. This special field attaches a MIME type (like text/HTML) to the data sent to the server and is used based on the specific cgi's requirements. This field is rarely used, and in the majority of forms placed on Web pages, the Settings section can be left blank.

Creating a Feedback Form

The best way to get the feel of forms is to create one. On the Executive Performance Web page, a special page has been set aside for the form called the *Feedback page*, as shown in Figure 16-13. In addition, a second page, acting as a child of the Feedback page, was also created — the *Thank You page* (see Figure 16-14). After the person visiting the site has filled out the form and clicked the Send button, he or she is taken to the Thank You page, which gives him or her visual feedback that the form was successfully sent.

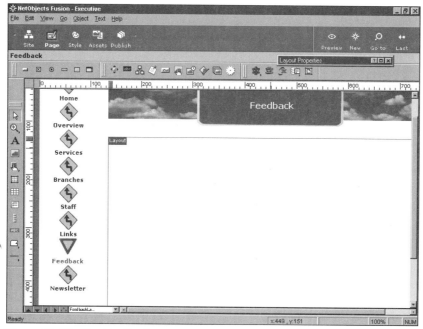

Figure 16-13: The Feedback page.

If the user makes an error — for example, if he or she doesn't fill out one of the mandatory fields expected by the Perl script — the script can generate an error page, allowing the user to backtrack and correct the error.

The form will contain a mixture of all the form controls allowed, which include the following:

✦ Text fields for Name, E-mail Address, and Company Name

✦ A multi-line text field for Comments

✦ A combo box for Position

✦ A radio button for Gender

✦ A checkbox for whether the user would like to be added to the mailing list

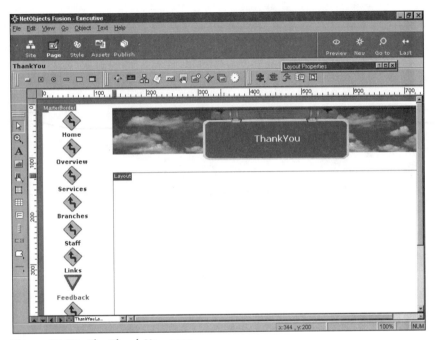

Figure 16-14: The Thank You page.

Adding a form area

As you will remember, before you can place a form on a page, you must define a Form Area. The quickest way to do this is with the Layout Region tool. You can also define a Form Area using the Form Area tool. Using the Form Area tool, a dialog box opens, asking you whether the form area is to be a region, table, or text box (see Figure 16-4). By directly using the Layout Region tool and checking the Layout Region is a form checkbox on the Properties palette, you can bypass this dialog box.

Adding a text field

The first field you will add is a text field that enables the person filling out the form to enter his or her name. Select the Forms Edit Field tool on the Forms toolbar.

Tip

If the Forms toolbar is not visible, select its option from the View ➪ Toolbars command on the menu bar.

Add the field to the page the same way as with any other tool—simply drag the mouse pointer inside the Layout Region you previously defined and where you roughly want to place the field, as shown in Figure 16-15.

Danger Zone

Make sure the form element you are placing lies inside the fuzzy blue line defining the Form Region. If the form element isn't inside the region, the form element—field, checkbox, combo box, and so on—will display a red exclamation mark.

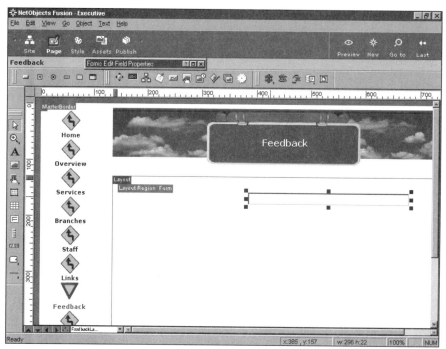

Figure 16-15: Adding a Forms Edit field.

Danger Zone

If the field is not created inside the Layout Region defined earlier, Fusion generates a warning message.

The actual length of the field is relevant. Fusion will make the field as long as the dimension you draw it, but you can later modify this value on the Forms Edit Field Properties palette. The field is always only one line in height, however.

Convention varies as to how many characters you should use for a Name field. I consider a length of 30 characters to be more than enough. Visibly—in other words, the length of field that appears on the screen in the Web browser—I personally believe that 20 characters is quite adequate.

At this time on the Properties palette it is also necessary to name the field. Fusion gives each field a default name, but more than likely the script to control a form expects something different.

If the script that controls the form uses this field, the name *must* be exactly the same as the script expects it to be. For example, the Perl script that will control this form requires a field called `from`, which will be applied to the e-mail address of the sender field. The Name field you have just added is not mandatory for the script and therefore can have any name you like.

Danger Zone

This convention applies to *only* the particular script you will be using for this form. Other scripts will most certainly require other naming conventions for the fields you place on the form. If you don't know the names required for a particular script, contact the developer of the script for this information. The generic script you are using for this form will suffice for the majority of simple forms, and it is freely available from `www.frostbyte.com.au/`. The script is called `mailto.pl`. A variation on this script (also called `mailto.pl`) is available from my server at `www.shazian.com.au/cgi-bin/mailto.pl`.

Finally, the Text box on the Properties palette for the field allows you to type the default text for the field. When the page is displayed in the Web browser, the text entered into this box is displayed in the field. The person filling out the form can then overtype this text. For a Name field, such text might be

```
Please type your full name here
```

If you want to prevent others from reading information "over the shoulder" when a visitor to your site is entering information into a Text field, clicking the Password field checkbox forces the Web browser to display asterisks in the field when information is being typed into it.

Field descriptions

Although you have named the field and placed it on the form in the location required, it is not immediately obvious what this field is for because the name of the field does not appear on the Web page. To allow the person filling the form out to fully understand what data is expected, you must create a simple text box with the name of the field in it. You then place this text box at a location where the user can identify the data to be entered into the field. Figure 16-16 shows the Name text field completed with all the parameters entered into the Properties palette, as well as a descriptive name created next to the field on the page, identifying its purpose.

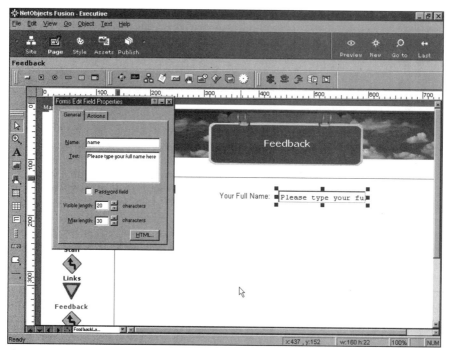

Figure 16-16: The completed Forms Edit Field and its Properties palette.

Creating other text fields

One nice thing about Fusion is that it allows you to be a little lazy! Instead of going through all the previous steps to create the other two text fields (for e-mail and company name), you can instead copy these fields and then simply rename the appropriate sections on the Properties palette.

To do this, you can use the standard multiple-select method (by holding down the Shift key and clicking both the text-descriptive field and the text field), select Copy, and then paste the contents of the Clipboard back to the page. A faster method is to Shift-click both the descriptive and the text field to select them all and, once selected, hold the Ctrl key and drag these two fields to a new location on the Web page. The result is a duplicate of the existing fields that you can then rename and have their attributes changed on the Properties palette. To create the two new text fields for the e-mail address and the company name, you need to do this twice.

Figure 16-17 shows the Name field duplicated on the Web page to create the E-mail field and the Company Name field.

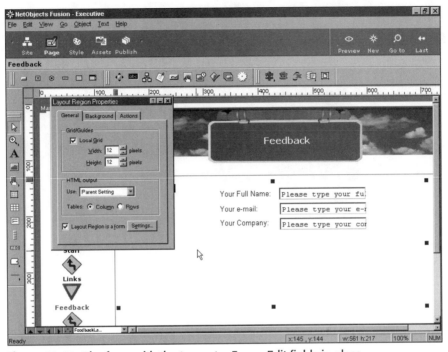

Figure 16-17: The form with the two extra Forms Edit fields in place.

Note

Remember that the Perl script to be used for this Feedback form requires the e-mail field to be called *from*. The company name field can have any name you want.

Adding a combo box field

The next field needed on the form is one allowing the person filling out the form to select or enter his or her job description or position with the company that employs them. The best type of field for this is a combo box field.

To add a combo box field, select the Combo Box tool from the Tools palette and draw the location of the field on the page at the approximate location required. Figure 16-18 shows the basic combo box added to the page.

The default height for a combo box field is five lines, and the Properties palette (shown in Figure 16-18) enables you to enter several default values by clicking the plus (+) key and typing the text of the entries that can be selected. The first field in the dialog box is the label that will be displayed on the Web page when the list is selected. The second field is the value that will actually be sent as part of the feedback form to the destination designated in the Perl script (the *to* field that will be defined later in the Hidden fields section).

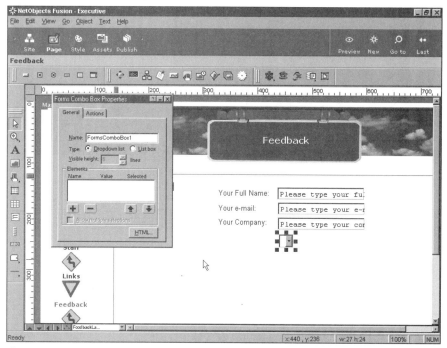

Figure 16-18: The combo box added to the Layout Region.

Figure 16-19 illustrates an example of entering one of the values (in this case, **Manager**) for the combo box list. In this case both the displayed value and the sent value will be one and the same.

Note The actual width of a combo box on the Web page is determined by the width of the largest entry in the list you define for it.

If you want the entry you have created to be the default entry, make sure you check the Selected by Default checkbox. Similarly, if in this field it is useful to allow the person filling out the form to choose multiple selections, you need to check the Allow Multiple Selections checkbox.

Danger Zone Multiple selections can be applied *only* to combo boxes set as list boxes. Multiple selections cannot be applied to drop-down lists.

If after making an entry into the list you decide this is not an option you need or is not applicable to this list, you can remove the entry by selecting the entry on the Properties palette and clicking the minus (–) button.

Finally, to change the order of entries you have created, selecting any single entry followed by clicking the up or down arrow buttons on the Properties palette moves that entry in the direction of the arrow in relation to the other items in the list.

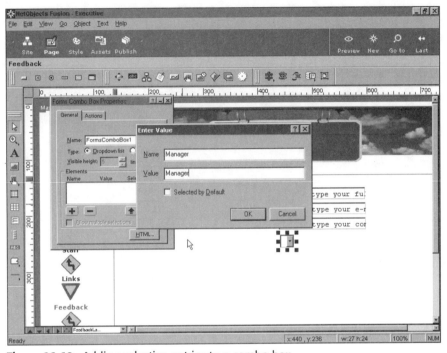

Figure 16-19: Adding selective entries to a combo box.

Figure 16-20 shows the completed list for this field in the Properties palette, and Figure 16-21 displays the Web page in the browser with its drop-down list in place. Notice that the width of the largest size entry in the list automatically dictates the width of the field.

Figure 16-20: The completed list for the combo box.

If a drop-down list, rather a spinner list, more suits your taste or the style of the page, click the radio button on the Properties palette for this option. (The default combo box style is list box, where spinner controls are used to select a value.)

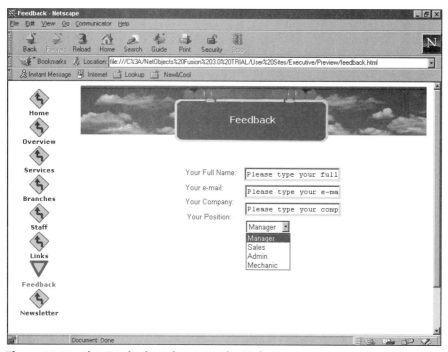

Figure 16-21: The Combo box shown on the Web page.

Adding a radio button field

The next field to be added is a radio button field, allowing the person filling out the form to select his or her gender. In this case two fields are needed: one for each gender type. To ensure that the site visitor can select only one radio button, you need to assign the same Group Name to the two radio buttons you place on the page.

Once you have selected the radio button tool from the Forms toolbar and placed it on the page, as shown in Figure 16-22, the Properties palette changes and shows the Forms Radio Button Properties. The first field on the Properties tab that you need to specify is the Group Name. The Group Name is an arbitrary title that has no other significance other than to describe the title of the single field (which applies to any number of radio buttons) sent to the form's destination. In other words, although, for example, you may have eight different radio buttons, all with different labels, the value sent is the Group Name along with the text placed in the Value Sent field of the radio button that the user has checked.

If this sounds a little confusing, all will be revealed! Figure 16-23 shows the settings for the second radio button. Figure 16-24 shows the two buttons, complete with the text label in place to their right.

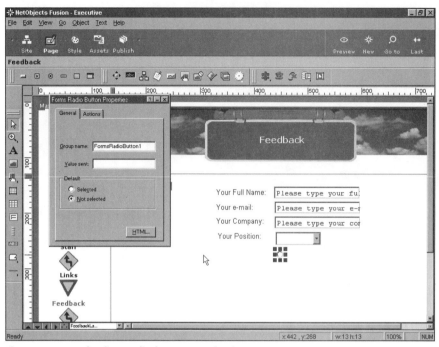

Figure 16-22: The first radio button on the form.

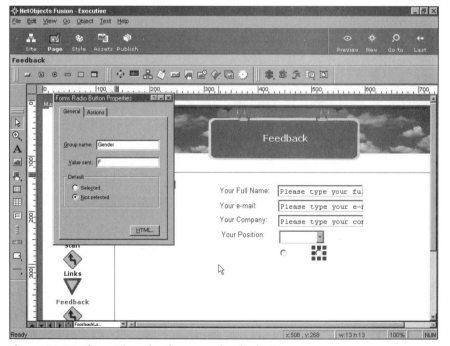

Figure 16-23: The settings for the second radio button.

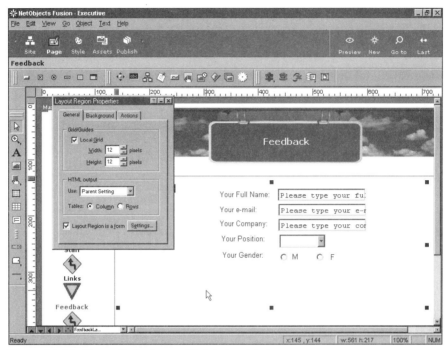

Figure 16-24: The radio buttons with labels added.

Note

Fusion does not supply any text labels for radio buttons (or checkboxes). To supply a label so that the person filling out the form knows the reason for the radio buttons (or checkbox), simply place a text label next to the radio button.

Adding a checkbox field

Unlike a radio button, a checkbox field is a standalone feature. You can add any number of checkboxes to a form, and the individual values for each checkbox are sent when the form is transmitted to the recipient.

Note

A series of checkboxes is useful when you have a sequence of questions that do not lend themselves to a single answer (as with radio buttons). For example, a form may ask for feedback on what magazines you read and allow you to choose a series. Radio buttons, on the other hand, allow you to answer only one question out of a series.

A checkbox is added in exactly the same way as a radio button. Choose the Forms Checkbox tool from the Forms toolbar and draw the checkbox at the location required.

On the Executive Performance Feedback form, a checkbox will be useful to ask people whether they object to having unsolicited mailings sent to them. If they check the box, this means they wish to receive information.

Figure 16-25 shows the basic checkbox after being added to the form with the checkbox tool from the Forms toolbar. Notice the settings in the Properties palette, in particular that the default value sent if the box is left *unchecked* is No.

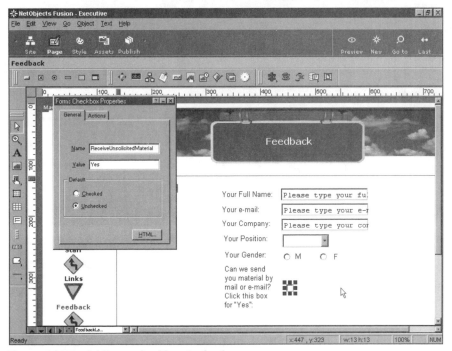

Figure 16-25: Adding a checkbox to the form.

Adding a multi-line field

The last field you need to add is a multi-line field allowing people filling out the form to send any comments they wish. Adding a multi-line field is similar to adding the text field. The only difference (as you can see in Figure 16-26) is that the Visible height section on the Forms Multi-Line Properties palette sets the number of lines visible in the field on the form. In real terms, however, the number of lines the user can type is unlimited. The Visible Height section only defines how many lines will be seen on the form.

Note   Unlike earlier versions of Fusion, in version 3, with a multi-line field, text entered automatically wraps to the next line.

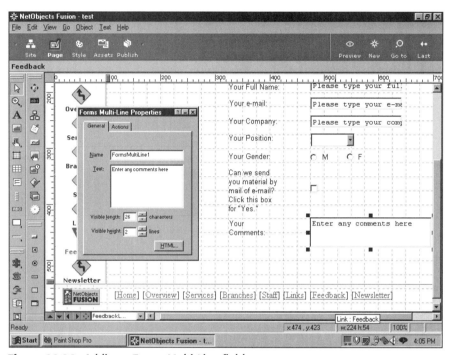

Figure 16-26: Adding a Forms Multi-Line field.

Also, as mentioned, be aware that due to aesthetics, some adjustment may be needed to make a multi-line field line up correctly with the rest of the fields due to the addition of the vertical and horizontal scroll bars. Also remember that Netscape Navigator and Microsoft Internet Explorer display these particular types of fields differently.

Adding Submit and Reset buttons

To complete the form you need to add two buttons. The first is a Submit button, which confirms that the user wants the form sent to the recipient defined in the Perl script—as set in the Hidden Fields section (I'm getting to that, I promise!) The second button is a Reset button, which lets the user cancel his or her input, clear all fields, and start over.

The Submit button is the most important one. You place it by selecting the Button tool on the Forms toolbar and setting the appropriate controls for it. Figure 16-27 shows the button placed on the form and the settings on the Properties palette for a Send button.

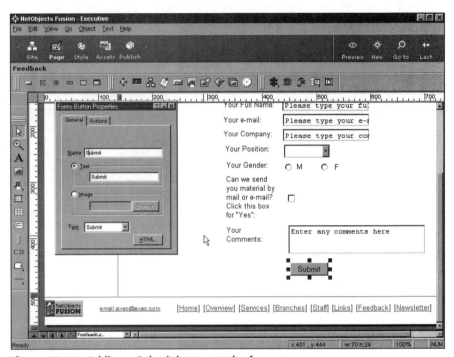

Figure 16-27: Adding a Submit button to the form.

Figure 16-28 shows the same settings for the Reset button. The only difference between the two is the Type field on the Forms Button Properties palette. The Submit button is set to Submit and the Reset button to Reset. While this may seem obvious, bear in mind the names of the buttons that appear inside the button on the page can be anything you like. In this case, for example, you may choose to call the buttons "Send" and "Cancel," respectively.

Tip

The width of the actual buttons on the page is determined by the length of the value you supply as the Text name of the button on the Forms Button Properties palette. The longer the name, the wider the button.

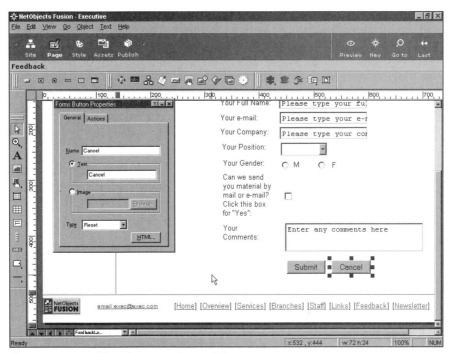

Figure 16-28: Adding the Reset (Cancel) button.

If you want to use an image in place of the standard Windows buttons, clicking the Image radio button lets you choose an image file to replace the button via the Browse button associated with it. All other parameters still apply.

Inserting hidden fields

The Perl script that invokes the action for this form requires several standard *fields* in order to work correctly. These are either fields on the form or hidden fields named as follows:

- ✦ to
- ✦ from
- ✦ subject

In the body of the form you already have a from field (the e-mail address of the sender), so the remainder of the fields need to be added as hidden fields. This process resembles adding the selectable lines in the combo box you created earlier.

After selecting the Form Region, clicking the Settings button on the Properties palette opens the Forms Settings dialog box, which lets you add the required hidden fields. See Figure 16-29.

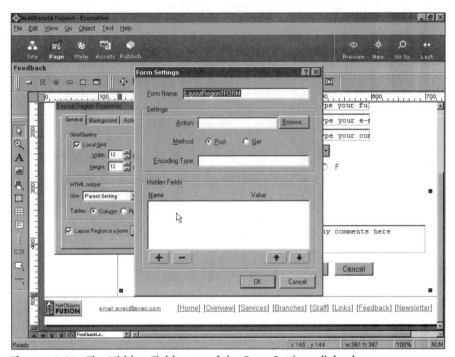

Figure 16-29: The Hidden Fields area of the Form Settings dialog box.

As before, when adding the lines to the combo box field, clicking the plus (+) sign lets you add a new hidden field, as shown in Figure 16-30. The first value in the Enter Value dialog box that opens is the name of the hidden field. The second value is sent to the recipient of the form (the person specified in the from field).

In the example shown, the name of the field is to and the value to be sent is david@ shazian.com.au. This e-mail address is where the contents of the form (consisting of an e-mail message comprising the field name, a tab, and the contents of the field followed by a carriage return) are sent.

Figure 16-31 shows the Hidden Fields settings completed with the to field, the subject field, and an optional nexturl field added. The nexturl field contains the URL of the page next displayed in the browser of the person filling out the form, after he or she has clicked the Submit button. (In this case, as you might guess, this page is the Thank You page.)

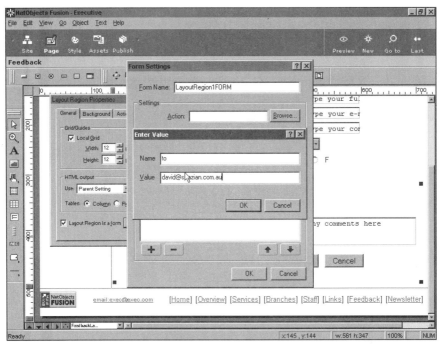

Figure 16-30: Adding hidden fields.

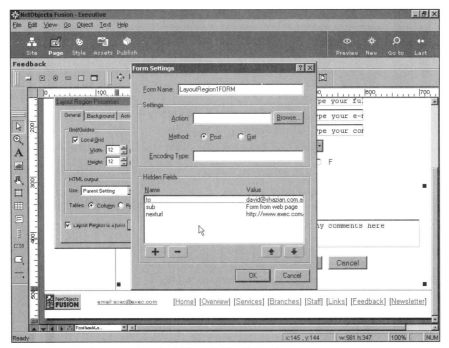

Figure 16-31: The completed Hidden Fields dialog box.

Note These hidden fields are required by the particular Perl script you are using to process this form. Other Perl scripts probably can and do require different parameters or fields. If the Perl script is of a generic nature, and many are available free of charge from the Internet (see Appendix B for details of locations of these scripts), check the documentation supplied to see which one you need to use.

Examples of differences include where multiple destinations are allowed or where processing depends on the data entered. For example, the Perl script driving the form at `www.coates.com.au/html/contact-us.html` checks the State field and directs the e-mail to the Branch Office in that state.

Adjusting the settings

The final step in creating a feedback form is to adjust the settings. In the form you are using here—allied with the type of Perl script to be used for this form—adjusting the settings is an easy step. You just need to place the URL of the Perl script that will process the form in the Action field (accessed after clicking the Settings button—select any field on the form). To make this easy, I have placed such a script on the server, found at `www.shazian.com.au/cgi-bin/mailto.pl`.

To complete this form, simply place this URL in the Action section. Even if your Internet service provider does not support Perl scripting, you will be able to use NetObjects Fusion to create feedback forms, or any other sort of mailto: style of form for that matter!

Figure 16-32 shows the correct settings for the Settings dialog box for this form and the associated Perl script.

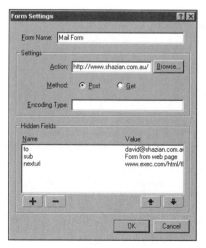

Figure 16-32: The Settings section showing the location of the Perl script that will activate the form when the Submit button is clicked.

Viewing the completed form

Figure 16-33 shows the completed form displayed in Netscape Navigator. If you have followed the instructions correctly, even though you may not have direct access to cgi and scripting capability, the `mailto.pl` script allows you to place forms on your sites that let you incorporate an e-mail feedback capability. This script was created by Steve Frost (`www.frostbyte.com.au`) and generously made available for this book. His Web site contains several other scripts that may prove useful for sites you develop. It is well worth a visit. Tell him I sent you.

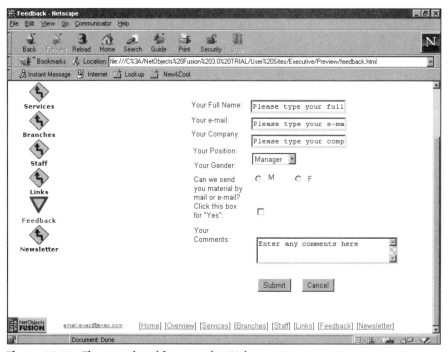

Figure 16-33: The completed form on the Web page.

The nexturl parameter

An optional Hidden Field is the `nexturl` field. The Perl script you are using uses this parameter to tell the browser the location of the next Web page to load (URL) after the Submit button is clicked and the form processed.

Call it a copout if you will, but this field is up to you. If you did not do so in earlier chapters, simply create a child page off the forms page. This page is then referenced by the `nexturl` parameter of the script placed as a hidden field. Figure 16-34 shows a standard example of a Thank You page.

Note

When published, the Thank You page will be placed in the html folder on the server. Due to this, the full URL of the page is required by the `nexturl` parameter. If, for example, this page was being published to `www.shazian.com.au`, the full URL for the Thank You page would be `www.shazian.com.au/html/thankyou.html`.

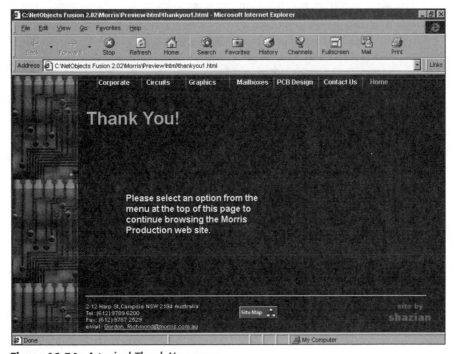

Figure 16-34: A typical Thank You page.

More Info

Forms are simple to set up. The feedback form developed here is the most basic sort of form, using a simple but effective Perl script. Before creating forms, no matter what the complexity, check the documentation of the script (or if developing it yourself, test, test and test again) to make sure it does what you want. Again, check Appendix B of this book to find resources for scripts you can use. You may also want to leap ahead and have a look at the Forms handler component (accessible off the Components toolbar) in Chapter 25.

Summary

✦ Forms are used to gain feedback, perform actions, or manage other interactive aspects of a Web site.

✦ Forms are controlled in their actions by scripts.

✦ The most common scripting language is Perl.

✦ The basic elements of a form are single line and multi-line text fields, combo boxes, radio buttons, checkboxes, and buttons.

✦   ✦   ✦

Using Scripts

As I have stated before, for the most part you do not need to have an understanding of the hypertext markup language (HTML) to use NetObjects Fusion. Fusion's Standard tools take care of the HTML for almost any element you want to add to your Web site, no matter whether you want to add text, images, sound, video, animation, Java applets, or ActiveX components.

Notice that I said *almost* any element.

Note

As powerful as Fusion is, some elements you might want to include may need to use a small snippet of raw HTML code to make them work or look or act just the way you want them to on your Web page. Adding some exotic Rich Media objects, for example, requires special code. See Chapter 22 for examples of special scripts required to embed RealAudio players in a page.

Many situations that can use scripting are normally not necessary for the average Web site, with the possible exception of adding Meta tags (see "Adding Meta Tags" later in this chapter for more information regarding Meta tags).

The advent of the newer technologies that have broadened what is possible with HTML-based pages means that a program such as NetObjects Fusion cannot cover everything. Some classic examples of what is not covered include:

+ Working with advanced forms
+ Adding Meta tags
+ Using JavaScript
+ Adding Inline RealMedia (audio and video)
+ Adding customization to a site where tools do not exist in Fusion for a particular task

These particular examples require custom HTML to make them work successfully. Fusion cannot be expected to create this sort of code because it has no way of knowing what code is required or what parameters may be needed.

Scripting is not a language, but don't be put off by the word *script* in this case. Unlike the plethora of languages that have appeared since the Internet (and the Web in particular) became popular, Fusion does not expect you to learn a derivative of Java, a subset of Visual Basic, a new way of writing macros, or yet another UNIX language! Scripting in Fusion terms is the addition of normal HTML code to existing objects on a Web page. These objects can include graphics buttons, images, text blocks, MasterBorders, and even sections of the page itself.

To demonstrate the addition of scripting, I will use two examples: adding Meta codes for the Internet search engines to use and adding a pop-up window containing a picture.

Adding Meta Tags

When developing commercial Web sites, one of the most important parts of the total project is to register the existence of the site with major search engines such as Yahoo!, AltaVista, HotBot, Lycos, WebCrawler, Infoseek, Anzwers (in Australia), and so on. Back in the good ol' days, registration was simply a matter of telling the search engine the location of the URL and supplying a description to explain the nature of the site. This was what the search engine displayed when your site appeared in someone's search list.

Times change, however, and these days it is necessary to encode certain parameters into a site's structure that the individual search engines use to index a site. These parameters contain basically the same information you used to give the search engine manually — the description of the site and a number of key words or phrases by which the search engine indexes the site. The coding used to do this is known as a *Meta tag*. An example of a standard Meta tag appears in Listing 17-1.

> **Listing 17-1: An example of Meta tags used to describe the contents of a site to an Internet search engine.**
>
> ```
> <META HTTP-EQUIV="Description" NAME="Description" CONTENT=
> "Alessi, the World's best known Design Factory. View information
> of their designers, new products and other relevant information
> on Ventura Design's Home Page">
> <META HTTP-EQUIV="Keywords" NAME="Keywords" CONTENT="Alessi,
> Alberto Alessi, Philippe Starck, Michael Graves, Aldo Rossi,
> Susan Cohn, Alessi Spa, Homewares, FFF, Alessandro Mendini,
> Girotondo, King Kong, Richard Sapper, Tendentse, Twergi,
> Ritzenhoff, Ventura, Ventura Design">
> ```

In this example the http://www.venturadesign.com.au site specializes in the wholesale marketing of goods manufactured by an Italian Design factory called Alessi. Consequently, the Description Meta tag explains what the site is about, and the Keywords Meta tag contains those words by which the owners of the site wanted it to be indexed. (For readers who may be interested in such products and designs, the majority of these keywords are the names of the individual designers of the goods that Alessi manufactures.)

After you register the site's URL with the search engines, robot indexers look at the site at their own leisure, grab the description and the keywords, and use this information to index the site. In this sense *robot* is a term that describes a sophisticated program that trolls the Web, grabbing the information contained in the Meta tags and adding the data to its database.

Okay, so how is this information embedded into a Fusion page?

For the Meta tags to work successfully, you have to embed this information into the Between Head Tags of the HTML code.

Whenever you right-click a Fusion page in Page view mode and in a MasterBorder, one of the options in the pop-up menu is Master HTML, as shown in Figure 17-1. Another, and easier, way is to click the HTML button on the Properties palette; however, you must have no objects selected for this to work. If an object is selected, you will instead be adding HTML for that object and not the page (no Between Head Tags tab will be visible if you click the HTML button when an object is selected).

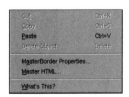

Figure 17-1: When right-clicking a page, a pop-up menu appears with the Master HTML option.

By selecting this option, a Page HTML window opens, as shown in Figure 17-2, which lets you enter HTML code manually into one of three locations: Between Head Tags, Inside Body Tag, or at the Beginning of Body.

Depending on what you are trying to do with the script dictates into which section you will place it. As mentioned, you need to place the Meta tag script in the Between Head Tags, so you type this code into that location.

Tip

To make life easier, I keep a copy of this script in a standard text file and copy and paste it as needed, changing only the Meta information as required.

Figure 17-3 shows the completed script for the Meta tag entered into the Between Head Tags section of the Page HTML window.

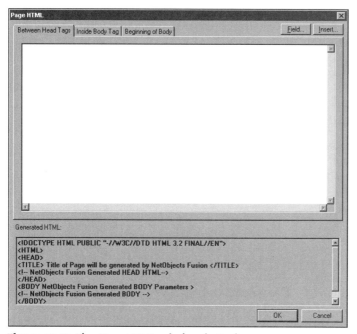

Figure 17-2: The Page HTML window in Fusion.

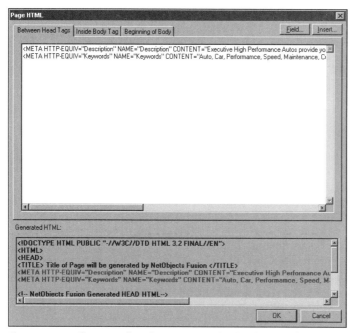

Figure 17-3: The completed Meta tag script in place in the Between Head Tags section.

After you have entered the script, you can close the Page HTML window. The site is now ready for indexing by any of the major search engines.

 In most cases it is necessary to add only the Meta tags to the Home page (index.html).

 If you right-click inside the Layout section on a page, an option called Layout HTML is available. This option opens a dialog box similar to the Master HTML dialog box. If your Home page is *not* using frames, you can place the Meta information using the Layout HTML option. If you do use frames, you *must* use the Master HTML option.

Adding a JavaScript Script for a Pop-up Window

Adding a Meta tag is one of the simpler types of scripts you can add to a Web site. A more complicated script — one that has visual impact — enables an object to act as a button to open a new browser window containing further information.

A good example of the use of this type of script is to place a thumbnail image or button on a Web page. When the visitor to the site clicks the thumbnail or button, a new browser window opens, containing a full-size version of an image. Figures 17-4 and 17-5 are examples of this type of script in use.

Figure 17-4: Here the Compressors button is used as a link . . .

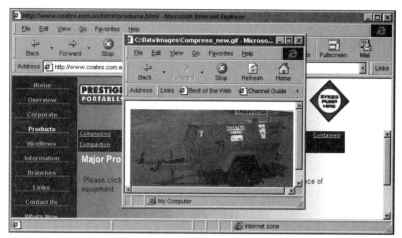

Figure 17-5: . . . to open a new browser window and display the image associated with the button's title.

This sort of script is ideal to place on the staff page of the Executive Performance Web site, for example. Here a brief description of key staff members is displayed along with a button. If the site visitor clicks the button next to the staff member, a new browser window opens to display a photograph of the person referenced.

This style of presenting information also has the side benefit of minimizing download time for visitors to the site. If visitors don't wish to see the photo, it is not downloaded unless they click the image button. In a site where many staff members may be listed, this can save huge amounts of downloading time.

The layout script

The first part of creating such a function is to create HTML code containing the JavaScript definitions and functions necessary for the script. Figure 17-6 contains the first script. This script is placed in the Between Head Tags section of the script editor, accessed by right-clicking in the Layout section of the page and selecting the Master HTML option or choosing the HTML button on the Properties palette.

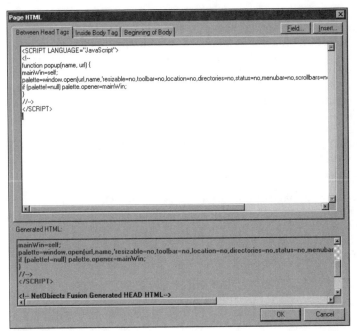

Figure 17-6: The JavaScript function script placed in the Between Head Tags section of the Layout Script.

Listing 17-2 shows the full script.

Listing 17-2: The complete script that defines the JavaScript code and parameters. (This function is called *popup*.)

```
<SCRIPT LANGUAGE="JavaScript">
<!—
function popup(name, url) {
mainWin=self;
palette=window.open(url,name,'resizable=no,toolbar=no,location=
no,directories=no,status=no,menubar=no,scrollbars=no,copyhistor
y=yes,width=295,height=252');
if (palette!=null) palette.opener=mainWin;
}
//—>
</SCRIPT>
```

The function of this piece of JavaScript code does as the name suggests (function *popup*) — it opens a new browser window. The parameters supplied to the new window include the commands not to display any toolbars, menu bars, scroll bars, and so on. In addition, the script nominates the height and width of the window.

After you enter the code into the script window, you can close it in preparation for the second step — adding a script to a button that will open the new window that has just been defined.

More Info

The basics of JavaScript are beyond the scope of this book, but Appendix B details some excellent sources of JavaScript reference if you want to learn more about the functionality and uses of JavaScript.

Figure 17-7 shows the Staff page of the Executive Performance Web site after placing a graphics button next to an employee's details. When this button is clicked (once the script has been added), a new browser window opens, containing a photograph of that staff member.

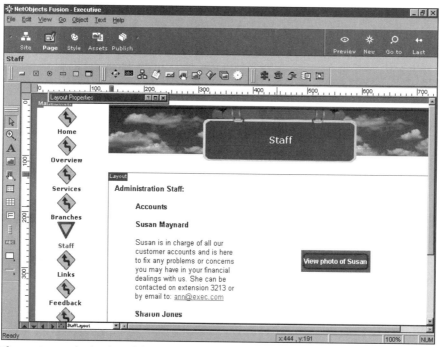

Figure 17-7: The basics of the Executive Staff page.

The button script

The second script that completes the coding side of the effect is added to the button itself. You place this script by selecting the button, clicking the HTML button on the Properties palette, and placing the contents of the script in the Before Tag section (as shown in Figure 17-8). Listing 17-3 shows the complete script.

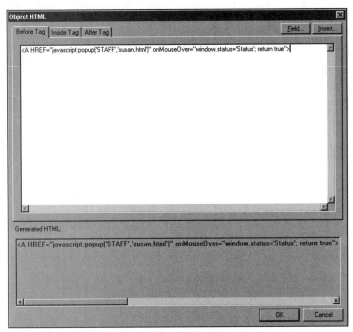

Figure 17-8: The Script window containing the script for the button to trigger the opening of the new window containing the image.

Listing 17-3: The complete script for the button.

```
<A HREF="javascript:popup('STAFF','susan.html')"
onMouseOver="window.status='Status'; return true">
```

A little explanation is needed here. When the site visitor clicks the button, the script of the button first obtains the JavaScript function from the script in the page's Layout section you created earlier. Using this function, a new window opens. The contents of the new window depend on the contents of an HTML file called susan.html. This HTML file is defined in the script attached to the button, as you can see in Listing 17-3. You can create this file as a normal Fusion page.

Tip

In this case, all you need to do is add a new page (below the Staff pages in the site's hierarchy). The sole content of this page will be a photograph of employee, Susan Maynard, as shown in Figure 17-9.

Figure 17-9: The Web page containing the photograph of an Executive Performance employee.

Tip

For best results, make sure the page created to display the photograph contains no MasterBorders or any other elements. You also need to adjust the sizes of the window as determined by the Layout portion of the JavaScript to accommodate the dimensions of the image. For example, in this case the photograph has the dimensions of 295 × 252 pixels, which is the value in the script shown in Listing 17-2. Simply vary these values depending on the size of the photograph.

That's all there is to it! Figure 17-10 shows the completed pages displayed in a Web browser. Visitors to the site first see the staff page, and when they click the photograph button next to Susan Maynard's name, the second window pops open, containing her photograph. Of course, you could add further functionality to this second window by placing further scripts into the body of the photograph if required. For example, you might pop open a third window that could be a floor plan of the office, showing where Susan sits.

Scripts and the use of them are only limited by your imagination and level of expertise in HTML or one of the scripting languages, such as JavaScript or VBScript. Many Fusion developers have created some interesting and snappy routines using scripts, but I stress again, it is *not* necessary to understand scripting fully to get the best results from Fusion.

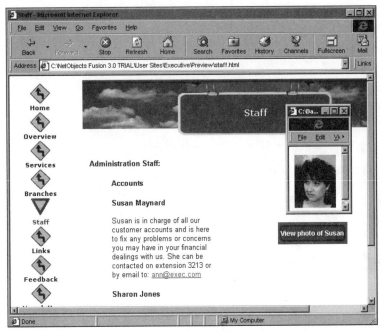

Figure 17-10: The Staff page complete with pop-up window.

New to 3.0

For users of earlier versions of Fusion, many of the tasks that required scripting to create an effect have now been made simple using NetObjects Fusion 3's Actions commands, which are described in Chapter 19.

Importing Existing HTML Pages into a Fusion Site

You may need to import existing HTML pages into a current Fusion site. An example of this occurs at www.haroldpark.com.au (shown in Figure 17-11). At this site, results of the race meetings each Friday are automatically generated as an HTML file by the electronic timing equipment and e-mailed to me as a document attachment. Using the External HTML tool on the Advanced toolbar is a monstrous time-saver in this regard.

To use the External HTML tool, select it from the palette and draw a placeholder on the page in Page view where the external HTML file is to be located. A dialog box opens, as shown in Figure 17-12, prompting for the file to be included. Enter the file name or use the Browse button to navigate to the file.

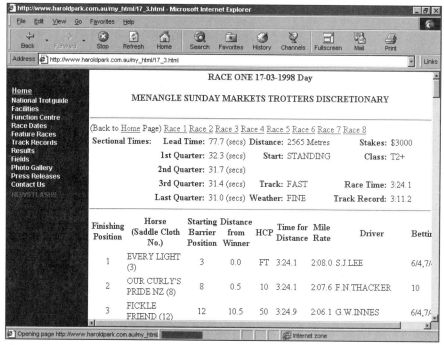

Figure 17-11: The Harold Park site that uses External HTML.

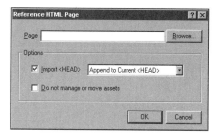

Figure 17-12: The Referenced HTML dialog box.

Note

You can only use the External HTML file for files on the local hard disk or a network drive. It cannot be used for remote pages.

There are two options on this dialog box. The first is a drop-down dialog box giving the choice of either appending the HTML code in the `<HEAD>` tag to the existing `<HEAD>` tag Fusion creates for the page or, alternatively, replacing the Fusion-generated `<HEAD>` tag.

The second option is to move or manage the assets in the External HTML page to be imported. If this option is checked, Fusion does not place the elements referenced on this page into its Assets list. This means *you* are responsible for making sure you don't have broken images on the page.

When you have selected the HTML file and set the options as you require them, clicking OK causes Fusion to import the page and add a placeholder for the referenced HTML on the Page view page, as shown in Figure 17-13.

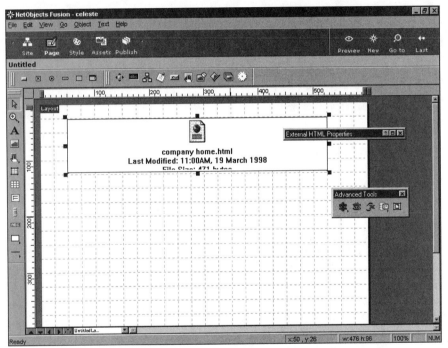

Figure 17-13: The Referenced HTML placeholder on the page in Page view.

Tip

If you wish to edit the HTML code, double-click the placeholder. The editor specified in the Preferences sheet opens. Figure 17-14 shows the Preferences sheet with Windows Notepad set as the preferred editor.

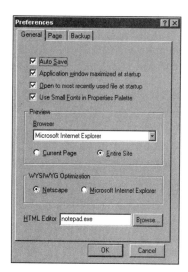

Figure 17-14: The Preferences sheet showing Windows Notepad as the preferred editor.

Using ScriptBuilder

If you are really serious about adding scripts to your pages — no matter whether they be JavaScript, VBScript, Jscript, LiveWire, or Dynamic HTML code such as required to create Microsoft Active Channel content — you can't get past an add-on tool available from NetObjects called ScriptBuilder.

Using ScriptBuilder, you can create both client-side and server-side scripts that will be supported by both Netscape and Microsoft browsers and their individual scripting technologies. Especially interesting about ScriptBuilder is a special tool called the *Inspector* that will check all your scripts as you create them and advise you of which versions of the individual browsers will be needed to run that script successfully.

You select language elements that you want placed as a part of a script from a section of ScriptBuilder called the *InfoDesk*. You can later place these inside the script using the *Map*. ScriptBuilder even provides a provision to replace text as you type with only key words needed as ScriptBuilder supplies the rest of the editable components.

Everything in ScriptBuilder is point and click. Even the library of scripts you have previously created and saved allows immediate access to these scripts, letting you insert them into a current document you may be working on.

Finally, any Web pages you have created via scripting using ScriptBuilder can be previewed in a flash. Also, of course, you can easily insert any scripts you've created into Web site pages you are creating in Fusion 3 using the HTML button available for most objects and elements.

I would say ScriptBuilder is a must-have, so we have included a trial copy for you on this book's CD-ROM! You can't ask more than that, can you?

By the way, if you come up with some really cool scripts, don't keep them to yourself. Share 'em with the rest of us in the NetObjects Fusion newsgroups at news.netobjects.com.

Summary

✦ Scripting allows further customization to Web pages and lets you add raw HTML when needed.

✦ In most cases scripting is not necessary when developing a Web site.

✦ Meta tags identify the subject matter of the Web site to Internet search engines.

✦ Scripts can contain HTML as well as JavaScript code.

✦   ✦   ✦

Using Frames

Aside from the introduction of tables, probably the next biggest Web development feature to cause a major impact was the introduction of frame technology to Web browsers. First to appear in Netscape Navigator, frames were quickly adopted into Microsoft Internet Explorer, and now they are in common use — some would say used too much — in Web sites everywhere.

Like most new things, at first the use of frames was grossly overdone. Everybody used them whether they were needed or not. Thankfully now, common sense has prevailed, and frames are mostly used only when the design structure of the site benefits from their inclusion.

So what's a frame?

Frames divide the Web browser window into separate areas, either horizontal or vertical. These individual areas of the window (or *panes*) can each display a separate HTML file. Figure 18-1 shows an example of a framed site.

Frames are very useful when you need to keep one section of a Web site in the visitor's view at all times. The most common use of frames as a design element is placing a menu bar or set of navigation controls inside a *static frame*. As the name implies, a static frame does not change: no matter which pages the site visitor navigates to inside the site, the frame containing these controls remains while other frames contain different information depending on the menu choices that the visitor makes. You can also employ frames in "shopping cart" applications, where for example, one pane displays the items the purchaser has bought, another tallies the running total of his or her purchases, and a third shows the "catalog" of items available to be purchased.

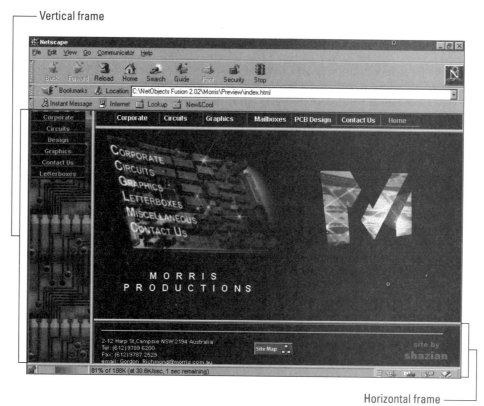

Figure 18-1: A Web site using both horizontal and vertical frames.

Creating Frames Manually

When designing a Web site manually by encoding the HTML commands in a text editor, creating a framed site is a little different than creating a normal set of HTML pages. The major difference is that you create the frames in a totally separate HTML file (called the *frame set*), where you define the different files that will initially appear in each pane. The frame set file can also contain some alternative HTML code to cater to browsers that cannot display frames.

For those who are not too familiar with HTML, the coding for a frame set is intimidating to say the least (see Listing 18-1).

Listing 18-1: **HTML code for defining a typical frame.**

```
<html>
<title>Mona Vale Christian Life Centre</title>
<frameset rows=="20%,80%,*" frameborder=0 framespacing="no"
frameborder="yes" >
<frame src="banner.gif"
name="scroll"
marginwidth=1
marginheight=1
scrolling="auto"
frameborder=0>

<frame src="index,html"
name="screen"
scrolling=auto
frameborder=0
marginwidth=0
marginheight=0>

<framesrc="airwaves.rpm"
name="navbar"
scrolling=no
frameborder=0
marginwidth=0
marginheight=0>
</frameset>
<noframes>
<body>

Your browser does not support frames.  Click below for:<p>
<a href="non-frame.html>Non Frames Version</a>

</html>
```

As you can see, this is not the simplest of code to follow. But now, having perhaps scared the life out of you and causing you to swear off the use of frames forever, let's look at the NetObjects Fusion way of doing things and ease the anxiety a little!

Adding Frames Using MasterBorders and AutoFrames

The key to using frames in Fusion lies in the MasterBorders. Any MasterBorder can change to become a frame area, and all this takes is one click of the mouse. This beats all that hand coding any day!

Figure 18-2 shows a standard Web page in Fusion in Page view mode. After selecting the left MasterBorder by clicking anywhere in it, you can see the MasterBorder palette as seen in Figure 18-3. Notice the options at the bottom of the Properties palette.

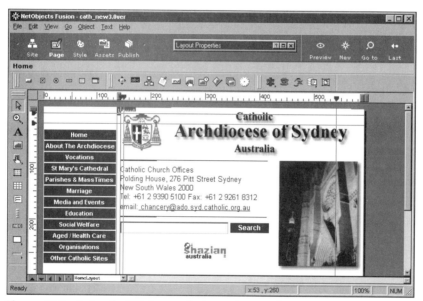

Figure 18-2: A standard Web page in Page view mode.

Figure 18-3: The MasterBorder Properties tab.

Clicking the Left button on the AutoFrames tab changes the left MasterBorder to a frame defined on the page. Figure 18-4 shows the same page as displayed earlier, but this time with the left MasterBorder being defined as a frame.

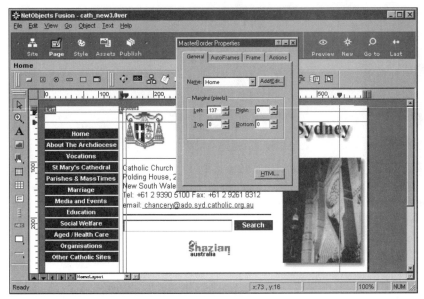

Figure 18-4: The same page after defining the left MasterBorder as a frame.

Using hidden frame borders

Many Web pages you have visited may contain framed information without you being aware of it. Likewise, many major sites make extensive use of frames, even though this is not immediately evident, as no distinctive border exists between the different frames on the pages. Figure 18-5 shows the Macromedia (the publishers of Flash and Director) home page for example.

This effect has been achieved by turning off the frame borders, thus making it look as though all the information is on one page. Again, this is a single-click operation on the Properties palette for the MasterBorder section as shown in Figure 18-6. The default for Fusion is to leave frame borders on.

Figure 18-5: The Macromedia Home page uses hidden frame borders.

Figure 18-6: Clicking the Generate HTML frame borders check box on the AutoFrames Properties palette sets the frame borders to on.

The Frame tab

Once you define a frame, a new tab appears on the Properties palette: the Frame tab. When you click this tab, a series of options become available for the frame (as seen in Figure 18-7).

Many of these options, such as Background style, are identical to the same options available for a standard Web page. This should not be surprising as a frame is in effect a stand-alone Web page: in this case, called Left.

Figure 18-7: The Frame tab on the Properties palette.

When posting a framed site to the Web server using the Publish options, you will find many more HTML files than usual. This is because every frame page becomes an HTML file, so it is not unusual to see the Fusion FTP client transferring such file names as *left_index.html* or *top_index.html*. In these two examples, the left_ index page is the left frame created on the Home page, and the top_ index page is the top frame.

Sometimes when clicking on the button to define any particular MasterBorder as a frame, you will receive a message in a dialog box stating that elements are at frame borders and therefore this command cannot be completed. The dialog box will then offer a fix for this problem. While you can accept this fix, I suggest finding the offending objects manually. Otherwise, your page could end up with elements all over the place. Find the offending elements and move them out of a frame edge's way. This usually occurs when setting left and right MasterBorder frames when elements in the top or bottom MasterBorder are inside what would be the resultant left or right frame area.

Scrollable frames

If you have a frame set up as a navigation control, it is sometimes necessary (or desirable) to lock the frame to stop it from scrolling. When a frame is not locked in this way, visitors to the site might inadvertently scroll the navigation controls off the page and without knowing they have done so may get very confused as to what happened to them!

To prevent this, the User Scrollable section, located on the Frame tab of the Properties palette (see Figure 18-7), provides a series of scrolling options:

- ✦ Setting the Yes option allows the contents of the frame to be scrolled up, down, left, or right using the scrolls bars. Scroll bars will always be added to the frame.

- ✦ Setting the No option locks the contents of the frame in place. Scroll bars are never displayed in the frame

- ✦ Setting the Auto option will cause horizontal or vertical scroll bars to appear if the contents of the frame cannot all be displayed on the screen.

If you lock a frame set so that it cannot be scrolled, make sure the entire frame is visible in all resolutions. Often — and quite often, believe me! — you can see all of the navigation controls in a frame in 800 × 600, but in the smaller resolution of 640 × 480, you won't be able to access any navigation controls at the bottom of the frame because the frame cannot be scrolled. If this may be a problem, selecting the Auto scrolling option will let the user resize the frame to the correct size when necessary.

Using Scripted Frames

Although using Fusion's AutoFrames option is the quickest and most simple method of creating frames, you can also define the frames manually on a page using scripting. This does require knowledge of HTML, however, and it may also be useful to review the preceding chapter on scripting before attempting to create scripted frames. If you have absolutely no knowledge of HTML coding, proceed with caution.

The major use of scripting to create pages is to define a frame structure that the AutoFrames feature of MasterBorders cannot accommodate. AutoFrames can only turn a MasterBorder into a frame. You cannot nest this to turn a MasterBorder into two separate frames using the AutoFrames feature. For example, you cannot split a frame into the two subframes as displayed in Figure 18-8.

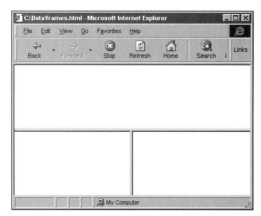

Figure 18-8: An example of a Web page framework using multiple frames that cannot be created with the AutoFrames feature of MasterBorders.

The frame set

As mentioned previously, the frame set is the heart of creating a set of framed pages. To refresh your memory, the *frame set* is usually — but not always — the top-level page containing the HTML code to define the layout of the frames and the source of the content for individual pages (HTML files) that will be displayed inside those frames. If you want your site to have frames on what ordinarily would be the index.html page, the page containing the frame set would be index.html, and the frame set commands would define the content of the frames from other Web pages.

Creating the frame set page is exactly the same as creating any other page in Fusion. It is simply added to the site using the Add Page button in Site view.

Note

Of course, you can also use the Home page that Fusion automatically generates when a new site is defined as your frame set page. In this case, as mentioned earlier, index.html would be the frame set page.

Once you have defined the frame set page, you need to add some HTML code—a script—to the page to supply the necessary definitions of each frame size and content. To do this, you must display the frame set page in Page view, right-click the Layout section, and click the HTML button on the Properties palette (as shown in Figure 18-9). This will open the Page HTML dialog box.

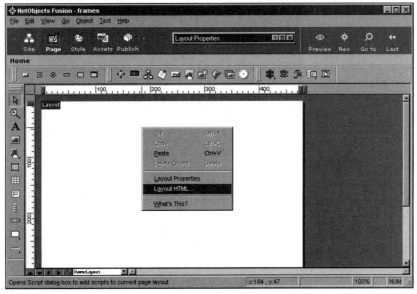

Figure 18-9: Selecting the HTML option from the popup menu while in Page view.

The frame set script

You need to place the frame set script in the Between Head Tags section. For example, to create the set of framed pages shown in Figure 18-10, use the frame set code in Listing 18-2.

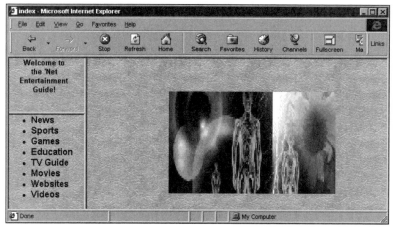

Figure 18-10: A basic framed page.

Listing 18-2: **The code to create the framed pages in Figure 18-10.**

```
<html>
<title>Mona Vale Christian Life Centre</title>
<frameset rows=="20%,80%,*" frameborder=0 framespacing="no"
frameborder="yes" >
<frame src="banner.html"
name="scroll"
marginwidth=1
marginheight=1
scrolling="auto"
frameborder=0>

<frame src="index,html"
name="screen"
scrolling=auto
frameborder=0
marginwidth=0
marginheight=0>

<frame src="airwaves.rpm"
```

```
name="navbar"
scrolling=no
frameborder=0
marginwidth=0
marginheight=0
</frameset>
<noframes>
Your browser does not support frames.  Click below for:<p>
<a href="non-frame.html>Non Frames Version</a>

</html>
```

Figure 18-11 shows the first four lines of code entered into the scripting window.

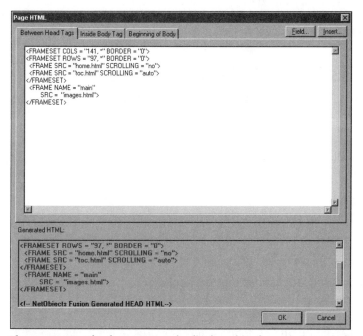

Figure 18-11: The frame set code displayed in the scripting window.

In this example, one of the pages is HTML-based (index.html), the second page contains an image map graphic (banner.html), and the third page contains an inline RealAudio soundtrack. You don't see any screen area for the soundtrack, but I'll have more on this in a second. (There's a neat trick here, trust me!)

I couldn't resist whetting your appetite here with the inline sound! See Part V for more on sound, video, and other rich media stuff. If you want to leap right ahead and follow this on your computer, you will need the RealAudio player from www. real.com.

Regardless of how individual content of pages is created, the frameset command always stays the same; only the src command differs depending upon the location of the content page.

The frameset rows command defines the percentage of the page for height of each frame. In this case, 20% is the height for the first frame, 80% is the height for the second frame, and the * lets the third frame use any remaining space. Of course, you cannot have more than 100 percent, so in this case, the sound file (the airwaves.rpm) file will play, but its controls will not appear. Neat trick, huh?

To assist in the creation of framed sites, it is useful to create in Fusion all of the source pages as children of the frame set page. This helps in planning and managing the links to these pages.

Creating links in scripted framed pages

When a link is placed in the content of a framed page and this link is clicked in the browser, by default the contents of the new page being linked to will appear inside the current frame. In many cases, this is neither aesthetic nor desirable. Consequently, the HTML specification allows the addition of different parameters to the definition of the link so that you can control how the page being linked to will appear. Four options are available to specify where you can force the linked target page to appear in either:

✦ The current frame

✦ Assumed display of the entire browser window: that is, ignore any of the frame set commands

✦ A frame that in the frame set has been defined as the default frame

✦ A frame specifically defined for that particular link

The current frame

As described earlier, if you do not define where the targeted link will appear, the linked page will appear in the frame of the current window. In this case, the current window is the frame that contained the link that was clicked. This is rarely used because it then may display pages that are designed for whole browser windows to appear in a very small frame. When this happens, the site visitor must endure much unnecessary scrolling of the frame to view the entire page. Worse, if the frame set has set this frame to No scrolling, the target page can only potentially have a small part of itself visible.

Defining a default frame

In the example shown in Figure 18-10, the largest of the three frames is called "main". This is the frame that will display all other Web pages navigated to by links clicked on in the Table of Contents frame (toc.html defined in the frame set). To force this, you need to add a script to the individual links in the Table of Contents page as shown in Figure 18-12. This script defines that all target pages will be displayed inside the frame called "main".

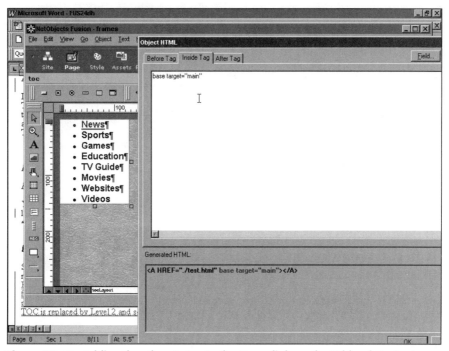

Figure 18-12: Adding the <base> tag to the News link on the Table of Contents page.

You add the <base> tag by opening the Table of Contents in Page view, clicking on a link, choosing the HTML button on the Properties palette, and placing the <base target = "main"> command in the Inside Body Tag section.

Defining a specific link

Sometimes it is desirable to target a specific link to appear in a specific named frame. This method does not affect any other links on the page, just the one containing the procedure. For example, all options but one will appear in the main frame (as defined above), but for developmental reasons, you may want the last link to appear in the banner frame. This is particularly useful when you have levels of menu pages, for example. Level one of the menu (image map graphic) is replaced by Level 2 and so on. To create such a link, use the Links button from the Properties palette as usual to create the link, but add a further parameter to the link specification. As you might have guessed, this parameter is the name of the frame to contain the link once the target of the link is loaded.

Let's say for example that you wish a page you are linking to be displayed in a frame called "special." The link is created as per normal, as shown in Figure 18-13.

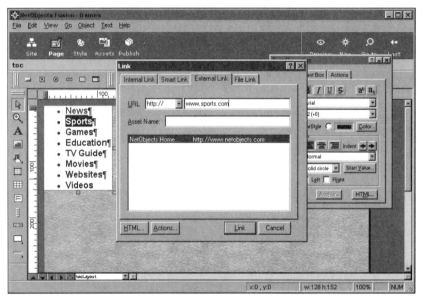

Figure 18-13: The link is created as per normal using the Links button on the Properties palette.

Secondly, you append the name of the frame you wish the target to appear in to the name of the link preceded by an equals sign (=) (as shown in Figure 18-14) using the HTML button on the Links palette. The code is added in the Inside Body Tag section (in the same way the `<base>` command was added).

Note   Using this method, you can instruct both internal and external links to appear in a specific frame. It is important, however, that if you mean to use an internal page as the target of the link, you *must still use* the External Link option, and the actual HTML page created by Fusion specified exactly, including its full path name on the server. Also note that quotation marks are *not* necessary. Fusion will automatically add these as needed.

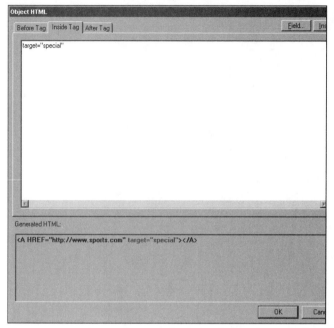

Figure 18-14: The target name is appended to the end of the link.

Displaying a link from a frame set in the entire browser window

To create a link that dispenses with the frame set definition entirely when the target page is loaded, the procedure is exactly the same as for nominating a specific frame. The only difference (as shown in Figure 18-15) is that the target frame has a special name in this case: _top. The first character here is the underscore character and not a dash.

Supporting Nonframes-Aware Browsers

Even in these enlightened times, some users out there still do not use *frames-aware browsers*. Good netiquette and Web authoring says that you should sympathize with these poor souls' disadvantage and add some HTML code that will allow these browsers to display alternative nonframes content.

This part is easy!

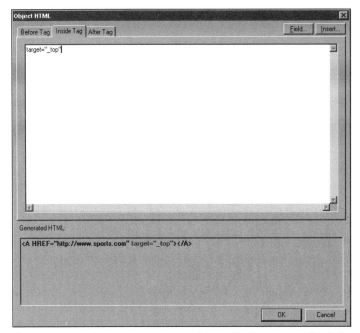

Figure 18-15: The `_top` parameter forces the browser to load the target page in the entire window and bypass the frame set commands.

The first thing to do is open the page containing the frame set commands. Using the scripting window, replace the closing `</frameset>` command with a new tag called `<noframes>` as shown in Listing 18-3's code.

Listing 18-3: Adding the code for browsers that don't support frames.

```
<body>
<noframes>
Your browser does not support frames.  Click below for:<p>
<a href="non-frame.html>Non Frames Version</a>
</noframes>
</body>
```

Secondly, for each page containing frame content, you must place a text box at the bottom of the page, as shown in Figure 18-16. This text box *must* be the last object on a page. If using MasterBorders, the text box even has to go below any MasterBorder content.

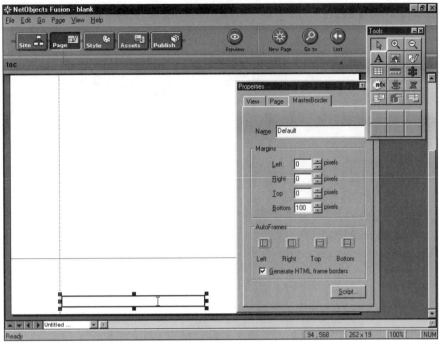

Figure 18-16: For <noframes> commands to work, a text box is added to the bottom of the page.

Finally, you add a script to the text box. Right-clicking the text box and choosing the Object HTML command from the popup menu allows the addition of this script to the After Tag field.

Be very sure to test this thoroughly with all the nonframes-aware browsers you are attempting to support. In fact, with any sort of scripting, good Web design policy says all scripts should be checked so that visitors to your site don't get any undesirable or unexpected results.

AutoFrames and Targeted Links

All that has preceded has related to hand scripted frames when the frame set definition you require is a frame architecture that cannot be accomplished using the AutoFrames feature. If you do use AutoFrames, though, and want total control over how and where linked pages appear inside frames, using the new Frame target option in Fusion 3 makes any scripting or adding target commands totally redundant.

In Figure 18-17, all of the buttons in the left frame refer to an anchor in the main body of the page (the Layout section). If an appropriate Frame Target option was not set, the resulting page would take over the entire browser window when any of these links were clicked (which is totally undesirable in this site).

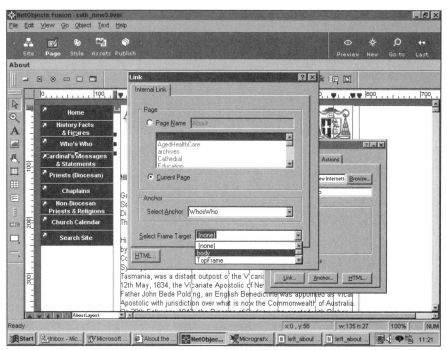

Figure 18-17: Each of the buttons in the left frame targets an anchor in the main body of the page.

Defining the target is performed in the Link dialog box as seen in Figure 18-18. In this case, the anchor to link to is selected from the dropdown list of available anchors, and secondly, the Frame target option body is selected.

The list of available targets will depend upon the Autoframes that have been defined for the page. In this example, there are both top and left frames, so these two options appear in addition to none and body. Notice the Frame Target has been set to body. This has been done so that when the "Who's Who" button is clicked and the page is reopened at the Who's Who anchor, this will be opened in the Body (Layout) frame thus leaving the menu in the left frame intact. If it was instead set to none, the page when reopening at the anchor would take over the whole browser window.

I am sure you will agree that this is much easier than all that hand coding!

Like any design tool, frames can be used or abused. The best guide really is to think carefully about the site and/or pages before adding frames. If frames don't add anything to the concept or design of the site, don't use them.

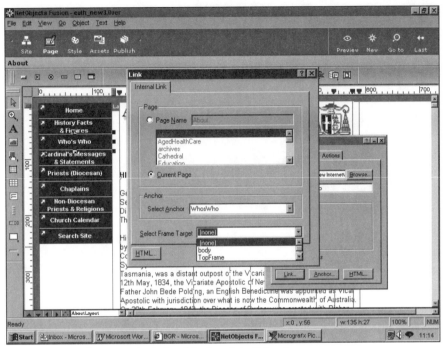

Figure 18-18: The target is defined in the Link dialog box.

Summary

✦ Frames divide a browser window into separate areas or panes.

✦ A frame's content is simply an HTML file either created with Fusion, by hand, or using cgi/Perl scripts, graphics images, or content created by JavaScript, VBScript, or a plug (such as RealAudio).

✦ Frames can have either their borders displayed or not displayed.

✦ Scroll bars in frames can be suppressed or shown as required.

✦ Fusion can easily add frames using the AutoFrames feature of MasterBorders with one mouse click.

✦ For more complex frame structures scripting must be added to pages.

✦ Targets of links can be added to any frame, a specific frame or defined to use the whole browser window.

✦ *Always* test your framing (or any other) scripts before publishing a site!

✦　　　✦　　　✦

Working with Actions and Layers

New to 3.0

Actions are one of the coolest new features of both NetObjects Fusion 3 and the HTML specification itself. A subset of this new specification referred to as DHTML (dynamic hypertext markup language), actions let the Web developer apply all sorts of terrific effects to pages and elements on pages.

To take full advantage of actions, the Web sites you develop should be published using the CSS and Layers option, which is specified in the Publish Setup dialog box (as shown in Figure 19-1). Be aware only version 4.0 and above of the popular browsers (Netscape Navigator and Internet Explorer, to name two) can translate the HTML code generated using this option.

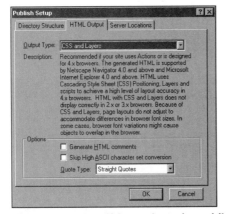

Figure 19-1: Specifying a site to be published using the CSS and Layers option.

More Info

For more information on Publishing and setting the CSS and Layers option, see Chapter 28.

Note Whereas using the CSS and Layers option is not an absolute imperative, actions you assign to a page or object may not work correctly or as expected in certain circumstances when you publish a site using, say, the Nested Tables option.

Applying Actions to a Page

So what is an action and how is it assigned? To demonstrate a very simple action, we'll use the banner of the Executive Performance Home page shown in Figure 19-2. You will see that very quickly, an action can be defined that will make this banner "fly-in" from the right side of the page when the page is loaded in a browser.

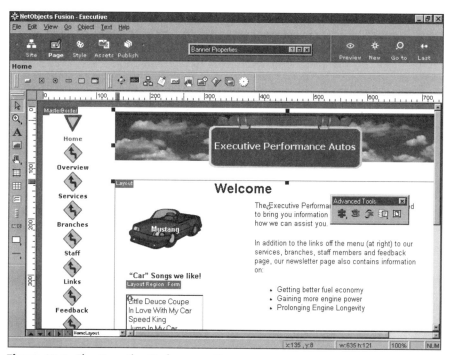

Figure 19-2: The Executive Perfomance Home page.

To create the action, make sure the banner is selected as shown in Figure 19-2. This will allow you to add the action using the Banner Properties palette and the Actions tab (as seen in Figure 19-3).

Figure 19-3: The Actions tab of the Banner Properties palette.

Any object that allows an action to be applied to it will have an Actions tab on its Properties palette. To add a new action, click the plus (+) symbol to open the Set Action dialog box (shown in Figure 19-4).

Figure 19-4: The Set Action dialog box.

Note

You can apply any number of actions to an object, and they will be performed sequentially. To change the sequence of actions, select an action on the Actions tab of the Properties palette and use the up and down arrows to change any Action's order in the sequence.

The first field in the Set Action dialog box lets you assign a name to the action. By default, Fusion supplies the name *Action1* to the first action, and will continue to name actions as they are added to the object by increasing the digit value (the second action will be called *Action2*, the third *Action3,* and so on).

I suggest giving your actions unique names that are meaningful to you. In this way, you can look at any action at a later stage and know what it is defined to do. For this first action, for example, let's use the name *Flying Banner*.

The second field, the When field, tells Fusion when the action you create will happen. By clicking the small right arrow button, a pop-out menu appears giving you the available choices shown in Figure 19-5.

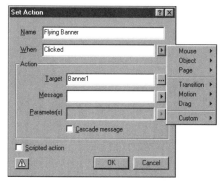

Figure 19-5: The When Action pop-out menu.

As you can see, there are lots of possibilities, and Table 19-1 describes them.

Table 19-1 The When Action pop-out menu options		
Trigger category	*Trigger event*	*What it does*
Mouse	Clicked	Detects Mouse left button down and up
	Mouse Down	Detects Mouse left button held down
	Mouse Up	Detects Mouse left button released
	Mouse Over	Detects Mouse cursor over an object
	Mouse Out	Detects Mouse cursor leaving the perimeter of an object
Object	Hidden	Detects whether an object is invisible
	Shown	Detects whether an object is visible
	Error	Activates when an object's source file cannot be found or loaded into the browser
	Loaded	Activates when an object has been loaded into a browser and is displayed
Page	Page Loaded	Activates when a page has been completed loaded into a browser
	Page Exiting	Activates when the current page is being replaced with a new page

Trigger category	Trigger event	What it does
Transition	Transition Started	The commencement of the current transition
	Transition Ended	The completion of the current transition
Motion	Motion Started	The commencement of the current motion
	Motion Ended	The end of the current motion
Drag	Drag Started	The commencement of an object being dragged (by the mouse)
	Drag Ended	The end of an object being dragged (by the mouse)
Custom	Edit	Creates a custom trigger using JavaScript or VBScript

As we want the banner to fly in from the right as the page is loaded, the When option we need is the Page option. When you select this, you're given a further pop-out choice of Page Loaded or Page Exiting. To complete the When action, choose the Page Loaded option.

Fusion automatically fills in the Target field with the name of the currently selected object: in this case, the page Banner. If you want to choose a different object to apply an action to, click the ellipsis field (...) to the right of the Target field. This will open the Object Tree from which you can select another object as seen in Figure 19-6. For this action, though, the currently selected object is the correct one.

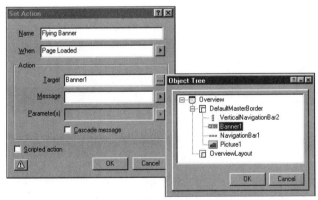

Figure 19-6: Choosing another object to apply an action to rather than the currently selected object.

The Message field is where the actual action is defined. It is called a "Message field" because this is the message that the browser will send to the object when the action occurs. Again, clicking the small right arrow button to the right of the message field pops out a menu with all of the messages available. Table 19-2 describes the messages and what they do.

Table 19-2
The Message Action pop-out menu options

Message type	Message	What it does
Object	Hide	Makes the current object invisible
	Show	Makes the current object visible
	Bring Forward	Brings the object forward one layer
	Send Backward	Sends the object back one layer
	Bring to Front	Brings the object to the top layer
	Sent to Back	Sends the object to the back layer
	Save Position	Saves the current position of object
	Restore Position	Restores the object to the last saved position
	Delay	Sends a custom message after a specified time to the object to which the Delay action is applied
	Set Image	Changes the image source file for a new one (does not change the image display). The new source file is associated to a keyword
	Use Image	Uses a new source file as the basis for an image based on an associated keyword (see Set Image)
Transition	Wipe	Hides or shows an object with a wipe effect
	Peek	Hides or shows an object with a peek effect
	Iris	Hides or shows an object with an iris effect
Motion	Fly	Moves an object from a specified window edge to its position
	Move To	Moves an object to a new or previously saved position
	Move By	Moves an object a defined number of pixels
Drag	Start Drag	Allows the object to be dragged around the browser window
	End Drag	Terminates a drag process (see Start Drag)
	Constrain Drag	Constrains a dragged object to the boundaries of its parent (default is no constraint)
	Set Collision Detection	Detects whether two objects overlap
	Clear Collision Detection	Terminates collision detection for an object

Message type	Message	What it does
Get Property	Get Top	Returns the top screen coordinate of an object
	Get Left	Returns the left screen coordinate of an object
	Get Position	Gets top and left coordinates of an object
	Get Z-Index	Returns the layer order number the object is on (Z axis)
	Get Clip Top	Returns the amount in pixels at the top of an object that is not shown (See Set Clip Top)
	Get Clip Bottom	Returns the amount in pixels at the bottom of an object that is not shown (See Set Clip Bottom)
	Get Clip Left	Returns the amount in pixels at the left of an object that is not shown (See Set Clip Left)
	Get Clip Right	Returns the amount in pixels at the right of an object that is not shown (See Set Clip Right)
	GetSrc	Returns the image source of an object
	GetLowsrc	Returns the low resolution image source of an object
Set Property	Set Top	Sets the top coordinate position of an object
	Set Left	Sets the left coordinate position of an object
	Set Position	Sets the top and left coordinate positions of an object
	Set Z-Index	Sets the layer number of an object (Z-Axis)
	Set Clip Top	Clips an amount from the top of an image in pixels. This area will be hidden
	Set Clip Bottom	Clips the amount from the bottom of an image in pixels. This area will be hidden
	Set Clip Left	Clips the amount from the left of an image in pixels. This area will be hidden
	Set Clip Right	Clips the amount from the right of an image in pixels. This area will be hidden
	SetSrc	Sets the source image for a picture object. Unlike Set Image, the image is not preloaded
	SetLowsrc	Sets the low-res source image for a picture object. Unlike Set Image, the image is not preloaded
Custom	Edit	Creates a custom message with JavaScript or VBScript

To cause the banner to fly in, we need a Motion message. Choose the Motion message as seen in Figure 19-7 and select the Fly option from the second pop-out.

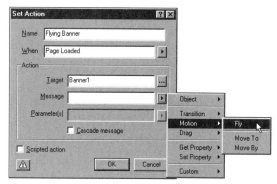

Figure 19-7: Choosing the Motion ⇨ Fly message.

The last step is to choose the Parameter. We have told Fusion what object to apply an action to, when to apply and what the object is to do. The parameter for the Motion message tells the object which direction to come from. The default parameter for the Motion ⇨ Fly message is In From Top. To change this to In From Right, click the small right arrow button to the right of the field and select it from the list as seen in Figure 19-8.

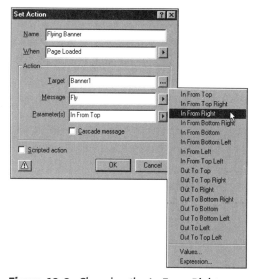

Figure 19-8: Choosing the In From Right parameter.

To complete the action, click the OK button.

Note

If not everything appears as it should when you preview the action, you can click the small yellow exclamation point button on the Set Action dialog box. It will display a series of useful hints as to what common action errors occur and how to rectify them. The Scripted Action parameter checkbox lets you add your own JavaScript or VBScript to an action. I'll get to the Cascade checkbox in a minute!

If all the fields have been filled in correctly and the appropriate parameters selected, the banner should now fly in from the right (as seen in Figure 19-9) when the page is previewed in a browser.

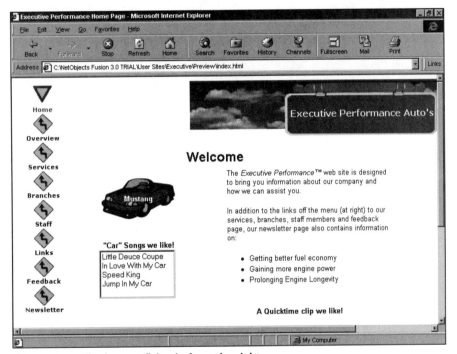

Figure 19-9: The banner flying in from the right.

Pretty snappy, huh?

Working with Layers

Using Layers in conjunction with multiple actions creates some very interesting possibilities. For example, using this combination, you can very easily simulate the "bubble" help or tool tips so common in today's software. You can use this to great effect in Web sites because you explain menu items, which are normally monosyllabic in content, much better to the site visitor. As the mouse pointer moves over a menu item, you can make a "pop-up" appear that gives this further explanation of the menu item's function.

Layers are the secret to this trick.

New to version 4.0 browsers, layers allow objects to be stacked on top of one another or overlap. Think of the layers as a series of transparent sheets. Each sheet can contain one object and are numbered. The number of the layer that an object is on is the *Z-Index parameter* of that object. You can move objects from layer to layer, effectively placing them either in front of or behind other objects on a Web page. No two objects can have the same layer number. To move objects in the layer hierarchy, use the Bring to Front (top layer), Bring Forward (up on layer), Send to Back (back layer), and Send Backward (down one layer) from the Arrange Objects command on the Object menu while in Page view.

This is not possible in version 3.0 browsers. While you can physically place objects in Fusion 3 on the page either on top of each other or overlapping, these objects' placement on the Web page will produce unpredictable results when such a page is seen in a lesser version browser than version 4.0.

The order of items that overlap or are stacked is important. To create the order of objects on different layers is achieved in a couple of ways:

✦ You can select an object and use the Arrange Objects command on the Object menu to move objects further up or down a layer as discussed earlier.

✦ Using the Object Tree window, select the object to move and drag it up or down the hierarchy to move it to a different level.

Creating a tool tip or bubble

To create the tool tips/bubble help function, we will place two graphics on separate layers, but one on top of the other. Using actions, the first item will disappear when the mouse pointer moves over it, and the object beneath it will appear. This will contain the text description of that menu object. When the mouse pointer moves out of the region encompassed by the second object, it will then disappear, and the first object will reappear.

To create this effect, we'll use the Built with NetObjects Fusion button graphic. This appears on a site automatically whenever you create a new site. If you can't find it on the page, it should be available in the Assets list or look for the BuiltByNOF file in the NetObjects Fusion 3.0\NetObjects System folder.

To place the button back on the page, use the Picture tool and create a placeholder on the page—the bottom MasterBorder is a good location. When the Picture File Open dialog box appears, click the Image Assets tab and select the BuiltbyNOF graphic. Click OK and the button will be placed on the page as seen in Figure 19-10.

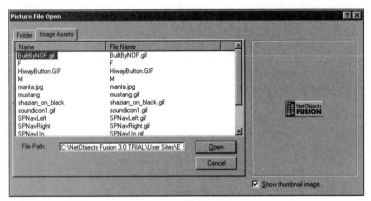

Figure 19-10: Placing the Built by NOF button.

Now we have to place the second graphic that will contain the description of this button's action when it is moved over a menu item. To do this, we'll use the Primary Button graphic used by the Hiway style. Again, place this using the Picture tool and in the Picture File Open dialog box appears, navigate to the NetObjects Fusion 3.0/Styles/Hiway/Primary Buttons folder and choose the file. Drag the button over the top of the Built by NOF button.

If you open the Object Tree, you can see that the Primary Button is above the Built by NOF button in the hierarchy as seen in Figure 19-11. To change this, and place the button below the Built by NOF button, drag it down so it is physically below the Built by NOF button as seen in Figure 19-12.

Figure 19-11: The Primary button above the Built by NOF button in the Object Tree.

Figure 19-12: After dragging it down the hierarchy so it is below the Built by NOF button.

To create the necessary effect, we need to add two actions to the Primary button and two actions to the Built by NOF button, as shown in Table 19-3.

Table 19-3 Actions to apply to the two buttons		
Action name	*Apply to*	*Action*
Hide NOF	Built by NOF button	When the mouse moves over the image, hide the Built by NOF button.
Show Primary	Primary button	When the mouse moves over the image, show the Primary button.
Hide Primary	Primary button	When the mouse moves out of the Primary button area, hide the Primary button.
Show NOF	Built by NOF button	When the mouse moves out of the Primary button area, show the Built by NOF button.

In addition, in the Picture Properties palette for the Primary button, uncheck the Object initially visible in browser option. This will hide the Primary button when the page is loaded.

Figures 19-13 through 19-16 describe the Actions dialog box for each of these actions. You might like to attempt them yourself before seeing how they are done. It's really easy, trust me!

Figure 19-13: Hide the Built by NOF button.

Figure 19-14: Show the Primary button.

Figure 19-15: Hide the Primary button.

Figure 19-16: Show the Built by NOF button.

Of course, to complete the exercise, you would put some explanatory text inside the Primary button using the Text in element option from the Picture Properties palette. To add some snap to the idea, you would also probably use a custom graphic that could mimic the graphic image used in balloon help or tool tips. The whole thing is so simple to do, many possibilities come to mind.

A quick browse through the actions commands shows that there are many ways of using the interactivity offered by this wonderful set of functions, but there are more to Actions than may immediately meet the eye!

For those who have used applications like Asymetrix Toolbook or Hypercard, you will be familiar with the concept of messages being passed from one object to another through a hierarchy. This is where it is important to understand the concept of the Object Tree.

Looking at the Object Tree shows the hierarchy of all objects on the page including the page itself, MasterBorders (and objects on the MasterBorder), and the Layout area. We'll now add a single action to a new button and see how this action passes down the Object Tree to all children of the target object (the one containing the Action). This can be a huge time-saver.

Using Actions for advanced messaging

To show a simple example of passing messages through from one object to another, we'll use a blank page in a new site with a left AutoFrame configured in the left MasterBorder. Instead of using a Navigation Bar or DynaButtons, the navigation controls placed in this left frame will be a series of graphic buttons created in an application like PhotoShop, Xres, or Picture Publisher.

To create a blank page, use the New Page button on the control bar, and click anywhere in the left MasterBorder to add the frame. Select the AutoFrames tab on the MasterBorders Properties palette and click the Left frame button.

Figure 19-17 shows an example of such a page.

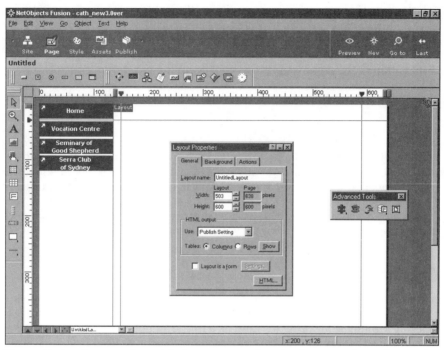

Figure 19-17: A page using a left AutoFrame and navigation controls made out of a series of graphics buttons.

The idea here is that whenever this page loads, the menu will drop down from the top of the page. Using Actions, you could of course add an action to each button, but it's much easier to add the action to the parent of the objects, and let this action pass down the Object Tree to its children. This means that you need only define the action once.

To do this, click the left frame to open its Properties palette, click the Actions tab, and fill it in as per Figure 19-18. Notice in particular the Cascade Message checkbox.

Figure 19-18: Adding an action to the Left MasterBorder.

The Cascade message checkbox is the key. When this is checked, any action you have defined will pass down to all of the object's children. In this case, we have told the left MasterBorder that when the page is loaded, it will fly in from the top of the page. Now of course, an AutoFrame cannot do this, so the message is passed down to its children: the graphics buttons making up the navigation controls.

These can fly down from the top, in unison, whenever the page is loaded, they do! Try it and see!

Whenever using effects like this, make sure the Object initially visible in browser checkbox is *not* checked. To do this, you will have to select each object subject to the parent's action, click the Actions tab and uncheck the box. If you don't, when the page is loaded, the object will appear then disappear before the action takes place.

This is a very simple example of passing messages down a hierarchy of objects but should give you a starting point for your own projects.

Creating a game

Actions can be used to add interactivity to a site. With so many possibilities available, I doubt that enterprising Web authors will not come up with some amazing examples, however for now, as a third example how about creating a very simple game that perhaps children visiting the Executive Performance Web site might like to play. To create this, we'll use the actions' ability to drag objects around the screen and place them where the visitor desires.

Look in the Examples folder on the CD-ROM packaged with this book. You'll find four GIF files:

  ✦ Body.gif

  ✦ Wheel1.gif

  ✦ Wheel2.gif

  ✦ Wheel3.gif

Place each of these on a blank page using the Picture tool as shown in Figure 19-19.

We'll add an action to each of these images so that the site visitor can drag them around the page with the mouse. It's like a puzzle: the site visitor needs to place all of the wheels in their correct position on the Volkswagen. When the page is exited, all of the images will revert to their original position so that the game can be played over and over.

We need to add two actions: one to allow the start of dragging an object and a second to return the objects to their original positions when the page is exited.

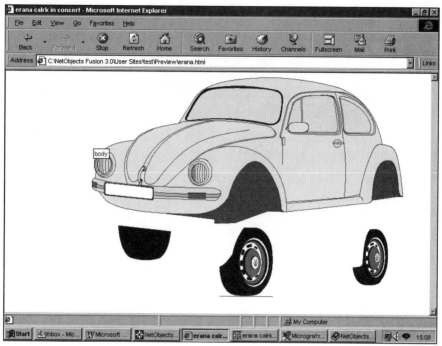

Figure 19-19: The four GIF pictures making up the car placed on a blank Web page.

To create the first action, a Mouse Down Action, follow these steps:

1. Select the body of the Volkswagen with the mouse.

2. Click the Actions tab on the Picture Properties palette.

3. Next, click the plus sign (+) to add a new action.

4. Click the arrow to the right of the When field. The When Action required is Mouse Down (as seen in Figure 19-20).

5. Once you have added the When section, it is now time to add the Message section of the action. In this case, it will be Drag ⇨ Start Drag (which you can see in Figure 19-21).

6. The default parameter for the Start Drag message is Until Mouse Up. In other words, the Start Drag message will continue to be sent to the object until the mouse button is released. This is exactly what we are after.

7. This is all we need for the first action for the body of the car and the OK button can be clicked to save the Action.

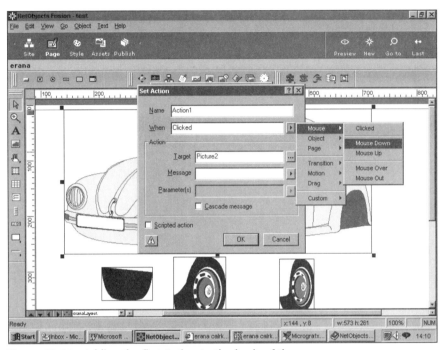

Figure 19-20: Adding the first Action to the body of the car.

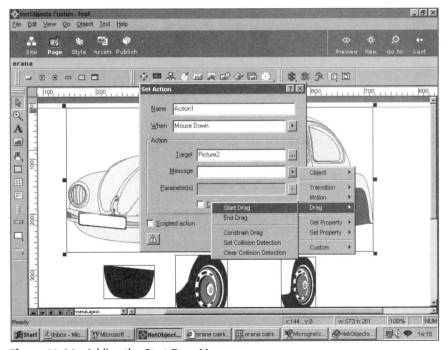

Figure 19-21: Adding the Start Drag Message.

We can now apply this same action to each of the three wheels. When the page is viewed in a browser, you should be able to move the four objects around the page by clicking and dragging any of them (as seen in Figure 19-22).

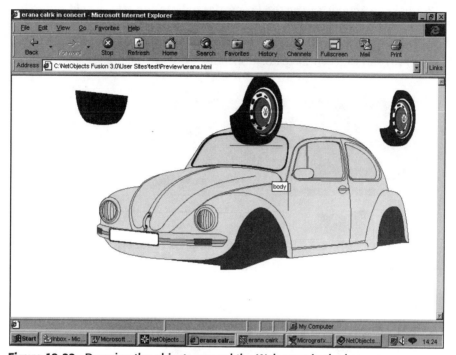

Figure 19-22: Dragging the objects around the Web page in the browser.

Pretty cute, huh!

Tip

To add more realism to the wheels in particular, use the Transparency option on the Effects tab on the Picture Properties palette to make the white background transparent.

We now need a final pair of actions that will return all of the components to their original starting point so that the game can be played again. Rather than use the same method of adding the Action to each object, we will use the Cascade capability to pass the message to all objects on the page.

This will require us to define two actions: the first will save the location of all objects on the page when it is first loaded and the second will return any moved objects back to their original position when the page is exited.

To create the first action, follow these steps:

1. Make sure the Layout is selected (either by clicking it or selecting it in the Object Tree window).

2. Click the Actions tab on the Properties palette and start a new Action by clicking the plus (+) sign.

3. This time we want Page ⇨ Page Loaded in the When field (as seen in Figure 19-23) and Object ⇨ Save Position in the Message field (as seen in Figure 19-24).

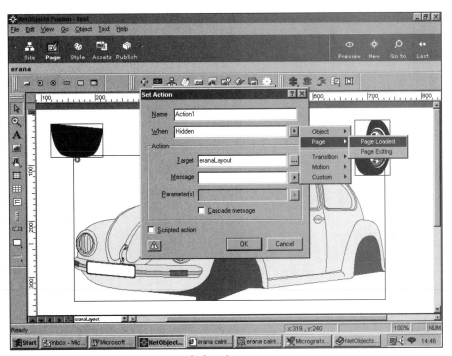

Figure 19-23: The When Page Loaded Action.

4. This will make sure all of the object's original positions are saved before any dragging occurs. To make sure the message is passed to all objects on the page, click the Cascade message checkbox and click the OK button.

We need one last action to complete the game: one that restores any objects to its original position (saved in the previous action when the page was loaded). Once again, click the plus (+) button to add a new Action and repeat. Figures 19-25 and 19-26 show the correct When and Message commands to add. Make sure to check the Cascade option!

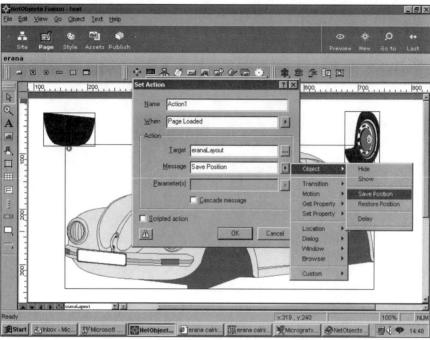

Figure 19-24: Adding the Save Position message.

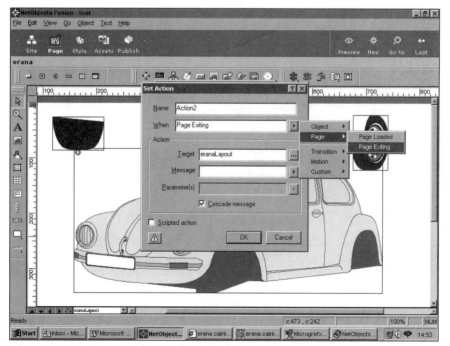

Figure 19-25: The When Page Exiting Action.

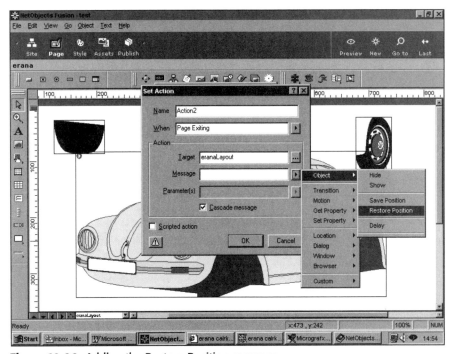

Figure 19-26: Adding the Restore Position message.

If you've done everything correctly, previewing the page will let you drag all of the objects around, and then a page Reload should place them back in the original starting positions.

OK, this is pretty basic as far as games go, but if you wanted to enhance it using actions, here are some things you could try:

✦ Use the Set SRC commands to give a choice of wheels or body.

✦ Use the Z-Index commands to change the order of object's layer position.

✦ Use the Set Image commands to allow on-the-fly changing of the car's components.

The possibilities provide endless fun for the entire family!

Actions and layers used in combination are very powerful tools. They provide welcome alternatives to enormous amounts of hand coding in HTML and JavaScript and are flexible enough to unleash the imagination of the Web developer.

To demonstrate the huge amounts of time that can be saved using actions in Fusion as against other coding methods, Listing 19-1 shows the code generated to define the switching buttons we created earlier in this chapter. To create this by hand and debug would take more time than I care to spend — not to mention that high-level JavaScript skills must be learnt first!

If you come up with some really cool actions, share them with us by making them available in the NetObjects Fusion newsgroups. Appendix B details the location of the various groups that are available.

Listing 19-1: HTML code for the switching buttons example.

```
<SCRIPT>
var
F_A,F_B,F_CH,F_CL,F_DB,F_E,F_F,F_L,F_MT,F_MV,F_R,F_SE,F_SU,F_U,
F_HR,F_MU,F_MD;
function F_e(){}
function F_n(){}
function F_onLoaded(){}
</SCRIPT>
<SCRIPT language="JavaScript1.2">
document.write("<SCRIPT src=\"file:///C:/NETOBJECTS FUSION 3.0
PRE-RELEASE/NetObjects System/script.js\"><\/SCRIPT>");
</SCRIPT>
<SCRIPT language="JavaScript1.2">
document.write("<SCRIPT src=\"file:///C:/NETOBJECTS FUSION
3.0/NetObjects System/effects.js\"><\/SCRIPT>");
</SCRIPT>
<SCRIPT>
function F_doLoaded(){
    document.main = new F_cMain();
    document.objectModel = new Object();
    F_OM('Layout','LayoutLYR', 'doc', '', new Array() );
    F_OM('Picture6' , 'Picture6LYR', 'img', 'Layout',new
Array(
    'Mouse Out','Picture6','Hide','',0,
    'Mouse Out','Picture2','Show','',0),'',0);
    F_OM('Picture2' , 'Picture2LYR', 'img', 'Layout',new
Array(
    'Mouse Over','Picture6','Show','',0,
    'Mouse Over','Picture2','Hide','',0),'',0);
    F_pageLoaded('Layout');
}
</SCRIPT>
<SCRIPT language="JScript">
document.writeln("<STYLE ID=\"NOF_STYLE_SHEET\">")
```

(continued)

Listing 19-1 *(continued)*

```
document.writeln("#LayoutLYR {position:absolute; top:2; left:2;
z-index: 1; VISIBILITY: INHERIT; }")
document.writeln("#Picture6LYR {position: absolute;
visibility: hidden; top:288; left:241; width:127; height:39; z-
index:1}")
document.writeln("#Picture2LYR {position: absolute;
visibility: inherit; top:295; left:276; width:70; height:29; z-
index:2}")
document.writeln("</STYLE>")
</SCRIPT>
```

Summary

✦ Actions add interactivity and animation to objects.

✦ Actions for an object are built using the Actions tab on the Properties palette.

✦ Actions consist of When, Target, Message, and Parameters functions.

✦ The actions options available will change depending upon the Object selected as the target of the action.

✦ Messages in an action can be passed down to the child objects of the target of the action by selecting the Cascade Message checkbox.

✦ Objects on a page can be placed on and moved between different Layers on a page.

✦   ✦   ✦

Data Publishing

In Fusion terms, *data publishing* is the act of taking information from an existing source, creating a set of Web pages based on this information, and publishing these pages to a Web server as part of an overall Web site. Common types of data that users publish include price lists, product catalogues, and corporate information.

The data to be extracted and published can reside in a standard PC or Macintosh database that is ODBC-compliant, such as Microsoft Access, Lotus Approach, or Paradox, and can even (with the correct drivers) be read from Excel spreadsheets or text files. As time goes on, even more facilities will no doubt become available to publish data using Fusion from other sources.

Fusion is able to extract and publish this data from other database applications by "reading" the existing database data file and creating a single Web page for every record in the database matching extraction criteria the developer has set. These special Web pages are called *stacked pages*.

Note

ODBC stands for *open database connectivity* and is a standard agreed upon by the major database developers. Special software drivers are used to connect other applications to an ODBC-compliant database to read the applications' information.

For example, in a database of company personnel you might find it advantageous to publish information about all departmental staff who are directly involved with the public (such as sales, accounting, or service). Other staff, such as administrative, manufacturing, or quality control people, would not need to be posted. Under this circumstance, Fusion would extract only the records meeting the search query

```
Department = sales OR accounting OR service
```

and would create Web pages for each of these records. This process is called *filtering*.

If at any stage you add, delete, or change a record, all stacked pages are updated automatically with any new information. At the same time, stacked pages of information from deleted records are removed, and stacked records for new records are added the next time you publish the Web site containing the database record information to the server. Once the definition of the stacked pages is complete, the rest is entirely automatic.

Internal and External Databases

Extracting information from an outside source such as a Microsoft Access database, called an *external data source,* will probably be the most common use of the Fusion data-publishing feature. Figure 20-1 shows an example of a Web page created from data residing in a Microsoft Access database. Fusion can also create stacked pages from an *internal data source.*

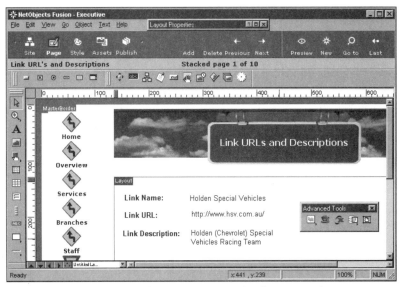

Figure 20-1: A page created using an Access database record.

An *internal database* is one where the information to go into the stacked pages is created within Fusion at the time of creating the stacked pages definition. As the definition of the internal database is created, the data for each stacked page is also added. Internal databases, in my opinion, are really only useful for small amounts of information, because the time involved to manually enter data precludes using them for more than perhaps twenty records. If the information is textual in format, it is often easier to import it into a spreadsheet application, as shown in Figure 20-2, and then connect this spreadsheet as an external database.

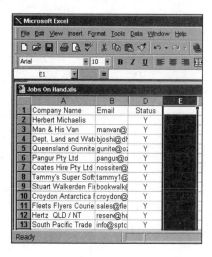

Figure 20-2: Text data imported into a spreadsheet. You can then attach this spreadsheet as an external database.

What Applications Can I Use with Fusion to Publish Data?

As mentioned, Fusion can connect to any ODBC-compliant database/application. Examples of ODBC-compliant applications include:

✦ Microsoft Access

✦ Microsoft Excel

✦ Lotus Approach

✦ Lotus 1-2-3

✦ Paradox

✦ Quattro Pro

✦ FoxPro

✦ DBase

So that Fusion can connect to the data files these applications create, it is necessary to have the relevant software driver installed on the local computer. This *driver* is the method by which the data pointers are transferred from one application to the other — in this case from the data file to Fusion's NOD file. By default, most of the applications mentioned install the ODBC driver when the program itself is installed. When this is not the case, at installation time the particular application usually shows a dialog box of available drivers, allowing you to select the ones you require.

The data is not actually copied to the NOD file. The driver creates a pointer to the existing data in the database data file, and the Fusion NOD file stores that pointer. Fusion, however, is intelligent enough to notice whether any of the data changes, and whether this happens by records in the database being added, deleted, or changed. Fusion then updates the pointers as necessary. This may sound a little confusing, but rest assured this operation is totally automatic and does not need any intervention from the Web developer — you.

Attaching a Database to a Fusion Web Site

To demonstrate how an external database is attached to a Fusion Web site, I'll use a Microsoft Access database to place a series of stacked pages on the Executive Performance Web site Links page. This database contains a series of records, each containing an http:// link to an automotive-related Web site. This idea is perfect for a company such as Executive Performance — it gives interested site visitors information they would otherwise have to hunt for around the World Wide Web. Each record contains

✦ The name of the link

✦ The URL of the link

✦ A brief description of the link

✦ Potential for a graphic image to be included

The first and third fields in each record will be purely text-based information, but a cool feature of Fusion will turn the second field, the URL link, into a hyperlink in its own right once you have defined the stacked pages. The fourth field is initially a text-based field, but later I show you how you can convert this to an image field using a little trickery. Figure 20-3 shows the data in a Microsoft Access table.

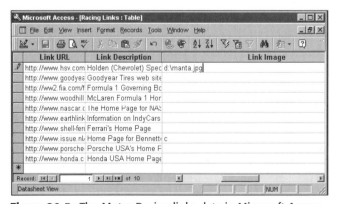

Figure 20-3: The Motor Racing links data in Microsoft Access.

Data objects, fields, and lists

Creating a series of stacked pages requires working with three distinct entities: the data object, the data list, and the data field. The *data object* is the reference to the external database itself and refers to the collection of fields and records from the database that will be used to create the stacked pages. After you have defined the data object, the *data list* is defined, which is the same as a table of contents. It appears on the page and lists a field or fields from each record. The site visitor can then select a record from one of the objects in the data list to view the entire record (the stacked page corresponding to that record). A *data field* is a single field inside each record.

Placing a data object

The first step in placing a data object is to tell Fusion what the data object is. Nominate the name of the data file to be used to create the stacked pages, and define all criteria, such as sort and select routines (called *filtering* in Fusion). To create the data object, select the New External Data Source tool from the Advanced toolbar, as shown in Figure 20-4. Draw the location of the data object on the page, and the dialog box shown in Figure 20-5 opens.

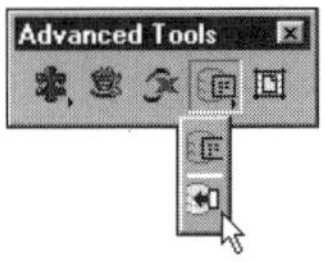

Figure 20-4: Choosing New External Data Source tool from the Advanced toolbar.

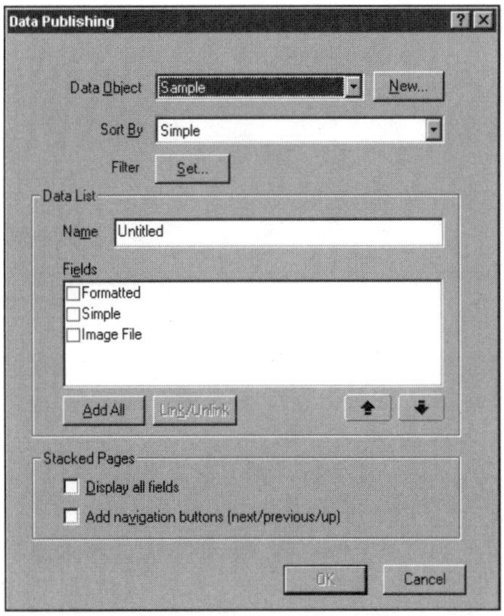

Figure 20-5: The Data Publishing dialog box.

The first thing you tell Fusion is what format the external data is in, as shown in Figure 20-6. The default option is Microsoft Access, which uses files with an .mdb extension. To choose the ODBC option, you would click the radio button underneath the Microsoft Access list box.

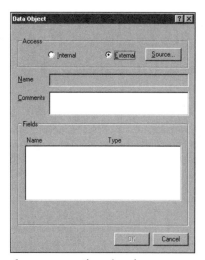

Figure 20-6: Choosing the source data file type for the data object.

Finally, using the Browse button, you can select the actual data file you want connected to the Web site, as shown in Figure 20-7.

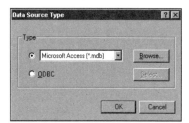

Figure 20-7: Selecting the source data file for the data object.

For some reason that seems to apply only to Microsoft products, you *must* close the source destination application and the data file before attempting to select it as a data object. If not, an error occurs.

After you have selected the data file, the individual tables in the database are displayed in the dialog box, as shown in Figure 20-8. To continue, simply choose the table you want to use (in this case, Racing Links) and click the OK button. The fields comprising the table are displayed in the Data Publishing dialog box, shown in Figure 20-9.

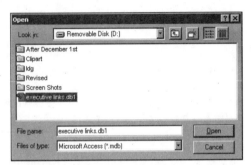

Figure 20-8: The individual tables comprising the Racing Links database with the Racing Links table selected.

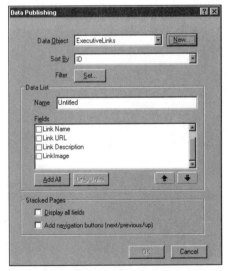

Figure 20-9: The fields comprising the Racing Links database table.

Note   Although this procedure seems awfully long-winded and complex, after you create a couple of data objects, it will become second nature!

The Racing Links database has five fields per record:

✦ ID

✦ Link Name

✦ Link URL

✦ Link Description

✦ Link Image

Selecting data fields

Selecting any field at this time only dictates which field or fields will appear in the Index of pages on the Executive Performance Links page. It does *not* affect which fields will appear on the stacked pages for each record. This process is entirely different and occurs later.

To select the field or fields to appear in the index, click the checkbox to the left of each required field, as shown in Figure 20-10. For your purposes here, you only need to check the Link Name. I'll explain why in a moment.

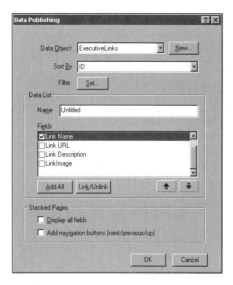

Figure 20-10: The required field selected in the Data Publishing dialog box.

Finally, you can set the options to specify sorting and search criteria. By default, Fusion sorts all the records according to the first field specified in the attached database, in this case Access. For this database, the first field is the ID field, which is a number Access allocates automatically but for any other purpose is probably useless. Consequently, sorting by this field has no relation to the data you will display on the stacked pages, so it makes more sense to sort by one of the fields that will be displayed. The Link Name field is the logical choice. You select this field as the primary sort field by choosing its name in the drop-down list shown in Figure 20-11.

At this time you can give the data list you are creating a meaningful title. If you are creating more than one data list from a single data object, naming the data lists is especially important because it enables you to identify previously configured data lists. For example, if you had a large number of motor racing links, a sensible approach would be to create separate data lists on the Links page for NASCAR, Indy car, Formula 1, touring cars, Go-carts, rally cars, and so on. Each of these data lists would be based on the same data object but would be created from separate filtering criteria. By naming the data lists accordingly, you can easily see which is which on the page.

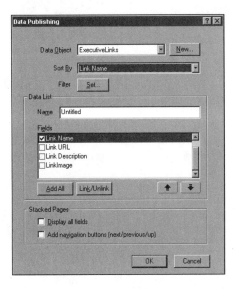

Figure 20-11: Selecting the field in the database by which you can sort the stacked pages.

Records can be filtered, although filtering is not necessary with this data object. *Filtering* is a method of telling Fusion which records to create as stacked pages by defining criteria for any single record to meet. For example, if you wanted to include only records from the Racing Links database where the Link Name field started with a letter greater than *G (equal or greater than H)*, you could define this in the Filters dialog box. Figure 20-12 shows another more complex data object with filtering criteria in place. You can set up to three connected filters using AND/OR relationships.

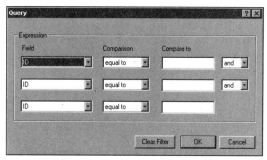

Figure 20-12: Filtering records from a database. Only those records matching the filter criteria will have stacked pages created.

As another example using the concept of different categories of motor racing, you could add a field in the database to identify which links referred to which type of motorsport. After doing so, you could then create separate data lists by extracting only those records that matched that category definition.

Filters are especially used and useful when more than one data list is created from a single data object. I have created Web sites with more than 40 data lists, all based on different filtering criteria but extracted from the one Access database.

Adding links to the data list

When this part of the sequence of creating stacked pages is complete, Fusion creates an index on the Executive Performance Web site Links page and a series of stacked pages. Each page contains the data from a single record in the database. So the user can select any individual stacked page to view from the list, one of the fields that will be displayed in the index needs to be linked to its stacked page. The field you have chosen to appear in the index is the Link Name field. To make this a link to the record, select it and click the Link/Unlink button. To indicate this record is linked, the word *Linked* appears next to the field's name in the dialog box.

Adding navigation buttons to stacked pages

Although not absolutely necessary, it is sometimes useful to let a site visitor browse one at a time through the records making up the stacked pages. To make this browsing easy, Fusion lets you automatically add a set of navigation buttons to stacked pages. These buttons are labeled Next, Previous, and Up. The first two are self-explanatory; they take you to the next or previous record in the stacked pages. The Up button returns you to the data list: the index. To turn this option on, click the Add navigation buttons checkbox. Figure 20-13 shows the completed dialog box for this data list.

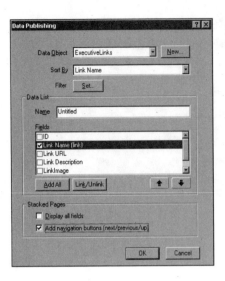

Figure 20-13: The Data Publishing dialog box with all selections and options complete.

Note

If the Add navigation buttons option is *not* checked (or the Display all fields option is also not checked), a series of blank stacked pages will be created, with each page corresponding to a record in the database that matches the filtering criteria (if any) you have set. Under this circumstance you have to use the Data List tool shown in Figure 20-14 so that you can individually place the fields you want onto the first stacked page and then format it as required. Each of the stacked pages in the data list will then conform to the formatting applied to the first page. It is, however, much quicker to let Fusion create a basically formatted page with all the fields in place, and then edit the stacked page later to achieve the look you want.

Figure 20-14: Using the Data List tool to place fields onto a stacked page.

You can now close the dialog box, and Fusion will create the data list on the Executive Performance Links page as shown in Figure 20-15.

Let's quickly examine what is on the page. First, Fusion has created a table with the first column containing an icon and the second containing the information from the Link Name field of each record. (You cannot see the data as yet; the data can be displayed only when previewed or published.)

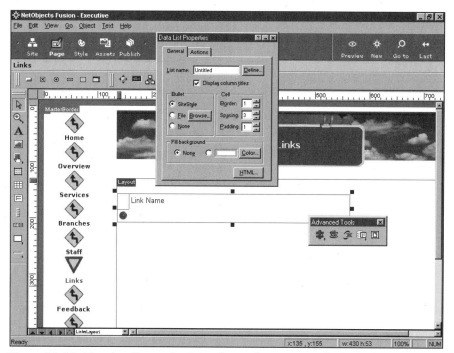

Figure 20-15: The data list on the Executive Performance Web site Links page.

The Data List icon is defined in the current Style View attached to the Web site. The current Style is Hiway; hence you have the Hiway Data List icon.

You can format the data list just like any other table on a page. This means you can modify the table column and row dimensions, change the data list icon, apply background colors to cells, and so on. In addition, you can also select the option to display column titles. You make all these options available by selecting the table that is the data list and Properties palette will appear as shown in Figure 20-16.

Figure 20-16: The Data list Properties palette.

The only things you *cannot* change in the data list are the font style, attributes, and color of the text. This text automatically assumes SiteStyle for the page (in this case, Hiway). To change these attributes, you'll have to go to Style view.

To make the data fit in the table for this data list (some of the Link Names are longer than the second column is wide), select the table and expand the width of the second column by dragging it to the right.

Tip Remember, to select a table, click the table and hold down the mouse button for a moment until the selection handles turn black. You can then resize the row and column borders accordingly. Another method of selecting a table is to draw a marquee around it by holding down the mouse button and drawing a square around the table. For large tables, though, this can be difficult. Consequently, the first method is preferable. Figure 20-17 shows the resized table.

Now you can see exactly what all this handiwork has produced. To see the completed data list, preview the current page by pressing the Preview button. Figure 20-18 shows the previewed page in Internet Explorer.

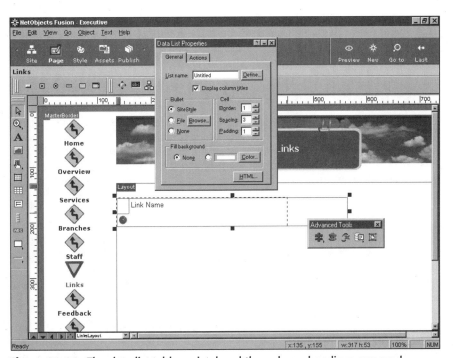

Figure 20-17: The data list table resized and the column headings removed.

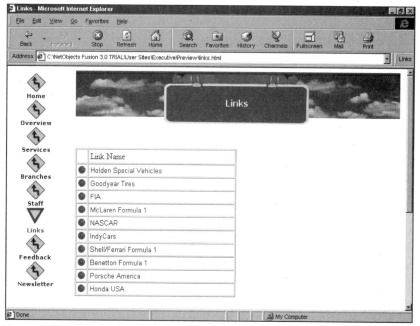

Figure 20-18: The Links page showing the completed data list (index).

Designing the stacked pages

Okay, the hard work is done. All you have left to do is the creative and fun bit — designing the stacked pages the way you want them. If you return to Site view at this time, you can see that Fusion has added a new page icon below the Links page (see Figure 20-19). This icon is a little different because it simulates several pages. These pages are the stacked pages Fusion created after the data object and data list were defined.

Stacked pages are just like any other pages in Fusion. You can apply any sort of formatting treatment to them you want. The only difference is that any formatting you apply to one stacked page applies that formatting to all the other stacked pages.

To edit the stacked pages, double-click the icon in Site view to enter Page view as shown in Figure 20-20.

The first thing to do is add the fields required on the stacked page using the Data List tool as shown earlier in Figure 20-14. By selecting this tool and drawing on the page (just as if you were creating a text field), the Data Field dialog box opens, letting you choose a field to place on the page. Figure 20-20 shows the page with all the fields in place as well as text description fields. After a field is placed, it automatically assumes the data from the corresponding record in the attached database.

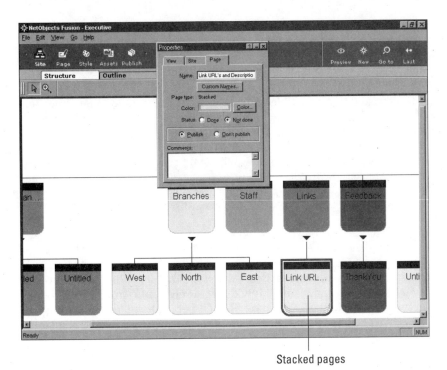

Stacked pages

Figure 20-19: The stacked pages shown in Site view.

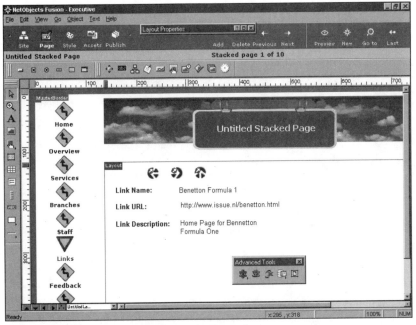

Figure 20-20: The first stacked page in Page view.

Note   Fields only have to be entered onto the first stacked page. They automatically appear on all other stacked pages together with the data from the corresponding database record.

To edit the stacked pages, double-click the icon in Site view to enter Page view as shown in Figure 20-21. Notice that a new detail lies across the top of the icon bar showing which stacked page you are currently viewing out of the total number of stacked pages in this data list. To change from page to page in the stacked pages list, simply click the left or right arrow. When you reach the end of the stacked page list, the next stacked page will wrap. For example, if there are ten stacked pages, when you are viewing number ten and click the right arrow to view the next page, the first page displays. The reverse of this also applies.

If you "select all" at this time (by pressing Ctrl+A or choosing Edit ⇨ Select All from the menu bar), you can see that each element on the stacked page is a separate entity. You can move these elements around at will, placing them wherever you like and formatting them individually. Using the standard formatting procedures you have used before, you can format individual text elements with regards to font style, color, type, alignment, and so on. Remember that any formatting applied to any entity on a stacked page is reflected in the same entity on *every* stacked page in the data list. Figure 20-21 shows an example of how these stacked pages may look after formatting. Figure 20-22 shows the stacked page in Preview mode. Note the Navigation (Previous/Next/Up) icons placed by Fusion.

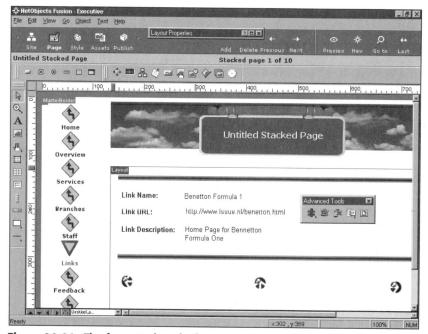

Figure 20-21: The formatted stacked page.

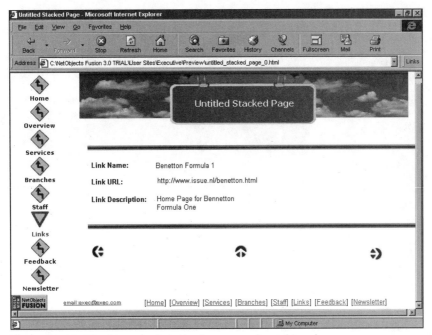

Figure 20-22: The formatted stacked page previewed in a browser.

Turning a stacked page field into a clickable object

At the moment, each field in the stacked pages is a straightforward text object. Because this is a page showing a potentially interesting link, it would therefore make sense to have the text box showing the individual site URLs as a clickable link. Doing so would save site visitors from having to copy the text of the link to their browsers and manually relocating to the page defined in the link. Instead, visitors could simply click it and be transported to the site nominated in the field.

This procedure is easy and uses a sneaky way of using the Add HTML feature of Fusion. Stay tuned!

What you need to do is surround the existing data with HTML code. The problem, of course, is that the actual data in the field is potentially changeable because it comes from a database. If the database content changes ('cause the link does), you need a method to make sure the Web page is correctly updated with the new information. To achieve this result, you need a combination of Fusion variables and HTML scripting. Follow these steps:

1. Delete the existing text field Fusion has placed for the Link URL data (see Figure 20-23).

2. Replace this field with a blank text field and make sure it is in insert mode (see Figure 20-24).

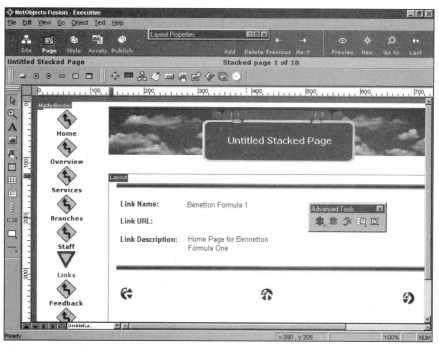

Figure 20-23: The page after deleting the Link Field.

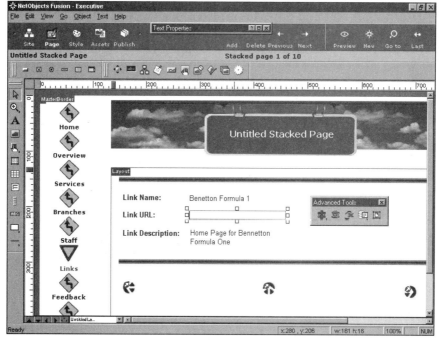

Figure 20-24: Place a new empty text field and make sure it is in insert mode.

3. From the Text Properties palette, click the HTML button (see Figure 20-25).

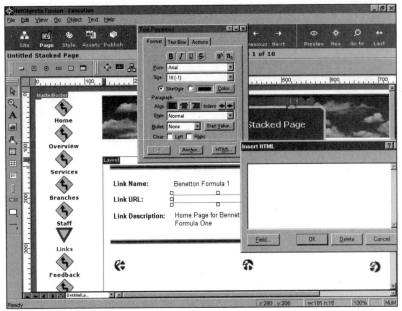

Figure 20-25: The HTML button on the Properties palette.

4. Enter the initial HTML code into the dialog box (see Figure 20-26):

```
<a href="
```

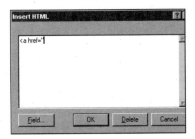

Figure 20-26: Insert the initial HTML code into the dialog box.

5. Click the Insert Variable button. From the drop-down list, choose the Data Object option and select the Link URL field from the list (see Figure 20-27).

Figure 20-27: Inserting the Data Object field variable for the Link URL.

6. Enter the middle part of the HTML code (see Figure 20-28):

```
">
```

Figure 20-28: Entering the next section of HTML code.

7. Once again, click the Insert Variable button and repeat Step 5.

8. Complete the HTML code (see Figure 20-29) by entering

```
</a>
```

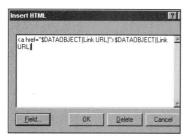

Figure 20-29: Completing the HTML code.

9. Click OK.

If you now preview the page as shown in Figure 20-30, you can see the data from the database is still there, but it is now a clickable link. If the database that supplies the text of the field on the Web page changes, because you are using a variable attached to the database, the field text is automatically updated the next time you publish the site.

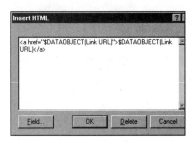

Figure 20-30: The previewed page showing the link for the Link URL field in place.

This is pretty clever, huh? It required a little bit of work, but the end result is worth the effort.

Adding Images

If your database supports the use of *binary large objects (BLOBS)*, you can import them into a stacked page the same way you can for any other field from the database. But if this is not the case, you can still import .GIF files and .JPEG images into a field on a stacked page. The trick is the way the database treats the reference to the original image, and how Fusion's Assets Register sees the definition of a field holding the details of the path name to the file you want displayed.

Note   Binary large objects (BLOBS) are a particular definition for images that can be stored in a database. To see whether your database does indeed accept this format, check your database documentation.

Sound confusing? Once you know how, it's easy! Here is where the Link Image field comes into play. I told you it would be useful and all would be revealed!

Say you have stored the image that belongs to the HSV record on the local hard disk. The full path to the file is

```
D:\mantra.jpg
```

The first step to including this image in the Web page is to place the full path name of the image in the Image Link field in the database, as shown in Figure 20-31.

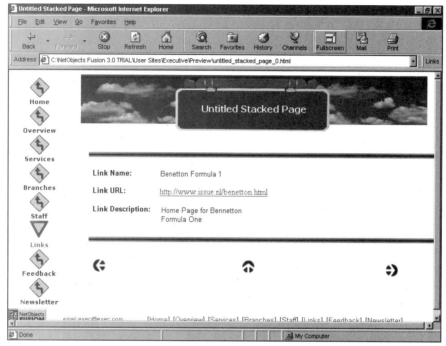

Figure 20-31: The database showing the field holding the path to the image.

Before continuing, if you added the original Link Image field earlier, delete it from the stacked page definition. This step is not always needed, but sometimes it overcomes a quirk that makes it refuse to accept the next step. This is the step that changes the format of the text field imported into the data list from the Access database to a Picture field. As you might guess by now, the picture that will be displayed on the Web page is the image referred to by the text path in the original field.

To change this attribute, open the Assets list for the Web site by clicking the Assets button on the icon bar and clicking the Data Objects button. The list of the data objects in the site opens, as shown in Figure 20-32. (There is always one data object asset called Sample; ignore this one.)

By double-clicking the name of the data object you have placed (Racing Links in this example), a dialog box opens, showing each of the fields in the database and their attributes. Double-clicking the Link Image field opens a second dialog box, and here you can change the field type to Image File. Figure 20-32 shows the Data Object dialog box, and Figure 20-33 shows the Data Field dialog box.

If you receive a warning dialog box stating that two fields cannot have the same name, change the name of the field in the top of the Data Field dialog box. When you place the new field on the Web page (remember you deleted the original), choose the one from the list that contains the new name.

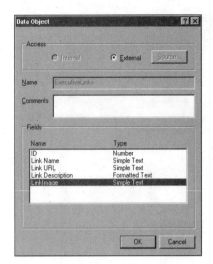

Figure 20-32: The Data Object dialog box.

Figure 20-33: The Data Field dialog box.

When you have changed the field attribute (and perhaps the name), you can return to Page view for the stacked page and add the Link Image field using the Data List tool. The image referenced in the path will now be displayed as shown in Figure 20-34. This applies to the field in every stacked page in the list. If the field in a stacked page refers to a path to an image, and that image exists, it displays correctly in Page view. The image file is also moved correctly to the Web server when posted.

Using the data publishing features of Fusion imparts a powerful new tool into the capabilities and functions afforded to Web authors. The possibilities and flexibility of data publishing are limited only by the imagination. When all the basic criteria have been set, no more work needs to be done. As long as the connected database is kept up-to-date, Fusion automatically and faithfully records all changes to the stacked pages for you every time you publish.

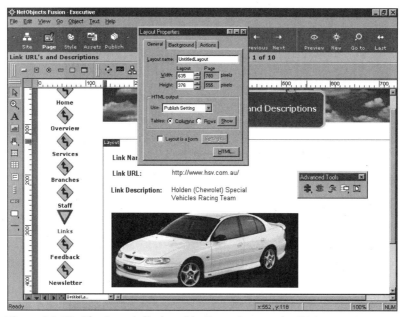

Figure 20-34: The image displayed in Page view on the Web page.

Summary

✦ Any ODBC-compliant database can be connected to a Fusion Web site.

✦ Other databases, such as ISM and SQL Server databases, can be included as long as the appropriate drivers are installed.

✦ A database connected to Fusion is a *data object*.

✦ The list of key fields displayed as an index is a *data list.*

✦ *Filtering* allows only selected records to be published.

✦ Stacked pages can be formatted in the same way as a standard page. Fonts, colors, images, backgrounds, and rich media objects all can be added to stacked pages.

✦ Any formatting applied to a stacked page applies to *all* stacked pages in that data list.

✦ Using Fusion's Insert HTML and variable options, any field can be made into a hyperlink.

✦ Graphics can be added either as binary large objects (BLOBS) or using the Assets view to change Data Field types to Images from the path names supplied.

✦ All records (stacked pages) created using data objects are updated automatically at publish time.

✦   ✦   ✦

Using Rich
Media

◆   ◆   ◆   ◆

◆   ◆   ◆   ◆

I have to confess that this is my favorite section of the book and was the most fun to write, albeit the technology had a tendency to try and outpace my typing! Rich media is what has made the Web come alive. Just 18 months ago, adding sound, complex animation, and video to Web pages was rare. Now it is commonplace.

In this section, I show not only how to add rich media components to Web pages using Fusion, but I also discuss the ramifications and potential pitfalls of doing so. The trick is to not create a situation where the visitors to your site are drumming their fingers, waiting for a page to load; at the same time you want to give them quality content in any of the media types that Fusion so easily allows you to add.

Adding Sound

Like any of the rich media elements you can add to a Web page, sound can have a large overhead, depending on the type of files you incorporate. In simple terms, there are three basic sources of sound files: *AU files, WAV files,* and *MIDI files*. A WAV file is a digitally stored sample of sound, and a MIDI file is an electronic representation of sound. The names WAV and AU come from the filename suffix such as BOING.WAV or CLICK.AU. A more specialized file type is the RA file—for RealAudio.

Of these files, MIDI files are more efficient by far in their storage and file size, but the drawback is that MIDI files are only good for music. As mentioned, WAV and AU files are digitally saved, actual recordings of speech, music, and so on. A MIDI file, on the other hand, is a sequence of instructions to a computer to play certain notes in certain ways. If you look at the documentation that comes with many of the popular sound cards, you will notice that they have a special chip or processor specifically designed to play these sequences.

A MIDI file does not contain a recorded sound of, say, a violin. Rather, it contains a set of instructions telling the computer to play a sound that *approximates* a violin. Because of this, if you want to place the climax of the 1812 Overture as an opening sound on your Web page, you can do so with MIDI, but it won't have the ambiance and depth of a real recording.

For speech, wave files (most commonly .WAV and .AIF files) are the only option. To give you a good idea of the potential size of these files, a five-second talking wave file at good quality (FM Radio quality) is approximately 250K in size. The higher the quality, the bigger the file size. Even at lowest quality (Telephone), the file would still be in the 100K+ size.

The quality of the sound file is determined by its frequency. At 44 kHz Stereo, the sound quality is roughly equivalent to a compact disc. As the frequency level drops in value, so does the quality of the sound (and the corresponding file size). At telephone level, the frequency is approximately 11 kHz Mono.

For a Web site to have sounds with any sort of decent quality, and to keep the file size manageable so that the site visitor doesn't have to wait an eternity before hearing anything, the sound bytes that can be added to Web pages must be small in duration. In this sense, small really means small, probably no more than a couple of seconds.

Having said that, over the last year or so, emerging technologies that started at a snail's pace and are now galloping are addressing this problem by using compression techniques to make the sound files smaller while retaining the quality. The best example of these technologies (and by far the most popular) is RealAudio from Real Networks. I discuss RealAudio and encoding sound files to compress them later in the chapter. Also under development, again with Real Networks at the forefront, is *streaming*. Under normal circumstances a site visitor has to wait until the sound file is fully downloaded before hearing the sound. With streaming the sound starts playing immediately, with the sound player accepting the data from the Web server as it is downloading instead of first storing it.

The only file type that Macintosh users cannot play is the .WAV type.

.WAV and .AU Files

For many sound file requirements, you can download and use literally thousands of public domain files available on the Internet.

Enclosed on the CD-ROM accompanying this book is a trial version of the Macromedia Flash program that also contains a variety of sound files you can use for effect.

If you want to create your own sound files, or even edit existing ones, you need a copy of a good sound-editing program. Some of these programs are available as shareware off the Net, whereas others are commercial packages. As in all cases with software, "you get what you pay for!"

GoldWave

GoldWave is a shareware Windows 95 sound editor with a bundle of features. GoldWave is supplied as a trial version available from the Net and as a full commercial version.

Not all of the features are available in the trial version, but for basic sound creation and editing, the program will suffice in most cases. You can import or save many different sound file formats, and the program caters well to adding special effects such as echoes, reversing sound tracks, cutting and splicing, and so on.

You can obtain GoldWave at www.sharewarejunkies.com/goldwave.htm. Figure 21-1 shows GoldWave with a speech sound file loaded and ready for editing.

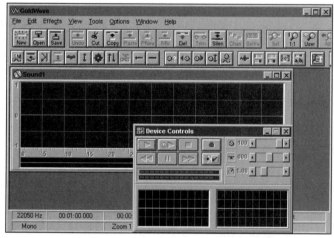

Figure 21-1: GoldWave audio-editing shareware.

Sound Forge XP

Sound Forge XP is a commercial application; it has no freeware or shareware version, so you must purchase it. Alternatively, many users have discovered Sound Forge XP because it is bundled with the Windows 95 version of Macromedia Director, but you can also buy a standalone version. Being a full commercial program, Sound Forge XP can take anything the amateur or professional can throw at it and is highly recommended, as you can see from the extensive list of options shown in Figure 21-2.

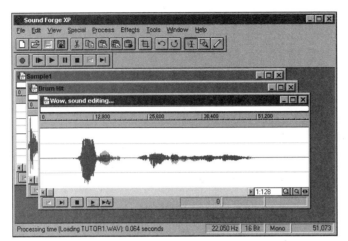

Figure 21-2: Sound Forge XP audio-editing software.

Because Sound Forge XP is such a comprehensive program, you're best off having some knowledge of audio editing, although it is fun to learn as you go. Removing pops and clicks from recorded sounds, for example, means you need to know about the various audio terminology and commands employed in Sound Forge XP.

For more information on Sound Forge XP, have a look at www.sfoundry.com.

RealAudio Encoder

While not strictly a sound-editing program, probably the most popular method of storing audio files involves RealAudio from Real Networks. To get the full benefit of the capabilities, such as streaming and high compression, you need access to a RealAudio server; for smaller files you can trick the system, as you'll see later in this chapter. Figure 21-3 shows the RealVideo Encoder, and Figure 21-4 shows the RealPlayer.

Having played at length with RealAudio (and its sibling RealVideo), I am convinced this is the way to go. In fact, a recent survey showed that in the vicinity of 80 percent of the top Web sites in the world have either RealAudio or RealVideo elements on their pages. The possibilities are endless and not just limited to news or sports broadcasts.

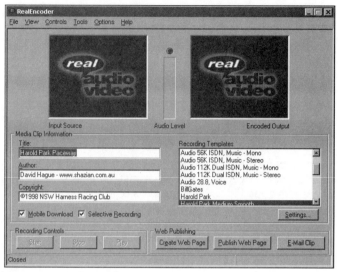

Figure 21-3: The RealVideo Encoder.

Figure 21-4: The RealPlayer.

In fact, a new development — also from Real Networks — lets you add audio files to Microsoft PowerPoint presentations and convert them into movies. Now, I ask you, how many millions of corporate PowerPoint presentations are out there that can go on a company's Web site? A picture is worth a thousand words; this must make a movie worth a million! I'll provide more on this later.

You can obtain more information on RealAudio from www.real.com.

MIDI Files

All the previous applications are designed to create wave or special compressed audio files that can contain speech or music.

Because of the huge file size used by WAV files, most developers who place music tracks on their Web sites use the MIDI format. MIDI is highly compressed in comparison. For example, three or four minutes of MIDI music may be only 30K or less in size.

If you are keen and have an ear for music plus the necessary equipment, you can create your own MIDI files using keyboards and other instruments that are MIDI-compliant. If not, you can download literally thousands of MIDI tracks from the Net. If you have a favorite piece of music, use any of the search engines, such as Yahoo!, Excite, or AltaVista, to perform a search using keywords such as **Oldfield+MIDI**. This search, for example, would find any MIDI tracks that are copies of any music by Mike Oldfield.

Note

Just in case you are wondering, Mike Oldfield wrote, directed, produced, and played every instrument on "Tubular Bells." For a MIDI copy of this and many other Mike Oldfield tracks, have a look at www.upv.es/~jlbalmas/oldfield.html (as shown in Figure 21-5).

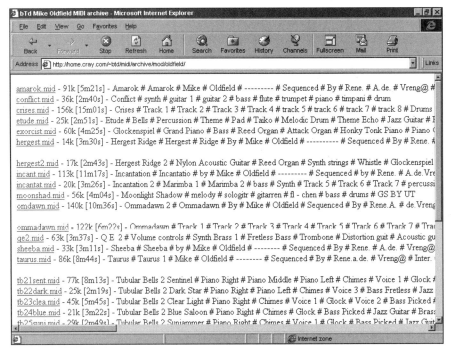

Figure 21-5: The Mike Oldfield MIDI site.

Adding Sounds to Web Pages

The preceding information was not designed to turn you into a sound engineer overnight; it was merely designed to give you an overview into the sorts of technologies available in the digital sound area. If you would like to know more, many books and even training courses in many cities are available.

However, you don't need a degree in rocket science to add any sorts of sounds to a Web page, as you will soon see.

A background MIDI track

To see how easy it is to add a sound file (WAV or MIDI) to a Web page, you'll add a background MIDI track to the Executive Performance home page. This track automatically plays whenever someone browses to this page. This is the easiest form of placing a sound file. To place a MIDI track on a Web page, follow these steps:

1. Click anywhere in the Layout section to make sure the Layout Properties palette appears, and choose the Background tab. Here you see an option for Sound (shown in Figure 21-6).

2. Click the check box to open a dialog box prompting for the location of the file to be added as a background sound, plus the option to loop the sound. For the sake of this exercise, you'll use a sample MIDI file supplied with Fusion called demo0001.mid.

Note

   The dialog box to select the sound file defaults to an .AIF file. To change this file and view all the sound files in this folder, select All Files in the Files of type drop-down list.

3. Click the Browse button and select the demo0001.mid file in the NetObjects Fusion 3.0/Samples/Content/Sounds folder.

4. Close the dialog box and click OK.

5. Play the file by previewing the page in a browser. Press Ctrl and click the Preview button.

Danger Zone

Looping means that when the file has finished playing its sequence, the browser starts the sound file once again — no matter whether it is a wave or MIDI file — and continuously replays it until the site visitor moves on to another page. My own feeling is that it is best to avoid the looping facility. If nothing else, when testing the page you will become heartily sick of the soundtrack, and it is a fair bet that regular visitors to the page will feel the same after a while. Bear in mind that visitors have no option to turn off the sound, short of turning down the volume!

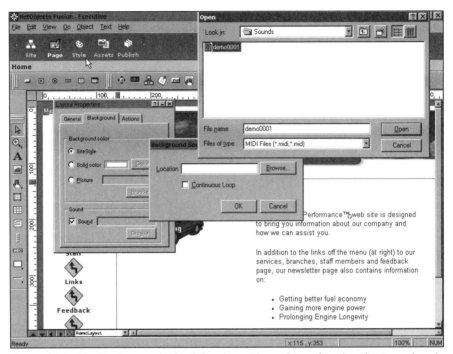

Figure 21-6: The Background tab of the Properties palette showing the Sound options and the dialog box selecting the MIDI file.

Using rich media tools for sound

Using the rich media tools gives you great control over the placement and usage of sound files. These tools enable you to link or embed sound files on Web pages against simply having a background sound play when the page loads in a Web browser.

To place a file using these tools, select the Media tool (the button that looks like a puzzle piece) on the Advanced toolbar, shown in Figure 21-7. From the pop-out menu, the last of the available options is the Sound tool. Choosing the Sound tool and drawing a rectangle on the page shown in Figure 21-8 opens a dialog box that prompts for the location of the file. After you select a file, the Sound Properties palette appears.

Figure 21-7: Selecting the Sound tool from the Media tool on the Advanced toolbar.

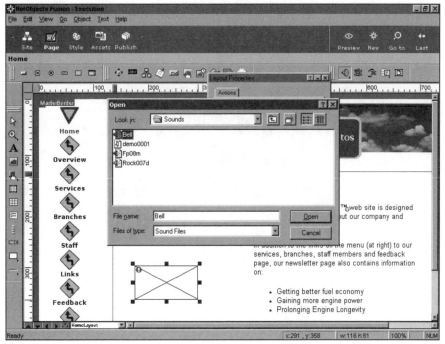

Figure 21-8: The Open dialog box prompts you for the location of the sound file you wish to place.

As an example, place the bell.wav file, which is in the same folder as the MIDI file placed earlier. Here's how to do it:

1. Select the Sound tool from the Media tool pop-out on the Advanced toolbar (as shown in Figure 21-7).

2. Draw its location on the page, and the Open dialog box appears.

3. Make sure the Files of type drop-down list is set to All Files, and select the bell.wav file from the NetObjects Fusion 3.0/Samples/Content/Sounds folder. Then click Open.

4. The Sound Properties palette appears. The dialog box presents you with three options for a sound file:

   • You can store the sound file as an inline sound.

   • You can display one of three Fusion icons.

   • You can display a picture (image file) from a file stored on the hard disk.

5. Select an icon option and preview the page in a browser by pressing Ctrl and clicking the Preview button in the icon bar.

Of the three icon selections in the Display area of the Sound Properties palette, the first option places the sound file as an *inline* file. When you use this option, a graphic control similar to that of a CD player (as shown in Figure 21-9) displays on the page at the location where you placed the Media Sound object.

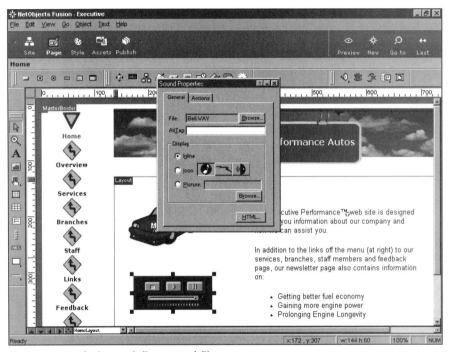

Figure 21-9: Placing an inline sound file.

Instead of automatically playing the file, the site visitor can start and stop the sounds or move forward or backward in the file at any time. The Web page showing the rich media inline graphic for the sound file is shown in Figure 21-10.

The second option lets you select one of three Fusion icons to show the location of a sound file. When the user clicks the icon, the sound plays. The third option is similar to the second option, the difference being that it lets you supply your own icon from a file. After the icon is placed, by selecting the image file from a dialog box, the user can also click the icon to play the attached sound file.

Note   Make sure the image file you use is a .GIF or .JPG file.

Figure 21-10: The inline sound shown in the Web browser.

No matter what your preference in the style of placing a sound file on a Web page using the Rich Media Tool, as with all graphics, don't forget to fill in the Alt tag on the SoundProperties palette when the graphics icon for the sound file is selected.

Note

In this case, the Alt tag refers to the graphic icon that the site visitor clicks to play the file, but it should still reflect the sound to be played (such as the "Wedding March" or "Gentleman Start Your Engines").

Creating and placing a RealAudio file

As promised, now is the time to learn how you can use a cheat to place a RealAudio file on a Web page without the need for a RealAudio server. Before you can do this, you need a copy of the RealEncoder shown in Figure 21-11, available from `www.real.com/products/creation/index.html`. The Real Encoder encodes both RealAudio and RealVideo, by the way. In fact, although in the past the two file types were quite different, they now both come under the banner of *RealMedia*.

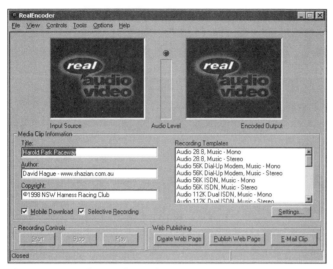

Figure 21-11: The RealEncoder.

When you have the RealEncoder loaded, you need to set it up correctly for audio only. Follow these steps:

1. Open a new session by selecting the New Session option from the File menu. A dialog box opens as shown in Figure 21-12.

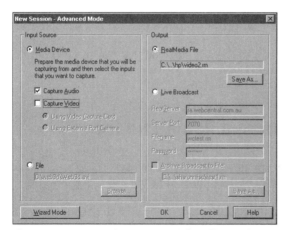

Figure 21-12: Creating a new RealMedia session as Audio Capture.

2. When creating a new session, the RealEncoder assumes you will be making a RealVideo file. So that only audio is expected, change the Capture Video option to Capture Audio (as Figure 21-12 shows) by unchecking the video checkbox.

3. Choose a filename into which the compressed audio is saved by clicking the Save As button at the right side of the dialog box, as shown in Figure 21-13. Type a new filename in the dialog box, and click Save to close the box.

4. After saving the file, you can press OK to close the open session dialog box.

Note

Make sure the Live Broadcast radio button is not selected in the New Session dialog box.

Figure 21-13: Creating a new output file for the captured RealMedia content.

The Properties section of the RealVideo Encoder window (shown previously in Figure 21-11) contains options to enter information for the Title, Author, or Copyright of the sound you are encoding. The listing on the left is where you select the type of compression required. The folks at Real Networks — the developers of RealAudio, RealVideo, and RealMedia — have made selecting compression easy by listing the choices as styles rather than techie-type terms. For most audio only, the Audio at 28.8 is quite adequate, although you may want to experiment with this under your own particular set of connectivity and hardware/software combinations. If you like to tinker, you can also tweak more options under the Settings button.

The final two options of the Mobile Download and Selective record checkboxes are optional. In short, if unchecked these checkboxes stop people listening to the audio so they can either download your audio file or record sections of the file themselves.

Now that you've set up all the parameters, it is time to start recording your audio by clicking the Start button. Of course, for this to work, it is necessary to have an audio source connected to the Line Input port of your sound card.

All the compression is done in *real time*, meaning that if you are compressing 15 minutes of audio, it will take 15 minutes to capture all the data from the audio source. When completed, you need to place the file onto the Web page in Fusion Page view mode.

This is where the trick comes into play!

Say you want to place the location and name of the saved *.rm file you have created with the Encoder at `www.shazian.com.au/real_audio_file.rm`. You need to create a simple text file, called a *META file*, that contains the string of the name (without quotes) of the *.rm file, as shown in Figure 21-14. The META file in this case would be called real_audio_file.ram. You manually send this file to the Web server using an FTP program such as WS_FTP, or Fetch on the Macintosh. For this to work, you must place the *.rm file (the text file) in the directory that contains the RealAudio file (which you must also do manually).

Figure 21-14: Creating the RealMedia META file.

Note   An FTP program such as WS_FTP is used to copy files from your local computer to the Web server. NetObjects Fusion 3 has an FTP program built in, and the mechanism to transfer files is pretty much a point-and-click affair. Using programs such as WS_FTP is a little more difficult, but no more difficult than using the Windows Explorer program or the Finder on a Mac. In most FTP programs, two windows display the contents of the local hard drive and the server respectively. To transfer files from one to another (assuming you are connected to the Web server) is as simple as dragging from one window to another. You can obtain WS_FTP from `www.softwarejunkies.com`.

Finally, to complete the process you must link any object on the Fusion page pointing to the URL of the META file, *not* the RealAudio file, as shown in Figure 21-15. This can be a text link or a graphic link. The basics are exactly the same as for any other link you have created so far, with the exception that instead of using an HTML page as the destination, you enter the full path of the *.rm file as shown.

That's all there is to it: streaming audio without a RealAudio server.

Note   The same process works if you encode a complete RealVideo file instead of a RealAudio file. If you do this, you will probably need to play around a lot more with the settings for the capture file to get the best results for your particular hardware/software combination.

Of course, to create a RealVideo, as well as an audio source, you need a video source. I have had excellent results using a standard Canon 8mm camcorder and a VideoBlaster Capture card.

Hot Stuff   If you want a Real Audio file to play inline (immediately as the page opens without the user having to click a button or link to start it), the sample HTML code in Listing 21-1 will play the file for you.

Figure 21-15: Creating the link to the META file.

In this case, the .rpm file is the same as the previously used "ram" file: a text file pointing to the URL of the *.rm file. (It is called *rpm* because it uses the RealMedia plug-in technology.) Create the file the same way as the ram file; just save it with the .rpm extension. The rest of the controls define the height, width, and so on of the RealPlayer controls and depend on your local situation. This code should give you a good starting point, however.

To place the code, first create a text field in Fusion where you want the player controls to be located. Then select the field, click the HTML button on the Text Properties palette, and paste this code (suitably amended for your situation) into the dialog box.

Listing 21-1: Example HTML code to enable embedded RealMedia to play when a Web page is opened.

```
<embed src="020298am.rpm" console="clip1" width=176 height=144
controls="Imagewindow" border=0 autostart="true"><br>
<embed src="empty.rpm" console="clip1" width=176 height=20
controls="StatusBar" autostart="false" embed="center">
<br><embed src="empty.rpm" console="clip1" width=176 height=30
controls="ControlPanel" autostart="false" embed="center">
<NOEMBED>
Your browser can't display plug-ins so you can't hear our Real
Audio. Have you thought about updating your browser?
</NOEMBED>
```

Tip

For an even fancier effect, assuming you have more than one RealAudio file you want visitors to choose from, you can place the descriptions of each audio file in a list box, as shown in Figure 21-16. Site visitors can then select which file they would like to hear. After selecting a file, visitors are taken to a page where the inline audio is stored, and the show starts immediately.

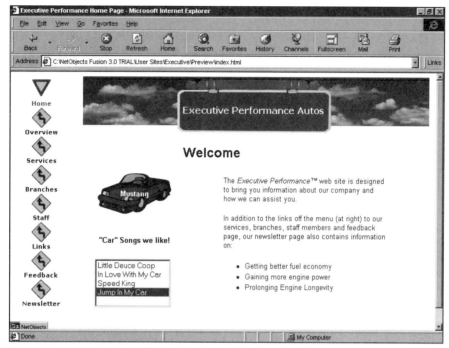

Figure 21-16: Selecting a file to play from a list (combo) box.

Follow these steps to create the list box:

1. Create a new page for each file to be played, and embed the RealPlayer file.

2. Go to the source page (where you'll place the list box).

3. Create a Form Area, and then select the Forms Combo Box tool from the Form toolbar. Place a combo box on the page in the Form Area (see Chapter 16 for more information on Form Areas).

4. Use the Name field to add the descriptives for each audio file. Use the Value field to add the destination URLs for the actual page (each *must* be the full path name) as shown in Figure 21-17. When you have created each destination, click OK to close the Enter Value dialog box.

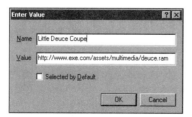

Figure 21-17: Entering the URLs of the pages to navigate to.

5. When you have finished adding all the Elements of the Combo Box, select the combo box control on the page and click the HTML button on the Forms Combo Box Properties palette. Click the Inside Tag tab and enter the following code in the large area:

```
onchange="top.location.href = this.options[this.selectedIndex].
value;"
```

6. Close the Object HTML dialog box by clicking OK.

Now, when a visitor selects an option from the list box, he or she will be taken to the page containing that audio or video file, which will start playing immediately.

Adding sounds to a page can add dramatically to the Web experience of visitors to your site. Always be wary that sound files (especially .WAV and .AIF files) can take some time to download. This can be irksome to some people, especially if the file is placed as a background sound where they have no control over the choice of whether to play the sound.

Tip

Investigate and learn all that RealMedia has to offer. Its Web site is at www.real.com. While you're surfing, have a look at www.timecast.com/audio/index.html for some really cool uses of RealAudio!

Summary

✦ Sounds are usually either .WAV, .AIF, or .MIDI files.

✦ .WAV and .AIF files can be used for music or speech.

✦ .MIDI files can only be used for music

✦ Sounds can be placed as background sounds that play automatically as a Web page is loaded (with a looping option).

✦ Sounds can also be inline, where the visitor to the page physically has to switch on the sound by clicking a graphic.

✦ RealAudio files can be added to pages using links to special META files. Inline RealAudio gives the user a system of controls to fast forward, rewind, stop, or pause the audio stream.

✦ ✦ ✦

Adding Animation

Shockwave is a relatively new addition to the Web site developer's toolbox. Initially developed by the Macromedia Corporation for its Director multimedia development package, Shockwave is a technology designed to allow the addition of Director and Flash "movies" to Web pages.

Since Shockwave's initial appearance, Macromedia has expanded the technology to encompass not only its Director multimedia authoring package, but also Flash 2, a lower-level animation package (a trial version is included on this book's CD-ROM), and Authorware, Macromedia's high-level authoring program. The availability of these programs adds to a Web site potential functionality that was unheard of only a year ago.

You can add full-motion graphics and synchronized sound, animation, and video to Web pages in NetObjects Fusion by including files created by either of these programs. The individual applications develop the content you require, and the Afterburner component supplied with each of these products then applies the Shockwave technology to make the resultant content Web-savvy. It is this Web-savvy resultant file that you add to the Web page in Page view, as shown in Figure 22-1.

Figure 22-1: Shockwave content on a Web page.

Shockwave consists of two components:

✦ Afterburner "shocks" the output of Director, Flash, or Authorware to create a Shockwave file.

✦ The client installs an ActiveX control or Netscape plug-in to view the shocked files in the browser.

The major advantage of Shockwave content is its streaming characteristic. Because the resultant shocked files are created in chunks (not very technical, I know, but you get the idea), they can start playing immediately when downloaded to the browser, while the rest of the file downloads in the background. As a result, you can create large applications using these powerful Macromedia tools and take full advantage of the functionality afforded you.

Shockwave Considerations

There are no special considerations when embedding Shockwave content into Web pages — apart from the necessity (mentioned earlier) that the people viewing the page have the appropriate ActiveX control or plug-in installed in their browsers. You can obtain both ActiveX controls and plug-ins from the Macromedia Web site at www.macromedia.com, as shown in Figure 22-2. In some cases you won't even need to download these, because later versions of Netscape Navigator and Microsoft Internet Explorer come with the control or plug-in already included.

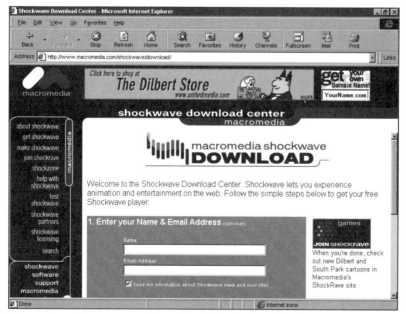

Figure 22-2: The Macromedia ActiveX/plug-in download page.

Adding Shockwave Content

As you may have guessed by now, adding Shockwave content is a simple affair and exactly the same as adding sound or video to a Web site. In fact, the Shockwave tool is on the same section of the Advanced toolbar as the Sound and Video tools, as shown in Figure 22-3.

Figure 22-3: The Shockwave tool on the Advanced Tools palette.

To place any Shockwave component, follow these steps:

1. Select the Shockwave tool that appears in the pop-out menu of the Advanced toolbar.

2. Draw the location on the Web page where you want to place the Shockwave content.

3. In the dialog box that appears, select the file that is the Shockwave content and click OK. An icon appears at the location of the placed file, as shown in Figure 22-4.

4. Enter the name into the Properties palette for the Alt tag to be applied to the Shockwave content.

Figure 22-4 shows an example of a Shockwave file placed on a Web page. This component, an Under Construction sign complete with sound effects, is supplied and installed from the Fusion CD-ROM. It is stored in the Shockwave folder within the Content folder.

Note

The addition of the Under Construction graphic demonstrates the addition of a Shockwave file to a Web page. In reality, I do not subscribe to using an Under Construction graphic at any time because it broadcasts a sloppy attitude towards Web development. In other words, if pages are not completed, don't place any of them in an area where they are accessible by the browsing public.

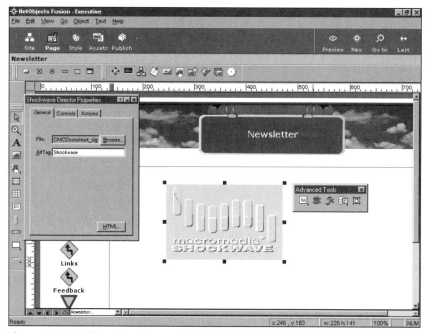

Figure 22-4: Adding Shockwave content to a page in Page view.

Incorporating Flash Movies

Although not immediately obvious, you can also use the Shockwave tool to embed Flash 2 (previously known as FutureSplash) movies into Web pages. Simply follow the same steps as for a Director movie. When the dialog box opens for you to select a Director file, navigate instead to the required Flash 2 movie file. You may need to change the filename suffix in the drop-down list to help in finding the file.

For those keen to try out Flash 2, seen in Figure 22-5, a trial version of the program appears on the CD-ROM that accompanies this book.

There is no doubt that the addition of Director, Flash, and Authorware content will set your Web pages apart from the simple HTML-only-based ones. As you have seen, adding this content is simplicity in itself (as are all things in Fusion when you get the hang of them!). The same cannot be said for the development of Shockwave content, however.

Flash 2 is a relatively easy package to learn, although its metaphors as a drawing program are totally skewed in their direction to other illustrative-type programs. In essence, you have to forget all you have learned with Illustrator, Freehand, Designer, or whatever. Flash is inexpensive (for good examples of Flash at work, have a look at www.msn.com) and very effective at what it does.

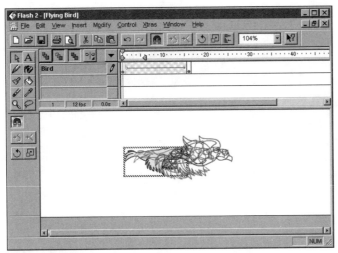

Figure 22-5: A flying bird in Macromedia Flash 2.

Director (shown in Figure 22-6) — and Authorware (shown in Figure 22-7) even more so — requires a huge learning curve to get the best results from it. When you are there, it is well worth the effort. One major drawback for the casual developer, however, is the cost of these applications, as they can set you back over $1,000 in some places.

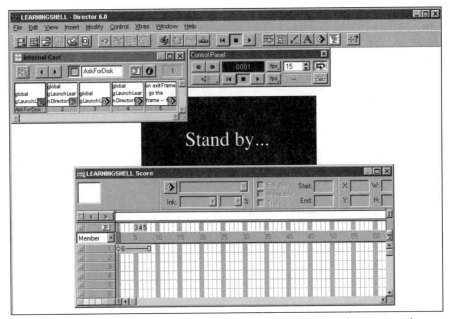

Figure 22-6: Macromedia Director showing a Director movie under construction.

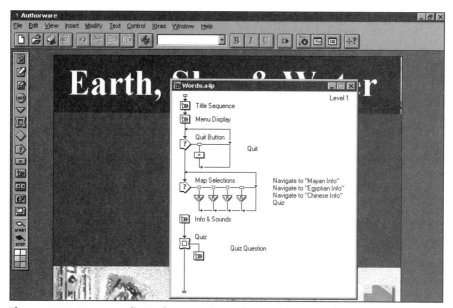

Figure 22-7: Macromedia Authorware is used to make interactive computer training applications that can be "shocked" and placed in a Web site.

Adding Other Rich Media Types

From the Advanced toolbar's Media plug-in tool, a number of other objects can easily be added to Web pages in NetObjects Fusion, including Virtual Reality files, Adobe Acrobat documents, and panoramic images. The methodology of placing these objects follows the same pattern as for adding sound video or Shockwave files.

Maybe I am biased, but of all the types of objects, I find the inclusion of panoramic photographs on a Web site to be the most exciting. If you haven't yet come across this technology, let me explain.

Remember when you used to take a whole series of photos of a landscape or cityscape? When the photos came back from the laboratory, the clear tape and the scissors were brought out to "stitch" the photos together to make a w-i-d-e panorama single photo.

Well, this technology is now available digitally. A number of applications exist to do this, and the one I prefer is PhotoVista from LivePicture (see www.livepicture.com). The difference, however, is that by using the mouse, you can "pan" the photograph inside the window — even turning a full 360 degrees. The application of this technology in real estate, entertainment, and hospitality industries is mind-boggling!

An example of a PhotoVista image in a Web page is shown in Figure 22-8.

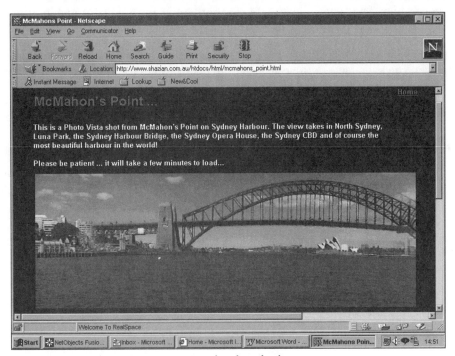

Figure 22-8: A PhotoVista panorama of Sydney harbor.

The steps to add a PhotoVista panorama are simple:

1. Create the image to be placed using the PhotoVista software (two files are output — a .JPG file containing the image and an .IVR file containing the panorama information).

2. Using the Media tool, draw the location on the Web page where the panorama shot is to be placed.

3. From the dialog box, select the .IVR file (*not* the .JPG file) you want to place.

4. Switch to Assets view. Using the Assets ⇨ Load File command from the menu bar, load the corresponding .JPG file into the Assets Register. When you publish, make sure the .JPG file is placed in the same folder as the .IVR file. (See Part VI for full details on publishing your Web site.)

Voilà! That's all there is to it.

Note   You will need a plug-in for your browser for PhotoVista panorama files to be viewed successfully. This plug-in is available for both Netscape Navigator and Internet Explorer 4 from the LivePicture Web site, as is a trial version of PhotoVista.

Have a look with PhotoVista; it is a lot fun and the possibilities are endless. Images placed can even have *hotspots* assigned to take viewers to other panorama shots. This technology is evolving all the time.

Summary

✦ Shockwave is a technology used to compress and segment applications built in Macromedia Director, Flash, and Authorware.

✦ Shockwave content is added using the Shockwave tool on the Rich Media tools palette.

✦ Before Shockwave content can be viewed in a browser, an appropriate ActiveX control or plug-in is needed.

✦ Panorama photos, Adobe Acrobat documents, and Virtual Reality images can all be placed into your Web sites as Rich Media.

✦   ✦   ✦

Adding Video

If using audio files causes a dilemma due to large file sizes, video takes this problem and multiplies it by a factor of ten! Even 30 seconds of video at the highest possible compression will be quite more than 1MB. Research and development divisions of many companies are searching for a satisfactory way of adding video to Web pages seamlessly and with minimal file sizes. Once again, Real Networks stands at the forefront, but Apple's QuickTime format is also worth considering as it has matured considerably of late.

Tip

Another company doing great work in video is Iterated Systems (www.iterated.com). This company apparently did the donkey work to create the compressor engine that Real Networks uses. In addition, it has created its own network that can be used in conjunction with Adobe Premiere for highly compressing .AVI files. The rendering of such files takes a *very* long time, but the resulting files are small and very clear. You can find an example of an .AVI file compressed with the Iterated Systems Clear Video plug-in at www.shazian. com.au/htdocs/html/video_ie3.html (for Internet Explorer 3 and 4) and www.shazian.com.au/htdocs/ html/videonetscape.html (for Netscape users). You'll need the Clear Video plug-in (which is accessible from either of these two pages).

In the concept of a Web page, the term *video* is generally used to describe a file format more than actual video (as in moving "real" pictures). Because of this, video is accepted as including high-resolution animation as well as video footage taken from a camcorder or VCR.

Video File Formats

The two primary file formats for video used on PC and Macintosh platforms are .AVI (Audio Video Interleave), developed by Microsoft, and .QT (QuickTime), developed by Apple Computer. For Web purposes you'll usually use source applications to create the file with either of these two formats, and you'll apply special compression routines from third-party companies (such as Real Networks or Iterated Systems) to minimize the file size. For example, you can use Infini-D, a high-end 3D authoring program, to create a "movie" of an animated logo, save the file to an .AVI format, and compress and encode it using RealVideo.

Although the use of these compression routines can certainly aid in bringing down massive file sizes to a relatively workable size, the drawback in many cases is that the viewer of the page must have a corresponding plug-in for his or her browser before seeing the video. Because of this, many people who surf the Web don't bother to view video — it is just too much of a nuisance until some major standards are set in place.

Many useful graphics applications use either .AVI or QuickTime as their default file format, and you can quite successfully apply the output from these formats to Web sites. Examples of such applications include the aforementioned Infini-D and Cinema 3D. Even Macromedia Flash can be exported to .AVI files.

All the programs I have mentioned share a common factor — they support either the .AVI or QuickTime format. You can place these file types "natively" on a Web page because they are without further compression, and standard players such as the Windows 95 Media Player will recognize these file types. (For Windows 95-equipped machines, you may have to download a QuickTime player from www.apple.com/quicktime).

Be aware that the computer resources necessary to create video are high. A minimum 32MB of RAM, a fast hard disk, and *lots* of hard disk space are necessary. In addition, the tools (software) you need to produce the very best of what is possible are in the higher price bracket. A large hard disk is just that, by the way. Without at least 5GB to store your movies, you will not be able to create anything of length.

None of the packages discussed here are shareware. Some of them, such as Infini-D, have trial versions available, but they are all commercial packages varying in price from a couple hundred dollars to more than a thousand.

You'll find a trial version of Infini-D and Macromedia Flash for both Macintosh and Windows 95 users on the CD-ROM with this book.

Tools to Create Video Files

There are many great tools on both the Windows and Macintosh platforms to create files. While not a complete list, in the following sections I discuss a number of these tools I have used over the years.

Web 3D

Web 3D from Asymetrix is a low-end, 3D animation-generation application mainly suited for creating 3D animated text. It is not particularly flexible, but you can generate 3D logos quickly and apply animation to them. You can then add different backdrops and surfaces to completed video sequences, define motions, and place lights at strategic points to gain effect. Only one camera is available for "filming" your animation, and it stays in a fixed position.

The default output format for Web 3D is an .AVI file, but, if required, you can easily import the resulting file into animated .GIF-generation programs and convert it accordingly. Figure 23-1 shows Web 3D with a graphics logo being created.

Figure 23-1: Web 3D.

Simply 3D

Simply 3D from Micrografx is an excellent lower-end application for generating 3D .AVI scenes. Part of the Graphics Suite 2 bundle of applications, you also get the advantage of gaining a top-flight image-editing and drawing program thrown in for a reasonable price.

Simply 3D is only available for Windows 95. For more information, take a look at www.micrografx.com.

Macromedia Extreme 3D

Macromedia Extreme 3D is one rung up the ladder in capability from Simply 3D and three rungs up from Web 3D. You can apply much more complexity to objects, and unlike Web 3D but similar to Simply 3D, you can build entire 3D models using the tools supplied. You can define multiple cameras to film separate views of the animation, and Extreme 3D also has a Macintosh as well as a Windows 95 version. Files are saved in either .AVI or QuickTime format.

Full details on Macromedia Extreme 3D are available from www.macromind.com.

Infini-D

Infini-D (shown in Figure 23-2 and available in both Macintosh and Windows 95 versions), in my opinion, is the granddaddy of the 3D/animated video-generation packages. With time, imagination, and more time, nothing is impossible with Infini-D. In fact, if you had that much time (and a fast PC or Mac), you could make a complete Web version of the movie *Toy Story* if you wanted.

Infini-D is not for the faint-hearted, however, because the learning curve is very steep. Because it's quite capable of creating a simple, spinning logo to broadcast-quality video animation, in my opinion, the serious Web developer cannot surpass Infini-D.

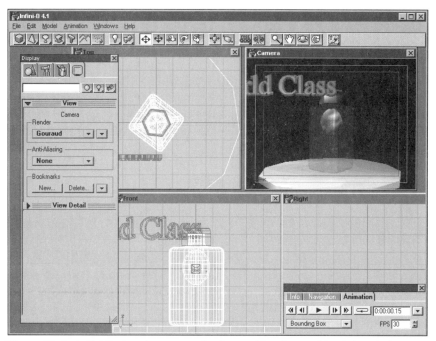

Figure 23-2: Infini-D showing a complex logo with a "space" backdrop being created. Note the multiple cameras and lights.

Macromedia Director

Macromedia Director has become the standard application for generating Web-based multimedia, and you can incorporate .AVI or QuickTime files into Director's final output, as well as graphics, text, and sounds (see Figure 23-3). Director has excellent tools for creating images and manipulating text, and it even has its own language, called Lingo, to control the flow and pace of the resulting animation or movie.

Strictly an industrial-strength package for the commercial developer, Director has a large learning curve and a price tag potentially beyond the reach of the casual user.

Figure 23-3: Macromedia Director was used to create this interactive CD-ROM to teach school children the intricacies of the taxation system.

Adobe Premiere

For final manipulation of .AVI or QuickTime files — whether they be animated or video files — Adobe Premiere is the tool of choice for most professionals (see Figure 23-4). Incorporating the digital version of the video-editing suite, Premiere provides a range of possibilities using digital video that you will never exhaust. And I have to say, Premiere is a lot of fun to play with, too! Premiere comes in both Windows 95 and Macintosh versions.

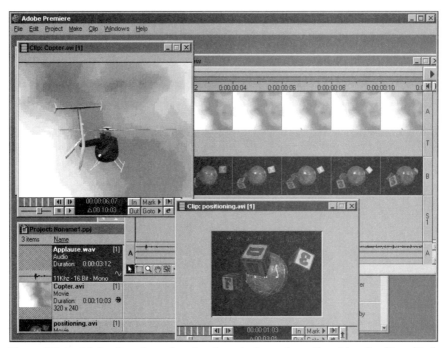

Figure 23-4: Adobe Premiere showing the window where the video final is edited and special effects are added. Each track can contain a video clip, soundtrack, or special effect.

Adding Video Files

Incorporating video files into a Fusion Web site is similar in concept to adding sound. Because of the two different formats and the separate parameters available for both, the Media: Plug-In tool on the Advanced toolbar contains tools for both QuickTime and .AVI (labeled Video) placement.

To place either of these file types on a Fusion page, follow these steps:

1. Select either the QuickTime or Video tool from the Media: Plug-In tool on the Advanced toolbar.

2. Choose the location on the page to place the video.

3. From the Open dialog box that opens, select the video file to be placed and click Open.

4. Set the appropriate parameters for the playback options on the Properties palette.

The Video and QuickTime Properties palettes

The Properties palettes for both Video (which includes RealVideo) and QuickTime are shown in Figures 23-5 and 23-6. They are very similar; in fact, the Video Properties palette is identical to the Sound Properties palette. The exception on the QuickTime Properties palette is its Controls tab, shown in Figure 23-7. Table 23-1 describes the commands on the Control tab.

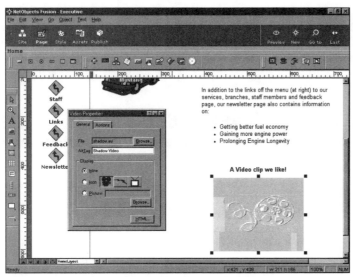

Figure 23-5: The Properties palette for Video files.

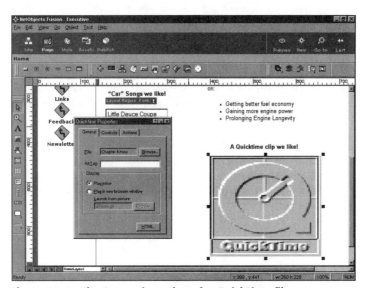

Figure 23-6: The Properties palette for QuickTime files.

Figure 23-7: The QuickTime Controls tab on the Properties palette.

Table 23-1
Controls tab commands on the QuickTime Properties palette

Command	What it does
Hide all	This command plays only the soundtrack of the movie in the background. No controls are visible.
Controller	This command displays a control bar allowing the viewer to start and stop the movie.
Auto Start	The movie starts playing whenever the viewer loads the page.
Loop	The movie replays continuously.
Keep movie in user's cache	This command keeps a copy of the movie on the local computer. If you return to the page containing the movie, you do not need to download it again.

As I mentioned, placing a video file on a Web page in NetObjects Fusion is identical to placing a sound file. Only the tools used are different — the Video tool for .AVI and RealVideo files, and the QuickTime tool for QuickTime files.

To see the concept of adding video to a Web page, add an .AVI file to the Executive Performance Web site. The site's Newsletter page makes a good candidate to add such a video. As the Web is such a dynamic medium, using videos on these types of pages gives the newsletter "life" over and above what a paper-based copy can offer. Figure 23-8 shows the page with the completed video added to it.

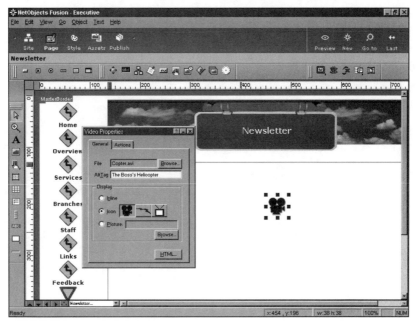

Figure 23-8: Video embedded as an icon on the Executive Performance Newsletter page.

Here's what you need to do to place a video file:

1. Choose the Video tool from the Media Plug in pop-out from the Advanced toolbar.

2. Draw the location of the video on the page in Page view.

3. Select the file to be placed. (On the CD-ROM that accompanies this book is an .AVI file called news.avi that you can place, for example.)

4. Fill in the parameters on the Properties palette for file name, icon type, and so on. Figure 23-9 shows the Properties palette for placing a video object.

Figure 23-9: The Properties palette for a video object on a Web page.

As with sound, you have three options for a video file:

✦ Display one of three Fusion icons.

✦ Display an icon from a file stored on the hard disk.

✦ Store the video file as an inline video.

The first option lets you select one of three Fusion icons to show the location of a video file (as shown in Figure 23-10). When the user clicks the icon, the video either starts to play (in the case of a *streaming format* such as ClearVideo) or downloads.

Tip

ClearVideo is a video compressor available from www.iterated.com. It highly compresses an .AVI file, thus making it much smaller, and also allows it to stream as it downloads. By *streaming*, I mean the video plays as it downloads; visitors to the Web site don't have to wait for the complete download. The downside is that the compression takes quite a bit of time (in the hours vicinity), and a plug-in is required for the browser.

The second option is similar to the first, with the difference being that it lets you supply your own icon from a file on the hard disk. Once placed, the user can click this icon to play the attached video file.

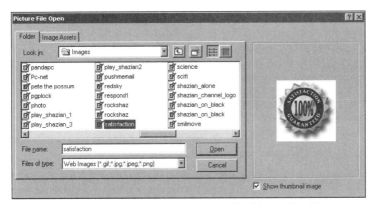

Figure 23-10: Choosing an icon for the embedded video file.

My personal preference for the Properties palette options is inline video. Although the icon uses more Web page real estate, I feel the icon is a more acceptable image for the viewer in regard to what video *should* look like — that is, a video recorder.

When an icon linked to a video file is clicked, the browser launches the video inside the video-playing *helper* application you have nominated. For example, in Windows 95 the helper application is the Windows Media Player. Figure 23-11 shows a video playing in the Windows 95 Media Player.

Note

Under normal circumstances, Web site visitors must wait until the video file is fully downloaded before their systems can play back the video. Conversely, *streaming* allows the video to start playing immediately, with the video player accepting the data from the Web server as it is downloading instead of storing it first.

Most streaming video technologies, such as RealVideo and ClearVideo, use their own special players to view the video. In these two cases, a special plug-in for the browser is necessary because the Windows Media Player cannot handle the streaming effect.

Figure 23-11: The Windows 95 Media Player.

The third option places the video file as an inline object. When you use this option, the video is embedded into the page and starts to play as soon as the site visitor accesses the page containing the video. In most cases this option is not desirable because it automatically forces the browser to start downloading files that are usually large without any choice by the visitor to the site.

More Info

Chapter 21 gave the details of how to create a RealAudio file. You can take the same steps to create a RealVideo file, with the only difference being to make sure the Video Capture option is checked, as shown in Figure 21-12 in Chapter 21.

To create RealVideo, you also need a video capture card such as the Creative Labs VideoBlaster IE500. To play back the video in the browser, you need to have the RealMedia player installed. You can obtain the RealMedia player from www.real.com.

Note   Because of the time it takes to upload a video file to a server and then download it again (if it's not streaming), it is a good idea to preview a page containing video to make sure you have all the parameters set as they should be or as you want them. See Chapter 27 for more information about previewing your site before posting it to a server.

As with sound, adding video to a page can add dramatically to the Web experience for visitors to your site. The technology, however, is still young, so don't expect too much in terms of speed and quality of presentation, and *don't* force your Web visitors to endure waiting for a video to download by making it inline. Wherever possible, give your visitors the option to play or not to play.

Summary

✦ Web-based video files are usually either .AVI or QuickTime files compressed using a third-party compression routine.

✦ Many third-party applications exist with which to create video files.

✦ You can show videos as icons. The visitor to the page must physically switch on the video by clicking a graphic or inline where the videos play automatically when the Web page loads.

✦ It is preferable to preview a page containing video before uploading it due to the time involved.

✦   ✦   ✦

Adding Java Applets and ActiveX Controls

Gone are the days of flat HTML pages. It is surprising to think that less than two years ago, all that we developers had to play with were the HTML language, image maps, and — for those brave enough — Perl scripts.

Mind you, some amazing Web pages appeared despite the limitations: a bit like some of the programs that were around when 4K memory was a lot! Enterprising developers work better under adversity, I say.

Strange, isn't it? Back in the good old days, VisiCalc, the father of spreadsheets and strange capitalization inside words, worked inside 48K memory and still left 32K for data. 1-2-3 and Excel, still pretty much supply the same basic functions supplied by VisiCalc — and most people would be happy with just those basic functions — but these programs now need 16 MB in the computer just to load.

Java and ActiveX have changed all that, though.

Unless you've been stuck on a desert island for the past two years, you've probably heard of at least one of these technologies. For those that may have (been stuck on a desert island, I mean), both allow the developer to add dynamic content to Web pages. *Java* is a language developed by Sun Microsystems and embraced by Netscape (and just about everyone else), whereas *ActiveX* is a Microsoft development based upon the older Visual Basic controls.

In one sense, the "war" between Netscape and Microsoft has probably helped rather than hindered Web development because it accelerated the availability of content creation tools far more quickly. As Java technology from Sun leapfrogged ActiveX, the catch-up teams from Microsoft swung into action to bring the ActiveX back to the forefront, and vice versa. Now, to cover bets, most developers release the ActiveX component for Internet Explorer at the same time as the Netscape plug-in. Recent examples include Shockwave, RealMedia, and ClearVideo.

Never before has this spate of development continued with such a pace — not even in the days of Microsoft Word versus WordPerfect was the life cycle of applications so short.

I won't be drawn into the "which is better" argument at this point. It seems the law courts are going to do this, anyway. Suffice it to say that Java and ActiveX each have their own pluses and minuses, and each I believe has its own place. It *is* true that ActiveX is trailing: at the time of this writing anyway, Netscape does not natively support ActiveX components. I am sure this will change quickly, however, and this can only be good for Web developers.

Adding Java Applets

To broaden the range of functionality, Fusion lets the developer embed third-party Java controls (or applets) into Web pages. This lets the developer take full advantage of the literally thousands of applets available.

Java applets are available for just about every task you might imagine. Just doing a quick search on the Net using AltaVista with the key words **Java+Applet+List**, for example, brought up over 250,000 possible pages of applets ranging from games, to banner displays, to event alerts.

To show you how to place a Java applet on a page, we'll add the Catchy applet (which is included on the CD-ROM supplied with this book).

The Catchy Java applet

As Catchy requires no special treatment beyond applying its parameters via the properties sheet, it is a good example of placing a Java applet into Fusion. Similar to the TickerTape NFX control, Catchy lets you place a scrolling message on the screen at a specific location in the browser. Where it differs is in the amount of flexibility it affords. Unlike the TickerTape NFX control, Catchy lets you:

✦ nominate the font type

✦ nominate the font size

✦ nominate the font style

I cover the TickerTape NFX control in Chapter 25.

An important option (especially when a client of a Web developer wants easy access to change the content of the scrolling message) is the capability to *attach* a text file to the applet containing the scrolling message content. To change the message, the client simply needs to change the content of the text file.

To place the Catchy applet, select the Java tool from the Advanced toolbar (as shown in Figure 24-1). The width of the location drawn on the page determines the width of the scrolling message. The height will dictate the actual height of the box (background) of the applet but does not affect the font size unlike the TickerTape NFX control. Consequently, it is advisable to make the height required fractionally larger than the resultant font size.

Figure 24-1: Selecting the Java applet tool from the Advanced toolbar.

Once you've drawn the location for the applet on the page, you need to configure several parameters to the applet that are defined on the Properties palette. Table 24-1 shows the parameters and the values to enter.

<table>
<tr><td colspan="3">Table 24-1
Parameters for the Catchy applet</td></tr>
<tr><td>*Name*</td><td>*Description*</td><td>*Value*</td></tr>
<tr><td>msg</td><td>message</td><td>Welcome!</td></tr>
<tr><td>speed</td><td>speed</td><td>-8</td></tr>
<tr><td>font</td><td>font</td><td>dialog</td></tr>
<tr><td>style</td><td>style</td><td>bold</td></tr>
<tr><td>size</td><td>size</td><td>10</td></tr>
<tr><td>fgcolor</td><td>foreground color</td><td>ff8000</td></tr>
<tr><td>bgcolor</td><td>background color</td><td>000000</td></tr>
<tr><td>msgfile</td><td>message file</td><td>The URL of the text file containing the message appended to the msg parameter</td></tr>
</table>

Figure 24-2 shows the Properties palette completed for the Catchy applet.

Figure 24-2: The Properties
for the Catchy applet.

You add these parameters one by one to the Java applet tab on the Properties
palette (as shown in Figure 24-3). To add a new parameter, click the plus (+) sign.

Figure 24-3: Adding the Catchy
Java applet parameters to the
Properties palette.

The first parameter (msg) is a hard-coded message that you cannot change without
changing the parameters of the applet. The message file (msgfile) parameter in
contrast, points to a text file on the server containing a supplementary message.
If no message parameters are defined, the Catchy applet simply displays the date
and time.

For the foreground and background colors, you must enter the hexadecimal value
of the required color (for example, #ffffff is the hexadecimal color for black).

Hot
Stuff

To obtain the list of hexadecimal colors that are "browser safe," use the Color
Picker available in Fusion. Simply place a rectangle anywhere on the page using the
Draw rectangle tool and on the Properties palette select the Color button.
Whenever you click on a color the hexadecimal value is shown at the bottom right
of the Color Picker as shown in Figure 24-4.

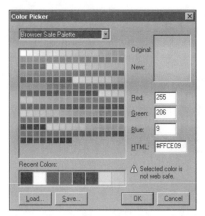

Figure 24-4: The Color Picker showing a color's hexadecimal value. (Notice that the Browser Safe Palette is selected from the drop-down list and the top of the dialog box.)

If all the parameters are completed correctly, the applet should scroll the message when displayed in the browser. Figure 24-5 shows an example of the Catchy applet in place with a welcome message.

The Catchy Java Applet

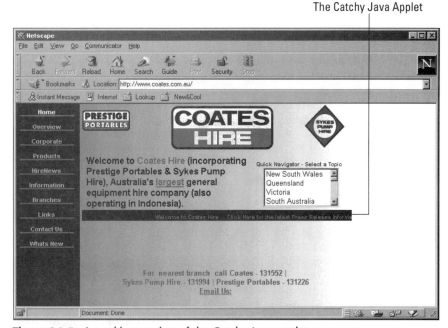

Figure 24-5: A working version of the Catchy Java applet.

For those visitors who don't have Java-aware browsers or who have decided to turn Java compliance off in their browsers, it is a good idea to add the following script to substitute the scrolling message. This is especially important if the message is a vital component to the site. To add this script, select the Java applet on the page in Page view, and on the Properties palette choose the HTML button. You need to place this script in the "Inside Tag" portion of the script window:

```
<a href="html/newsroom.html"><font size=+1 color="#FF0000"
face="Arial,Helvetica">The scrolling message text goes
here.</font></font></font></a>
```

The closing > and the opening </a at the start and end of the code indicate that the script is embedded inside existing HTML.

Adding an ActiveX Control

In many cases, ActiveX development has duplicated Java development in the functionality afforded. This occurred primarily as Microsoft was initially using ActiveX as a "Java-killer." Lately, however, sanity has prevailed, and ActiveX use and capability have broadened dramatically.

At the time of this writing, ActiveX controls are only supported by Microsoft Internet Explorer versions 3.0 and above (although a Netscape plug-in by NCompass available from www.ncompasslabs.com/product.htm allows this functionality in Netscape Navigator).

From a slow developmental start, thousands of ActiveX controls are now available for a multitude of uses. A good place to start looking is on the Microsoft home pages where there are links to many developers of ActiveX controls plus freeware controls that you can download. Be aware, however, that although many of the controls are classified as freeware, a large number of them have licensing restrictions. Many controls are also designed for Visual Basic and Office 97 use and therefore in many cases are totally unsuitable for Web-related work.

The ActiveX Control Pad

ActiveX controls tend to have a history of instability. The general rule of thumb is that if they work under test in the Microsoft ActiveX Control Pad, any ActiveX control should be stable in a Web environment.

The ActiveX Control Pad, available for free from the Microsoft Web site, is a testing application for ActiveX controls. It is available from www.microsoft.com/ sbnmember/download/download.asp, but you must be a member of the Microsoft SiteBuilder Network to obtain the Control Pad. See www.microsoft.com/ sbnmember/download/download.asp for more details on joining the Microsoft SiteBuilder Network.

To add an ActiveX control, just select ActiveX Control from the Advanced toolbar and draw it on the page in Page view (as in Figure 24-6). You then add the necessary parameters via the Properties sheet, and that's all there is to it. The tricky part is knowing exactly what parameters are expected.

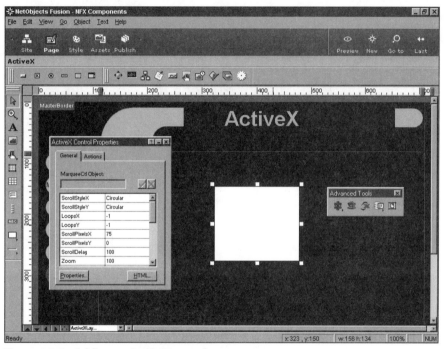

Figure 24-6: Adding an ActiveX control.

ActiveX controls are many and varied, and their implementation is just as diverse. Some let you fill in parameters via the Properties palette (as shown in Figure 24-7), and yet others require complex scripts (such as the one shown in Listing 24-1).

Figure 24-7: The ActiveX Control Properties palette.

When scripting is required, you'll need to do some experimentation as to exactly where you need to place the correct properties included in the script. As a rule of thumb, press the HTML button on the ActiveX Control Properties palette and try the Before Tag section in the layout script as seen in Listing 24-1. This script shown manages the ActiveX control for the tab menu feature in Figure 24-8. At this level, adding ActiveX controls is not for the faint hearted! Thankfully though, many ActiveX controls are not only easy to add but very functional at the same time.

Read on!

Listing 24-1: **The script for the tabbed ActiveX control.**

```
<script language="VBScript">
<!--
Sub Window_onLoad()
CNTab.Additem "TEXT: Home, HREF:tabs_about.htm, FRAME:main"
CNTab.Additem "TEXT: Overview, HREF:tabs_who.htm, FRAME:main"
CNTab.Additem "TEXTCorporate, HREF:mailto:team@auscomp.com.au,
FRAME:main"
CNTab.Additem "TEXT: Products, HREF:www.auscomp.com.au,,
FRAME:main"
CNTab.Additem "TEXT: HireNews, HREF:tabs_need.htm, FRAME:main"
CNTab.Additem "TEXT: Information, HREF:tabs_inc.htm,
FRAME:main"
CNTab.Additem "TEXT:Branches, HREF:tabs_sabt.htm, FRAME:main"
CNTab.Additem "TEXT:Links, HREF:tabs_sfrm.htm, FRAME:main"
CNTab.Additem "TEXT:Contact Us, HREF:tabs_sidx.htm, FRAME:main"
CNTab.Additem "TEXT: Copyright, HREF:tabs_copyright.htm,
FRAME:main"
end sub
-->
</script>
<center>
<p><font face="Arial Narrow"><strong>Content Navigator - TAB /
Online Documentation</strong></font></p>
<OBJECT ID="CNTab" WIDTH=500 HEIGHT=80
classid="clsid:A75550A4-6ABD-11D0-86E9-0080AD11822F"
codebase="CNTabs.CAB">
</OBJECT>
```

As you can see, this ActiveX control uses a different approach to navigation than is commonly seen on Web pages. Certainly, it could be created using graphics and image-mapping, but this is a much more elegant solution and shows off the ActiveX technology very well. The downside is that this lies at the pointy end of ActiveX technology, and I for one would not like to unravel all this code when it will only generally work on Internet Explorer pages anyway!

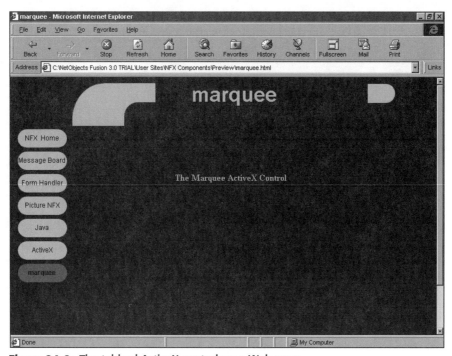

Figure 24-8: The tabbed ActiveX control on a Web page.

An Acrobat ActiveX control

So is there an easy ActiveX control that we can quickly place to perform a useful function? Well yes there is.

Since its inception, Adobe Acrobat has become the de facto standard for the delivery of documents both across the Internet as well as intranets. As long as you have the Acrobat Reader, which is free, you can view any document created by anybody on any platform. It probably comes as no surprise that you can actually place an Acrobat ActiveX control to embed documents into your Web pages instead being displayed in the separate reader.

Note

To download Adobe Acrobat, jet over to its Web site at www.adobe.com.

Say, for example, you want to display an Excel spreadsheet (such as seen in Figure 24-9) on your Web page and allow the person viewing it to scroll around, zoom, and all those other things that make Acrobat so cool. Just create the Acrobat format of the document, and then embed the document into the Web page using Fusion's ActiveX component tool.

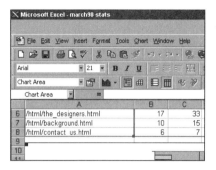

Figure 24-9: An Excel spreadsheet
to be embedded into a Web page.

To add the ActiveX control, first choose the ActiveX Control tool from the
Advanced toolbar and draw the area of the control you require on the page. You
need to make the area created large enough to fit the document: the size you draw
will be the viewable size of the embedded document. Once you have defined the
area, the Insert ActiveX Control dialog box opens (Figure 24-10) letting you choose
the control you wish to place. In this example, the Acrobat reader control is at the
top of the list and selected. It is also wise to check the Set Codebase box so that
Fusion knows where the control is stored at Publishing time.

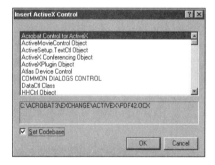

Figure 24-10: The Insert ActiveX
Control dialog box.

Once you have selected the control and clicked the OK button, the ActiveX Control
Properties palette is shown as seen in Figure 24-11.

Figure 24-11: The ActiveX Control
Properties palette for the Acrobat
Reader ActiveX control.

This particular control requires only four fields for parameters, and Fusion has filled in the Codebase one for us. The first field (src) specifies the location on the hard disk of the actual Acrobat document to be posted to the server (and, of course, subsequently embedded into the Web page). You must enter this manually as there is no navigation dialog box with which to enter this information. Once you have entered the source file, the Acrobat document specified will be shown on the page complete with the Acrobat Reader menu bar allowing all functionality that Acrobat affords (as shown in Figure 24-12).

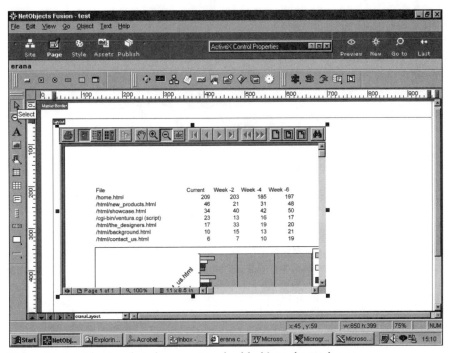

Figure 24-12: The Acrobat document embedded into the Web page.

The only field that you need to fill out for this particular control is the Alt tag field.

Done! Now you can publish the page to the server. Figure 24-13 shows the completed page in Internet Explorer.

You can also Preview the page to see how it will look prior to posting, but don't make the mistake that many do. When the previewed page is displayed, nothing is showing! It may be the bleeding obvious, but this is usually caused by setting Fusion's preferences to Netscape Navigator as the default browser, and of course Navigator doesn't support ActiveX controls. You wouldn't be the first, and you certainly won't be the last if this happens to you.

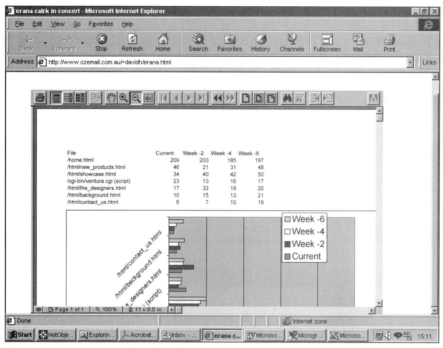

Figure 24-13: The completed Web page.

The use of Java and ActiveX controls is something that you have to experiment with, but most times, it is effort well spent in creating more intuitive, interesting, and — dare I say — compelling Web pages. Be prepared to spend a lot of time in frustration, however. It is not uncommon for the documentation supplied to be either sparse or nonexistent (try finding out about the parameters for the Microsoft Marquee ActiveX control, for example).

The actual placement of Java and ActiveX in Fusion is the easy part!

Summary

✦ Java applets and ActiveX controls are placed using their tools from the Advanced toolbar.

✦ Both Java and ActiveX require parameters to be supplied.

✦ Some parameters may need to be added via scripting for both Java and ActiveX.

✦ ActiveX will work with Microsoft Explorer browsers, but unless the NCompass plug-in is installed in Netscape Navigator, they will not (at this time) work in Netscape. Even then, problems may be encountered.

✦   ✦   ✦

Adding NetObjects NFX Components

Just like Sun Microsystems and Microsoft, NetObjects has also stepped into the add-on component fray with its technology called *NFX components*. In effect, an NFX component (accessed from the Component toolbar as shown in Figure 25-1) is simply a sophisticated way of applying certain Java applets or Perl scripts to a Web page.

Figure 25-1: The NFX components selected on the Component toolbar.

Fusion comes already equipped with several NFX components:

✦ DynaButtons — navigation controls that change depending upon their state (such as, pressed or mouse over)

✦ TickerTape — a clickable moving message much the same as the LED displays seen in many shops, banks, and airports

✦ SiteMapper — a Java applet showing a map of the Web site letting the site visitor click a page in the SiteMapper to navigate directly to that page

✦ Message Board — a full-featured bulletin board allowing users to post and read posted messages

✦ Form Handler — a Submit form where all the scripting is created automatically (This means that the developer does not need to know a scripting language such as Perl.)

✦ Picture Rollover, Time Based Picture, Picture Loader, and Rotating Picture applets — used to change images based on criteria

Most of these are easy to install, while the Message Board and Form Handler can be a nightmare!

This is no fault of the good folk at NetObjects; it's more usually a problem with the way the Internet Service Provider structures its system. In the case of the Message Board and the Form Handler, most of the problems occur when the ISPs do not allow you to set some of the parameters that these components require. Most notable are the strict hierarchies of directory (folder) structures they require and access to a cgi-bin.

Note

A *cgi-bin* is a special directory on the Web server allowing a developer to access external languages (most usually Perl 4 or 5) for transactional processing. Both Message Board and Form Handler require you to have a cgi-bin.

The basics of adding an NFX component are pretty standard for all of them, with the caveat mentioned earlier regarding those that require cgi-bin access.

Adding DynaButtons

DynaButtons are a useful NFX component, but require a little forethought because generally you will be replacing a Navigation Bar with them. Consequently, as certain restrictions apply when using DynaButtons, not all updates you may make to the site will be reflected later in the DynaButton navigation controls.

A *DynaButton* is a Java applet that uses the Primary button from the currently nominated style as a navigation button in exactly the same way a standard Navigation Bar does. When the mouse pointer moves over the button, however, it will automatically change to the highlighted Primary button style. Move the mouse pointer away again, and it changes back to the Primary button style.

Figure 25-2 shows a site using DynaButtons. Take special note of the last button in the list (labeled "Mandorin Goldfields"). All the other buttons are linked to pages inside the Fusion created site, but the last item in the list on the left is a link to an external site.

DynaButtons

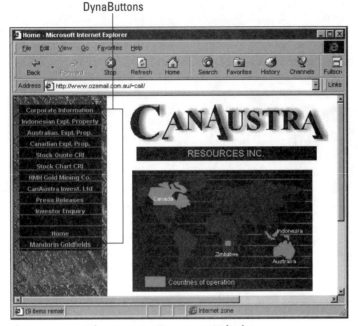

Figure 25-2: Using DynaButtons on a Web site.

The button's text is not using a custom name as this cannot be applied to external links. To do this, requires another method. Read on because DynaButtons are in my opinion one of the best parts of Fusion and, when you are comfortable with them, can be a great substitute for Navigation Bars in giving great (and imaginitive) interactivity.

Here's how to add DynaButtons:

1. Select the DynaButtons button from the Component toolbar and draw the location on the page (horizontally or vertically).

2. The DynaButtons Properties palette will open, where you'll select the Number of Buttons. Use a number that matches the number you require on your page.

3. For each button number on the Properties palette, click the field (i.e. Button 1) and click on the button containing ellipsis (...) next to the field name at the top of the palette (see Figure 25-3). This will open the Link dialog box.

4. Create the local link for each DynaButton as you would any other local link using the Internal Link or Smart Link tabs.

For external links, create the link as you would for any other link, but to put a meaningful name in the button (remember you cannot set custom names for external links), make sure you fill in the Asset Name field. This will become the text value in the button. Figure 25-4 shows the Properties palette and Link dialog box for an externally linked DynaButton.

Figure 25-3: Clicking the ellipsis button on the DynaButtons Properties palette.

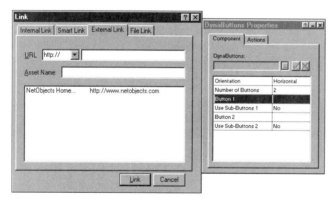

Figure 25-4: The Properties palette and Link dialog box for an externally linked DynaButton.

The DynaButtons in Figure 25-2 use the Primary and Secondary buttons from the Tech style. If the mouse pointer passes over the button, the horizontal line three-quarters of the way down the button changes from a purple line to an orange dashed line. This gives the site visitor visual feedback as to what is happening.

More Info

Different DynaButtons perform different visual actions. In effect, the button switches between the Primary button in the Style view to the Secondary button when a mouse over action is performed. Of course, this makes it very easy to define your own DynaButtons by defining your own style (copying an existing style) and substituting your own images. For more details on styles, refer to Chapter 7.

You can also apply sub-buttons to DynaButtons. When you choose this option from the DynaButtons Properties palette, clicking a DynaButton opens a second series of buttons allowing further links available to the visitor (as seen in Figures 25-5 and 25-6). This option is useful when the primary DynaButton links to a parent page with the sub-buttons linking to child pages of the parent. See Figure 25-7 to witness the sub-buttons in action.

Figure 25-5: The basic DynaButton . . .

Figure 25-6: . . . and with sub-buttons added.

Figure 25-7: The sub-buttons in action.

DynaButtons versus a Navigation Bar

When you place a Navigation Bar on a page, adding new pages to the site in the hierarchy the Navigation Bar is pointing to (child level, current level, and so on) will automatically add new buttons to the Navigation Bar. This is not so with DynaButtons. You must manually add any new pages and/or links required.

Note

You cannot see any DynaButtons (or any other component for that matter) when previewing a page. You must either publish to a server or locally before you can see them. If you do attempt to see what a component does by clicking it, you will get a gentle error message (as seen in Figure 25-8).

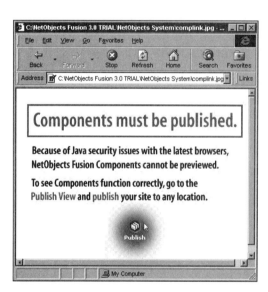

Figure 25-8: The component error message shown when attempting to preview a component's output.

Danger Zone

Be aware that for DynaButtons to work, the site visitor must have a Java-capable browser!

Adding the TickerTape Component

One NFX component that should work for everyone is the TickerTape. When placed, it allows the developer to define up to 50 messages that scroll across the screen in a predetermined position such as seen in Figure 25-9. You can select the colors for the background, the frame, and text from an available palette of colors. Also, the messages can be clickable: you can define a URL so that when a visitor to the site clicks on a scrolling message each message can link to that address.

TickerTape

Figure 25-9: An example of the TickerTape component.

The electronic LED signs that simulate the TickerTape component are used in shops and so on to catch the eye of the customer and to advise of specials, important information, and the like. The TickerTape component is also well suited to this task. One location I have successfully used the TickerTape component is on a Links page, advising visitors I've recently added a new link that I think will be of interest to them. This is much sexier than a flashing "NEW" graphic!

To add the TickerTape component, click its tool on the Component toolbar and draw the location of the TickerTape message on the screen. With the TickerTape, the physical size you draw the box will be the size of the message in both height and width. Figure 25-10 shows a TickerTape drawn on the Executive Autos Links page.

Once positioned, a graphic appears in the box telling you what this control is. To define the properties of the TickerTape component, you must use its Properties palette and enter the parameters on the Component tab (as seen in Figure 25-11).

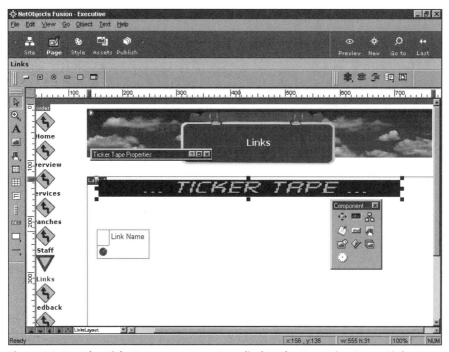

Figure 25-10: The TickerTape component applied to the Executive Autos Links page.

Figure 25-11: The Properties palette for the TickerTape component.

Now, simply enter the message (you can have up to 50 messages and they will scroll one after the other) and select the destination URL (if any), speed, and colors in the appropriate fields on the Properties palette. To enter this information, click on the parameter and enter the details into the field at the top of the tab. Some parameters allow you to select a choice — for example, colors and the number of messages. Figure 25-12 shows the finished result of the TickerTape for the Executive Autos Links page.

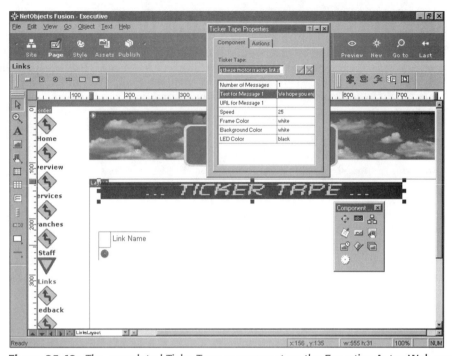

Figure 25-12: The completed TickerTape component on the Executive Autos Web page.

Note

You cannot change the font style and size on the TickerTape component. The font style is fixed to the "LED" style seen in Figure 25-12. The font size is dictated by the height that you drew the component box for the TickerTape on the page. If you want to create a TickerTape-type scrolling message but define your own parameters beyond what the Fusion NFX component allows, see "The Catchy Java Applet" section in Chapter 24.

Hot Stuff

Here's one enterprising use of the TickerTape component one of my clients thought of:

The client scouted out all the Internet sites of its competitors. Where the pricing for their products was more expensive, it added those URLs to the TickerTape with a "We are cheaper! See for yourself!" message.

Adding the SiteMapper Component

The SiteMapper component is a beauty! It immediately gives your site visitors feedback as to exactly where they are in the site. For large sites, this is especially important. SiteMapper also allows people to navigate to any section of a site immediately without having to perhaps wade around trying to find just the page they want.

Adding the SiteMapper is simplicity itself.

Simply select the SiteMapper component from the Component toolbar, draw a rectangle at the location required for the SiteMapper icon, and that's it!

On the Properties palette, only one option is available to you: to change the graphic image used. To change the SiteMapper graphic supplied with Fusion, click Image parameter and click the ellipsis (...) button next to the default graphic name, Sitemapper.gif (see Figure 25-13). In the dialog box that opens, select a new graphics image.

Figure 25-13: The SiteMapper Properties palette.

When a page containing the SiteMapper component is viewed in a browser, clicking the image used (see Figure 25-14) will open a separate window with a graphical view of the site (as seen in Figure 25-15). To navigate to any page in the site, point at it with the mouse (the icon for the page will change color and show the name of the page on it), and click it.

Figure 25-14: The SiteMapper icon.

As useful as this is to see the structure of a site, even more goodies are now available to the site visitor. The graphic view of the site can be altered in the window by selecting either the Structure or Outline buttons. Each of these displays is identical to those of the same name in Site view mode.

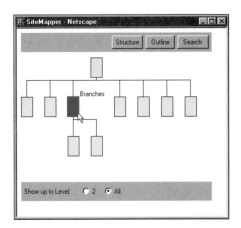

Figure 25-15: A view of a Web site using the SiteMapper component.

Using the Search button at the top right of the SiteMapper window lets you enter a search string that is part of a page name. Once the search text has been entered into the field at the base of the window, all pages that have this text in their name will be listed in the window. Again, simply clicking a page title in this list will open that page in the browser. The last option, Show up to Level, adjusts how many levels the site visitor wants to view.

Adding the Message Board Component

If you want a full-featured message board on your Web site where visitors can leave messages and participate in conversations (threads), this component is for you. This especially applies if you have no inclination to learn Perl, JavaScript, and all the other things necessary to create a message board (also called a bulletin board) from scratch.

For the message board component to work, there are a few necessary requirements and restrictions:

✦ You must have access to a cgi-bin directory that will process scripts with a cgi extension.

✦ If the server you are publishing to is a UNIX-based server, it must have Perl 5 installed. Windows NT may or may not have Perl 5 installed as the cgi scripts invoked on a Windows NT server are NT Binary files.

Note

Most standard ISP user accounts do not allow cgi executable files to run; you pay more for this privilege.

✦ There should be no proprietary schemes on the Web server for executing scripts.

✦ The Page Title parameter on the Message Board Properties palette (see Figure 25-17 in a few pages) cannot contain a single quotation mark ('). For example, a Page Title parameter of Bob's Message Board will cause the Message Board to fail.

✦ Double quotation marks are not allowed when entering a Message in either the Name or Subject field.

✦ A JavaScript-compatible browser must be used as a client to the Message Board (Netscape Navigator or Internet Explorer versions 3 or greater have been tested satisfactorily).

The following UNIX servers have been tested with the Message Board component:

✦ Netscape FastTrack 2.0 (Solaris)

✦ Netscape Enterprise 2.0 (Solaris)

✦ Apache (LINUX)

The following Windows NT servers have been tested with the Message Board component:

✦ Netscape FastTrack 2.0 (NT 4.0)

✦ Netscape Enterprise 2.0 (NT 4.0)

✦ IIS 2.0/3.0 (NT 4.0)

To add the Message Board component to a Web page, just select it from the Component toolbar and place it on the page. The icon in Figure 25-16 will appear.

Figure 25-16: The Message Board icon.

The Message Board Properties palette contains several options that configure the Message Board system. It is imperative that you configure these correctly for your local situation. Of particular importance is the Publish to parameter, which does not signify what server you are posting to but which version of the scripts (Windows, UNIX, or Macintosh) are uploaded to the server.

You may need to contact your ISP and obtain the details of these first two as it does vary from ISP to ISP.

Apart from that, as I said, installing what is an elegant Message Board system rivaling the best is a snap to create. In fact, if you are lucky enough to meet all of the criteria required in the Properties palette by default, adding this message board to a site is a one-click effort!

Note

I use a "vanilla" Internet service provider, OzEmail, and the only parameter I needed to change was the cgi-bin directory.

Note

There is no simple way from within Fusion to change the Message Board button graphic. You will need to replace the file C:\NetObjects Fusion 3.0\Components\ BBSComp\bbs\image\BBSComp.gif.

More Info

You can apply only one Message Board to any single Fusion NOD file. To test this component, you must publish the site to a server. Previewing a site will not let you test the MessageBoard component. In addition, when publishing a site with a Message Board, you should turn off the Publish changed assets only option on the Publish Site dialog box. For more information on publishing a site, see Chapter 28.

Installing the Message Board component is simple. Select the Message Board component tool from the Component toolbar and draw a rectangle where you would like the button for the message board to be located on the page. Figure 25-17 shows the Message Board button in Page view.

The Message Board icon

Figure 25-17: The Message Board button on the page.

Note

A *thread* is a series of messages that follow each other. For example, an original message may have many replies, and each of these may also have replies, thus building up a hierarchy of messages that are not all necessarily on the same topic but are in the same "thread."

When the site visitor clicks this button, the underlying Perl script and JavaScript will create the page seen in Figure 25-18 and read in all the messages that are stored in a text file on the server.

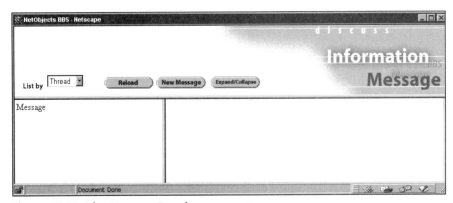

Figure 25-18: The Message Board component.

After the Message Board is installed, site visitors can leave a message or read existing messages. Site visitors can also sort messages by thread, subject, author, or time.

Site visitors can expand threads (to show all of the individual messages) or collapse them (only showing the subject matter).

Adding the Form Handler Component

Another useful time saver is the Forms Handler component, again especially if you have no inclination in getting into the nitty-gritty of creating processing scripts for forms.

Remembering back to the chapter on forms (Chapter 16), we used a Perl script that already existed to send the form to an e-mail address. This script is activated when the Submit button is clicked.

Tip

That script is called mailto.pl and is available from www.frostbyte.com.au/ frostbyte/cgi-bin/.

NetObjects Fusion also comes with a predefined script that you can use on forms. You can place this on the page containing the form using the Form Handler component. The mailto.pl script sends the output of the form to an e-mail address. In contrast, the Form Handler component can send the form to a nominated text file or to an e-mail address. You can nominate the destination with the Publish to option on the Form Handler Properties palette.

To use the Form Handler component to create a form (as seen in Figure 25-19), create the forms as usual (remember you have to define a Layout region with the region tool or define a table or the Layout as a form by clicking its checkbox on the properties palette) and place all the elements of the form as per usual. This could include single and multi-line forms edit fields, combo boxes, check boxes, and so on. You must also add the Cancel button manually.

Note

All the server restrictions and requirements needed by the Form Handler component are identical to those mentioned earlier for the MessageBoard.

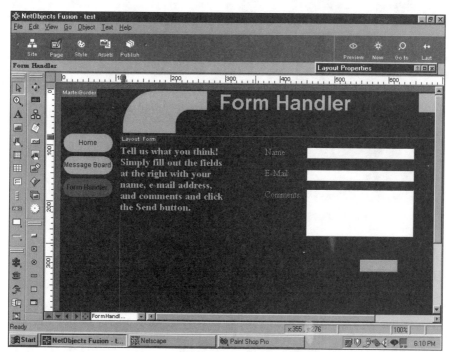

Figure 25-19: The basic form on the page.

The Form Handler component controls the Submit button for that component. In other words, use the Form Handler tool from the Component toolbar to draw the Submit button for this form. Do *not* use the standard Submit button from the Form toolbar. To add this, choose the Form Handler component from the Component toolbar and draw on the page where you want to place the Submit button within the form. The Form Handler Properties dialog box will open as seen in Figure 25-20.

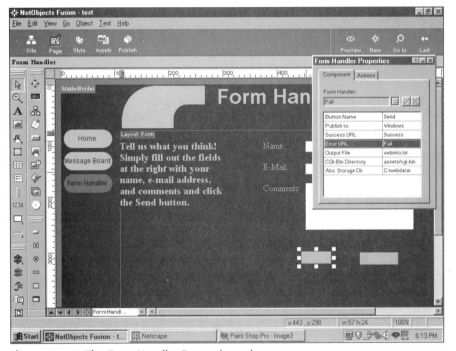

Figure 25-20: The Form Handler Properties palette.

All that is remaining is to fill in the appropriate parameters:

✦ The Button Name (label) you want on the button, The default is Submit.

✦ The type of Web server you are publishing to: Windows NT, UNIX, Macintosh, or e-mail. If you choose to have the output sent to an e-mail address, an additional field appears where you can nominate the address to send to in the format *name@domain.com*. A valid example of an e-mail address is david@shazian.com.au.

✦ The URL to load if the message is sent correctly. This is selected using the familiar Link dialog box. If this URL is a local page (part of this Web site in Fusion), you will have to create it, of course.

✦ The URL to load if an error occurs. An error is usually caused by the person filling the form in not filling in a required field. Again, this URL is selected using the familiar Link dialog box. Again, you may want to create the page if the error URL page is part of the Fusion site.

✦ The name of the Output File to contain the message. Note here, do not enter a path, just the file name you want to use.

✦ The Required Fields that the user must fill in on the form. If one of these is missed, the Web page specified in the Error URL will be loaded.

All of the fields on the form must be named using a sequential numbering sequence. For example, the first field must be called *1*, the next *2*, and so on. Make sure you have no other naming conventions or the component will not work correctly. The Submit and Reset buttons do not need to be a part of this numbering sequence.

You will also need to enter the appropriate paths for the UNIX Perl directory (if using the UNIX option), cgi-bin directory, and the Storage directory where you want the Output file to be located. For the Path to Perl and cgi-bin directory settings, you may need to contact your ISP and get these details as it does vary from ISP to ISP.

Once all these parameters are in place and the site is published, your visitors can now fill out the form and send the information. All you need to do is open the Output text file to read them. What could be easier?

If you do have problems setting up the Form handler, the most common causes are

✦ lack of cgi capability on the Web server

✦ incorrect setting for path to Perl setting

✦ incorrect permissions settings on the Web server

✦ nominating directors/folders that do not exist

Unfortunately, there are many, many permutations that ISPs use for this side of things at the server end. Because of this — and potentially to save a lot of time — it is best to first confirm with your ISP what all these settings are. This applies equally to the Message Board component.

Adding Picture Placement Components

The next four tools on the Component palette are all Java applets that allow you to control an image or sequence of images:

✦ Picture Rollover

✦ Time Based Picture

✦ Picture Loader

✦ Rotating Picture

The Picture Rollover component

The first of these components, the Picture Rollover component, works in the same way as a DynaButton. When the mouse moves over an image placed using the component, it will change to a second image. When the mouse pointer leaves the image, it can then either revert to the original image or even display a third.

First, select the Picture Rollover tool from the Component toolbar and place it where you want on the page. The Picture Rollover Properties palette initially shows two parameters, but expands to four (as seen in Figure 25-21) as soon as you set the first one.

Figure 25-21: The Picture Rollover Properties palette.

Just specify an Initial Image to be displayed on the page. When you have entered this parameter, the Properties palette will then request two more images: the first to replace the initial image when the mouse pointer "rolls over" the image and the second for the image to replace this second image when the mouse pointer leaves the image or "rolls out." Of course, the third could simply be the original or if wanted, an entirely new picture. It's your choice.

Finally, an optional Link URL parameter lets you define the image as a link. This is added using the Link dialog box. Only one link is added, and this will apply equally to all three images.

The Time Based Picture component

The Time Based Picture component lets you specify up to 24 images, each to be displayed during a certain time frame. Links can be individually added to each image. While there is a certain amount of "cuteness" to this component, there is a very good time when this can be used.

Note

One has visions of personal Web sites showing different images based on the time of day. When the person who owns the site is asleep, an image of a teddy bear may appear, for example.

A more valid example, though, might be for those companies who run 24-hour support systems that "follow the sun." When it is daytime in Australia, for example, all support calls, e-mails, and the like are routed to an Australian office from right around the world. When it is night there but day in the United Kingdom, the system automatically switches all calls to the London office, and so on.

Using the Time Based Picture component and its Links attributes, different images (and e-mail links) can be shown for different times of the day and support e-mails can automatically be sent to the office that is on support alert. This would need some careful planning based on time zones, but the end result is an interesting concept.

The Time Based Picture component accepts three parameters per image:

✦ The Image file

✦ The URL link applied to the image

✦ The Start Time for the Image

Figure 25-22 shows a typical Properties palette for the Time Based Picture component.

Figure 25-22: The Time Based Picture Properties palette.

The Picture Loader component

The Picture Loader component places an image on your site that may exist elsewhere. The most common cause of this situation is for advertising banners.

Once you've selected the Picture Loader tool and placed it on the page, it accepts only one parameter (as shown in Figure 25-23): the complete URL of the image to be loaded.

Figure 25-23: The Picture Loader Properties palette.

The Rotating Picture component

The Rotating Picture component is very similar to the Time Based Picture component. First, as with the other components, select the tool from the Component toolbar and place it where you want on the page. In the Rotating Picture Properties palette (shown in Figure 25-24), you can define a sequence of images and the amount of time before loading the next image. You can also assign a link to each image. You can add a maximum of 50 images.

Figure 25-24: The Rotating Picture Properties palette.

Adding Additional NFX Components

The last tool on the component toolbar is a generic Component placer. A development kit known as the NetObjects Fusion Component Development Kit allows developers to create their own components, which you can place using this last tool. A dialog box opens (as seen in Figure 25-25) letting you select the component to install.

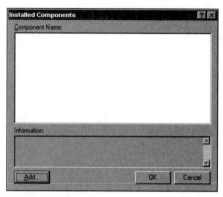

Figure 25-25: The Generic Component placer dialog box.

Summary

✦ NFX component controls are Fusion-supplied objects that can be used on Web pages.

✦ Some NFX component controls require access to a cgi-bin directory for Perl script execution.

✦   ✦   ✦

Publishing a Web Site

Until a site is published, it is not really a site. It is just a series of HTML documents or a Fusion NOD file sitting on a hard disk somewhere. In the past, publishing a site meant also having to learn a third-party program such as WS-FTP before being able to publish.

Fusion has eliminated all these problems. Not only is it easy to publish a Web site, Fusion also gives you maximum control of all the assets in a site such as graphics or sound files and where they will be placed. Part VI covers all these areas in detail.

Using the Assets Register

The Assets view mode of NetObjects Fusion (shown in Figure 26-1) lists all the objects, according to their type, used as the content of a site. Each type has a separate button on the icon bar labeled Files, Links, Data Objects, and Variables.

Using Assets view can be a tremendous time-saver in site management when, for example, you need to change an image that applies to many Web pages in the site across-the-board, or when you need to delete an object a site no longer uses.

Changing Column Widths

When displaying any of the sections of the Assets view, several columns across the window describe various attributes of the asset, including its name, type, size, location, and whether it is in use. If you need to modify column widths so that you can see more or less of any particular column, place the mouse pointer over the separator bar in the heading as shown in Figure 26-2. When the pointer is in a position allowing the column width to be altered, it will turn into a horizontal double-headed arrow and let you drag the column separator to a new location.

Each Asset type (File, Link, DataObject, and Variable) is accessed by clicking the relevant tab at the top of the main window.

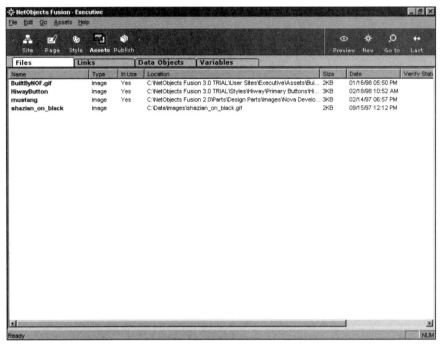

Figure 26-1: NetObjects Fusion Assets view.

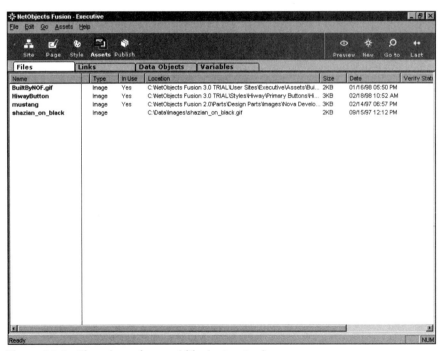

Figure 26-2: Changing column widths in Assets view.

Tip

In Assets view, if you see an asset not in use (the In Use column will be blank for that asset), it is best to delete it. Deleting an asset in Fusion does not remove it from your hard disk; only its references in the Fusion NOD file are removed. To delete an asset, select it with the mouse pointer and press the Del key. A warning dialog box informs you that you cannot reverse this operation. Click OK if you are sure you want to delete the selected asset. If you have a large number of unused assets in a site, you can also use the Delete All Unused File Assets function from the Assets command on the menu bar.

Note

It is also advisable from time to time to verify the validity of all Assets. Although you can manually check the file's status on your hard disk with the information appearing in Assets view, there is an easier way. Simply choose the Verify All File Assets option from the Assets menu. Fusion then verifies all assets and details the verification in the Verify Status column (you may need to scroll to the right to see this column).

Even though you can, deleting assets marked as in use by the site is not recommended. Figure 26-3 shows several assets not in use by the site.

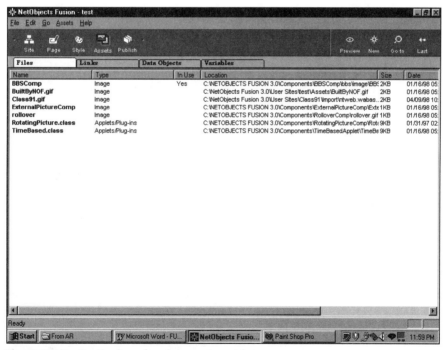

Figure 26-3: Assets view showing assets not in use.

Gaining Asset Information

While the listing of assets is a valuable resource to see exactly what is being used in a site, even more power and flexibility lie below the surface. When you double-click an asset, a dialog box opens, providing further information on the individual asset used by the Web site (see Figure 26-4).

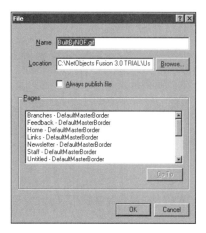

Figure 26-4: The File Asset dialog box.

Listed in the File Asset dialog box are the asset's name, location on the hard disk, and a list of the pages in the site on which the asset is used. This dialog box can save hours of time when an asset changes.

For example, say a Web site contains 100 pages, and on each page in the site a graphics image of a company logo appears. If this logo changes due to an update, under the old method of creating Web sites the Web author would laboriously have to update every single page with the new logo manually. In NetObjects Fusion the Web author would just need to locate the asset, double-click it to display the File Asset dialog box, and reallocate this asset to the new graphics file using the browse button and the navigational dialog box (shown in Figure 26-5). All occurrences of the asset in the site are then updated automatically with the new image.

Of course, you can employ the same net effect with the use of MasterBorders. If the company logo were in a MasterBorder common to all 100 pages in the site, simply changing the image in the MasterBorder would apply to all pages, the same as changing the asset. In practice, however, most large sites (and many smaller ones for that matter) use a variety of MasterBorders. The more proficient you become with MasterBorders, the more you will find you use them. Of course, it is also not necessarily safe to assume that the image will appear only in a MasterBorder. It may also appear in other sections of the site, and changing it carte blanche may make changes to the site you hadn't anticipated.

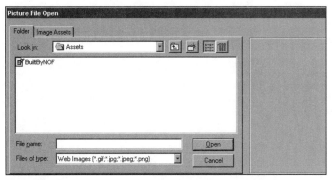

Figure 26-5: Browsing for a replacement asset file.

The File Assets dialog box is also useful to find information or locations of objects in a site. Using the same type of example as before, assume that whenever you have placed the telephone number of the company on a page, you have also placed a small telephone icon next to it. If the telephone number changes, as this is text, you cannot simply modify a single entity. You have to change every incidence of the telephone number's text string (with the caveat of MasterBorders mentioned earlier). Locating the telephone icon file in the File Asset list and using the Go To button in the dialog box, however, enables you to navigate to each page containing the telephone icon and change the number accordingly.

Tip

For static information such as telephone, fax, 800 numbers, and so on, using NetObjects Fusion variables is a much better way. Assigning a telephone number to a variable means you can place the variable where required on pages. When the value of a variable changes (such as a telephone or fax number), you can then alter it by modifying the associated variable using the Variables section of Assets view. Then all instances of that variable are updated everywhere in the site. See Chapter 13 for more information on creating variables.

Files

The Files listing of Assets view (shown in Figure 26-1) lists all external files used as part of the site. These files include images, multimedia objects (such as Shockwave files), NetObjects Fusion plug-in components, CGI scripts, Applets/Plug-ins, and background sounds.

In the Files mode of Assets view, much information is available about any individual asset. This information is grouped by the column headings across the top of the main window. In addition to an asset's name, other information available includes:

✦ Type

✦ In Use (signified by a Yes or No status)

✦ Location (on the hard disk)

✦ File Size

✦ File Date

✦ Verify Status

When adding new assets in Assets view, the file types choices in the Open File dialog box determine what "type" the added asset is listed under. If no type is specified, the asset is listed as an Image type.

Links

Clicking the Links button in the icon bar while in Assets view changes the window from displaying all the files used in the site to a complete listing of all links that have been defined in the site. Figure 26-6 shows the Links section of Assets view.

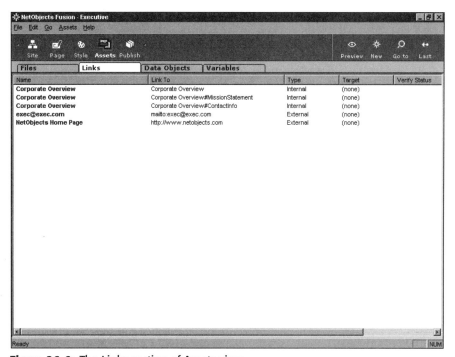

Figure 26-6: The Links section of Assets view.

Again, the Links window is divided into a series of columns, with information on each link displayed relating to its name, what it is linked to, and the link type. The columns used in the Links view are

✦ Link Name

✦ Link To (URL , page, or anchor name)

✦ Type of Link

✦ Link Target

✦ Verify Status

Links have four types: Internal, Smart, External, and Local File. Internal and Smart links point to pages within the structure of NetObjects Fusion and are restricted to that capability. Smart links are differentiated from regular Internal links by the fact that they follow links according to the structure of the site. For example, a Smart link might be First Child Page. This means that whatever page is in the "first" position as a child of the page containing the link is the one to which the link goes. It doesn't matter which page is placed here; the link always goes to the first child page.

Smart links also do not have anchor options; only Internal links have anchor options. External links give you the option to link to any URL anywhere. The link can be internal to the site if you want, but it is not necessary. External links allow you the variety of prefix choices, including http://, ftp://, and mailto:. File links enable you to link to any file, using a standard http:// link. If a file requires an embed tag, you need to use the multimedia tool. Targets are available for all links when Autoframes are available. If a link has a target, it is listed in Assets view.

Internal links

When you double-click an Internal link type, a dialog box opens, detailing the link's name and the pages on which it appears (see Figure 26-7). The only option available here is to select a page containing the link and, using the Go To button, navigate to that page. You cannot modify internal links in any way while in Assets view. If any modifications are required for an internal link, you must perform these on the link itself on the page in which it appears. To make the modification, use the Link button on the Properties palette after you have selected the link.

Tip

To keep track of exactly which objects are links (including graphics and text), use the Object Icon option on the View menu to show a visual indicator of links in the site.

Figure 26-7: The Internal Links dialog box in Assets view.

External links

Double-clicking an external link *does* allow modification of the destination URL of the link. To change a destination URL for an external link, change its value for the URL displayed in the External Links dialog box, shown in Figure 26-8.

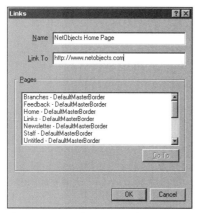

Figure 26-8: The External Links dialog box in Assets view.

Note   If you have separately named two external links but both point to the same URL, Fusion only displays the last link created. Making a change to this destination URL in the External Links dialog box affects both named links, however. The names you apply to external links are for your reference, and Fusion is smart enough to look after the physical links itself and update any other references in the site as you change any one of the URL references. This does not apply, however, to links that share a name but point to different destinations. Changing the name of one link does not affect the other.

Data Objects

Data objects are not *objects*; strictly speaking, they are more correctly a *definition*, descriptions of what and how sections of a linked database are to appear in the Web site. Chapter 20 covers the creation and definition of data objects in detail. Figure 26-9 shows the Data Objects tab of Assets view. Listed are two Data Objects. The first is a connected Microsoft Access Database and is called an *external data object,* and the second is a default *internal data object* Fusion creates when a new site is defined.

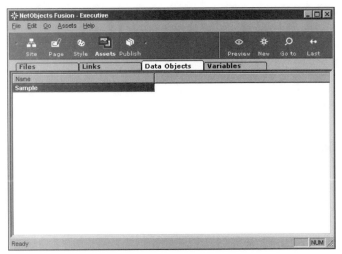

Figure 26-9: The Data Objects section of Assets view.

Double-clicking a data object in Assets view opens a dialog box (shown in Figure 26-10), which lists all the fields, as well as their type, that the author is extracting from the database. You can add fields using the plus (+) sign on the dialog box. You can also rename a field by double-clicking it to open the Field dialog box (displayed in Figure 26-11).

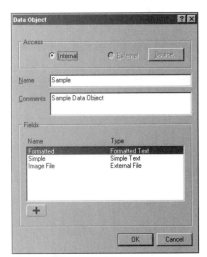

Figure 26-10: The Data Object dialog box in Assets view.

Figure 26-11: Changing a Data
Objects field name and type.

Variables

The final Asset type is the variable. *Variables* are internal objects either maintained
by Fusion (such as Web site author name, number of pages in the site, date last
updated, and so on) or defined by the user as briefly described earlier in this
chapter. The Variables section of Assets view (shown in Figure 26-12) displays
only those variables created by the Web site author.

Tip   Variables are also known as *fields* in NetObjects Fusion version 3.

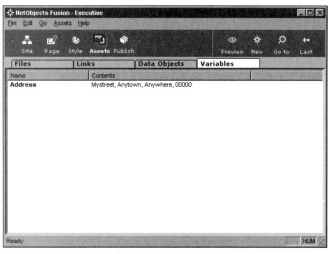

Figure 26-12: The Variables tab in Assets view.

The Web Site Author Name variable is defined on the Site tab of the Properties palette in Site view. Other variables, such as Date Last Modified, Creation Date, and so on, are internally managed by Fusion and cannot be altered, although you can place them on pages. Refer to Chapter 12 for information on creating and using variables in Fusion.

You can modify variables in Assets view by double-clicking them to open the dialog box displayed in Figure 26-13. In the example shown, a variable has been set for a telephone number (+61 2 9310 5544). After you have defined a text block, you can place it anywhere on any of the pages in the Web site using the Insert Variable option from the Text command on the menu bar.

Figure 26-13: Modifying a variable's value.

Summary

✦ Assets view displays all files, links, data objects, and variables used in a site.

✦ An asset's details are viewed and, when allowable, modified by double-clicking the required asset in the list.

✦ You can change the source files for file assets.

✦ You cannot change internal links, but you can assign different URLs to external links.

✦ Duplicate external links pointing to a single URL are only displayed once.

✦ Duplicate named links pointing to different URLs are listed separately.

✦ You can alter the values of user-defined variables in Assets view.

✦   ✦   ✦

Previewing a Site

To see what a page or the entire created-in-Fusion site will look like in a Web browser before publishing it to the Web is called *previewing*. On the icon bar in every module of Fusion is the Preview button. When the Preview button is clicked, Fusion displays the current Web page in the preferred Web browser as defined in the Preferences sheet.

Note In the Preferences options (accessed by selecting Preferences from the Edit menu) you can configure Fusion so that only the current page is previewed when the Preview option is chosen. After the preferences are set, holding down the Ctrl key when previewing has the opposite effect — Fusion previews the whole site. If the preferences are set to preview the whole site, the reverse happens when the Ctrl key is held down — only the current page is previewed.

By default, clicking the Preview button once causes Fusion to generate the HTML code for every page in the site. These pages can then be navigated to as if they were sitting on a Web server by using the navigation controls you have placed on the page(s). Sometimes, however, generating the full site is not opportune or desirable — there may be many pages, and the full site could take some time to generate, for example.

It does not matter which mode you are in — Site, Page, Assets, or Publish view. The Preview button is always available, and the currently selected page is the one Fusion shows in the preferred browser.

Previewing Your Site

When the Preview process is invoked, Fusion performs a number of tasks "behind the scenes." The only operation evident to you is the display of a dialog box (shown in Figure 27-1) informing you which page(s) are being generated.

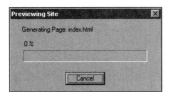

Figure 27-1: The Generating HTML dialog box.

At the same time, however, Fusion also creates a folder in the C:\NetObjects Fusion 3.0\User Sites*User Site* folder (where *User Site* is the name of the current site) called Preview. In this folder, all the pages being previewed are stored as HTML-generated files. These files are loaded into the Web browser.

Note At any time the Preview folder can be deleted because it will be re-generated every time the Preview option is chosen. This folder is most usually deleted to save disk space.

Setting the Preferred Browser

Before you can use the Preview facility of Fusion, you need to make sure you have supplied the correct parameters to the program so that Fusion knows which browser to use to preview the page or pages of the site. To tell Fusion which browser to load at Preview time, you must specify it on the General tab of the Preferences sheet, accessible from the Edit command on the menu bar shown in Figure 27-2.

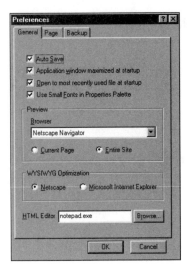

Figure 27-2: The Preferences sheet showing the General tab.

On the General tab you have the choice of setting your preferred browser to either Netscape Navigator or Microsoft Internet Explorer via a drop-down list box. In addition to assigning your preferred browser, an option is also available to specify whether Fusion will preview all of the site's pages or just the current page when the Preview button is clicked. I tend to choose single page only. In a large site especially, previewing the entire site can take some time. To close the Preferences sheet, click the OK button.

Tip

You can simulate the single page only command by holding down the Ctrl key when clicking the Preview button on the icon bar.

The "no more links.gif" file

When previewing single pages, it is easy to forget that when the page has been rendered into the browser, you have no ability to use or test any of the hypertext or other links appearing on the page. You may accidentally click a link, which isn't hard to do because for all intents and purposes, the page looks as if it were on the Web itself.

Consequently, Fusion has built in a gentle reminder if you do inadvertently click a link on a previewed page. This is called the No More Links reminder, which is a .GIF file loaded into the browser once an illegal link attempt has been made. To return to the Preview page, simply click the Back button of your browser.

Why pages look different in Navigator and Internet Explorer

Both Netscape Navigator and Microsoft Internet Explorer render HTML code differently. Because of this difference, Web pages may show anything between a subtle difference and a dramatic difference when viewed between the two browsers. This difference is why it is so important to preview any pages or sites you create in both browsers, especially for a Web site open to public viewing.

Whereas you should not detect too much difference between the two browsers with a basic Web site consisting primarily of text blocks and simple graphics, when a page contains tables and complex formatting, some inconsistencies will most assuredly occur.

Why a gap appears at the top left of the page

One common question concerns a gap that exists at the left-hand and top edges of a page when you view it in a Web browser. This gap occurs even though the elements on the page in Fusion are flush to the left and top of the page.

Both Netscape Navigator and Internet Explorer place a margin approximately ten pixels wide on the left and top of the current page being viewed. To fix this margin, use the Add HTML button on the Layout Properties palette and enter the following HTML code inside the BODY TAG section. (Note that Fusion does this already if the Background image offset preference is left unchecked. If it is checked, Fusion includes the values supplied for the margins.)

For Internet Explorer:

```
TOPMARGIN="0" LEFTMARGIN="0"
```

For Navigator:

```
MARGINWIDTH="0" MARGINHEIGHT="0"
```

Setting WYSIWYG Optimization

The WYSIWYG section of the Preferences sheet General tab provides information regarding optimization. Both Netscape Navigator and Microsoft Internet Explorer have their own idiosyncrasies when it comes to displaying Web pages. Because of this, the WYSIWYG (What You See Is What You Get) option lets you choose to optimize the page for the browser you prefer when previewing.

For example, the lengths of fields on a form appear shorter in Explorer than they do in Navigator, as shown in Figures 27-3 and 27-4. More important, for the same HTML code, Internet Explorer and Navigator render spacing between text differently. It is wise to set this option to your browser, because with the WYSIWYG option on, the spacing that appears in Page view is exactly the same spacing you will see when the page is previewed in the browser.

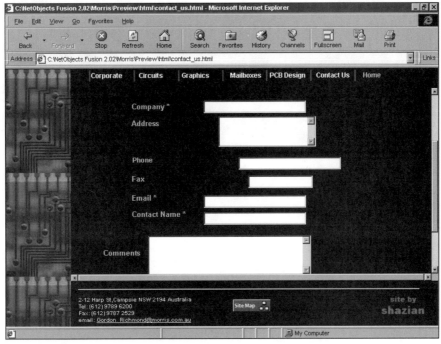

Figure 27-3: A form page shown in Microsoft Internet Explorer.

Tip

Whether your allegiance is towards Microsoft or Netscape, it is always a good idea to preview your pages in both browsers prior to publishing to the Web server, just in case there are any nasty discrepancies when the pages are rendered between the two browsers against the way they look in Fusion. It is a simple matter to set the preference options for one browser and preview the page, and then change the options to the other browser and preview the page again. Previewing in both browsers can save a lot of heartache later — not to mention some rather unflattering emails! Of course, this means you have to have both browsers installed, but the amount of disk space needed is more than offset by the time-saving obtained later, believe me.

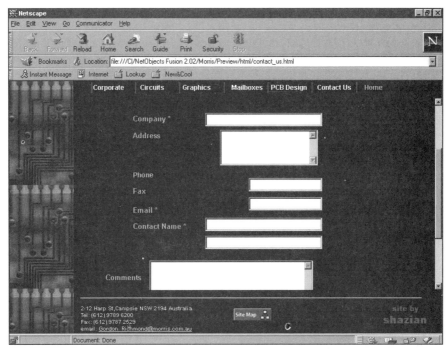

Figure 27-4: The same page shown in Netscape Navigator.

Summary

✦ Previewing is used to show the current page or site in a Web browser before publishing.

✦ Preview creates a Folder called Preview in the User Sites folder.

✦ WYSIWYG optimization sets the appearance of Page view to match the preferred browser.

✦   ✦   ✦

Using Fusion's Publishing Tools

Publishing is the act of generating the HTML to create the
Web pages and electronically transferring the sites and
pages created with NetObjects Fusion to a Web server or
intranet server. Publishing a site generally occurs when the
entire site has been completed.

When you have completed a Web site, you need to move it
from your local computer to a server. Commonly, this server
is a Web server at a remote location. Increasingly more
common, this server can also be a network server acting
as an intranet host.

At publishing time Fusion creates all the HTML code for each
page in the site, transmits these pages and any associated
graphics or other files to the Web server, and stores all these
files in a special folder structure. Figure 28-1 shows Fusion's
Publish View.

Note

The trial version of NetObjects Fusion 3 on the CD-ROM that
accompanies this book is limited in functionality — it does not
enable publishing.

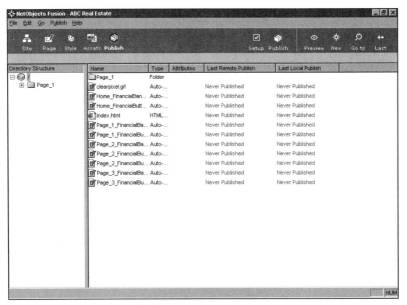

Figure 28-1: Fusion's Publish View.

Publishing Your Site via FTP

In most other Web-authoring programs, to publish a site you move the files to a Web server with a third-party application such as WS_FTP, shown in Figure 28-2. With an FTP (File Transfer Protocol) program, the Web author must make sure all files are moved to the correct locations in the directory structure of the Web server. Additionally, all supporting files, such as graphics, sound, Java Applets, and so on, must be transferred.

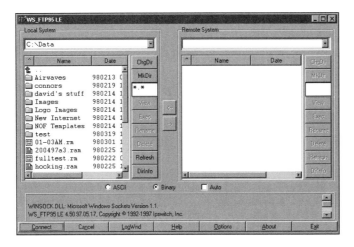

Figure 28-2: The WS_FTP program for Windows.

With Fusion, however, the FTP program is a built-in function. When all the settings for publishing have been set, transferring all files (not just the HTML ones) is a one-click operation. A bonus is that Fusion also takes charge of placing the files in exactly the correct locations on the Web server, ensuring that nothing is missed or misplaced. The correct file location, therefore, guarantees the accuracy and integrity of the Web site.

Tip

Where possible, avoid the This Site Currently Under Construction temptation. Many surveys have shown that when visitors to a site see this message, most leave immediately. You wouldn't stay in a hotel that was still under construction, so try not to offend your visitors with the same type of situation. Most experienced Web authors work on the "If it's not finished, don't publish it" edict.

Setting Options

Fusion requires certain parameters to ensure it has all the information needed to transfer the completed files successfully. The information required includes the location of the Web server, a user login name and password, and other optional requirements, such as the name of the home (index) page and file extensions.

A major component of these settings is the Base Directory setting. While this setting does vary from ISP to ISP, it's an important aspect of making sure your published documents go to the right location. As an example, I'll use the most common Base Directory setting, which is public_html. (Another common setting is htdocs.)

While this setting does not appear in the actual URL of the final published site, it is implied. Thus, when publishing a site to www.shazian.com.au, the Base Director is public_html. If the full path was used as it appears on the Web server, the index.html file would then be www.shazian.com.au/public_html/index.html.

If you are publishing to a folder separate from the root folder, as demonstrated in the previous example, the Base Directory needs to be modified accordingly. For example, if you are publishing to a folder called *newsite*, the Base Directory would then be *public_html/newsite* and the full path on the Web server would be www.shazian.com.au/public_html/newsite.

Just remember, the Base Directory does *not* show in the URL of the completed site.

For further details on this subject, you may need to contact your ISP to see what its special requirements (if any) are.

Publish view shows two window panes. The left pane shows a hierarchical view of the site. Each of the folders displayed is a page in the Web site. As you click each of these folders in turn, the right pane displays the assets on the selected page and their current status. Figure 28-3 shows Publish view. Notice that the home page is selected in the left pane, and the right pane displays all the objects you have placed on that page, with the details on whether the item has been published and when clearly shown.

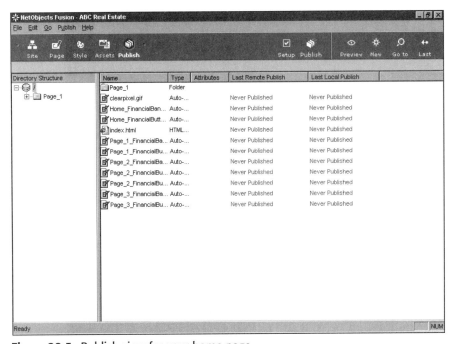

Figure 28-3: Publish view for your home page.

The Publish Setup dialog box

The Publish Setup dialog box (shown in Figure 28-4) contains the various fields you need to fill in so that Fusion knows exactly where and how to publish the site. You access this dialog box by clicking the Setup button on the icon bar.

The Publish Setup dialog box contains three tabs marked Directory Structure, HTML Output, and Server Locations. To move between each tab, simply click the one required.

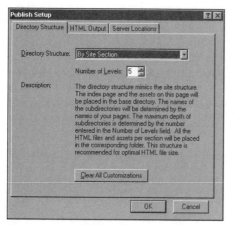

Figure 28-4: The Publish Setup dialog box.

The Directory Structure tab

In NetObjects Fusion versions 1 and 2, the Web server directory structure was fixed — it could not be changed in any fashion. In version 3.0, however, using one of the options on the Directory Structure tab lets you define the way the files and folders are organized on the Web server.

The Directory Structure tab contains a single drop-down list. This list lets you select how the various files and folders in Publish view are displayed and therefore published to the server. The list contains three options, which I explain in the sections that follow:

✦ Flat

✦ By Asset Type

✦ By Site Section

Even after selecting one of the preconfigured types available from the drop-down list, you can still move any of the folders around in the left pane just as you can in the Windows Explorer program. You have complete freedom as to how you configure your site for publishing. After all, you may have a personal preference as to how you want to post the files to the server, or your Web server may require that you use a particular structure.

You can also dictate how many nested pages can be used by setting the Number of Levels box on the Directory Structure tab. The default is 5.

Flat

Selecting the Flat option displays all items on all Web pages as single entries belonging to the site. In this case, the site is shown as a single icon in the left pane. The right pane, as seen in Figure 28-5 shows all of the elements, including the actual pages, as being children of the site. When the site is posted, all pages and objects reside in a single base directory on the Web server. The exception to this are any applets or other components which require their own folder and support files. In this case, these elements are placed into their own folder.

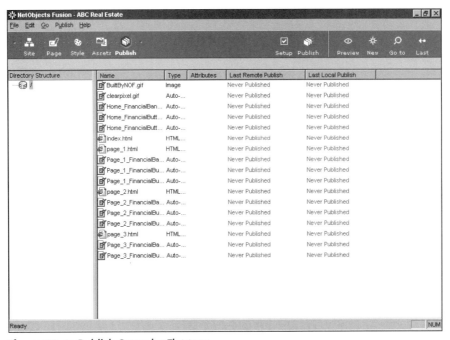

Figure 28-5: Publish Setup by Flat type.

By Asset Type

Selecting the By Asset Type option displays all items in the left pane by the type of object. Figure 28-6 shows a fully expanded list in the left pane, where you can clearly see the different types of folder groupings for each object type. As you select each of these folders in turn, the right pane displays all objects in that particular folder. For example, selecting the Images folder in the left pane displays all the images you have used in the site so far in the right pane.

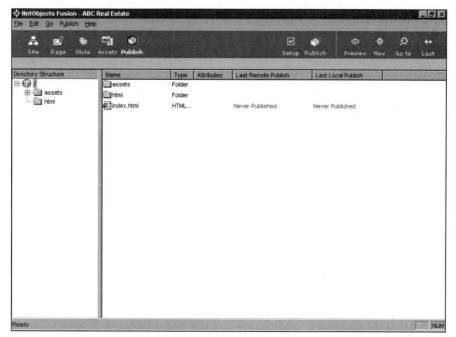

Figure 28-6: Publish Setup by Asset Type.

When you post the site to a Web server, the index page will be in the base directory, and two subfolders, labeled html and assets, will contain the rest of that site's elements. As the folder names suggest, the generated HTML files will be placed in the html folder, and the other assets (including images, sound files, and video) will be placed in the assets folder in separate folders according to their type. (This is the folder setup used in NetObjects Fusion 2.0.)

By Site Section

Displaying Publish mode By Site Section is the default mode, as shown in the dialog box in Figure 28-7. When the Publish windows are displayed in this way, the left pane shows the Web site in a hierarchical fashion similar to the familiar Site view map. Each folder in the left pane is a Web page, and each of these folders when selected show all the objects on that page in the right pane.

When you publish the site, the index page and its assets are placed in the Base Directory of the Web server. All subsequent pages have their own folders (which will contain their respective assets).

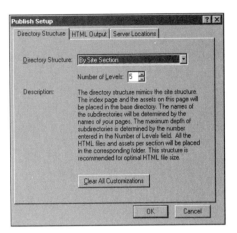

Figure 28-7: By Site Selection is the chosen Directory Structure in the Publish Setup dialog box.

The HTML Output tab

The HTML Output tab (shown in Figure 28-8) contains options that let you configure the type of HTML code generated when you publish the site.

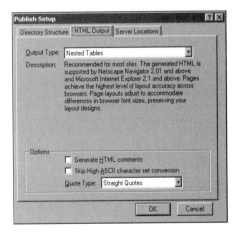

Figure 28-8: The HTML Output tab.

"What? There are different types of HTML?" you ask. Well, yes, sort of. For the first two types, at least, everything comes down to the complexity of the table code that Fusion generates.

Nested Tables

The first of the Output Type options is Nested Tables, which is the default. From experience, this option is currently the best to use on most Web sites. The HTML this option generates is compatible with Netscape Navigator version 2.1 and above and Internet Explorer version 2.1 and above. The Nested Tables option also provides the best accuracy for your layouts so that the objects you place on a Web page end up in relatively the same location you placed them, taking into account that different browsers render pages in different font sizes.

Regular Tables

The HTML that this option generates is compatible with Netscape Navigator version 2.1 and above and Internet Explorer version 2.1 and above. If you find that the Nested Tables option is giving site browser errors or objects are not appearing in locations they should, change the Output Type option to Regular Tables. This creates "looser" HTML that is more browser-independent and friendly and will usually eliminate any problems.

CSS and Layers

Danger, Will Robinson! While this option will create the most accurate rendition of your Web masterpiece in terms of layout, it is only available for browser versions 4.0 and above. (In this case I'm talking about Netscape Navigator and Internet Explorer.) Site visitors viewing the site in an earlier-version browser will assuredly get inconsistent results. Although the majority of users have migrated to version 4.0 of the popular browsers, if you are creating a site for an intranet, you may find that, due to policy, browser version 3.0 or less is still the norm.

The very way CSS and Layers works means that huge differences may occur when a site is viewed in a browser not supporting these specifications. For example, using Layers, elements on a page can be placed on top of one another and, using actions, be made to "switch" positions under specific circumstances. Earlier browsers do not support elements sharing the same space, so to speak, and will therefore "repel" them when viewed. This means your carefully placed overlayed objects will suddenly appear side-by-side.

You may also get font inconsistencies when using the CSS option, which can also cause elements to overlap in some cases.

Generate HTML comments

Those who have dabbled in writing programs using any of the multitudes of available computer languages are well aware of the advantages of adding remarks or comments to code. Not only do remarks or comments provide a clear description of how and why you wrote the code the way you did, but they also aid in debugging any errors that may occur.

The same applies to HTML. While technically not a language, having comments in HTML also presents advantages for the same reasons, although no debugging with Fusion-generated code should be necessary!

Fusion lets the Web author decide whether he or she wants these comments generated at Publishing time. Checking the Generate HTML Comments box on the HTML Output tab triggers this function.

Figure 28-9 shows an example of Fusion code with the HTML comments added.

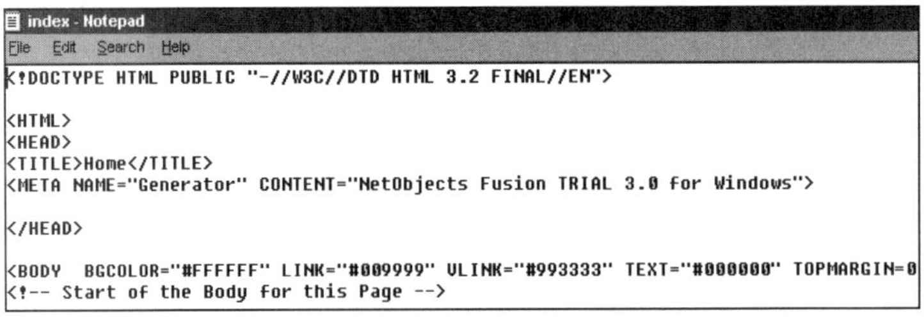


```
<!DOCTYPE HTML PUBLIC "-//W3C//DTD HTML 3.2 FINAL//EN">

<HTML>
<HEAD>
<TITLE>Home</TITLE>
<META NAME="Generator" CONTENT="NetObjects Fusion TRIAL 3.0 for Windows">

</HEAD>

<BODY  BGCOLOR="#FFFFFF" LINK="#009999" VLINK="#993333" TEXT="#000000" TOPMARGIN=0
<!-- Start of the Body for this Page -->
```

Figure 28-9: HTML generated by Fusion with comments.

Skip High ASCII character set conversion

In general, unless you're using special character sets such as Kanji, leave this box unchecked.

Quote Type

This option depends heavily on personal taste and is browser-dependent. Simply, if you use quotation marks in your Web site, you have the opportunity of telling Fusion which type to use. Straight Quotes (") are the default, showing just vertical marks; Curly Quotes (“) are the type used in typesetting and “curl” differently, depending on whether they're at the beginning or end of a word; and Newspaper Quotes (') are single straight quotes.

In general, the site visitor's browser font settings will control the appearance of these quotes in his or her browser, so I suggest simply leaving the Curly Quotes default turned on.

It's your call. You might want to experiment with your local setup and see what works best.

The Server Locations tab

So where do you want to post the Web site? You must provide a server location no matter whether it's your local hard disk (for testing purposes) or an intranet or Internet Web server. The Server Locations tab is where you supply this information (see Figure 28-10).

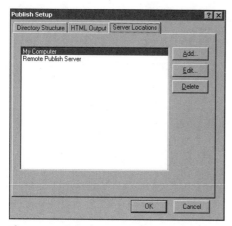

Figure 28-10: The Server Locations tab.

You can add as many server locations as you like to this tab. Click the Add button, and the Location Properties dialog box appears. In the Server Name field enter a name that is meaningful to you, such as OzEmail FTP server or ZIP Secure Server, for example.

If you're testing (also called *staging*) your site, make sure the Local radio button is selected and specify where you want to place the site on your computer. You can use the Browse button to find the location as well.

To select only a single remote server, just click the Remote radio button and fill in the blanks.

Tip   If you don't know the necessary information, you need to contact your Internet service provider, Webmaster, or network administrator for the necessary data. An example of the settings required for a standard (Is there such a thing?) ISP is shown in Figure 28-11. Notice the Base Directory setting discussed earlier.

The Remote section of the dialog box contains fields for details of the user account on the Web server. If you check the Remember Password option, Fusion stores this password in the NOD file. If not, the field remains blank, and at publishing time a dialog box opens, requesting the password before Fusion will transfer the files to the server. If you do tell Fusion to Remember Password, you will be able to enter the password into the field, which will be displayed as a series of asterisks (*) for security reasons.

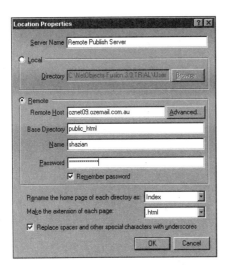

Figure 28-11: Configuring the Location Properties dialog box.

I don't recommend having users store their passwords in Fusion. There is a slim chance someone could hack it.

All information — not just the password — entered into this dialog box is stored permanently in the NOD file. Due to this, if you make any changes to your account, such as a change of password or user name, you must update this dialog box by using the Edit button.

The Advanced button opens another dialog box that enables you to fine-tune the Location Properties further. This section is very much ISP-specific. Again, if you're unsure what should be entered here, check with your ISP, Webmaster, or network administrator.

At the bottom of the Location Properties dialog box is a small section reserved for naming conventions of the home page and the extension to be used for all pages. This section of the dialog box is optional.

Rename the home page of each directory as
The first of these options changes the name of the home page from its default of Index.html. Why would you change from Index.html?

Some Web servers require the home page to be called a different name than most people would consider normal (Index.html). A common example is the normal index.html page being called home.html. I have never come across this myself, but in the Fusion newsgroups this appears to be a common practice, in particular for some ISPs in the United Kingdom.

A second reason to change is when using multiple NOD files in Fusion for a single site. The current home page (what Fusion classifies as the home page for this site) may not be the home page on the Web server but instead the top page of a section of the Web site. For large sites especially, you're better off breaking down the site into separate NOD files for both practical and backup reasons.

Your other options are Current Page Name, Default, and Home. The current page name is the name you have applied to the page when naming it. For example, the top page in Site Structure might be called "top_page." When this option is selected, the normally named index.html would be published as *top_page.html*. The "default" option is for the page to be called default.html, no matter what name you have given it (this also applies to the Index and Home options).

Make the extension of each page

To change the Home page from index.html to another name, select the option you require from the drop-down list in the Files section, as shown in Figure 28-12. To change the file suffix to *htm* or *shtml* rather than *html* (these three options are the only ones for this field in the current version of Fusion), once again choose the alternate option from the drop-down list. (Remember, custom names always override the publish settings.)

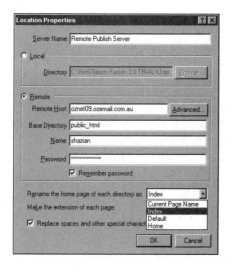

Figure 28-12: Changing the name of the Home page.

Replace file name spaces with underscores

Whereas some Web servers require a different home page name than index.html, many more cannot cope with having spaces or special characters as part of a filename. If this is the case with the Web server you are publishing to, or the final published site produces strange errors when clicking hyperlinks, you may need to check the Replace file name spaces with underscores option in the Location Properties dialog box. When you have entered all the Location Properties information, you can close this dialog box.

Posting your site to a Web server

Now that you've set all the necessary parameters, close the Setup sheet and click the Publish button on the icon bar. In the dialog box that opens (shown in Figure 28-13), you can select the server to post to from the drop-down list.

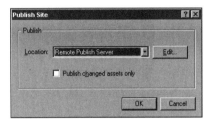

Figure 28-13: The Publish Site dialog box.

An important option here is the Publish changed assets only checkbox. If this box is checked, only the assets that have changed since the last post to the server will be sent. When posting to the Web server for the first time, leave this box unchecked. On subsequent posts, click this box to check it. Once you check the box, only the changes you have made to the site will be posted to the server, which is a huge time-saver.

While you may have made what seems on the surface only a minor change, you may notice that Fusion is posting more files than you would have thought. This is because even subtle changes may cause changes to the site you have never thought of. For example, changing some element in a MasterBorder requires all pages using that MasterBorder to be reposted. You may have only changed a graphic, but this change is relevant to all the HTML of those pages; therefore, Fusion reposts all the pages that contain that graphic.

If you need to make changes to the Server Location setup at this point, clicking the Edit button lets you make these changes on-the-fly.

Note   This is the Publish button on the right side of the icon bar, not the left!

Fusion now generates the HTML for all pages you have selected to publish, contacts the Web server, and moves the pages via its built-in File Transfer Protocol (ftp) program. If you make any subsequent changes to the Web site, all the parameters you have set remain in place, and, apart from perhaps selecting new sections or files to post, reposting your site should be a one-click affair. When completed, Fusion displays a Transfer Complete dialog box.

Summary

✦ Publishing sends completed Web pages to an Internet Web server or intranet server.

✦ Different directory (folder) structures can be defined for how the files are placed on the server.

✦ The complexity of the HTML code can be set to cater for different browsers.

✦ As many Web server locations as necessary can be configured.

✦ It is possible to republish only assets (pages, images, and so forth) that have changed since the last post to a Web server.

✦   ✦   ✦

How Do I Install Fusion?

NetObjects Fusion System Requirements

To make Fusion available to the widest market possible, the developers of the program have created two versions of Fusion: one for the Microsoft Windows 95 or NT platform and the other for the Macintosh environment.

For Windows 95 and NT

Here is a list of what you need to install NetObjects Fusion on Windows 95 or NT or later system:

✦ PC with a 90MHz or faster Pentium-based processor

✦ Windows 95 or Windows NT 3.51 or later

Running Fusion on Win32s under Windows 3.11 will not work.

✦ A minimum of 32MB of RAM is necessary (and 20 MB or greater is highly recommended); for a full installation, which includes all of the supplied templates, styles, clip art, and so on, 100 MB of hard disk space is recommended

✦ 32MB of actual RAM required (64MB recommended to run NetObjects Fusion with an HTML 3.*x*-compatible browser) with 15 MB available for NetObjects Fusion

✦ Minimum video display of 800×600 pixels at 256 colors or more

✦ TCP/IP compliance for Internet connectivity

✦ 32-bit ODBC drivers for external database connectivity

✦ Mouse or compatible pointing device

✦ A CD-ROM drive

You will also need a Web browser. NetObjects Fusion 3.0 is optimized for:

✦ Netscape Navigator 2.01 or later

✦ Microsoft Internet Explorer 2.1 or later

✦ Other HTML 3.0-compatible browsers or later

✦ To use actions and layering, you should use Netscape Navigator 4.0 or later or Internet Explorer 4.0 or later.

For Macintosh

What follows is a laundry list of what you need to install NetObjects Fusion on your Macintosh:

✦ Power Macintosh or 100-percent compatible (Power Macintosh 8100 or faster recommended)

✦ Mac OS 7.5.1 or later (7.6 recommended)

✦ 90 to 120 MB available hard disk space for full installation

✦ 32 MB of actual RAM required (64 MB recommended to run NetObjects Fusion with an HTML 3.x-compatible browser) with 15 MB available for NetObjects Fusion

✦ Minimum video display of 800 × 600 pixels at 256 colors or more

✦ Internet access for publishing

✦ A CD-ROM drive

You will also need a Web browser. NetObjects Fusion 3.0 is optimized for:

✦ Netscape Navigator 2.0 and higher

✦ Microsoft Internet Explorer 2.0 and higher

✦ Other HTML 3.x-compatible browsers

✦ To use Actions, and layering, you should use Navigator 4.0 or later or Internet Explorer 4.0 or later.

Note

This is the most up to date information I have as this book goes to press. The Mac version of Fusion 3 is completing the development stage, so I have included ranges for the areas in which the requirements may change.

Upgrading from Previous Versions of Fusion

If you have an earlier version of NetObjects Fusion installed, it is recommended that you upgrade to version 3 using the following steps:

1. Export all existing User Sites as templates (NFT) files.

2. Uninstall version 2 using the Control Panel Add Remove Programs option.

3. Install version 3 from the CD-ROM.

4. Open any existing User Sites as templates.

Note

If you don't export any existing sites as templates as per step 1, when you attempt to open a NOD file created in an earlier version, Fusion 3 presents you with a dialog box. This will ask you if you would like a copy to be made of the original NOD file before it converts it to version 3 format. It is strongly suggested you *do* make this copy.

Installing from the CD-ROM

If you've bought the full version of NetObjects Fusion 3, just pop the CD-ROM in the drive and consult the section that applies to your particular platform: PC or Mac.

Danger Zone

The folks at NetObjects warn us not to install Fusion 3 on a network, Zip, or Jaz drive. You're better off sticking to your hard drive.

On your PC system

1. Click Start, and then click Run (as seen in Figure A-1).

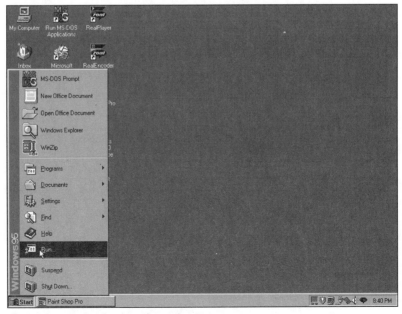

Figure A-1: Selecting Run from the Start menu.

Note

2. Type **D:\Setup.exe** in the Open field, and click OK (as seen in Figure A-2).

   D: is the usual designation for the CD-ROM drive. Yours may be different. If so, select the Browse button and find the drive from the Look in field.

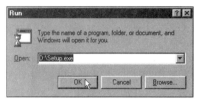

Figure A-2: Typing the install file in the Run dialog box.

3. The NetObjects Fusion Installer splash screen will appear (as seen in Figure A-3). Select Next.

Figure A-3: The first screen of the NetObjects Fusion Installer.

4. Select Yes after reading the License Agreement (as seen in Figure A-4).

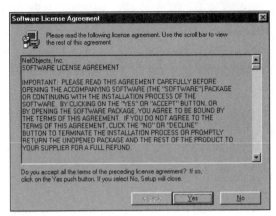

Figure A-4: The Software License Agreement.

5. A general disclaimer will appear (as seen in Figure A-5); just select Next.

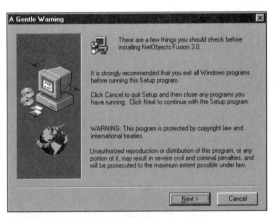

Figure A-5: A Gentle Warning screen.

6. In the User Information dialog box (as seen in Figure A-6), type in your Name, your Company's Name, and the Serial Number found in the software package. Press Next.

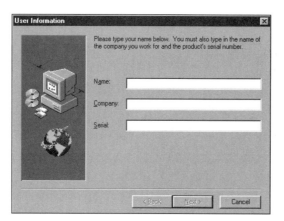

Figure A-6: Enter your information in the User Information dialog box.

7. The Installer program will ask you to confirm the information you entered (see Figure A-7). If everything's kosher, select Next.

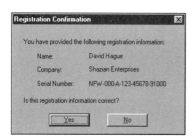

Figure A-7: The Registration Confirmation dialog box.

8. Choose a directory to install NetObjects Fusion 3. I'd use the default destination, but you can use the Browse button to locate one you prefer (see Figure A-8). Select Next.

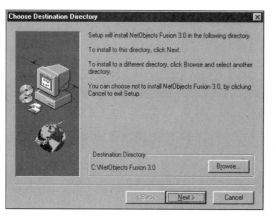

Figure A-8: Choosing the directory to place Fusion.

9. If the folder does not exist, you'll see the dialog box in Figure A-9. Create it now by selecting Yes.

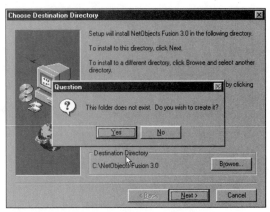

Figure A-9: Creating a folder for Fusion.

10. The Installer will then ask you whether you would like to install the Full or Compact version of Fusion (as seen in Figure A-10). If you've made the disk space available, just click Next.

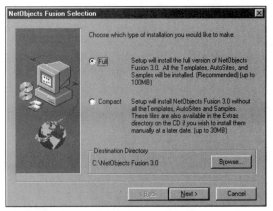

Figure A-10: Choosing which version of Fusion to install.

11. NetObjects Fusion will begin to install the files (as seen in Figure A-11).

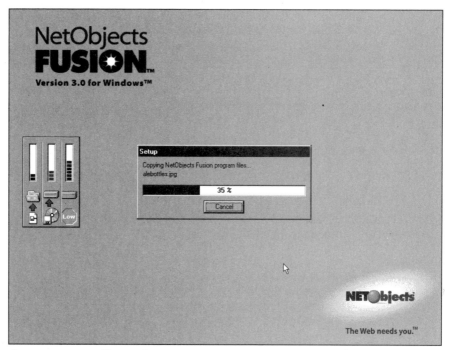

Figure A-11: Installing Fusion.

12. To install TrueType Web Fonts (as shown in Figure A-12), select OK.

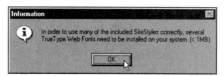

Figure A-12: Installing TrueType Web Fonts.

13. Select Yes after reading the TrueType License Agreement (as seen in Figure A-13).

14. Review the Readme, and select Yes.

15. Select if you would like to restart your computer now or later, and click Finish.

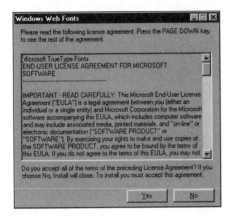

Figure A-13: The TrueType License Agreement.

On your Macintosh system

To install the full version of NetObjects Fusion 3 from a CD-ROM, follow these steps:

1. Insert the NetObjects Fusion 3 CD-ROM.

2. Double-click the NetObjects Fusion 3 CD icon on your desktop.

3. Double-click the NetObjects Fusion 3 Installer icon.

4. Click Continue in the NetObjects Fusion 3 Installer splash screen.

5. Read the License Agreement and click Accept to continue.

6. Use the dropdown menu in the top left corner to install the full version (Easy Install) or selected components (Custom Install).

7. Select the install location. For best performance, accept the default which is currently set to the root of your hard disk.

8. Click Install.

9. Click Continue to close any open application, acknowledge the notification, and continue with the installation. When the installation is finished, a message appears indicating that the installation was successful. You now have the option to quit the Installer, continue installing more components, or restart you Macintosh.

10. If you chose Easy Install (in step 6), click Restart.

After your Macintosh has restarted, a NetObjects Fusion folder appears on you hard disk. Be sure to read the Read Me file before starting. It contains important, late-breaking news about NetObjects Fusion.

Note This is the most up-to-date information I have as this book goes to press. The Mac version of Fusion 3 is completing the development stage, so some steps may be different; consult the documentation that accompanies the product.

Installing from this Book's CD-ROM

To install the NetObjects Fusion 3 for Windows, Limited Functionality trial version from the CD-ROM that accompanies this book, you must:

1. Once you have downloaded the appropriate configuration to your hard disk, double click the NOF30_LFTrial.exe.
2. Select Setup. The file will then begin to self extract.
3. Select Next
4. Select Yes after reading the License Agreement.
5. Select Next.
6. Type in your Name and your Company's Name.
7. Select Next.
8. Choose a directory to install NetObjects Fusion 3 trial. I'd use the default destination.
9. Select Next.
10. If the folder does not exist, create it now by selecting Yes.
11. NetObjects Fusion will begin to install the files.
12. To install TrueType Web Fonts, select OK.
13. Select Yes after reading the TrueType License Agreement.
14. Review the Readme, and select Yes.
15. Select if you would like to restart your computer now or later, and click Finish.

Installing from a Web Download

You can download trial versions of NetObjects Fusion from the company's Web site at www.netobjects.com/download/index.html. The trial version contains all the features and functionality of the full version except the ability to stage or publish the sites that you build with that version.

You'll be asked to enter your e-mail address, choose a software version to download, and then asked to enter personal information (only your name, ZIP code, and e-mail are required). You'll then be asked if you would you like NetObjects and selected third-parties to contact you concerning sales and promotional information and some marketing questions.

You have two options when downloading:

✦ Download a single compressed file

✦ Download a series of small files

You'll have several sites from which to download Fusion, some based on where you live.

If you have any problems with the downloading or uncompressing of the files, check the NetObjects Web site (at www.netobjects.com) on tips for downloading on your particular hardware platform.

Tip

On the NetObjects Web site, you can also find a whole bunch of extra Templates, Styles, graphics, and so on. They are downloadable from www.netobjects.com/extras/index.html. There are also links to other applications that complement Fusion 3 from their site.

Downloading the single compressed file

For both Windows and Macintosh, the file saves to the Desktop by default. Just follow the procedures in the previous section entitled "Installing from this Book's CD-ROM." The file will automatically decompress and start the installation procedure.

Downloading from a series of files

To install the NetObjects Fusion 3 for Windows, Limited Functionality trial version you must:

1. Download all the files to a temporary directory. The name and location of the directory are not important. Do not install from the desktop. Place all four components in a folder, and double-click on the NOF3.0_LFTrial_1of4.

2. Select OK, the Installer will automatically unzip the files.

3. The remaining steps (3-15) are the same as for downloading the single compressed file.

For Macintosh, do not install from the Desktop. Place all the components in a folder and double-click on the Installer icon after uncompressing the files.

Registering NetObjects Fusion

It is always a good idea to register software as this is the only way the company—NetObjects in this case—is able to keep you in touch with any updates, patches, and so on.

To register Fusion, you can either:

✦ Mail in the Registration card supplied with the program.

✦ Register online at `www.netobjects.com/registration/html/registernof3.html`.

✦ Select the Registration command on the Help menu (which will take you online to the above URL automatically. (You must have an Internet connection to use this function.)

Don't forget to also register any applications that are bundled with Fusion such as HomeSite.

Summary

✦ Extra Styles and Templates are available from the NetObjects Web site.

✦ Links are also available to other applications that complement NetObjects Fusion.

✦ If using a previous version of Fusion, either save all User Sites as templates or accept the copy option when upgrading sites to version 3.

✦ Uninstall version 2 to save disk space after saving any User Sites as templates.

✦ Don't forget to register! This includes any add-on programs supplied with Fusion.

✦   ✦   ✦

Additional Information

◆ ◆ ◆ ◆

In This Appendix

NetObjects Fusion
resources

Language resources

Applications
resources

Other useful
information and
resources for Web
development

◆ ◆ ◆ ◆

In various places throughout this book I have mentioned
extra resources you will find useful for using NetObjects
Fusion 3; creating Web sites in general; information on
languages such as JavaScript, Java, Perl; and many other
subjects. In this appendix you find this information.

NetObjects Fusion Resources

This section categorizes resources that are available as an
adjunct to Fusion 3 or relate directly to the application.

The NetObjects Web site

Obviously the best place to get the most up-to-date information
on NetObjects Fusion itself is the NetObjects Web site (www.
netobjects.com). The site contains all sorts of goodies, hints,
tips, new ground-breaking documentation, and so on. There
are also special offers for users wanting to upgrade to newer
versions and announcements of new products. The NetObjects
Web site changes often, so it is worth bookmarking and
checking regularly.

Newsgroups

For support purposes — and I have said this many times in the
book — in my opinion NetObjects provides the best support
of any product I have ever used since I started in this industry
in 1979. The place to find this wonderful support is in the
NetObjects newsgroups. Before you fire up your newsreader
and search for NetObjects, you won't find it in the general
run-of the-mill newsgroups, because it is hosted on a special
server by the folks at NetObjects.

To access the NetObjects newsgroups, you have to point your
newsreader to news.netobjects.com and download the
newsgroups current at the time.

Language Resources

Three major languages are used in Web work for scripting are Perl, JavaScript, and Java. I have come across a number of useful resources I am sure will be helpful.

Perl

Without question, the best Perl-related Web site is at www.extropia.com. This site is created and maintained by the acknowledged gurus of the Perl world: Selena Sol (aka Eric Tachibana) and Matt Wright. In conjunction with Gunther Berzniecks, they also have a superb Perl book called *Instant Web Scripts with CGI/Perl* published by MIS/MIT. Selena has one rule: you can use anything on their site free-of-charge as long as you acknowledge where it came from *and* you in some way help someone else. This idea is simple, effective, and in the original spirit of the Internet.

Other useful books include:

✦ *Foundations of World Wide Web Programming with HTML & CGI* (IDG Books Worldwide, Inc., 1995)

✦ *Web Programming Secrets with HTML, CGI, and Perl* (IDG Books Worldwide, Inc., 1996)

✦ *CGI Bible* (IDG Books Worldwide, Inc., 1996)

JavaScript

The best-of-the-best at JavaScript is Danny Goodman. His Web site at www.dannyg.com contains heaps of information that parallels his excellent book, *JavaScript Bible* (IDG Books Worldwide, Inc., 1997).

Java

What can I say? In the twelve months it took to write this book as Fusion 3 developed, more has happened with Java than probably any language in history! If you're new to Java, I recommend *Java Programming for Dummies* (IDG Books Worldwide, Inc., 1997), and for the experienced user, *Foundations of Java Programming for the World Wide Web* (IDG Books Worldwide, Inc., 1996).

Another excellent book for beginner to intermediate is *Creating Cool Web Applets With Java* (IDG Books Worldwide, Inc., 1996).

For the best Java Web site, have a look at www.javaworld.com and sign up for their regular newsletter. It contains heaps of Java-related information.

Applications Resources

In addition to NetObjects Fusion, of course, a Web author's toolbox is not complete without a number of other Web-authoring applications. There are literally hundreds of programs out there that cater to almost any need, so I'll restrict my discussion to the programs I consider to be indispensable and/or the ones I use or know others have had great success with.

3D Graphics

Infini-D

In my opinion this is the best program available for both the Mac and the PC. (A trial copy of Infini-D is on the CD-ROM accompanying this book). Its Web site is at `www.metacreations.com`. There is also a third-party — and very active and informative — listserv newsletter available by subscribing via `www.metacreations.com/products/infini-d/resources.html`. On this page are also heaps of links to other resources, including image files, tutorials, newsgroups, and so on.

Web 3D

For quick and dirty 3D text and generic 3D images, it 'is hard to get past Asymetrix Web 3D. Sorry, it's PC-only at this stage, but Web 3D allows you to quickly create 3D .GIF files in a program that is very inexpensive — about US$50, I believe. The Web site is `www.asymetrix.com`. A companion product, 3D/FX, is also very useful.

Graphics and image retouching

Micrografx Designer and Picture Publisher

Most people swear by Photoshop for both the Mac and the PC. I guess it depends on what you are brought up on, and I cut my teeth on Micrografx products (see `www.micrografx.com`). Using Designer and Picture Publisher is now second nature to me, as I am sure Photoshop is to other users; however, for value for your money, these programs are hard to beat in my opinion. A bonus is that you also get ABC Flowcharter and Simply 3D 2 in the same package.

Macromedia Freehand 8 and Xres

A relative new kid on the block is a new version of an old favorite. Freehand 8 at a cursory look seems to have some interesting attributes and benefits. And Xres cannot be surpassed when dealing with large graphics files. Even Photoshop enthusiasts say that! See `www.macromedia.com`.

Flash

When you need animation, nothing can touch Macromedia Flash. It's elegant, simple to use, and consists of small file sizes when shocked. Flash — of which a trial sample is enclosed on the CD-ROM that accompanies this book — is *the* standard for Web animation. You can find more information at www.macromedia.com.

Director

When more animation/multimedia is needed, and you have the time and the learning curve energy, Macromedia Director is the way to go. Just about anything can be created in Director due to its ability to import just about any animation/video file format and its use of the Lingo multimedia language. Again, see www.macromedia.com.

Video and Imaging Resources

Adobe Premiere

For creating and editing .AVI or QuickTime files, Adobe Premiere is to video as PhotoShop is to a graphic artist. It just can't be beat and is a lot of fun to boot. It helps to have an understanding of video and its creation, not to mention heaps of hardware resources at your disposal. A Pentium 200MMX or equivalent, 64MB RAM, and 5GB or better of hard drive space free is the minimum. However, and I quote from the rec.desktop.video newsgroup, "You can have the best equipment in the world, but if you can't write, light, shoot or script, forget it!" (As an adjunct to Premiere, when only a small video is created and you want to turn it into an animated .GIF, use GIF Construction Set, available as shareware from www.mindworkshop.com. This converts .AVI files to animated .GIF files.)

For more details on Premiere, see www.adobe.com.

RealMedia

As you may have guessed from the chapter on RealAudio and RealVideo, I am very excited about this technology, and anyone can use it! To get all the low-down, have a look at www.real.com. To create both RealAudio and RealVideo, you need the free downloads of RealPlayer and Real Encoder, and there is now even a limited freeware Server application.

If you're experienced in Adobe Premiere, a new addition to the RealMedia catalog is a plug-in to convert Premiere files to RealVideo or Audio files. For PowerPoint aficionados, another plug-in lets you convert PowerPoint presentations to RealVideo format.

PhotoVista

To generate those really cool panoramic photos that enable the viewer to pan the image inside a browser window, PhotoVista is king. Available as a trial download (it works fully; it just places a watermark on the image until registered and paid for), PhotoVista is one of those rare programs that is both fun and useful. Available for both Mac and PC, I find PhotoVista indispensable. See www.livepicture.com.

Clear Video

Clear Video is a Premiere (or for any programs that generate .AVI files) plug-in that creates extremely compressed but very clear streaming video files for the Web. Although the rendering takes quite some time, the end results are well worth it as there is little sacrifice on quality from the original. See www.iterated.com for more details on Clear Video plus lots of other video resources.

Video Director

This is a bit of a hybrid. If you do not have the hardware resources, the time to learn, or the money to buy Adobe Premiere but still want to add homegrown video to your Web sites, Video Director may just be what you are looking for. A "black box" that controls your camcorder and VCR, Video Director stores only the start and stop times of edited videos from the camcorder. When it is time to create the finished VHS tape, it controls both the camcorder and the VCR, plus it allows titling, music overlays, graphics insertion, and much more. The final edited tape can then be imported using a video capture card (I use the Creative Labs IE500) straight into RealVideo.

Video Director costs about US$250 and can be learned in minutes, giving professional results. See www.pinnaclesys.com for more details.

Avid

If you have a full wallet, the necessary hardware, and want the best you can get for video production, Avid Systems provides the best of the best. Available on both Mac and PC, Avid is accepted as the world leader in desktop video editing and production. Some of the most awesome movies of all time were edited on Avid (such as *Titanic* and *Babe* — *Babe* was Australian, you know).

Avid is not cheap, but it is for those who *must* have the best. See www.avid.com.

Other Resources

This last section is for stuff that doesn't really come under any other logical heading. It contains information I have picked up along the way.

World Wide Web Marketing

I read a copy of *World Wide Web Marketing* (John Wiley & Sons, 1995), and my wife, Sharon, saw the author, Jim Sterne, speak at a conference. What this man does not know about Web marketing is not worth writing. Do yourself a favor and grab a copy.

Canon MV-1 Digital Video/Still Camera

I am in love with it. For amazing picture quality and ease of use (and showing off to your friends), this is the best combination of digital video and digital still camera I have ever used. See www.canon.com for details.

Nikon Coolpix 300

If all you want is a digital still, however, my favorite is the really cool Nikon Coolpix 300. Doubling as a tape recorder (Really! It stores sounds as well), the Coolpix can handle up to 128 640 × 480 pixel, 256-color JPEG images and is a breeze to attach to a PC or Mac for downloading. It's a bit heavy on the batteries when downloading, but the optional powerpack fixes that.

Rama, Riven, and Starfleet Academy

When you have had enough and want some mental inspiration, want to get rid of some pent-up aggression, or just want to drool over the graphics, I highly recommend Rama (from Sierra), Riven (from Cyan), and Starfleet Academy (from Interplay). They're just the trick!

✦   ✦   ✦

About the CD-ROM

Included in the back of this book for your enjoyment, edification, fun, and to take away yet more evenings from your wife/girlfriend/husband/boyfriend is a CD-ROM that contains a trial version of NetObjects Fusion 3 as well as what I consider extremely useful complementary applications and add-on components to Fusion. Also included are sample Fusion templates and what I call the "parts," which are the text, image, database, and other files used throughout the tutorial sections of the book.

Contents

The CD-ROM is divided into the following folders:

+ Software
+ Examples
+ Templates
+ Web Sites
+ NFX Components

Software

While Fusion by itself is without question the greatest boon ever to Web authoring I know of providing just about every facility you may ever need, there is always a place for additional programs to assist. These are used to create custom graphics or animation, or even just applications that assist you in using the Web to find or relocate sites that are a valuable resource for further information.

Well, here we have provided you with samples of some of the best! On the CD-ROM is the following trial software:

◆ Trial version of NetObjects Fusion 3

NetObjects Fusion is, in my opinion, the best Web-authoring development program available today. It is a powerful tool that enables you to build, design, and maintain full-featured, professional Web sites without having to be well-versed in HTML.

◆ Trial version of NetObjects ScriptBuilder 2.0

ScriptBuilder from NetObjects is a powerful, dedicated script editor for the Web. It maintains a point-and-click environment that makes script development easy. With ScriptBuilder, you are able to write dynamic scripts for Web pages, preview scripted pages, and navigate to embedded functions and objects.

◆ Trial version of Infini-D from MetaCreations

Infini-D from MetaCreations is one of the programs that even just a few years ago would have cost thousands of dollars and required very expensive high-end hardware just to run. Using Infini-D, highly detailed and complex 3D models and animation can be built to use in Web pages. Infini-D also enables you to export animation as AVI or QuickTime files and incorporate them in RealMedia or QuickTime movies.

◆ Trial version of Flash 2 from Macromedia

Macromedia Flash has become the de facto standard for creating animation for Web pages. From simple buttons to fully fledged cartoons, Flash is easy to learn, fun to master and creates a myriad of possibilities to make any Web page stand out from the rest. Both a Macintosh and Windows version of the trial version of Flash are included on the CD-ROM.

◆ Trial version of ISYS HindSite from Odyssey Software

You saw something on the Web, but you can't remember where, and you didn't make a bookmark. ISYS HindSite remembers everywhere you've been and everything you've seen. ISYS HindSite offers Netscape Navigator and Microsoft Internet Explorer users the unique capability to perform full text searches on the contents of previously accessed Web pages. Versions for both Netscape and IE are included on the CD-ROM.

◆ Trial version of ISYS for Intradisk from Odyssey Software

Lots of people are realizing the advantages of publishing information in a platform-independent, vendor-neutral form such as HTML. While many people are publishing information in this format, all of them are doing so with the aid of a "search button" in their publication. ISYS for Intradisk brings back the Search button!

◆ Trial version of Universe Image Creator from Diard Software

Ever wondered how those "spacey" backgrounds are made in the popular television science fiction programs like "Babylon 5" or "Star Trek"? Well now you too can create wonderful galactic backdrops for your Web pages using Universe Image Creator. Easy drag and drop to add planets, stars, clouds and more make each Universe image totally unique.

✦ Microsoft Internet Explorer 4 and Netscape Navigator

For your convenience, Microsoft Internet Explorer 4 and Netscape Navigator Web browsers have been supplied on the CD-ROM.

Examples

All of the "parts" referenced in the book during our creation of various Web site elements, such as the Executive Performance Web site, are stored in the Examples folder on the CD-ROM. When placing the text on the Company Overview page of the Executive Performance Web site, for example, the file to use (if you want to of course as you can always type it!) is co.txt. A complete list of all these parts follows:

✦ Welcome.txt

✦ Co.txt — the company overview text in the Executive Performance Web site

✦ Car.gif — the "mustang" to go on the Home Page of the Executive Performance Web site

✦ Usa.gif — the map used for image mapping in the Executive Performance Web site

✦ Catchy Java Applet — example used in showing Java Applets

✦ Executive links.db1 — Racing "links" database used in the Executive Performance Web site

✦ Manta.jpg — optional image for the Racing "links" database

✦ Tubular.midi — Mike Oldfield MIDI soundtrack (optional)

✦ "Under Construction" Shockwave file

✦ body.gif, wheel1.gif, wheel2.gif, and wheel3.gif — used to create a basic drag and drop game when learning Actions

Templates

I have supplied a number of tried and tested Fusion templates you may like to use in any future projects. These include:

✦ Harness Racing Template — used to create a site for a harness racing (Trotting) club

✦ Hire Company Template — useful for any company that hires out machinery, building equipment, and so on

✦ Markets Newsletter — a template that was created for a produce market authority

✦ Motor Industry Software Template — used for a company that develops software and has trial versions of the software downloadable from their Web site

✦ MVCLC Template — a template for a church Web site

Web Sites

In the Web Sites folder on the CD-ROM is a Fusion site called "weblist." This contains links to all of the Web sites that are referenced in the book. From many of these information on third-party programs that are useful adjuncts to Fusion is available, and also in many cases demonstration versions are downloadable. There are also links to sites that contain great resources such as Perl scripts you can use to help in building Web sites.

NFX Components

In the NFX Components folder are the following NetObjects Fusion components, pre-built mini applications designed to add functionality to your Fusion 3-created Web sites:

✦ Demo version of **The Data Drill** (Lite Edition) (Coolmaps.com)

✦ Demo version of **RollOver** (Coolmaps.com)

✦ Demo version of **LinkMaster** (Coolmaps.com)

✦ **BetterPictureLoader 2.0** (Apollon-Components)

✦ **LinkDropDown 2.0** (Apollon-Components)

✦ **Image Rollover** version 1.1 (WebObjects, Ltd.)

✦ **SiteSearch** version 1.1 (WebObjects, Ltd.)

For more information about the specific components and the companies that created them, refer to the readme file in the individual components folders.

Installation Instructions

To install the *Fusion 3 Bible* CD-ROM, follow these steps:

1. Insert the Fusion 3 Bible CD-ROM into your CD-ROM drive.

2. Click the Start button.

3. Select Programs ⇨ Windows Explorer.

4. Double-click the CD-ROM drive icon to view the contents of the CD-ROM in the right window.

Software

For each of the trial versions of software supplied on the CD-ROM, navigate to its folder within Windows Explorer and double-click the Setup icon to start the installation process. Follow the onscreen prompts. Once you have installed an application, it is always wise to read the readme file so that any late changes, updates, or further information can be seen.

Examples

In the Examples folder are a number of files that are referenced throughout this book. If you decide to follow the tutorial examples, you will need to copy the contents of this folder to your hard disk.

As an example of the folder structure I use, I keep each Web site I am creating (the Fusion NOD file) in the default User Sites folder that Fusion creates when the site is initially created. Second, I created a folder called "Data" on the hard disk under the root directory (usually the C:\ directory) and in this Data folder, create a folder for each Web site. In here, I place all the elements used in the Web site such as graphics, sound, and video files.

Templates

In the Templates folder are a number of pre-created Fusion templates you can use. Each of these templates is in a compressed WINZIP file. I suggest copying all these files to a new, separate folder on your hard disk before Unzipping them. For example, create a folder called "Xtra Templates," copy each of the ZIP files into this folder, and extract them. Each template will be placed in its own folder under the "Xtra Templates" folder.

Web Sites

The Web Sites folder contains a Fusion NOD file and ancilliary files that make up a Web site containing details and links to all the URLs mentioned in this book. To access this site, create a new folder in the C:\NetObjects Fusion 3.0\User Sites folder called "Web Sites." Copy the ZIP file from the CD-ROM into this folder and Unzip it. The site can then be opened using the File Open command in Fusion.

NFX Components

For each of the NFX components, to install them on your hard disk (I don't recommend using them in a Web site by importing them from the CD-ROM), select the EXE or SETUP file (as necessary) for each of the components you want to install and follow the onscreen prompts. As with the trial versions of applications, make sure you also read any readme files for late information or changes.

✦   ✦   ✦

Index

(continued)

(continued)

(continued)

(continued)

(continued)

IDG BOOKS WORLDWIDE, INC.
END-USER LICENSE AGREEMENT

READ THIS. You should carefully read these terms and conditions before opening the software packet(s) included with this book ("Book"). This is a license agreement ("Agreement") between you and IDG Books Worldwide, Inc. ("IDGB"). By opening the accompanying software packet(s), you acknowledge that you have read and accept the following terms and conditions. If you do not agree and do not want to be bound by such terms and conditions, promptly return the Book and the unopened software packet(s) to the place you obtained them for a full refund.

1. **License Grant.** IDGB grants to you (either an individual or entity) a nonexclusive license to use one copy of the enclosed software program(s) (collectively, the "Software") solely for your own personal or business purposes on a single computer (whether a standard computer or a workstation component of a multiuser network). The Software is in use on a computer when it is loaded into temporary memory (RAM) or installed into permanent memory (hard disk, CD-ROM, or other storage device). IDGB reserves all rights not expressly granted herein.

2. **Ownership.** IDGB is the owner of all right, title, and interest, including copyright, in and to the compilation of the Software recorded on the disk(s) or CD-ROM ("Software Media"). Copyright to the individual programs recorded on the Software Media is owned by the author or other authorized copyright owner of each program. Ownership of the Software and all proprietary rights relating thereto remain with IDGB and its licensers.

3. **Restrictions on Use and Transfer.**

    (a) You may only (i) make one copy of the Software for backup or archival purposes, or (ii) transfer the Software to a single hard disk, provided that you keep the original for backup or archival purposes. You may not (i) rent or lease the Software, (ii) copy or reproduce the Software through a LAN or other network system or through any computer subscriber system or bulletin-board system, or (iii) modify, adapt, or create derivative works based on the Software.

    (b) You may not reverse engineer, decompile, or disassemble the Software. You may transfer the Software and user documentation on a permanent basis, provided that the transferee agrees to accept the terms and conditions of this Agreement and you retain no copies. If the Software is an update or has been updated, any transfer must include the most recent update and all prior versions.

4. **Restrictions on Use of Individual Programs.** You must follow the individual requirements and restrictions detailed for each individual program in Appendix C, "About the CD-ROM," of this Book. These limitations are also contained in the individual license agreements recorded on the Software Media. These limitations may include a requirement that after using the program for a specified period of time, the user must pay a registration fee or discontinue use. By opening the Software packet(s), you will be agreeing to abide by the licenses and restrictions for these individual programs that are detailed in Appendix C, "About the CD-ROM," and on the Software Media. None of the material on this Software Media or listed in this Book may ever be redistributed, in original or modified form, for commercial purposes.

5. **Limited Warranty.**

   (a) IDGB warrants that the Software and Software Media are free from defects in materials and workmanship under normal use for a period of sixty (60) days from the date of purchase of this Book. If IDGB receives notification within the warranty period of defects in materials or workmanship, IDGB will replace the defective Software Media.

   (b) **IDGB AND THE AUTHOR OF THE BOOK DISCLAIM ALL OTHER WARRANTIES, EXPRESS OR IMPLIED, INCLUDING WITHOUT LIMITATION IMPLIED WARRANTIES OF MERCHANTABILITY AND FITNESS FOR A PARTICULAR PURPOSE, WITH RESPECT TO THE SOFTWARE, THE PROGRAMS, THE SOURCE CODE CONTAINED THEREIN, AND/OR THE TECHNIQUES DESCRIBED IN THIS BOOK. IDGB DOES NOT WARRANT THAT THE FUNCTIONS CONTAINED IN THE SOFTWARE WILL MEET YOUR REQUIREMENTS OR THAT THE OPERATION OF THE SOFTWARE WILL BE ERROR FREE.**

   (c) This limited warranty gives you specific legal rights, and you may have other rights that vary from jurisdiction to jurisdiction.

6. **Remedies.**

   (a) IDGB's entire liability and your exclusive remedy for defects in materials and workmanship shall be limited to replacement of the Software Media, which may be returned to IDGB with a copy of your receipt at the following address: Software Media Fulfillment Department, Attn.: *Fusion 3 Bible*, IDG Books Worldwide, Inc., 7260 Shadeland Station, Ste. 100, Indianapolis, IN 46256, or call 1-800-762-2974. Please allow three to four weeks for delivery. This Limited Warranty is void if failure of the Software Media has resulted from accident, abuse, or misapplication. Any replacement Software Media will be warranted for the remainder of the original warranty period or thirty (30) days, whichever is longer.

   (b) In no event shall IDGB or the author be liable for any damages whatsoever (including without limitation damages for loss of business profits, business interruption, loss of business information, or any other pecuniary loss) arising from the use of or inability to use the Book or the Software, even if IDGB has been advised of the possibility of such damages.

(c) Because some jurisdictions do not allow the exclusion or limitation of liability for consequential or incidental damages, the above limitation or exclusion may not apply to you.

7. **U.S. Government Restricted Rights.** Use, duplication, or disclosure of the Software by the U.S. Government is subject to restrictions stated in paragraph (c)(1)(ii) of the Rights in Technical Data and Computer Software clause of DFARS 252.227-7013, and in subparagraphs (a) through (d) of the Commercial Computer—Restricted Rights clause at FAR 52.227-19, and in similar clauses in the NASA FAR supplement, when applicable.

8. **General.** This Agreement constitutes the entire understanding of the parties and revokes and supersedes all prior agreements, oral or written, between them and may not be modified or amended except in a writing signed by both parties hereto that specifically refers to this Agreement. This Agreement shall take precedence over any other documents that may be in conflict herewith. If any one or more provisions contained in this Agreement are held by any court or tribunal to be invalid, illegal, or otherwise unenforceable, each and every other provision shall remain in full force and effect.

my2cents.idgbooks.com

CD-ROM
Installation
Instructions

To install the *Fusion 3 Bible* CD-ROM, follow these steps:

1. Insert the Fusion 3 Bible CD-ROM into your CD-ROM drive.
2. Click the Start button.
3. Select Programs ⇨ Windows Explorer.
4. Double-click the CD-ROM drive icon to view the contents of the CD-ROM in the right window.

Software

For each of the trial versions of software supplied on the CD-ROM, navigate to its folder within Windows Explorer and double-click the Setup icon to start the installation process. Follow the onscreen prompts. Once you have installed an application, it is always wise to read the readme file so that any late changes, updates, or further information can be seen.

Examples

In the Examples folder are a number of files that are referenced throughout this book. If you decide to follow the tutorial examples, you will need to copy the contents of this folder to your hard disk.

Please note that when you copy a file from a CD-ROM to a hard disk, that file will retain a "read only" attribute. If you get an error saying that Fusion can't access a file, you will need to remove the "read only" attribute. To do this, right-click the file and select Properties. Uncheck the "read only" box, click Apply, and then click OK.

As an example of the folder structure I use, I keep each Web site I am creating (the Fusion NOD file) in the default User Sites folder that Fusion creates when the site is initially created. Second, I create a folder called "Data" on the hard disk under the root directory (usually the C:\ directory) and in this Data folder, create a folder for each Web site. In here, I place all the elements used in the Web site such as graphics, sound, and video files.

Templates

In the Templates folder are a number of precreated Fusion templates you can use. I suggest copying all these files to a new, separate folder on your hard disk.

Web Sites

The Web Sites folder contains a Fusion NOD file and ancilliary files that make up a Web site containing details and links to all the URLs mentioned in this book. To access this site, create a new folder in the C:\NetObjects Fusion 3.0\User Sites folder called "Web Sites." The site can then be opened using the File Open command in Fusion.

NFX Components

For each of the NFX components, to install them on your hard disk (I don't recommend using them in a Web site by importing them from the CD-ROM), select the EXE or SETUP file (as necessary) for each of the components you want to install and follow the onscreen prompts. As with the trial versions of applications, make sure you also read any readme files for late information or changes.